WILLIAM GRAHAM SUMNER

WILLIAM GRAHAM SUMNER

WILLIAM GRAHAM SUMNER

BY

HARRIS E. STARR

NEW YORK
HENRY HOLT AND COMPANY
1925

PREFACE

THE life of William Graham Sumner is the story of what an American youth of resolute purpose can accomplish in the world in spite of obstacles and abuse. His career was so intimately associated with public affairs during the last quarter of the nineteenth century that it was far less simple and monotonous than that of most college professors; and his investigations were so thorough-going, and were carried on with such interest in their practical bearings, that no one concerned with modern social and political problems can afford to ignore them. The beginning of this biography was in a study made several years ago and presented to the Graduate School of Yale University for the degree of Doctor of Philosophy. The author is greatly endebted to Mr. Eliot Sumner, Mr. Graham Sumner, and Mrs. Alice Sumner Camp for access to Professor Sumner's private papers. Acknowledgment is made to Messrs. Ginn and Company for permission to quote freely from "Folkways," and to the Yale University Press for similar permission with respect to the "Collected Essays." Thanks are due to the staff of the Yale University Library for many courtesies, and to Mr. William Adams Slade of the Library of Congress for help in finding material in newspapers. Before all others, the author is under obligation to Professor Albert Galloway Keller, Professor Sumner's colleague and successor at Yale, at whose suggestion this work was undertaken, and with-

v

out whose constant encouragement and advice its accomplishment would have been impossible.

H. E. S.

New Haven, Connecticut,
March 20, 1925.

CONTENTS

Kinship is a fact which, in the forms of heredity and race, is second to none in importance to the interests of men.

Folkways.

CHAPTER I

BACKGROUND

WILLIAM GRAHAM SUMNER owed much to the economic forces which he spent his life in studying and describing. By the exercise of an indomitable will he made himself what he was, but they gave him his opportunity. To them his birth in America was directly due, and from this came his main chance. Had it been his lot to grow up in the land where his parents were born, amid the conditions existing in their class in the middle of the nineteenth century, it is not probable that anything but a limited and obscure career would have been his. It was the economic pressure in an old country, pushing rugged individuals out into the less thickly populated areas of the earth; the abundance of land and the demand for labor in a new country, together with the democratic conditions which these create, that made it possible for the son of a poor working man to develop the powers which were in him and become a widely recognized leader in one of the most important of fields.

Both William's father and mother were English immigrants. The former came to America of his own volition; the latter was brought hither by her parents. They were Lancashire folk, of humble but worthy antecedents. Their predecessors had tilled the soil, tended the loom, or practiced some handicraft. With books they had had little acquaintance; for personal cultivation they had had neither the time nor the means. The earliest of the Sumner line of whom we have certain

1

knowledge were weavers. William's grandfather, from, whom he took his name, was a block-cutter, and his father, Thomas, a blacksmith mechanic. His mother's father, Joseph Graham, was a locksmith and petty farmer.

But if his ancestors were unable to endow him with the advantages which generations of culture create, they did give him the sturdy qualities which Lancashire fostered in the best of its people. Lancashire stock was good stock from which to spring. "Leaving London out of question, and perhaps also excepting Devonshire," boasted the *Manchester Courier* in 1874, "no country has produced so many remarkable men or so many men who have exercised an influence upon the history of the nation."

The natural conditions of the region were of a character to develop the qualities for which achievement calls. The coal fields, extensive forests, and water power, which gave it industrial opportunity, limited its agricultural possibilities, and made resourcefulness, self-discipline, and perseverance necessary in those who preceded the industrial era. These qualities the artisans and textile workers who succeeded them inherited. Their virility and directness were reflected in a dialect noted for its terseness and vigor, and a hard-headedness characterized them such as Robert Peel, the grandfather of the Prime Minister, displayed when he dropped the final "e" from his name, "for no better reason," his grandson asserts, "than the utilitarian which he assigned, that it was of no use as it did not add to the sound."[1] Subtlety of reasoning and the mystical were foreign to their practical, straightforward type of mind. For compromises they

[1] "Lancashire Worthies," second series, Francis Espinasse, London, 1877, pp. 51, 52.

had no use, and when they had once arrived at a conclusion they did not lightly abandon it. "There is no
class of people in England," said John Bright in the
House of Commons, "more determined and more un-
conquerable, whichever side they take, than are the
people of the country from which I come." Their
enterprise and leadership were acknowledged in the
proverb, "What Lancashire thinks to-day, England
says to-morrow."

Since their lot was cast in a region predestined by
nature to become a great manufacturing center, it was
inevitable that Lancashire people should turn their
minds chiefly to industrial needs and to economic and
social problems. As a result, many of the inventions
which caused the industrial revolution of the eighteenth
century appeared from their midst. Henry Cort, dis-
coverer of the processes of puddling and rolling iron,
which did much to stimulate the British iron trade,
was a Lancashire man. Richard Arkwright's native
town was adjacent to that in which Thomas Sumner
was born, while at Blackburn, a few miles away, had
lived James Hargreave, by means of whose spinning
jenny his fellow townsman, Robert Peel, grew rich.
It was in Lancashire that modern economic problems
came first to be defined; here factory and temperance
reforms had some of their sturdiest advocates; and
here the anti-corn-law league, which overthrew the
corn laws and undermined the protective system of
England, had its headquarters.

Thomas Sumner was a typical Lancashire artisan,
hardheaded, strong willed, independent, enterprising.
His home was at Walton-le-Dale, on the banks of the
Ribble River, about twelve miles from the Irish Sea.
Here he was born, May 6th, 1808, according to his
son William, though the baptismal records of the parish

church give the date as May 4th.[2] Walton-le-Dale
was then a small town of between four and five
thousand people, but just across the river was Preston,
with a population of almost twenty thousand, destined
soon to be one of the great cotton centers of England.

Not only was this region one of the most attractive
in the industrial portion of Lancashire, it also abounded
in historic associations. At Walton, Thomas saw the
remains of a minor Roman station. Here, as a boy, he
attended St. Leonard's Church, built originally in the
11th century, summoned thither by chimes widely renowned for their sweetness. "Proud Preston," so
called because on every side it had to be approached
from below, had formerly been the winter resort of
the gentry of the county. A tradition prevailed that
during one of his forays into Lancashire Robert Bruce
had partially burned the town. A stronghold of
Catholicism, and loyal to King Charles, it was taken
by the Parliamentary forces in 1643, but was soon
recaptured by the Earl of Derby. At the battle of
Preston, the principal seat of which was at Walton-
le-Dale, Cromwell, in 1648, defeated the Duke of
Hamilton. Here, in 1715, the Jacobites met stubborn
resistance from Parson Woods and his parishioners,
and the forces of the Pretender surrendered.

For four or five generations at least, William's ancestors had lived in this locality. His father once told
him that he had seen his own great-grandfather, who
was a Lancashire weaver. In the records, both of
Walton-le-Dale and of Preston, Sumner, Sumpner, or
Sompner, is a frequently occurring name. As early
as 1603, according to the Preston parish register, the

2 "Registers of the Parish of Walton-le-Dale," transcribed by Gerald
E. C. Clayton, printed for the Lancashire Parish Register Society by
Strowger & Son, Clarence Press, 1910.

son of a Richard Sompner was baptized.[3] In 1646,
1652, and 1666, the mayor of Preston was a Thomas
Sumpner, and in 1654, a Richard Sumpner.[4] Thomas
Sumner's grandfather was a Preston man, and it is
not improbable that the line of weavers and artisans
to which he belonged was an offshoot from some of
the seventeenth century Sumpners, but no connection
can be positively established.

The village of Walton-le-Dale lies between the river
Darwin and the Ribble, into which it flows. The well-
watered country thereabout affords good pasturage
and opportunity for gardening. That Thomas Sumner's father was a farmer in a small way, as well as
a block cutter, is indicated by a rough drawing of his
old home which Thomas sent to William while the
latter was in England, just after his graduation from
college. It represents a long, low, stone house, for
two families, of the type common in rural England,
with a barn and two dwellings in the back "foult,"
or yard. Thomas' father seems to have been a man
of industry and ability, for he had built up a good
business; but like that of many of his neighbors it
was ruined by the improvements made in machinery
during the last part of the eighteenth century, and the
development of the factory system.

As a result William's father was born to poverty
and struggle. He had no more schooling than was
necessary to enable him to read and write and figure
a little. He never learned to spell or to write gram-
matically. Eager to get what knowledge he could
and to make the most of himself, he read such books
as he could secure, and availed himself of the libraries,

[3] "Records of the Parish Church of Preston," Thom. C. Smith,
London, Henry Gray, 1892, p. 82.
[4] "History of the Parish of Preston," Henry Fishwick, London,
Elliot Stock, 1900, pp. 78, 79.

lectures, and courses of instruction which Working
Men's Institutes afforded. Stimulated perhaps by
the historic associations amid which he grew up, his
interest turned to English and American history.
Upon these and upon constitutional law he informed
himself thoroughly. His habits were the best possible
and he showed himself capable of indefatigable industry.

In him were the instincts of the reformer. Among
his contemporaries, born in Walton-le-Dale fourteen
years earlier, was Joseph Livesey, one of the pioneer
temperance advocates of England, a sturdy free trader,
highly commended by Cobden for his contribution to
the agitation against the corn laws. A possible relationship between Livesey and Thomas Sumner is suggested by the fact that the latter's mother was a Livesey. Intemperate indulgence in drink was perhaps the
worst of Lancashire vices. The villagers of Walton-
le-Dale, Livesey says in his biography, "thought well
of drink." "Weavers crowded the public houses."
"We had a sad, wet lot connected with the Church.
The grave digger and his father were both drunkards;
ringers and singers, both were hard drinkers. I remember the latter singing in my father's kitchen, one
Christmas morning, in a most disgraceful condition.
When the church clock was standing for want of wind-
ing up in a morning, as was often the case, the remark was, 'The clock was drunk again last night.' " [5]

In order to alter such conditions for the better,
Livesey started a movement in behalf of total abstinence which spread rapidly all over England. With
his spirit and aim Thomas Sumner was in complete
accord. He became and remained a teetotaler, and by

[5] "Autobiography of Joseph Livesey," National Temperance League
Publication, London, 1885, p. 8.

argument and persuasion did what he could to get his fellow working men to give up drink. Once he ventured to make a speech. The attempt was a failure and he never tried again.

The years of Thomas' youth and early manhood were the trying ones following the Napoleonic wars. "It would be hard to convince the present generation," wrote Livesey, "of the hardships endured in the past —from about the years 1810 to 1832." With peace had come, not prosperity, but disaster, unemployment, and poverty. In manufacturing districts, such as Lancashire, the people faced both the general hardships of the times and also the evils which accompanied the growth of the factory system. The influx into these districts had been great and still continued. Housing facilities became inadequate. Conditions in the factories were disgusting. Food was dear and wages were low. From boyhood Thomas Sumner had been accustomed to see the cotton factory apprentices, reputed to have been recruited from a foundling hospital in London, marched into church each Sunday, many of them crooked legged, because of the habit of stopping machinery by placing the knees against it. As much as parents may have disliked to do so, they were forced to put their children to work along with such foundlings in order to secure sufficient incomes to support their families.

Thomas was too ambitious and resolute a man to submit to such conditions and raise a family among them when there was a chance of bettering himself. Accordingly, in 1836, the year of the memorable "spinners' strike" in Preston, when he was twenty-eight years old, he joined the stream of those who for some time had been seeking relief though immigration, and set his face toward the United States.

Forty-five years earlier, due to the activities of Alexander Hamilton, who felt that there could be no proper independence of Europe until the United States manufactured its own textiles, there had been incorporated in New Jersey "The Society for the Establishment of Useful Manufactures," and what is now Paterson chosen as the site of a great industrial center. Cotton mills, paper mills, and iron works were built there. For some time Lancashire people had been coming thither. One of the suburbs was called Manchester, and another, Oldham. Knowing that he would find people of his own kind there, perhaps already having friends in the vicinity, the future father of Alexander Hamilton's biographer came to Paterson.

Some eleven years before, there had arrived in Oldham, New Jersey, from Oldham, Lancashire, Joseph Graham and his wife, Elizabeth Pidock. About the Grahams, unfortunately, little is known, save that they had the vigor and the courage to leave old things behind and seek a larger life on this side of the Atlantic. Like Thomas Sumner, they came from a great manufacturing center, and had been subject to similar molding influences. Joseph Graham had established himself on a small farm, which he worked as best he could while pursuing his trade as a locksmith. His characteristics, also, seem to have been those of the county whence he came. He was industrious, frugal, and vigorous of mind. His spare time he spent in studying astronomy and making observations. He had a daughter, Sarah, one of eleven children. This daughter became the wife of Thomas Sumner, and on October 30, 1840, their first child, William Graham Sumner, was born.

The value and importance of the family sentiments, from a social point of view, cannot be exaggerated. They impose self-control and prudence in their most important social bearings, and tend more than any other forces to hold the individual up to the virtues which make the sound man and the valuable member of society.

Challenge of Facts.

CHAPTER II

HOME AND EARLY TENDENCIES

Thomas Sumner's arrival at Paterson had been in a rather unfortunate period. He sought to escape wretched circumstances at home; he found hard times here. In 1837 Paterson suffered an almost complete stagnation of business. Failure and fire visited the iron industry. Although conditions improved, this independent, practical-minded Englishman was not certain that New Jersey was a place where he wished to remain and raise a family. Against one thing he rebelled,—the custom of "store pay." For the work he did he wanted cash, with freedom to trade where he chose. Then, too, in so big a country, one would be foolish to settle down without making a survey of the possibilities offered. Thomas was not one to stay, in spite of everything, where the home folk were or to take the path of least resistance. He determined to look about, and to decide rationally where he could do the best for himself and his family.

Accordingly, he took his wife and young son and started out prospecting. For several years they traveled from place to place, crossing New York and Pennsylvania, and going on into Ohio. All the while the family was increasing. In 1842, another son, Joseph Graham, was born, and a year or two later, a daughter, Esther Elizabeth. Finally, Thomas returned, having become persuaded that if a man would live as poorly and educate his children as badly in the East as in the West, he could live as well in the

11

East. To avoid the tyranny of "store pay," he shunned New Jersey, however, and came to New England.

After a brief stay in New Haven, during which they lived first at 104 Wooster Street, and later in the rear of 50 East Street, the Sumners moved on to Hartford, where Thomas secured a position in the shops of the Hartford and New Haven Railroad. Here he worked for years. Pay vouchers in the archives of the New York, New Haven, and Hartford Railroad, of which those on page 13 are examples, indicate that his particular job was that of repairing locomotive wheels.

The wages which Thomas Sumner received were never large, and it was in a humble, working man's home where economy and self-denial were necessary and trouble often came that William was reared. Security and comfort were achieved there only after hard struggle. During the first ten years of their residence in Hartford, shifting circumstances caused the Sumners to change their abode with frequency. Soon the three small children were left motherless. Attacked by what would probably now be diagnosed as appendicitis and the patient's life saved, Sarah Graham died, December 15, 1848, and was buried in the old North Burying Ground, where a stone to her memory bears the trite but, in this case, appropriate inscription:

> If mortal worth demands a tear,
> Then pay the grateful tribute here.

His mother's death when he was but eight years old unquestionably affected greatly William's circumstances and happiness. She was a woman of great

HARTFORD AND NEW HAVEN RAILROAD COMPANY

1855. To sgd. Thomas Sumner Dr.

Nov. 30 For 16¼ days' work in shop this
month 1.62½ $26.40
For turning "Orion's" Tyer 10.00
For turning "New York" Tyer 5.00

$41.40

Received Hartford, Dec. 3, 1855, from
the Hartford and New Haven Railroad
Co., forty-one................40/100
dollars in full for the above account.
sgd. Thomas Sumner.
Correct————

HARTFORD AND NEW HAVEN RAILROAD COMPANY

1857 To Thomas Summer Dr.

Sept. 30 For 15 days' work in M. Shop this
month at 1.62½ $24.38
For turning off "Victory's" wheels ... 5.00
For turning off "Connecticut's" wheels 5.00

$34.38

Received Hartford, Oct. 5, 1857, from
the Hartford and New Haven Railroad
Co. thirty-four................38/100
dollars in full for the above account.
$34.38 sgd. Thomas Sumner.
Correct————

goodness and charm, and she left an indelible impression upon her children's memories. The journal which William kept as a student abroad reveals a hunger for the affection which she gave him, and he never knew again until he had established his own home. Years after her death, when his half-sister was born, he insisted that she be named Sarah, and though she was not commonly known by it, that name was given her. There is a tradition that in his later life he once spoke with much feeling of his mother's simple faith and the religious training which she gave him.

Left with three children to care for, Thomas married, a few months later, Eliza VanAlstein of Liverpool, New York, by whom he had another son. This child lived but a few months, however. Eliza was an extremely capable woman, but had all the hardness which sometimes goes with feminine strength and executive ability. It was in no small measure through her aid that Thomas Sumner succeeded in getting on his feet financially. In this achievement he was helped by an association formed with the Graham brothers, Thomas and Richard. The former's wife, Catherine, was the sister of Sarah Graham, and had married a man of the same name, but unrelated. Both men were engineers on sugar plantations in Cuba, and had acquired some capital which they invested in Hartford real estate. They bought several houses on Atlantic Street, which Thomas Sumner looked after in their owners' absence, and in one of these, number 20, a two-family brick house, now standing, the Sumners made their final home.

No sooner were they established here in comfortable circumstance, however, than death came again to the household. After eleven years of married life,

barren and toilsome, during which she had brought
Sarah Graham's children to the threshold of manhood
and womanhood, Eliza VanAlstein died, January 4,
1859. Very shortly after, Thomas took for his third
wife Catherine E. Mix, of West Hartford, by whom
he had two children of his old age, Henry and Sarah
Alice. There followed a long period of domestic happiness and comparative prosperity. With respect to
character Kate Mix resembled William's mother. In
a letter written to William in 1866, his father speaks
with warmth and tenderness of her sweetness and unselfishness. "If Esther did not fall into the hands of
a good Samaritan when Kate Mix came here," he
exclaimed, "then I don't know what a good Samaritan
is. She has all of a dozen times refused to get new
things for herself so that Esther might have her wants
supplied, saying Esther was young, and clothes are
everything to young girls. She never used a harsh
word in my hearing in her life. All that she ever asked
was that we should be satisfied with her endeavors to
please. I hope when you get married, as I think and
hope you will marry some day, you will never forget
mother who has been such a source of enjoyment."
Unfortunately, it was only as a student home for
vacations and as a later visitor that William came
under this stepmother's influence. As time went on,
however, he acquired a deep affection for her, and at
his father's death he brought her to his own home in
New Haven and took care of her.

The domestic felicity of these later days was troubled somewhat by Thomas' increasing physical dis-
abilities and financial reverses. Fellow workmen led
him home from the shops one day, blinded in an eye
by a piece of flying steel. Later he was badly lamed
by a fall. His hearing failed. Increasingly sensitive

to his appearance and limitations, he mingled with people as little as possible. When William was married he declined to be present at the ceremony, stating his reasons in the following pathetic words:

> Hartford, April 2, 1871.
> DEAR WILLIAM:
> Yours of the 29 ult. came duly to hand. I think it will not be convenient for me to come to New York to see you married. I am quite busily engaged on my Broad Street property. Besides, as you are aware, I could neither see nor hear, so as to form any judgment as to how you looked or what was said. So you see it would not be very gratifying to me as I could only guess what was going on. . . .

Some time before this letter was written, Thomas had given up shop work and devoted himself to the management of the Graham property and building enterprises of his own. With what little capital he had been able to acquire, some help from Thomas Graham, and numerous mortgages, he succeeded in erecting a number of dwellings in a growing section of the city. For a period this speculation proved profitable, but later, owing in part to his failing mind, his affairs became sadly involved, and at his death, April 8, 1881, he was almost as poor as when he came to America.

Whatever advantages the home of Thomas Sumner may have lacked, it was a wholesome one. There William derived a first-hand knowledge of the toil and hardships of the common people, and learned the worth of what he later called the "economic virtues." Industry, thrift, and self-denial were exemplified. Unproductiveness and waste Thomas Sumner could not tolerate. Girls no less than boys should work was his conviction. "You know as well as Joe and I do what father thinks about girls working," Esther wrote to William in a letter in which she asks him to urge her father to let her visit the Grahams in Cuba. "He told me one day that I was as able to earn my living as he." "He belonged to the class of men," declared William, in later years, "of whom Caleb Garth in 'Middlemarch' is the type." [1] Simple, honest, of few words, profoundly impressed with the wonderfulness and importance of the industrial organization, he applied his utmost sense to "fruits of diligence and not to faiths and polity." Hard work and perfect workmanship were his religion, and the worth of these he impressed upon the young at every opportunity. Meanness he hated, and with mean and evil men he would have nothing to do. With his fellow workmen, after a day's body-racking, begriming labor in the shops, he would discuss politics, capital, wages, and working conditions, and William heard his father, with his Lancashire background of free trade and "laissez faire," express himself on social and economic questions. "In early life," William wrote, "I accepted from books and other people some views and opinions which differed from his. At the present time, in regard to these matters, I hold with him and not with the others." [2] He was one of those many worthy, independent, self-supporting individuals, who mind their own business, ask no favors, and, though "weighed down with the costs and burden of the schemes for making everybody happy, with the cost of public beneficence, with the support of all the

[1] "Autobiographical Sketch of William Graham Sumner," in "A History of the Class of 1863, Yale College," New Haven, 1905, reprinted in "Earth Hunger and Other Essays," edited by Albert Galloway Keller, Yale University Press, 1914.
[2] *Ibid.*

loafers, with the loss of all the economic quackery,'' make no complaint. He was his son's "forgotten man.''

It is safe to say, however, that William's youth was not an altogether happy one. It was too lonely and self-centered. The neighbors thought him odd; his own family offered him little companionship, sympathy, or encouragement; few liked him. With his father, probably, he had most in common, but Thomas Sumner was not a particularly expressive individual. Had his mother lived longer, or had it been his fortune to have Kate Mix mother him, his lot would have fallen in pleasanter places, and his nature would have been modified by influences, from the lack of which he always suffered. But fate decreed that he should grow up under the cold, stern régime of Eliza Van-Alstein. Her rule was one of iron, and her temper, somewhat shrewish. Any craving for sympathy and love which William may have felt never found waters of refreshment in her. Her economies bore heavily on the children, and they were deprived of privileges and pleasures which many of their associates enjoyed. The first book which William ever owned came, not from his father or mother, but from a Sunday School teacher, George Buck. It was a little American Sunday School Union publication, entitled, "Self-dependence.'' Subsequently, William loaned it to the North Grammar School, Hartford. Nearly fifty years after, the late Charles D. Hine, then Secretary of the State Board of Education, found the book in the school, and returned it to Professor Sumner, who preserved it among his most valued papers until his death. The practical in Thomas Sumner approved his wife's thrift, but the father in him resented her severity. Long afterward he wrote: "We all know that there was not one woman in a thousand could keep house with her or manage domestic concerns so economically.'' But, he adds, ''My heart has ached a thousand times for you children, when you little dreamed of such a thing, brought on by this very economy.''

With neither his brother nor his sister did William have much in common. In a letter which Esther, or ''Chet,'' as she signs herself, wrote to him during the first years he was abroad, she complains with some petulance:

> I cannot (now I have begun this letter) think of anything to write. When Joe was away, every single Sunday I could write him a letter a great deal longer than I can write to you in a month. You know so very few folks that I know, and I can hardly think of anything or anybody to write about.

Esther was a high-strung, quick-tempered, tempestuous girl, who enjoyed considerable popularity. She was good-looking, vain, pleasure-loving, and extremely sensitive. Warm hearted and generous, she had a deep affection for William, who plainly did not approve of her and often hurt her cruelly by his attitude and criticisms. Her pride and quick temper kept her in a continual turmoil, so that her early career was a trying one. Finally, she married happily and went with her husband to live in Canada.

Joseph was a youth straightforward, honest, and chivalrous, much liked in Hartford by all who knew him. He wrote with fluency of expression, and a beauty of penmanship which aided him to secure more than one position in an era before the typewriter had destroyed the profitableness of that art. In his letters to William he often expresses strong convictions regarding current events, but his reasoning shows none of the former's power of mind. With most of his companions, he entered the Northern army during the Civil War, and was always inclined to look down upon William for not doing likewise. After serving out his term of enlistment, he became chief clerk in the Adjutant General's office in New Orleans, and was later associated with various Federal agencies there. Marrying a widow of that city, he continued to live in the South. Somewhat lacking in stability and business sagacity, though always optimistic in the extreme, he never attained any great success.

With this good-natured, easy-going, socially inclined brother and this excitable, proud, pleasure-loving sister, William grew up, quite different in temperament, tastes, and ambitions from either. From childhood he displayed great seriousness of mind. To him life was real and life was earnest in a degree often irritating to his associates. He took himself seriously, was dignified in carriage, and as punctilious about his personal appearance as his circumstances would permit. The only sport in which he is known to have engaged was skating, one which does not necessarily involve sacrifice of dignity or complete cessation of thought on more important matters. His sobriety cast a shadow which the healthy minded resented. As he walked up Atlantic Street when home from college, invariably dressed in dark clothing, his countenance as somber as his raiment, impertinent youngsters would sometimes cry after him, "Mister, why don't you smile?" At his appearing, it is said, all the joyousness of an occasion was likely to take flight. The neighbors thought him conceited and overbearing.

But back of all this seriousness there was a keen

sense of propriety and strong moral feeling, which if they made a prig of him in his youth, were to make him a noble exponent of righteousness later. Frivolity, waste of time, neglect of opportunity, were even in his early days abhorrent to him. Instinctively he was a champion of the right and a hater of all that was underhanded, mean, or dishonest. Along with these characteristics went a pronounced tendency to criticize and reform, which made him disliked and feared. There was a sting in his words, says a somewhat younger contemporary who lived across the street from the Sumners, which was very unpleasant. The speaker himself had frequently come under William's correction. Once he had gone into the Sumner cellar, where a barrel of sugar sent by the Grahams from Cuba was kept, and had just put a little into a rusty pan with the intention of taking it away for private enjoyment, when William, home from college, suddenly confronted him. "I never heard," he states, "a denunciation of thieves and stealing, clothed in such terse and cutting terms as was that which I straightway received." But after the lecture was over, William went upstairs and presently returned with a clean receptacle, which he filled with sugar and gave it to the boy, saying, "If you want any more, come and ask for it. Don't steal it." Joseph and Esther were constantly subjected to his rebuke, and even his parents were not exempt. The Sumner home was on the side of a short hill, down which in winter the children, and sometimes their elders, were accustomed to coast. Coming home one day, William found his father and step-mother engaged in this sport, and upbraided them for their lack of dignity and waste of time, remarking that mature people ought to be in better business.

Early in life he showed unusual eagerness for
knowledge and an untiring zeal in acquiring information on all subjects. The library of the Young Men's
Institute was his constant resort. Here, when only
thirteen or fourteen years old, he was studying with
great avidity Harriet Martineau's "Illustration of
Political Economy." In these didactic stories, tedious
enough to the modern reader, he learned that "capital
is something produced with a view to employment in
further production," and that "labor is the origin
and saving is the support of capital." They also impressed upon his mind that "property is held by convention, not natural right"; that "increase of population is necessarily limited by means of subsistence"; and that any degree of restriction "on the
natural direction of labor and capital is ultimately
injurious to every class in the community." In free
trade principles, also, he became schooled, being
taught that "as the general interest of each nation
requires that there should be perfect liberty in the
exchange of commodities, any restriction on such
liberty, for the sake of benefiting any particular class
or classes, is the sacrifice of a larger interest to a
smaller,—that is, a sin in government;" that legal
provision for the indigent is economically unsound
was demonstrated to him with equal clearness and
force. The interest which these "Illustrations"
kindled never waned. "In college," he wrote many
years later, "we read and recited Wayland's 'Political Economy,' but I believe that my conception of
capital, labor, money, and trade, were all formed by
those books which I read in my boyhood." [3]

3 "Sketch of William Graham Sumner," *The Popular Science Monthly*,
Vol. XXXV, 1889. Reprinted in "The Challenge of Facts and Other
Essays," edited by Albert Galloway Keller, Yale University Press, 1914,
p. 5.

Efforts to express himself in literary form began almost as early as his reading, and several examples of such attempts he carefully preserved. When only eleven years old he wrote "Fernando, the Chieftain of Northern Corsica." It is an ambitious tale of mysterious caves, bands of robbers, pirates, and fighting, disclosing a wholesome love of adventure, and, in spite of its crudeness, ability and a capacity for painstaking work not common in one so young. The other romance is dated April 27, 1858, and is entitled "Adventures at the Convent of the Great St. Bernard." It is written in the first person and narrates the rescue of a political prisoner being taken under guard to his country. A third experiment, "The College Scrape, a Farce in One Act," is a rather heavy production, but shows that, in spite of his seriousness and dignity, William was not altogether lacking in sense of humor. It is interesting to note that both romances are tales of chivalrous service. Fernando was a chieftain who, with his band of hardy followers, guarded the lives and property of the peasants from robbers and pirates. The person rescued in the Convent of St. Bernard was one under the ban of his government for holding republican principles.

The most fortunate influence which came into William's life was the friendship of Reverend Elias R. Beadle, D.D., from 1852 to 1863 pastor of the Pearl Street Congregational Church of Hartford. To him more than to any one else, perhaps, William owed his later career. Dr. Beadle was a scholar and man of affairs. He had been a missionary in Syria, and was accustomed to spend a portion of each year abroad. In Europe, as well as at home, he had a reputation as a scientist, his special field being mineralogy and conchology. He was a man of warm, evangelistic fervor, and his character, ability, and kindliness won him a large following among the youth of Hartford. Becoming acquainted with William, he took a deep interest in him and a lasting friendship resulted. Soon William left the Episcopal church, in which he had been reared, to become a member of the Pearl Street Church, and for a long time Dr. Beadle was his constant advisor.

Three things, in those critical years, William's pastor did for him. In the first place, he fired his ambition and fortified his will. He made him believe that with the help of God he could go far, if he only had the courage and the faith, and was willing to pay the price. He also persuaded him that the field to which his gifts and tendencies called him was the Christian ministry. That this sphere of activity already appealed to Sumner is probable. Questioned by one of his sons, in after years, as to his reasons for entering the ministry, he replied that he could never remember a time when the desire to do so had not possessed him. Furthermore, Dr. Beadle convinced William that he must not be satisfied with less than the best preparation possible. He must take no short cut. Whatever might add to his power and usefulness, he was to spare no pains to get. At this time William had left school and gone to work in the dry goods establishment of Collins Brothers, where he was very unhappy. Under the spell of Dr. Beadle's encouragement and confidence, he went back to school to prepare for college.

During this period he tried his hand at writing sermons, two of which have been preserved. They show that the writer held most earnestly the prevailing orthodox conception of God, the creation, sin, and the atoning work of Christ, and that future reward and punishment were very real and vivid things to him. One is on the text, "Have faith in God"; and the other on the somewhat funereal exclamation, "The Lord gave, and the Lord has taken away: Blessed be the name of the Lord!" The former sets forth the various applications of Christian faith. The latter does not deal with death, as the text might suggest, but with God's gifts in general and the significance of their loss. Gifts he classifies as duties and privileges, and as he later emphasized social obligations rather than rights, so here he gives greater space to duties than to privileges, remarking: "We have spent more time on the duties, because they are not acknowledged or considered, than on the privileges, which are new and fresh to the sense continually and need no argument." The writer's feeling of responsibility for the well-being of others is revealed in the pronounced evangelistic note of these discourses, almost clamorously sounded in the following extract.

The third duty incumbent upon us is to fit others for Heaven. 'Freely ye have received, freely give.' Yes, indeed, freely have ye received! All these blessings God has showered down upon you, my Christian friend, and you must give an account of their use. He has given you them and you may have thought they were very bountiful and have thanked him for them; but, Oh! have you remembered the accompanying duty to extend them to others. The Lord gave you the blessings, but he also gave you the duties. You have used the blessings, have you used the duties? . . . To all these suffering poor around you, all the poor sinners hungering and thirsting for righteousness, give freely; give of the spirit and blessings of God. . . . It is your bounden duty to extend the blessings of Christianity to your suffering, starving, and dying neighbor. Ah! do it; extend it to all, and press its importance upon all: thus shalt thou insure thyself a great reward. Let me quote some of those texts which bear upon this subject for your especial edification. 'But ye are a chosen generation, a Royal Priesthood and Holy Generation, a peculiar people, that ye should show forth the praises of Him who hath called you forth out of darkness into his marvelous light, which in time past were not a people, but are now the people of God; which had not obtained mercy, but now have obtained mercy.' This is the people we are, my friends, and the duties devolving upon us are obvious. And again, all the great joy and benefit of saving a brother! 'Brethren, if any man do err from the truth and one convert him, let him know that he who converteth a sinner from the error of his way shall save a soul from death and shall hide a multitude of sins!' And again: 'And they that be wise shall shine as the brightness of the firmament; and they that turn many to righteousness, as the stars forever and ever.'

We had instruction which was real and solid, which conceded nothing to show and sacrificed nothing to applause. We learned to work patiently for real and enduring results. We learned the faith that what is genuine must outlast and prevail over what is meretricious. We learned to despise empty display. We had also a discipline which was complete and sufficient, but which was attained without friction. There was no sentimentality, no petting, no affectation of free and easy manners.

Integrity in Education.

CHAPTER III

SCHOOL AND COLLEGE

WILLIAM's excursion into the dry goods business interrupted his schooling for two years, so that he was almost nineteen when he graduated from the Hartford high school. For the public school system, and especially for the schools of his native city, he always had the warmest regard. But for them the door to the life he was privileged to live would have remained shut.

Some of his teachers made a deep and lasting impression upon him. "When I look back upon my school days," he said, in 1897, at a dinner given in honor of Dr. Henry Barnard, long connected with the schools of Connecticut, "I know that two or three of my teachers had decisive effect upon my character and career. . . . We had one teacher whom I never saw put in a difficult position but what he extracted himself from it in such a way that we all felt that that was just the right way to act in an emergency of that kind."[1] In the high school it was his fortune to be under Mr. T. W. T. Curtiss, principal, and Mr. S. M. Capron, head of the classical department. Both were men of that candor, honesty, and unostentatious goodness which Sumner so frequently extolled. In methods they were ahead of their time; and Sumner often declared in public that, as a teacher, he was deeply indebted to the sound traditions which he received from these men.

[1] The address given at the dinner is printed under the title "The Teacher's Unconscious Success" in "Earth Hunger and Other Essays."

The first step in securing the thorough training which, under the influence of Dr. Beadle, had become William's fixed aim was now taken, and he was ready for the second, a college education. This was made possible for him by the stepmother at whose hands he had suffered so much hardship and unhappiness. Years afterwards he liked to tell in grim amusement how in boyish anger at her treatment of them he and his brother Joseph used to plot to kill her. "But," he always added, "I owed her much." By her good management and rigid economy she had succeeded in accumulating a little of the capital which Sumner so often declared to be the fundamental requisite for all material, intellectual, and spiritual advancement. The fruits of her severity Thomas Sumner, who was always ready to make any personal sacrifice for the good of his children, put at William's disposal. So scrupulously fair was he and so averse to any seeming partiality, that in his will, drawn up during the period of his real estate enterprises when he expected to die possessed of some property, he made the following provision:

> Whereas I have advanced to my son, William G. Sumner, large sums of money for his maintenance and education, more than to my other children, I will and direct that $1000.00 shall be deducted from the share above given to said William G. to go into the remainder of my estate.

The tuition at Yale College in Sumner's day was $45.00 per annum, and the college authorities estimated that from $230.00 to $320.00 a year would cover all necessary expenses, including fees, room, heat, board, laundry, and society taxes. Aside from what

Sumner When a Student

he might spend for luxuries, therefore, a thousand dollars would just about support a student during his entire course.

Accordingly, in the fall of 1859 William entered Yale. He went into college comparatively poor, with few friends, reserved and repellent in manner, mature beyond his years, with strong moral and religious convictions, and with no ambition but to get knowledge. He graduated with some of the highest honors in the gift of students and of faculty, little changed in personal characteristics, not well known to many, but beloved and greatly respected by a few who had been able to penetrate to the admirable qualities and warm heart which lay beneath his cold and hard exterior, among whom, as it happened, were some of the ablest and wealthiest men in his class. They had unlimited faith in his future, and were ready to invest in him heavily.

Regarding his habits, Mr. Samuel Huntington, for three years his roommate, writes:

I roomed with Sumner for the first three years of our college course. In freshman year we lived in a frame house at the northwest corner of Chapel and High Streets. Then for two years we inhabited 'South Middle, North entry, third story, back middle room.' Then I separated from him because my younger brother entered college. Sumner spoke rather contemptuously of my taste in leaving him 'for a freshman.' While we roomed together we were rather apt to do our studying at different times, as he would study for a recitation in the first hour, or hour and a half available, and spend the remainder of his time in reading, while I devoted the last hour or more to preparation for the recitation. He took very little exercise, wherein also we differed. He was not athletic. Perhaps if he had done more in the way of bodily

exercise he would have lived longer. I saw very little of
him after we graduated.

The house in which Huntington and Sumner roomed
as freshmen was the home of a widow, Mrs. George
Lewis Selden. The original building may still be discerned beneath the protuberances which commercial
ambitions have imposed. As a senior, Sumner lived
at 29 South.

Another classmate, Mr. J. Frederick Kernochan,
describes as follows some of William's characteristics:

He was by no means an unpopular man, but he had
so much of that New England reserve that he never could
have been a popular man among a lot of thoughtless
youngsters. Although he stood high among his friends
and, had he desired it, he would always have secured any
place he wished, because of his mental equipment, still
he did not have so many intimate friends as to give him
class popularity. I never knew him well until senior
year, but then I came to know that the New England reserve was only skin deep and to his intimates he was
always warm-hearted and genial. Although a very good
scholar he was not in any sense a 'grind.' I am sure the
little we were expected to learn in college, in those days,
came to him very easily. He seemed to grow into the
lighter vein more slowly and in every class meeting after
our graduation he seemed to be a much younger man than
when a boy at college: as the others seemed to grow older
after graduation he always seemed to me to be younger
every time we met. In many ways he was an old man
among the young and a young man among the old. It
may be that this idea of mine grew out of the fact that,
as I said, it was not until senior year that I really knew
him well. No man in the class stood higher in the estimation of the boys, and no man seemed to be more beloved than he in his own circle of friends, who were the
leading men in the class.

Yale was not at this time a large or live institution. In the academic department there were five hundred and two students, and in the professional departments, one hundred and thirty-nine. Sumner's class, that of 1863, was the largest which had ever entered, numbering one hundred and seventy-three. Notwithstanding the outbreak of the Civil War in the midst of its course, it graduated one hundred and twenty-two strong, superior in point of size, with one exception, to all its predecessors.

As in most institutions of the kind, the curriculum was then extremely narrow. The first three years were given up almost entirely to Latin, Greek, mathematics, and rhetoric. Juniors might elect a modern language or mineralogy. In the senior year there was instruction in history, United States Constitution, moral and political philosophy, history of philosophy, theology, astronomy, and chemistry. Throughout the course considerable attention was given to composition and forensic disputation.

The faculty, though small, was able; but the teaching was poor. Reverend Theodore Dwight Woolsey was president, Reverend Noah Porter, professor of moral philosophy and metaphysics, and Reverend William A. Larned, professor of rhetoric and English. The chair of Greek was occupied by James Hadley, and that of Latin by Thomas A. Thatcher. Hubert A. Newton was professor of mathematics, and William D. Whitney, professor of Sanskrit and instructor in modern languages, while the scientific courses were conducted by James D. Dana, professor of natural history, and Benjamin Silliman, Jr., professor of chemistry.

The probability is that young Sumner got far more out of his own hard study and broad general reading

than he did from the class rooms or personal contact
with members of the faculty. The former were dismal places, both physically and pedagogically; the
latter, it was difficult for any student to achieve. Mr.
Henry Holt, who graduated in the class of 1862, paints
the following picture of the conditions then existing.

The Yale of to-day is far different from the Yale of
my time. Then it was probably at its very worst in
mind, body, and estate. In mind it dated back centuries,
in body it was the old brick row, and in estate it was
squalidly poor. The general attitude of the faculty was
the puritanical mistrust of anything that had an element
of pleasure in it. To be a member of the Yale faculty
up to the late sixties, a man had to be orthodox, and before those times thinking men had begun to lose their
orthodoxy. The result was that while the Yale faculty
were generally good scholars and men of strong and high
character, they were to but a small degree thinking men.
The only one with whom I ever became intimate, and
that after graduation, was William D. Whitney, who was,
with the possible exception of Dana, the greatest of them
all; and in college he kept the widest of his thinking to
himself. . . . These belated Puritans, with all their
sturdy virtues, were not the men to have much influence
on boys. I can recall but one of the faculty who appeared ever to have been young, and if any other one
ever had been, the standard was against showing it. Outside the class rooms, we saw very little of them, especially
those of us who were not religiously inclined and needed
guidance most. They were good and learned men, but
most of them being 'stupid' not only inspired us with
little interest in our studies, and made faithfulness to
routine the main test of merit, but, being Puritans, they
actually for the sake of 'discipline' deliberately threw
obstacles in our way. The training in the classics was
almost all in the grammar, and while we were studying

chemistry they actually gave us a pamphlet of chemical formulas to learn by heart. Of course most of the boys of any spirit flunked it. In short, the most diabolical ingenuity could hardly have done more to make both religion and scholarship repulsive.[2]

Against the methods of instruction Sumner must have rebelled, for he had known good teaching; and any seeming hypocrisy upon the part of the faculty must have aroused his disgust; but it is doubtful if the conditions described irritated him as much as they did Holt. The latter was already a radical. Sumner was himself serious minded, puritanical, and conventionally religious. Whatever the limitations of curriculum and faculty, he saw abundant opportunity to get knowledge and training, and to the getting of them he applied himself rigorously.

Other interests were few. Places of amusement or social intercourse saw him but little. The oldest freshman society, Kappa Sigma Epsilon, enrolled him as a member. Originally a select society, limiting its initiates to twenty, in Sumner's day it competed with Delta Kappa for the largest membership possible, freshmen being met at trains and steamboats by rival committees and given no peace until they had pledged themselves. Membership, therefore, signified nothing. As a junior, William belonged to Psi Upsilon. His scholarship and the reputation which he had made as a writer and speaker brought him a place among the fifteen prominent men of the class elected at the close of the junior year to "Skull and Bones." His most intimate friends were his associates in the "Cher" Eating Club, whose motto was "Always a Unit."

[2] "Garrulities of an Octogenarian Editor." Houghton, Mifflin Co., 1923, pp. 34, 35, 36.

They consisted of Charles M. Gilman, Charles H. Wesson, Henry F. Dimock, and William C. Whitney.

Sumner took high rank as a scholar, though he did not lead his class. This honor fell to another embryo clergyman, Leander T. Chamberlain, a more brilliant but less able individual. In his junior year Sumner was elected to Phi Beta Kappa, and in the junior appointments he was given one of the high orations. At the junior exhibition, of which he was one of the ten managers, a long drawn out affair with afternoon and evening sessions, a speech by Chamberlain, preceded by one from Sumner, brought the program to its climax.

To Benjamin Silliman, Jr., Mr. George Sheffield attributes William's failure to take higher, if not the highest, rank. The course in chemistry was one of the most difficult in the curriculum. Professor Silliman had no pedagogical wisdom or gifts. What was clear to him, he assumed was equally so to his pupils, and he was accustomed to assign long lessons and put difficult problems on the board, expecting the whole class to understand them with very little elucidation on his part. The class, on the other hand, came to feel that such circumstances made any means of passing the course justifiable. Silliman's habitual obliviousness to what was going on in the classroom invited cribbing, and few declined the invitation. "I myself," Mr. Sheffield confesses, "was once given a question in an oral test about which I knew little. Having been granted a few moments for thought, I took Silliman's text book and read his own answer to him. 'Very good,' was his comment. 'I could not have stated it better myself.' In such practices Sumner stubbornly refused to join. Furthermore, his conscientious endeavors to understand and his persistent questioning

so irritated Silliman that the latter thought him a fool
and barely passed him.

It was in composition and public speaking that
Sumner shone most conspicuously. In the sophomore
prize competition in English composition he was tied
for first place in his division with his friend, William
C. Whitney. In declamations he was third, Whitney
being first. He also received one of the five Townsend
premiums, awarded for the best original compositions submitted by seniors. The two great debating
societies, Linonian and Brothers, were active then,
and Sumner was prominent in the latter, serving as
vice-secretary, secretary, and president. In the freshman debate of that organization he won the first prize
against nine competitors, supporting the negative side
of the question: "Ought the United States to interfere
actively in behalf of nations struggling for liberty?"
In the sophomore competition he was equally successful. The subject for discussion was: "Is the government of the United States better adapted for a
civilized nation than that of Great Britain?" No
false patriotism prevented Sumner from taking the
negative side of this question. There is no record
of a junior debate, but in the senior competition he
once more took first place, the subject being: "Has the
Order of the Jesuits tended to advance civilization?"
Unfortunately the manuscript of this argument seems
not to have been preserved. He was bitterly disappointed in not winning the DeForest Medal, awarded
for the best oration delivered by a senior. It went to
Chamberlain, Linonia's ablest writer and declaimer,
acknowledged by Sumner's friends to be a better
public speaker, if not so good a thinker. The medal
was of gold worth one hundred dollars, and the winner
invariably turned it into cash immediately. Sumner's

disappointment was probably due both to the fact that he hated to be beaten, especially by Chamberlain, and also to the fact that he was ambitious to study further and sorely needed the money.

One of the most notable tributes to Sumner's ability and literary gifts, perhaps, was his election in the fall of 1860 to the central editorial board of *The University Quarterly*. The *Quarterly* was an intercollegiate publication, conceived and brought into being by Yale students. Its purpose was to enlist the active talents of the young men in America and, so far as possible, in foreign universities, in the discussion of questions and the communication of intelligence of common interest. Each of the institutions participating in the enterprise elected a board of editors, to which were assigned a certain number of pages proportionate to the number of undergraduates in the institution and the number of institutions in the association. The board at the place of publication, which was New Haven, compiled, printed, and had general business management of the magazine. Some twenty-six American institutions, together with Cambridge University and the University of Heidelberg, constituted the association. Owing in part to the war, but more particularly to the difficulty of smooth coöperation, the life of the *Quarterly* was short, extending only from January, 1860, to October, 1861.

At Yale the Board consisted of three members from each of the three upper classes, the election being by general vote of the students. Sumner, Chamberlain, and a third prospective clergyman, Ebenezer P. Hyde, were chosen from among the sophomores. The office entailed a great deal of drudgery and necessitated the expenditure of much time. Two contributions are credited to Sumner. One is a news article regarding happenings at Yale, and the other, probably his first published work, a study of Charles Kingsley's "Two Years Ago." [3] Characteristically enough, he uses the novel as the basis for the discussion of a moral question. Is the reading of fiction justifiable? If so, upon what grounds? The essay discloses as its author a person very much in earnest, disposed to look at everything from the point of view of religion, and strongly inclined to analysis and argument.

The great argument against the reading of novels has been their enervating influence upon the mind. That fiction might sometimes be read to advantage, as a pastime or mental recreation, probably no one would deny; but the argument as generally stated is that this kind of reading fascinates the young, draws their minds from more important and more useful pursuits, tempts them to waste time that is truly valuable, and incapacitates them for close and deep thought. This statement is no doubt just, and the argument is most powerful. Let us analyze it, however, and discover its causes. We trust that we shall find that it only proves fiction subject to abuse. The great cause of the enervating influence of novel reading upon the mind is that so few novels demand thought either after or during the perusal. In the excitement which they produce, the mind is whirled away without effort or volition of its own. Through page after page the mind follows the struggles of the hero, or the sorrows of the heroine, absorbed and excited. At the close of the volume the tension ends; the whole aim of the work is accomplished, and even if there were anything in it that was worthy of a sober second thought, the reaction upon the mind unfits it for the exertion. This want of encouragement or necessity for a reconsideration of the work after it has been completed is perhaps even worse than the excitement or the want of thought

[3] Vol. 4, p. 269.

of the first perusal. It has the most disastrous effect upon the memory, and upon the power of mind to review and grasp a course of argument. We have, therefore, not only the danger of giving up the mind to frivolous and useless pursuits, but the further danger of incapacitating it for undertaking any of those severer labors by which its healthy action is encouraged. No doubt this is stating the argument as strongly as any one, even the most strongly opposed to novel reading, would desire. But is it necessary that a novel to be such should excite, as we have above supposed, and should whirl the mind away in such an unnatural excitement as to discourage and preclude thought, and afford no matter for subsequent reflection? We promptly answer that it is not, and we have placed at the head of this Article the title of a novel that may serve, as a single instance, to vindicate our position.

There follows an analysis of the principal characters. They are found to be such as justify the genuine usefulness of the standard novel. Men really live and hope and dare and struggle as we see them doing in this little world of the imagination. We may let these dream personages lead our thoughts through their careers, and show us where such aims and activities as theirs end. If they lead us aright, we may profit before it is too late by their examples.

And now speaks the uncompromising moralist and apostle of religion, cocksure in his judgments, perfunctorily dismissing the great, and declaring unworthy anything which merely gives pleasure.

If the only object of the novelist were to amuse, then would he be no better than the mountebank. If he aim only at popularity, his art must be degraded by those artifices, by which alone this can be obtained. The object must be different from these, and should be infinitely higher. It should be to arouse good and noble thoughts and desires. To place before a man, especially before a youth, a character that shall, of itself, attract him and prompt him to say, 'This is a noble man, such a one as I would like to become,' is to do him a great service. This the novel may do. This is its proper province, and all who undertake to write fiction should have this in view, or they degrade a truly noble means of usefulness. Kingsley seems to appreciate this. He has therefore written for us in a very different spirit from that of any other novelist; in what we might call a *spirit* of religion. There is no ostentatious parade of an intention to exert a Christian influence, but such an influence pervades the book and is felt by every reader. This no other novelist of our language has attained. Not, by any means, that the phrases and principles of religion are wanting from their works, but that the religion they teach is of a spurious kind that can accomplish no good. When an author who has little or no knowledge of experimental religion attempts to introduce anything of the kind into his works, it is probable that it will be such as would be far better omitted. Dickens, Bulwer, Thackeray, and Brontë have been raising the novel to a high position as a study of life and human nature. Kingsley has gone far beyond them in perfecting it, by clothing the whole with a mantle of pure piety and true religion.

Sumner's contributions to the discussions in Brothers, always carefully prepared and written out, disclose that his thought was much upon character and its development, and that the interest in political and social questions which Harriet Martineau's "Illustrations of Political Economy" had stirred still possessed him. Their titles are significant: "Candor," "Liberality," "Self-culture," "Independence of Thought," "The Laboring Classes," "Political Equality," "Shall the Suffrage be Universal?'' ''Did the French Revolution Advance Civilization?'' The thoroughness, carefulness of definition, keen analysis, concreteness, and candor, which give his more mature writings much of their value and power, are conspicuous, and he expresses his views with the assurance and firmness which come from wide reading and honest thought.

Unquestionably, the following utterances from the essay on ''Self-culture'' issued out of the youthful Sumner's own heart. He had come to see in life a splendid opportunity. The determination to improve it possessed and governed him. He counted that day lost whose low descending sun viewed no progress made.

> Men are all about us that seem to be living an aimless, purposeless life, unworthy indeed to be called life. It is mere existence. Life is in itself something teeming with thought and purpose. Intelligent beings alone can be said in the highest sense of the word to live. It implies the recognition of all those high purposes and vast capabilities to which our existence is but a subordinate circumstance. The man of purpose alone truly lives. Every moment, therefore, is a splendid opportunity; every individual is a grand achievement of the creating power endowed with the grandest capabilities. . . . Every moment lost is so much gone from our power to make the most of the capabilities of which we are conscious. Physical, moral, and mental strength are in the grasp of each one, but they must be grasped. The man therefore who has stopped to think must become conscious of a duty that makes life seem but a moment in which to accomplish the work of centuries. Everything about him is for his improvement.

That Sumner was not over puritanical is disclosed in an argument on the negative side of the question,

"Is the Use of Tobacco Opposed to Sound Morals?", in which he has some quiet fun with those holding opposite views. One page of the manuscript has a hole burned through it as if by the stub of a lighted cigar or hot pipe ashes.

In an essay on "Composition Writing" hatred of all superficiality and bombast appears, and also indications that Sumner was reacting critically on the methods of teaching then in vogue. Although declaring that "it is not my intention to indulge in any strictures upon the course of instruction to which we are subject or to criticize the policy of our instructors, however much I may believe them liable to such criticism," his frankness will not permit him to do otherwise. The first rule for composition writing which he lays down is that one should not write until he has some thought to express and feels that he can express it better than any one has hitherto done. This requirement, he admits, would sweep out of consideration "most of our college literature and *all* the college composition exercises." If, however, a "man should read carefully the work of mature minds and by encouraging the thoughts thus engendered in his mind and by reconsidering the arguments presented, produce for himself new thoughts and opinions," the rule would be observed and composition writing be saved from the superficiality and positive harmfulness which present class room methods encourage.

Already the fact that life is a ceaseless conflict from which both good and evil must forever flow had impressed him, and the following from an essay entitled "The Law of Change" is perhaps the first of the many shots which he aimed at foolish idealists who imagine that the world can be made over into something altogether good and fair:

There is no perfection in anything finite, no point can ever be reached so secure or so perfect that no evil or abuse shall proceed from it. Hence then we have a pointed rebuke for those who are ever striving to reform and improve hoping in some golden era to attain a state of infallible perfection. This certain law of change will carry on men and principles from the fondly anticipated heights to new and perhaps worse evils and abuses.

It is interesting to note also how the lines along which his social and political views were to run later were already forming. He tears to pieces the theory of equality, points out that our political and social democracy is due primarily to abundance of land in a new country, and prophesies that class rule will develop as the population increases. He criticizes the electoral system, and declares that "it is contrary to all our primary ideas of right that those who have least at stake in a government should have control over it." He argues that the government of Great Britain is better adapted for a civilized nation than that of the United States because it limits the suffrage by property qualifications, has a legislative system which is more flexible and more quickly responsive to the will of the people, and is not hampered by a written constitution with a supreme court attachment. He asserts that the United States should not interfere actively in behalf of nations struggling for liberty, on the ground that such interference could be neither intelligent nor successful, but would involve the United States in difficulties with all European nations, call for the establishment of a large standing army, and destroy its one great opportunity for service, that of demonstrating to the world the success of the great experiment which has here been begun.

If there is any salvation for the human race from woe and misery it is in knowledge and in training to use knowledge.

Purposes and Consequences.

CHAPTER IV

YEARS ABROAD

WHEN the class of 1863 graduated William Graham Sumner was not present. Excused from attendance on the exercises by vote of the faculty, he was already on the high seas en route for Europe and the advantages offered by its universities. His absence was a grievous disappointment to his father. "It was painful to us," he wrote, "to see Commencement in the newspapers and to know what a distinguished part you would have played had you been home. Professor Thatcher told C. Wesson that he could hardly say how much detriment your absence would be to Commencement."

William's determination to have the best education available had been greatly strengthened by his college experiences. To secure it he was now prepared to undergo any labor and to make every sacrifice. Dr. Beadle's son, Heber, was studying theology at Geneva, and thither William decided to go. The greatest obstacle in his way was lack of funds. This was finally overcome by his classmate, William C. Whitney, who persuaded his older brother, Henry M. Whitney, to advance a sum of money which, by strict economy, would support William for a limited period.

Matters were further complicated, however, by the fact that just before his graduation William was drafted for the army. He appears never to have had the slightest inclination to go into the service. Indeed, he seems to have regarded the draft as an unwarrant-

47

able interference with the career upon which he had
set his heart. A Hartford contemporary, Captain
James E. Smith, when asked why William did not become a soldier, replied: "I don't know, but I always
felt that he considered the matter unemotionally from
every angle and decided that he was too valuable material to be fed to the guns." This opinion is perhaps
not quite fair to Sumner, yet it is probable that with
his hard, practical, Lancashire judgment he did survey
the situation coolly and come to the conclusion that
he could be of more use in the world by continuing his
education than by going to war. In his predicament,
Mr. Whitney again came to his rescue by furnishing
the money necessary to buy exemption. The task of
finding a substitute William left to his father.
Whether any one actually served in his stead is doubtful. The following report which Thomas Sumner sent
his son reveals that the person secured, after having
received his money, bolted.

I have got a substitute for you, in fact two. One
was a deserter, the other skedaddled. They left him in
the American Hotel, and he jumped through the window. I think I shall get a certificate for all that. I
have spent three half days in looking after substitutes,
and paid $250. I sent $50 back to Mr. Whitney.

Upon leaving America, William carried with him
this letter of commendation from Professor Noah Porter, addressed to Mr. Cyprian Wilcox.

New Haven, July 24, 1863.
My Dear Friend:
Mr. William Sumner, who will give or send you this
letter, is a young gentleman of superior powers and mind,
a very fine scholar and writer, who goes to Europe to

spend a year or two in study. His means are limited, but he has a brave heart and a ready and self-helping hand.

I have advised him to go if possible into the family of some German or Swiss Pastor in the country, where he can live cheaply and be shut up to the necessity of learning German rapidly and it may be French.

Can you not name to him some such family or person? Is our old friend Vahllmeh not settled yet? Would he not aid him by taking him to his family if he has one?

Mr. Sumner would be ready to meet any reasonable expense, but cannot be extravagant in his outlays. If Mr. S. calls on you, will you not give him the counsel which your own remembrance and acquaintance so well qualify you to give? In doing so you will not only aid a very excellent and promising man, but will confer a personal favor on your old

Acquaintance and friend
N. PORTER.

Please fail not to commend me to Mrs. Wilcox and to friend Vahllmeh, whom I hold in true and warm regard.

In order to travel as cheaply as possible, William had planned to cross in the steerage of a steamer, but upon inspecting his quarters he found them intolerable, and secured passage in a sailing craft, the *Fidelia,* which he describes as the oldest ship of the Black Bear Line.

In letters to his classmate Charles Wesson, William gives an interesting account of life aboard ship.

At Sea, July 24, 1863.

DEAR CHARLEY:

Very many things that I would write to you I should also write to Dim (Henry F. Dimock) and Bill (William C. Whitney). It will save me very much repetition and also enable me to write much longer letters if I send them to you in turn and you send them around to each other.

I wrote you from New York telling you of my plans and movements up to the day of sailing.

24th.

We were to go to sea in the packet on Saturday, but the day of sailing was postponed until Monday. On Sunday I went to church with Mr. Whitney in the morning and in the afternoon we went up to the Park. Mr. Whitney proposed one good dinner together before I sailed, and we had it at Delmonico's, as good a dinner as I ever ate. The time appointed for leaving was 12 M. Monday, but the tug did not leave till one. It took us over to the ship, which lay off the Battery. We got away about 4 P.M., but the tug broke down and left us at anchor just below Staten Island for a whole day. Tuesday at 4½ P.M. we got away again and got to sea Tuesday evening. Wednesday morning it came calm and remained so until to-night. Now we have a breeze again and are off. I am very comfortably situated. Our lady passenger backed out and very glad I am for two reasons. First, she was not by any means a lady, and secondly, I got her stateroom all to myself. I have for fellow passengers two Germans and an Englishman. One of the Germans is a very nice fellow and has told me a great deal about Germany. The Englishman is not much, but he has talked about England considerable and has told me considerable about it. The Captain I like very much. He gave me a quadrant and showed me how he kept his reckoning and also gave me some paper and showed me how to make a chart so that I can keep the ship's reckoning from day to day. I am studying French a little so I get along very well. Time has not hung heavily upon my hands at all. I have not been sick yet. We have had no rough weather. I have only been a little squeamish and lost my appetite. To-day, however, I have felt better. I often think of you fellows. The captain is a very nice man. He is quite sociable and we have very nice times together. He gives us very good food and abundance of it though for my part I can eat scarcely any-

thing. I have not been sick yet, but I feel a little uneasy
at times and the idea of eating anything is disgusting.
From Wednesday morning until Friday night we were
becalmed and only moved about two miles directly north-
ward. Friday evening a breeze sprang up and to-day
(Sunday) we are buzzing along beautifully with all sails
set. The sun is shining brightly and it is altogether very
pleasant. I hope that you fellows will enjoy the Bacca-
laureate this afternoon. I should like to look in upon
you for a little while. In the second cabin we have 8 or
9 passengers. One is an old Irishman who brought the
Captain down on him by blowing around and making a
noise. No. 2 and 3 are a man and his wife (English).
The man has been in the army. He is an ignoramus and
('áya) thinks he knows everything. I never talk with
him, but I have heard him talking to others. His wife
is the homeliest woman I ever saw. She is cross-eyed
and innocent of either crinoline or soap. No. 3 and 4
are another couple with a child and prospects of another,
so imminent as to make it probable that we may bring
one more passenger into Liverpool than we took from
New York. The woman is dirty and ragged, and for that
matter so are they all. It is amusing to hear the stories
of the immigrants when they are coming over. The conclusion that I have come to is that going to Europe in a
packet may be very well, coming back is quite another
thing. We have seen no pirates yet and we are in the
very place for them. Neither have we seen any gunboats
which has been a cause of much grumbling on the part
of the Captain. He is a dogmatic old fellow, full of
crotchets and I have learned to let him talk his talk out
without noticing him. He has got his little boy with him.
A nice little cove, ten or a dozen years old, who runs
about the deck and makes boats. By the way, when we
were coming down New York bay I saw a little specimen
of the merchant service. Two of the sailors were drunk
of course. One of them came on board with his jaw
broken. He said his boarding master did it. The latter

individual came on board after nine. When they were weighing anchor the man didn't work to suit him, and he punched him awfully. After that the mates pitched into him and two others who were drunk, and bruised their faces all up. They have been going around here ever since with their faces all bruised up. One of them has one eye all shut up. It was the most disgusting thing I ever saw, but it seems to be the common thing in such cases. I have got a bet on the trip with one of the Dutchmen. He offered me two to one that we were *six weeks* out and I took him up. He did it in a fit of disgust during the calm, but he was in earnest. I thought I would take him up, but I shall never take his money on such a ridiculous wager.

Tuesday, 28th.

I have been sick for two days, but I am better this evening. I have not been sick at my stomach, but dull and drowsy with headache and languor. I have no appetite yet, but think I shall get one soon. The wind holds finely and we are getting along in fine style. . . . I have been laying out my trip through the British Isles by the aid of an atlas which I found on board. I am going by a shore line around through Northern Wales and Holyhead, and from there to Ireland. Then back to Liverpool and from there by steamer to Glasgow. Then I shall walk to Edinburgh, then to Abbotsford and Carlisle and back to Liverpool. My address will therefore be at Liverpool for a week or two after I arrive, but after you get this you had better direct to London. I have great help in laying out a cheap route from my English fellow passenger and think I shall be able to see a great deal of England at a slight expense.

In a similar letter, written to his father, William speaks more in detail of the Captain's kindness to him, and reveals his eagerness for knowledge of every kind.

At Sea, 23d.

Still calm. It is very dull lying here doing nothing, but we have not made five miles to-day. This noon the Captain gave me an old quadrant which he calls the 'pig yoke,' and let me take an observation. He also taught me to make the reckoning and gave me some paper to make a chart of the voyage. By studying a little French and so on I manage to get rid of the time pretty well. This evening I have had a good talk with some of the sailors about sailing and about ships. I have learned nearly all the ropes and sails in the ship and if we have as long a voyage as it seems likely to be, I shall know considerable about the ship before we get to Liverpool.

One of my German fellow passengers is a very nice fellow and is quite well educated and I enjoy his society very much. He has told me a great deal about Germany. Another passenger is an Englishman from Manchester. I don't think much of him. He came out he says for four months, just on a little visit, and is now going back. He has told me a great deal about England and the mode of living there. The Captain also told me a great deal. You will see that the Captain is very kind. He seems to be quite pleased that I know or care anything about navigation. I mean, however, to learn all I can about anything and everything I can. I shall certainly learn much more about a ship here than I possibly could on a steamer.

Upon arriving in England William carried out the plan of travel arranged on shipboard. Much to his father's delight, he visited Preston and Walton-le-Dale and sent home a detailed account of what he saw. The last of December found him ready to take up work at Geneva.

During the six months spent here Sumner worked incessantly. From the time he got up in the morning until well on toward midnight he gave every minute possible to his books. Short walks were his only exercise, and seldom did any form of amusement break his customary routine. He lived in a private family where he gave instruction in English to one of the household. Although attending some lectures in church history and allied subjects, he devoted himself almost entirely to French and Hebrew. He had no high opinion of the university instruction at Geneva and depended chiefly upon private tutors. From a journal which he kept during this period we get an idea of his manner of life.

Monday, Oct. 5th, 1863.

Rose at 7¾. Breakfast. Commenced to study at the beginning of Ollendorf's French, and studied from 8½ till 12¼. Dinner. French from 12¾ to 2. Lecture by Dr. Mede at the Oratoire from 2 till 3 on church history. French from 3¾ to 4¾. Walked with Mr. Beadle, Heber, and Mr. Brocher from 5 till 6½. Supper. French from 8 till 9½, learning avoir and être perfectly. Letter to Mr. Whitney from 9½ to 10½. Bible and list of words and journal till 11¼. Bed. Day very pleasant. We walked around the end of the lake and saw the sunset on Mont Blanc which was very fine.

Vendredi 9 Obre.

Rose at 8. Studied French 8½ to 12. Hebrew 1 to 3. Went to my first Hebrew recitation and found it decidedly 'one horse.' Mean to try and get private instruction. Went to see Heber, who was sick. Returned at 5, studied till 7. Evening English till 10. Studied till 11. Serenade by a very good chorus under my window. Bed at 12.

Mercredi le quatorze Oct.

Rose at 7½. Studied from 8 till 12 French. Do. from 1 to 5½. French lesson till 7. After tea Heber came in. Went into the dining room and saw some strange ladies, one of whom spoke English, confound her. From 9½ to 10 corrected Mademoiselle's exercises. 10 to 11 Bossuet, exercise, journal, and Tales of a Grandfather which I am to translate. Bed 11½.

Jeudi le 15 Oct.

Rose at 8½. Went to buy French Grammar. Went to post. No letters. Bought Grammar and Lexicon of Larousse. Studied from 10 to 12. Do. from 1-5. Went and paid for my pants and bought a Hebrew bible, also a novel, Ici et là. Studied from 6 till 7. After tea English till 9½. Studied from 9½ till 11. Bible and Journal. Read Ici et là till 12½.

So, with little variation, except that soon it is written in French, the journal continues. Not even on Christmas does William take a holiday.

Vendredi le 25.

Le jour de Noël. Je me levai à 9, Français à 3. Essayai de prendre un leçon mais M. Paton ne le voulait pas. Soirée en famille. Au lit à 10.

William had not been in Geneva more than two months before the limitations of the place created in him a strong desire to study in Germany. For some time he held back. Still ardently orthodox, and brought up to believe that those who hold differing theological views should be avoided, he hesitated to subject himself to influences reputedly heretical and destructive. Regarding the matter he wrote both to his father and to Dr. Beadle. The former advised strongly against putting one's faith in jeopardy.

I feel sorry to hear you are disappointed in your theological studies, and find it a one-horse concern. . . .

I should regret exceedingly if you should come back a confirmed German skeptic. I know from my own experience how unsatisfactory it is not to know what one believes, and yet I find nineteen-twentieths of my acquaintances in just that fix. The Germans are noted the world over for their heresies and isms, theorizing and philosophizing on every phase of religion, no doubt some with the purest of motives, but often led astray by searching for truth as it is called. My idea is, if Christianity is all a humbug, as some have asserted, it would be absolutely wrong to oppose it unless something better was ready to take its place. And my advice is to avoid everything that savors of doubt or distrust. Apply your own rule as you applied it to the Universalist church when I asked you about going one Sunday night. You then thought it best to avoid any place of doubtful reputation.

Dr. Beadle's advice was somewhat different. In a warmly affectionate letter, shot through with religious fervor, he does not oppose William's studying in Germany, but tries to fortify him against any attendant dangers.

Geneva, Oct. 31st, 1863.

DEAR WILLIE:

May God bless you in your work. Be patient and courageous, what the Scripture means by *strong of heart*. I have always urged you to *thorough* preparation. Now more than ever does this seem desirable, imperative. You need to be 'thoroughly furnished,' and remember, after all, that the best equipment is to be clothed with humility and filled with the spirit. If you keep near to God, I have no fear of Germany. German theologians have studied and searched on independent ground, much without God. If you go star-hunting, you will find only night, not day. Studying will not hurt you, speculation will not imperil your faith if your heart is full of the

Holy Ghost. But do not venture out upon doubtful ground unless you go with a firm grasp upon the hand of Jesus. It is good not even to look toward Sodom, better not to pitch the tent that way. Do not think I have fears about you. I have learned to leave you with God, and know that He will guide you and gird you for your work.

And now good-by,

With love more than ever,

E. R. BEADLE.

William's eagerness for knowledge was stronger than his fears for his faith, and though he persevered at Geneva through the winter, he left in April for Germany. Before going he wrote to Charles U. Shepard, a classmate at Yale, then studying medicine at Göttingen, regarding the merits of the different universities. From Shepard he received the following interesting reply:

Göttingen, March 17th, 1864.

DEAR BILL:

Your letter is just this minute received and I hasten to reply. I am going away this noon to Hanover, but will come back Monday, to remain three weeks, and then I leave for Dresden for a two weeks' absence. I will return after this second visit for the beginning of the ensuing term. (April 15th or 20th.) Now I will, if you give me instructions, make all the arrangements for your comfort and ease next semester. What say you? This University and Heidelberg are the two leading ones. This University is better than Heidelberg for the following reasons: 1st, there is more studying done here than anywhere else, and especially more than at Heidelberg, where the students do nothing but bumming. German students, as perhaps you know, devote their first two or three terms to bumming; these terms are spent in Heidelberg; afterwards they come here to finish and do real study. The best German is spoken at Göttingen. There will be few Americans here next term (*Thank heaven*), and none of them bummers. There are every summer about 100 of the loosest Americans residing in Heidelberg, besides as many English. Take my advice and beware of Americans on the continent, I mean 99 out of 100. Now for Halle. Halle is very *high school* in its theological view, approaching *Romanism,* and you *would have a hard time there.* This is not my own opinion, but obtained from the highest source I could consult. If you come to Göttingen you can immediately enter the University, thereby obtaining *sundry advantages;* and everything being cheaper for a student, it is really a great reason you should do so. You have no *examen* to pass, no *papers* to present, only your *passport.* Then you pay about $5 and you have a diploma stating your entry in the University. Also they give you a card which prevents any policeman in Germany from touching you. You can only be tried by the laws of the University, a copy of which is given to you, and you give your word to obey them. Lectures cost about $5 a course. Lessons in all modern languages the same. Oriental languages about the same. The greatest Sanskrit scholar in Germany (Prof. Ewald) is here. The greatest Hebrew scholar also, Prof. Holzhausen (a Jew), etc. etc. The views here are very liberal indeed. I can get you fine rooms for $60 the year, good ones for less. I think $50 is about what I should take. Of course you can have rooms for less time; as long as you want them. I write this much in a great hurry and could say more, but it is not possible now. Write me immediately with any questions you please. Come by all means so as *to begin the term.* Our library is 3d in the world. Come if you want to study, but don't unless that is your wish. There is nothing else to do here hardly. With my best wishes to aid you all I can, I am ever your old friend,

                                        C. U. SHEPARD, JR.

Conditions in Göttingen, as described in this letter, were just what William sought, and thither he went to spend two years among influences which did much to shape his attitude of mind and determine his career. He mastered the German language, continued his study of Hebrew, took up Old Testament criticism, developed a great interest in Egyptology, delved in theology, and listened to Lotze demonstrate his system of philosophy. For Professor Heinrich Ewald, whom it was his privilege to know with some intimacy, a rare scholar, and a man of the greatest warmth, earnestness, independence, fearlessness, and love of truth, he acquired the highest admiration. With the same assiduity and disregard for physical consequences that he had shown at Geneva he applied himself to his studies. After three or four weeks' residence in Göttingen he writes in his journal:

Mercredi le 27 Mai

Levé à 7½. De 8 á 1 Grammaire Allemand et composition. De 2 à 3 au musée. De 3 à 4 Composition. De 4 à 7½ avec Shepard et Ben. De 8 à 10½ 'Soll und Haben.' C'a été aujourd'hui le jour de naissance du roi, et à cause de cela congé dans l'universite. A midi il y avait de la musique à l'hotel de ville et une salve d'artillerie. On a vu aussi ici et là des drapeaux suspendu aux balcones et fenêtres. L'Allemand n'est encore difficile. Je lis l'histoire assez peniblement et 'Soll und Haben' est aussi assez difficile. Cependent je travaille et j'espere que je pourrai bientôt lire avec plus de facilité. Je fais beaucoup de places pour mes études theologique aussitôt que je pourvai les entreprendre. Je pense souvent aussi ces jours a l'Amerique et la vie qui me attend là bas. J'espere qui je pourrai me préparer bien ici pour cette vie et que je serai bien apprete à mon travail. A present je fais seulement des études de Allemand comme moyen le plus facile à poursuivre plus tard les études distinctivement theologiques.

He finds the hours of the day too few for the work he wishes to do, and so resolves to get up earlier in the morning.

Lundi le 30

Je me levai à 8. Cette manière de faire n'est pas du tout comme il faut. Je dois me lever de beaucoup meilleure heure car je ne trouve pas que j'aie assez de temps dans ma journée pour les études que je dois et que je veux faire. Je voudrais me lever au moins à 6 heures. Alors je pourrais commencer à etudier à 6½. Je vais essayer de faire ceci. Je commencai à étudier á 8½ et lis la grammaire jusqu'à 12. De 12 á 1 j'ecuvis de l'historie. Á 2 au musée. Encore des nouvelles des grandes batailles devant Richmond. Dieu donne que il nous gagne cette bataille. De 3 à 6½ j'etudiais l'Allemand. De 6½ à 7 Mr. Socin pais á chez moi. De 7 à 8 leçon. De 8 à 9½ au musée. De 9½ à 11 Jean le Trouveur. Au lit 11½.

Curiosity led him to witness several duels, but as soon as he found himself beginning to enjoy them he judged that it was time for him to see no more.

Samedi le 4

Je me levai à 6, et allai voir les duels. J'en vis trois dont un etait entre Mr. Storlling et un autre. Il est tout extremement fou. D'abord j'étais degouté; plus tard cependant j m'interessais et je verrai à comprendre comment on prend plaisir à ces affaires. Ça m'était bien assez de preuve que j'en avais vu autant qu' il eut an fallait.

These years in Göttingen were hard years. One of less grit and power of will would not have been equal to them. Incessant mental application with little exercise or recreation began to tell upon him and he had several attacks of sickness which occasioned considerable apprehension at home. "Be sure to observe your health," his father wrote him, "for of all men a broken down clergyman is most to be pitied." All the time, furthermore, he was worried about money. His father scraped together what he could for him, and his brother Joe, then drawing a good salary as chief clerk in the Adjutant General's office in New Orleans, forwarded one hundred and fifty dollars, but owing to the war the exchange was against them almost three to one. For a while, due to overwork and worry, William was in a state of extreme mental depression. He feared he would have to give up his work and go home, but with courage and resolution he forced himself to keep on. One day there came to him like a thunderbolt, he says, the thought that there would arrive a time when he would realize that he could be only what he was, and would ask himself how earlier, when he had his chance, he could have been such a fool. "Think only of what you will be if you are strong," he admonishes himself, "and that which you will not be if you are now weak. I have made my resolution. I think of that which is in the future and I have patience and hope." Upon hearing of his needs, Mr. Whitney again came to his aid, and the way was made clear for as thorough a preparation as he might desire.

Perhaps it was the effect of the war upon his own fortunes which stimulated his interest in political affairs at home. Certain it is that he talked them over with Professor Ewald and other Germans and got their point of view. He also discussed them in letters to his family and friends. His sympathies were with the Republican party and with the North in general, but he did not hesitate to criticize severely some of the government's policies. As was to be expected from his earlier advocacy of a limited franchise, he was strongly opposed to giving the right to vote to the negroes. His opinions called forth some rather warm retorts from his brother and father. The former, under date of September 1, 1864, wrote as follows:

I don't like the way you speak of the Government and war. Undoubtedly you see the uproar and noise and bustle of the great conflict, but you are too far away from the great pulse of the people to feel the encouragement which you would feel if here. The general impression seems to be that Grant will take Richmond, but it must take a long time. The Government has called for 500,-000 more men and I guess the Johnny Rebs will find there is no peace for the wicked. I don't wonder that the foreigners are neutral when our young men go over there and lose all their patriotism. You never had much anyway, but since you have got over there you are a little 'coppery.' No one denies the right to criticize our public men, but we must deny that it is policy to be continually squabbling about this, that, and the other, spending more of our time criticizing than in fighting rebels.

On August 20, 1865, he wrote:

In regard to the suffrage for the negro I think that any man who has used the bullet in the war *for the salvation of the Government* is entitled to the ballot. If secessionists, loud and open can
> Uncrook the hinges of the knee
> That thrift may follow fawning
and receive their pardon and acceptance as American citizens and vote, then the black soldier who lost his leg or arm fighting for my country has at least the same claim on her gratitude. I think you are like too many others

who say, 'Well! the nigger is free now, why can't you let him alone?' We can't let him alone,—our duty is to elevate him. Doing less, we surely fail in our duty as civilized Christian people, and after we have done as much to elevate him as we have done to degrade and debase him we may rest from our labors and see that progress has been made.

Evidently William and his father had had a spirited argument over the same matter, for on September 21, 1865, the latter wrote:

I think our nigger difference might as well suspend, as it is not very likely that you or I will change our views in consequence of anything either of us might say. I had a good deal thought out, but concluded it best to let it drop as not worth the paper.

William did not lose his faith under the pressure of German influences, but he became more critical, his evangelistic fervor was cooled, and his views regarding the Bible and theological dogmas underwent more or less change. He carried on long theological discussions with his friend, William C. Whitney. "I should hate to see you come back an atheist, or anything of that sort, and there is no danger," Whitney wrote, "but I don't care what a man believes if he has come to it honestly, and we are waiting to pin ourselves on to your coattails when you get back, for we know you, and know that you wouldn't dodge the issue for fear you would offend some dogmatic old woman or be unorthodox, and it is mighty important to us to have one theologian to swear by. We have all concluded that we shall have to suspend judgment on a good many of these topics until you get back to tell us what is the thing to believe."

The great value which these two years in Germany were to him, Sumner himself declares.

I enjoyed intensely the two years which I spent at Göttingen. I had the sense of gaining all the time exactly what I wanted. The professors whom I knew there seemed to me bent on seeking a clear and comprehensive conception of the matter under study (what we call 'the truth') without regard to any consequences whatever. I have heard men elsewhere talk about the nobility of that spirit; but the only *body* of men whom I have ever known who really lived by it, sacrificing wealth, political distinction, church preferment, popularity, or anything else for the truth of science, were the professors of biblical science in Germany. That was precisely the range of subjects which in this country was then treated with a reserve in favor of tradition which was prejudicial to everything which a scholar should value. So far as those men infected me with their spirit, they have perhaps added to my usefulness, but not to my happiness. They also taught me rigorous and pitiless methods of investigation and deduction. Their analysis was their strong point. Their negative attitude toward the poetic element, their indifference to sentiment, even religious sentiment, was a fault, seeing that they studied the Bible as a religious book and not for philology and history only; but their method of study was nobly scientific, and was worthy of rank, both for its results and its discipline, with the best of the natural science methods. I sometimes wonder whether there is any one else in exactly the same position as I am, having studied biblical science with the Germans, and then later social science, to mark the striking contrast in method between the two. The later social science of Germany is the complete inversion in its method of that of German philology, classical criticism, and biblical science. Its subjection to political exigencies works upon it as disastrously as subjection to dogmatic creeds has worked upon biblical science in this country.[1]

In May, 1866, William took up his residence at Oxford for the purpose of studying Anglican theology. Before leaving Göttingen he had practically made up his mind to return to the Episcopal Church. For some time his friend Whitney had been urging him to take this step. Writing in September, 1865, he made the following appeal in behalf of himself, Dimock, and Wesson.

> We are all of us Episcopalians, Bill, and you must be the same, can't you? I don't mean to say do it because we are, but don't you like it best? There is the greatest dearth of ability in the church here and I think we shall get to be pillars somewhere perhaps before you get back. The Presbyterian church leaves so much scope for individual peculiarities in the preacher that it isn't good as a system. Now and then an able man can carry the thing off, but generally they pray for things that you don't go with them on and their personality is so unpleasant that it don't work. The Episcopal Church is undoubtedly taking the best classes of society here and I think for the good reason that there is less to offend enlightened feelings in it.

How much William was moved by such reasoning it is impossible to say. In a fine spirited letter to his old pastor, Dr. Beadle, he frankly states the feeling which made him hesitate to become a minister in a Congregational or Presbyterian church.

[1] "Sketch of William Graham Sumner," *Popular Science Monthly*, Vol. XXXV. Reprinted in "The Challenge of Facts and Other Essays," p. 6.

84 St. Aldates St.,

DEAR SIR: Oxford, June 10th, 1866.

I wrote to you some time in January '65 since which time I have only heard from you indirectly as having been in Hartford or through some friend. My sister wrote me a few months ago that you had been at our house. It is also nearly a year since I heard from Heber. I wrote to him as he directed me in the care of Inman at Liverpool so that he would get it just before leaving, but I presume that he did not get it, as I asked him to write to me from America about the steps he took there and about getting settled, which he has not done. In the meantime I have been studying at Göttingen, as you have no doubt heard from my relatives, with great pleasure and profit. Göttingen is the only place at which I have yet studied which satisfied me. The thoroughness of their scholarship and the scientific accuracy of their methods are unrivaled. I shall rejoice all my life long that it has been my privilege to study there. I felt, however, very strongly, that I was out of the current of Anglo-American theology, that the thoughts and sentiments of the place were foreign to ours, and that I was not keeping up with our theological movements. I therefore determined to come to England for my last few months in Europe and read up English theology. I left Göttingen on the 10th of April and spent about ten weeks traveling. I went to Munich and Augsburg and from there around by Murenberg to Frankfurt and Mainz, then down the Rhein to Coblenz and Cologne. Then to Paris, where I stayed three weeks, and then to London, where I spent two weeks in Great Russell St. I came here about the 28th of May, got a room, and am now reading for the most part in the Bodleian. I had some letters from Göttingen to England which have secured me all the help I needed, and some other friends whom I have made have also been very kind, so that I am, I think, getting full advantage of all there is here. I must say, however, that I am greatly disappointed in English

theology so far as I have got into it. Books which I had
heard of as grand works in their departments turn out
shallow or unsatisfactory. I do not, I hope, feel contempt
for anybody or anything—that would be very unbecoming—but I had hoped and expected to find that their
works would repay more richly the time they require.
My trunks have not yet come from Göttingen and I am
not able to settle down to study as thoroughly as I want
to, but I expect them this week. This week is 'com-
memmoralia' and the town is very busy—after that it
will be very quiet and I shall be able to prosecute my
studies very undisturbedly. How long I shall stay here
I do not know. I now intend to stay until the first of
October and then to spend a few weeks in Scotland and
Ireland, and get home by Thanksgiving. It is very possible, however, that I may get tired of it and start sooner.
I may be home in September, though I do not think I
shall go so soon. This will serve to give you a slight
idea of what I have done and am intending to do. I cannot, however, give you any idea of the experience I have
had in studying theology. I do not intend to try to describe that now as indeed it would be impossible within
the compass of a letter, but I have been thinking for a
long time of writing to you about one decision at which
I have arrived and which under the circumstances I feel
bound to write to you about before I make it final. That
is, that I want to go back to the Episcopal Church. I do
not know whether this will be any great disappointment
to you or not. I sincerely hope not. At any rate the
perfectly gentlemanly and delicate manner in which you
have always treated me makes it possible for me to write
to you upon the subject openly and plainly. I have always remembered with pride and pleasure what you said
to me at Geneva, that you thought we had always understood each other perfectly. It is my wish that you should
always understand me. You know of course that when
I joined the Pearl St. Church I did not and could not
have any preference grounded on a conviction on doc-

trinal points. I was not of proper age and had not the
education to go into these things. I was led almost entirely by my respect and affection for you personally,
and by my desire to attend your church. I found out
soon after I left Hartford that my preference had been
for the Pearl St. before any Episcopal church in Hartford rather than for Calvinistic before Episcopal theology. I was contented, however, to let it remain so and
thought that it would make little difference. I did not
intend then at all ever to go back. Since I have been
in Europe, however, and have been studying Theology,
properly speaking, I have had a growing desire to do so.
At first I did not entertain the idea very seriously, being
deterred to a great extent by the thought of the disappointment it would probably be to you. It has, however,
grown upon me until I have decided to go back unless
you should very decidedly oppose it. I have not yet
stated the determination to any one, although some of
my friends in Germany know that I have been thinking
of it. I reserved writing to you about it until I should
know my own mind decidedly. I do not know whether
you will care to hear any of my reasons, but I will say
that they are not doctrinal. I do not care anything for
the differences in point of doctrine. The hierarchy is a
very convenient form of church government and has at
least seemingly no objectional features. The ceremonies
I do not regard as at all objectionable—rather the contrary. On the other hand I have never liked prayer meetings. I could not bear to lead one (as pastor) and hear
such bad taste and bad theology as one sometimes hears.
I do not like revivals and could never with honesty conduct one. I do not believe that I could ever cause one in
my church, and you know that that is generally the test
of the pastor's usefulness. I do not like the doctrine of
conversion as it is commonly taught. I say nothing of
predestination because I believe that it is not now held
by our American churches, at least in its rigor. Do not,
I beg you, whatever else you may think of this, believe

me guilty of ingratitude and neglect for people who have been most kind friends of mine. When I think of my career as a clergyman which now, I suppose, lies directly before me, I am forced to ask myself in view of my own tastes and feelings and opinions where I shall probably be able to work to the greatest advantage, and that is the only ground of my choice. It would be impossible for a Congregational clergyman to deprecate prayer meetings and revivals in which the very life of his church depends and I could never sincerely and honestly conduct either. It is a disagreeable thing for me to take this step because it makes me appear fickle and unsettled and I know that my father will blame me in this view of it worse than any one else when he hears of it. It would be a very great happiness to me if you should respect my feelings in this matter and understand them as I hope you will, so that I might do whatever seems to me the best and right thing without forfeiting at all your respect and friendship, which I value most highly. When I look back upon my life it seems very strange how I have been led and how friends have been raised up for me at every point. In such a retrospect you have a most prominent part and I must always look upon it as one of the most remarkable orderings of Providence that I owe in a great measure to that affection for you which led me to join your church that excellent education which I have enjoyed. I do not forget that if I had remained an Episcopalian all that would have been very different. Under these circumstances I should regret more than I can say if our friendship (for such it has been) should be diminished. I do not think it at all necessary that it should be and I hope soon to hear from you that you render me in this matter full liberty to do as I shall think best. Please remember me to Heber and Miss Susie. I should like to hear from Heber. Please write me as soon as you get this else I shall not be sure it has reached you. I have only your old address.

Very truly and gratefully yours, WM. G. SUMNER.

The reply to this letter which William in due time received was wholly in keeping with the spirit of his own, and reveals the bigness of the man who had befriended him as a youth, inspired him to make the most of himself, and directed and encouraged him in his struggles.

> Philadelphia, 205 South Sixth St.
> July 14th, 1866.

DEAR WILLIE:.

Your good letter from Oxford was refreshing to me. Amid my many and imperative duties I had lost sight of you, but had not forgotten you. I shall never do that. I am bound to you very tenderly and these ties strengthen with the going and coming of the years. Yes: go, and may God bless you and bless me also. I wish most of all to have you work where you will work the most naturally and the most effectually. Be only a *Christian* minister. Battle for Christ in the highest and noblest sense. If I was in your place I think I should follow the leadings of such Providence as seems to direct you. I expect to see you a strong man and a useful one. I hope you will improve your opportunities at Oxford. Your time there will be of much avail to you and tell well for you in this country. I cannot at this moment write you at length and hasten off this note to give you my words of love and approval at the earliest moment. Heber is settled in a parish in Bridgeton, N. J., and doing finely. Wife and one baby boy are just at this minute in Paris, but go soon to Switzerland. Write me soon again. Remember that one debt you owe to me is to let me keep abreast of your march and learn of all your weal and woe.

More than ever yours in Christ our Lord.

> E. R. BEADLE.

Sumner's conviction that the Episcopal Church was most congenial to his views and tastes was strengthened, he says, by a study of Hooker's "Ecclesiastical Polity," which he made while at Oxford. There, too, he had his love for political science reawakened.

I went over to Oxford in the spring of 1866. Having given up all my time in Germany to German books, I wanted to read English literature on the same subjects. I expected to find it rich and independent. I found that it consisted of second-hand adaptations of what I had just been studying. I was then quite thoroughly Teutonized, as all our young men are likely to be after a time of study in Germany. I had not undergone the toning-down process which is necessary to bring a young American back to common sense, and I underrated the real services of many Englishmen to the Bible as a religious book —exactly the supplement which I then needed to my German education. Ullmann's 'Wesen des Christenthums,' which I had read at Göttingen, had steadied my religious faith, and I devoted myself at Oxford to the Anglican divines and to the standard books of the Anglican communion. The only one of these which gave me any pleasure or profit was Hooker's 'Ecclesiastical Polity.' The first part of this book I studied with the greatest care, making an analysis of it and reviewing it repeatedly. It suited exactly those notions of constitutional order, adjustment of rights, constitutional authority, and historical continuity, in which I had been brought up, and it presented those doctrines of liberty under law applied both to church and state which commanded my enthusiastic acceptance. It also presented Anglicism in exactly the aspect in which it was attractive to me. It reawakened, however, all my love for political science, which was intensified by reading Buckle and also by another fact next to be mentioned.

The most singular contrast between Göttingen and Oxford was this: at Göttingen everything one got came from the University, nothing from one's fellow students. At Oxford it was not possible to get anything of great value from the University; but the education one could get from one's fellows was invaluable. There was a set of young fellows, or men reading for fellowships, there at that time who were studying Hegel. I became intimate with several of them. Two or three of them have since died at an early age, disappointing hopes of useful careers. I never caught the Hegelian fever. I had heard Lotze at Göttingen and found his suggestions very convenient to hold on by, at least for a time. We used, however, in our conversations at Oxford, to talk about Buckle and the ideas which he had then set afloat, and the question which occupied us the most was whether there could be a science of society, and, if so, where it should begin and how it should be built. We had all been eager students of what was then called the 'philosophy of history,' and I had also felt great interest in the idea of God in history, with which my companions did not sympathize. We agreed, however, that social science must be an induction from history, that Buckle had started on the right track, and that the thing to do was to study history. The difficulty which arrested us was that we did not see how the mass of matter could ever be so mastered that the induction could actually be performed if the notion of an 'induction from history' should be construed strictly. Young as we were, we never took up this crude notion as a real program of work. I have often thought of it since, when I have seen the propositions of that sort which have been put forward in twenty years.[2]

In June, 1866, Sumner was elected a tutor at Yale. The election was brought about, apparently, largely through the activities of his classmate and friend, David B. Perry, himself at that time a tutor and theological student, and entirely without any knowledge on Sumner's part. The latter welcomed it, however,

[2] "Sketch of William Graham Sumner," "Challenge of Facts and Other Essays," p. 7.

as affording an opportunity for further study and better acquaintance with church affairs in the United States, before taking up the actual work of the ministry. Sumner accepted the position in the following letter to President Woolsey:

84 Aldates St., Oxford,
July 11th, 1866.

REVEREND SIR

I received day before yesterday intelligence of my election as tutor. It is a letter from Mr. D. B. Perry to Mr. Wessen, dated June 14th, and was forwarded to me from Germany. As so long a time has elapsed and as an early reply was desired I address myself directly to you and by the first steamer. I was very much flattered by an honor which I had never expected. I have spent the last three years studying theology and was intending to come home in November and commence work as a minister. I suppose that in view of the preparation generally considered sufficient I am prepared to do so, but I am not at all in haste to assume the responsibility, and if I can spend a year yet in *America* before doing so I should be very glad. Such is the state of the case and so I reply that if I can come for a year without *binding* myself to stay longer I would like to come and will try to do the college the best service I can. I hope you will not think it unbecoming in me to set this condition, but the fact is that after getting so expensive an education for my profession it would not pay for me now to spend two or three years in any work aside from it. Mr. Perry did not write me any of the conditions at all, and I know nothing about them. I can quite well understand, however, that you should not like to have tutors come for just one year and if such is the case, please let me know and I shall be contented. I will make arrangements to be in America by the first of September unless I hear from you to the contrary. I wish I could know too what I am to teach. I thank you very much for thinking of me for the place at any rate, and am with great respect

Yours obediently,

WM. G. SUMNER.

Before returning to America Sumner had one great pleasure. At Göttingen, seemingly, he had met Lord Archibald Campbell, son of the Duke of Argyle. A warm friendship had sprung up between the two which was to last all their lives. Upon Campbell's suggestion they made a tour of Scotland, and William had the delight, not only of viewing its beautiful scenery, but of meeting many persons of rank.

William was not a person to be over-impressed by titles and social prestige, yet one of such humble antecedents, who three years before had crossed the Atlantic in a sailing craft, because he could ill afford passage in a steamer, would have been more than human, had he not been somewhat elated as he returned home with such experiences fresh in his mind. But of far greater satisfaction to William was the consciousness that he had got the knowledge and power for which he went. The struggle had been hard. There had been many a dark day. But he had been strong "to strive, to seek, to find, and not to yield."

We cannot fulfill our destiny by sitting still, by doing nothing, by suppressing discussion, by bragging about the Yale of fifty years ago. Drs. Woolsey and Porter have not exhausted all wisdom to the end of time, although such a statement, put into cold type, is likely to shake Yale to its foundations. Yale College is greater than any men. It is criminal to let it lose years out of its life by consideration for the interests or feelings of anybody. It must go on. The existing generation is just as competent to do its work and live its life as the last was.

Letter to the New Haven *Morning News.*

CHAPTER V

TUTOR AND COLLEGE REFORMER

The period which Sumner consented to spend at Yale, while he became better acquainted with ecclesiastical conditions in America, was prolonged until nearly three years had passed, and it was not until the spring of 1869 that he finally resigned his office as tutor.

The tutorial system in the late sixties was in ill repute, both with the students and with the alumni. No change was so generally demanded, declared President Woolsey, writing in 1871,[1] as its abolishment. The number of tutors varied from five to eight according to the supply, and they did about half the teaching work of the college. For the most part they were recent graduates, generally theologues, who, after a brief period of teaching, expected to take up some other occupation. Although they were young men of good scholarship, in other qualifications for the office many of them were almost wholly lacking.

From the typical tutor of the time Sumner was a striking variation. "It was refreshing to see him walk across the yard," says Professor Henry A. Beers, of the class of 1869, "well dressed, alert, and full of energy, a marked contrast to the shabby and doleful theologues to whom we were accustomed." Equally refreshing were his methods in the classroom. The first year he taught mathematics, not because he so desired, but because the ordering of things was such

---

[1] "Yale College: Some Thoughts Respecting Its Future," *The New Englander*, July, 1871, Vol. XXX, p. 506.

that a new tutor was compelled to teach what was not already assigned to some one else. It is said, however, that he made even courses in mathematics interesting. During the second and third years he gave instruction in Greek. Here he was at home, for ancient languages and history had been one of his principal fields of study, and to all who were under him, Professor Beers declares, "he made Greek a living language." Unlike the most of his contemporaries he was not a mere hearer of recitations, but a revealer of truths and an inspirer of interest. His course in Plato opened up to his students the whole world of Greek thought, and was as much an introduction to philosophy as it was practice in translation and drill in syntax. Furthermore, he taught directly and personally, utilizing his own independent knowledge of the subject no less than the content of the textbook. As old men his students remembered vividly the enthusiasm which he kindled in them.

But it was not success as a teacher or liking for his office which caused Sumner to tarry on at Yale. On the whole he seems to have found his life there rather uncongenial. The pettiness of much that was associated with it irritated him. Then, too, the college was as "squalidly poor" as it had been ten years before. In books and equipment, it was getting more and more behind the times. An ambitious scholar like Sumner, eager for the latest results of scientific research, would have been constantly annoyed by the limited acquaintance with them which the college could afford. The educational outlook was narrow. There was great reluctance to enlarge the curriculum, and much indifference to the fast multiplying social and industrial problems of the world without. The scientific spirit with which Sumner had become imbued in Germany was

regarded with suspicion and fear. There was still
what he called "a Puritan theological crowd," connected with the college. This was inclined to cut him,
he says in a letter to Reverend Charles E. Grinnell,
then pastor of a Unitarian church in Lowell, because of
his Episcopal affiliations.

No doubt for this coldness toward him there were
also other causes. He was not an easy-going con-
formist. His convictions were pronounced and he was
persistent and fearless in seeking his ends. In faculty
affairs he was independent and pugnacious. "The
faculty broke down yesterday in maintaining discipline," Professor Packard wrote to him after his departure. "Myself—I voted no, and longed for you."
Toward existing conditions he was frankly critical,
and in the presence of age and tradition, not always
respectful. To the conservatives, this forceful youth,
fresh from heretical Germany, with his aggressive air
and advanced ideas, was not altogether acceptable.
They were a little afraid of him.

The underlying cause of his discomfort as a tutor,
however, was the fact that in vision and educational
ideals he belonged to the Yale that was yet to be. An
epoch in the life of the institution had closed; a new
one was waiting to be born. No one was more conscious of this fact than President Woolsey. Writing
in the *New Englander,* in 1870, he declares that
"there is a somewhat general feeling, we believe,
among those who are most deeply interested in Yale
College that the institution is about entering on a new
era of its existence. The work of the last seventy
years, it is felt, has been a good and a great one, but it
is mainly accomplished." [2]

2 "Yale College: Some Thoughts Respecting Its Future," *The New
Englander,* July, 1870, Vol. XXIX, p. 448.

Those who felt this most strongly were, like Sumner, of the younger alumni. With increasing vociferousness they were calling for the changes which they believed would give Yale a new birth. The college was not keeping up to the spirit of the age, they said. Too little recognition was accorded to the sciences, history, political philosophy, and modern languages. The officers were out of touch with the general trend of affairs and unappreciative of the education required by those who were to enter the practical life of the day. The tutorial system had outlived its usefulness. The Corporation was too restricted in its composition. The shaping of its policies should not be left to a little group of Congregational ministers. Yale should be a national, not a Connecticut institution, with representatives of all sections of the country on its governing board.

It was soon recognized that the changes called for could not be effected unless the financial resources of the college were greatly increased. The way to enlarge them, it was believed, was by arousing the alumni to a hearty and sustained support of the institution, and the surest way of accomplishing this, it was argued, was by giving them a larger share in its management. As early as 1866, President Woolsey had suggested a change in the composition of the Corporation, with a view to securing this result.[3] That body was then made up of the Governor, Lieutenant Governor, six senior senators, the President of the college, and ten self-perpetuating clerical members. The state officials on the Board generally served but a year or two, became little acquainted with the affairs of the college, and had small interest in them. President Woolsey's

3 "Dr. Hedges' Address to the Alumni of Harvard," *The New Englander*, October, 1866, Vol. XXV, p. 695.

suggestion was that such legislation be enacted as would make it possible to replace the senators with representatives from the alumni.

In the agitation of "Young Yale" for changes in the college, greater participation in its government by the alumni came to be the central theme. The principal seat of this agitation was in New York City, where a vigorous alumni association was formed. At its first meeting, held at Delmonico's, January 29, 1869, the presiding officer, Hon. William M. Evarts, said in his address:

> How are we to keep alive this idea that this is a College of the whole Union, that the Alumni make up the College, but by following the wise suggestion of the head of the University that the Alumni associations throughout the land should have an opportunity of being represented in the working Corporation of the College. (Applause.) Nothing but benefit can grow from this, and everything that is good may be expected. There are no dangers and no evils. All that is wanted is a statute of the State of Connecticut.[4]

In this New York group Sumner, who had gone to New York upon leaving Yale, became a leading spirit. In later years, as a permanent officer of the college, he was to fight many a hard battle to accomplish reforms the need of which he had appreciated as a tutor. In the earlier work by the alumni which paved the way for them, he also rendered stalwart service both by speech and pen. His almost three years' residence at the college gave him an intimate acquaintance with conditions, which few of the other leaders possessed, and his power of analysis and fine balance secured for

[4] *New York Tribune*, January 30, 1869.

his utterances a respect which those of some of the agitators did not command.

It was at the alumni dinner held during the Commencement exercises of 1870 that the "Young Yale" movement reached its climax. Apparently the stage was all set for the event. Mr. C. G. Child, of the class of 1855, spoke of the aloofness of the faculty from the student body. "We know you to be genial gentlemen," he said, "full of kind sympathy, but we do not find it out in college, and I hail it as an auspicious omen that two members of the faculty have come down from the platform to smoke cigars and that President Woolsey offers the pipe of peace." [5] Following Mr. Child came Mr. William Walter Phelps, of the class of 1860, whose speech was the sensation of many days:

The younger alumni are not satisfied with the management of the college. They do not think that in anything, except scholarship, does it keep progress with the age. They find no fault with the *men;* they find much fault with the spirit of the management. It is too conservative and narrow. . . . The college wants a living connection with the world without—an infusion of some of the new blood which throbs in every vein of this mighty Republic—a knowledge of what is wanted in the scenes for which Yale educates her children—this living connection with the outer world—this knowledge of the people's needs that can be acquired only from those who are in the people and of the people. This great want can be supplied only by the alumni. Put them into your government. Get them from some other state than Connecticut, from some other profession than the ministry. Call them and they will gladly and eagerly come—call them and with the reform will pass away every appearance of alumni indifference. . . . Believe me, men who sit on the

[5] *College Courant,* July 23, 1870.

Supreme bench, who control the cabinet of the executive
—who in all moral and intellectual reforms are the leaders of their countrymen, Yale men who got their training
here, are as able to manage its affairs as Rev. Mr. Pickering of Squashville, who is exhausted with keeping a few
sheep in the wilderness, or Hon. Mr. Domuch, of Oldport,
who seeks to annul the charter on the only railway that
benefits his constituency.   Young Yale asks more—that
that worldliness which is not inconsistent with godliness;
which is an absolute condition of worldly success—that
tact—that recognition of human weakness and infirmity,
to which all successful men cater, and which gives a Yalen-
sian the largest and richest church in the metropolis,
which makes another the first law officer of a late administration, shall not forever by its utter absence check
Yale's growth.   Don't let Harvard, our great rival, alone
have benefit of it—let Yale condescend to be worldly
wise.   The son of a president is a young gentleman about
to enter college.   Saintly Yale folds her arms in true dignity of saintliness, and young Vicksburg goes to Harvard.   The press, in a telegram, carries the fact to ham-
let and prairie, and the name of Harvard enters a thousand households for the first time.   It is Commencement
time: Yale says—learning not festivity is the true object
of a college.   We will not cater to the weakness of alumni
by offering other attractions than philosophical orations
of the graduating class.   Five hundred Yalensians needing very little impetus to gather them under the old trees,
find nothing, and stay away.   Five hundred Harvard
men, needing the same impulse, pack their portmanteaus
and go to Cambridge because Lord Lacklaw and the
Hon. Mr. Blouse, distinguished senator from Alaska, will
be on the platform.   Harvard takes great poets and his-
torians to fill its vacant professorships—Yale takes boys
who have proved their qualifications by getting their windows broken as tutors.[6]

[6] *College Courant*, July 23, 1870.

This speech created a great furor. Dr. Leonard
Bacon, one of the clerical members of the Corporation,
published a scathing retort in the *New Englander,*
under the title, "A Voice from Squashville," signing
himself, Rev. Mr. Pickering.[7] Communications poured
into *The Nation,* until it was compelled to close its
columns to further discussion of the subject.

Perhaps the sanest and most thoroughgoing treatment of it was an article of some length, written by
Sumner, and printed in *The Nation,* September 8th,
1870. It has none of the bombast or sneering contempt which made Mr. Phelps' address so offensive.
It does not assume that a change in the composition
of the governing body will necessarily remedy existing evils. It analyzes the situation and points out the
fundamental need. The need is money. The writer
is one who appreciates that to all human well-being
material capital and right business management are
a prime requisite. He is a clergyman by profession,
but his point of view is that of the economist. Yale's
recitation rooms, it is true, are inconvenient and poorly
equipped. Its library, one of the most important of a
college's instrumentalities of education, is miserably
inadequate. The authorities know this as well as the
critics who urge it upon their attention. They would
be glad enough to make the proper improvements.
But where is the money to come from?

> The machinery of education has been improved as
> much within fifty years as the machinery of locomotion.
> The improved machinery, however, is expensive. A great
> deal of the fault which is found with the college resolves
> itself into this, that it is trying to turn out modern,
> highly-finished work with antiquated and clumsy ma-
> chinery. People are dissatisfied with it just as they

7 October, 1870, Vol. XXIX, p. 678.

would be with a railroad run upon strap rail, with spring-less and cushionless cars. The state of things can be improved only by the investment of capital, and the question is, how to raise the capital? It is simply a mercantile problem, neither more nor less, and as such it ought to be discussed.

If better instruction and a higher grade of education are to be secured, we are thrown back again upon this same vulgar necessity. In vigorous language Sumner sketches the teaching situation as he had lately observed it.

The 'tutorial system,' as it is called, although it is very far from being a system, is one of the most vulnerable points of the institution. It is one of the things upon which adverse criticism fastens most frequently and with the most pungency. It certainly is an antiquated and rickety machine for the work of education. The time when a college instructor fulfilled his duty if he looked on the book and saw that the young men repeated from memory what was written in it, has gone by. We now have a few men, at least, who hold another theory of the work of their office. The instructors who are now demanded are men of thought, research, and genius, who can *make* books or even dispense with them, and teach directly, personally from an independent and original knowledge of the subject. Only such men can inspire enthusiasm and awaken interest. They are as rare as the men of excellent qualifications for any other branch of work, but we need to find them and see that they are secured for their proper calling. A book is a dead thing. We have to make it answer because we cannot all come into personal relations with the scholar who wrote it and acquire the knowledge he has to impart with the added force and the added charm of his spoken words. A book which is crammed and recited to a man who hears it as a routine duty only is worse than dead, it is *killing*.

Now, it is impossible, in the nature of things, that a young man who has only been out of college for a year or two, and has perhaps spent those years in some foreign pursuit, should come to the task of teaching, at a month's notice perhaps, with either the knowledge of human nature, or the power to enforce discipline, or the scientific culture, or the plain matter-of-fact information in regard to the subject, which the position requires. Still less is it to be expected that any large number of the persons so chosen shall have talent for this kind of work. This much is bad enough, but it is not the whole story. The schools address the best of the young graduates and try to secure them as teachers. They offer salaries to men only one or two years out of college which are sometimes twice as large as the tutors receive. When, at the end of three years, the college elects tutors, it finds that the most desirable men are either engaged in other pursuits, or are employed as teachers at such salaries that to take a tutorship would involve a heavy pecuniary sacrifice. Once the college could make its own terms. It could take only graduates of three years' standing, and could insist that they should stay for at least two years. Now it has to take men of two or even one year's standing, and they will not bind themselves to stay more than a year. What does this mean? Simply this: that the college offers remuneration which is below the market price for the article it wants. All things considered, the amount of labor, the 'position,' the opportunities for other work, the amount of compensation, etc., the place is not attractive to the men who are desired. There may have been formerly a class of men who had the requisite talents and attainments, and who were willing to devote them gratuitously, or almost gratuitously, to the work of preparing the young men of the country to win fame and wealth in the learned professions. If such a class ever existed, it is now extinct. The law of supply and demand, of the relation between price and quality, rule here as everywhere else. If you will not pay the market price of the article you want, you must take the inferior article, which your money will buy. Professors or potatoes, the law is universal. If, therefore, this country does not want the higher education, let us ascertain that fact, and then it will make little difference whether the colleges are bad or good, and we can stop talking about them. If college and university education of a high character is wanted, let us make up our minds that we have got to *pay* for it in the money which it is worth.

If then the great question of increased efficiency is one of ways and means, what can be done about it? Why not try the *business* plan? asks Sumner. In outlining this he anticipated the Alumni Fund with its yearly contributions.

In the first place, when we get tired of waiting for the rich man's thousands, we can begin to take the poor man's dollars. We have examples enough before us of success in business which has been won by seeing that there was more money to be made out of the pennies of the million than out of the dollars of the upper ten thousand. No graduate of the college has ever paid in full what it cost the college to educate him. A part of the expense was borne by the funds given by former benefactors of the institution. A great many can never pay the debt. A very few can, in their turn, become munificent benefactors. There is a very large number, however, between these two, who can, and would cheerfully, give according to their ability in order that the college might hold the same relative position to future generations which it held to their own. The sense of gratitude, the sense of responsibility, the enlightened interest in the cause of education, which are felt by these men, constitute a resource which has never yet been tried, but which would yield richly. They stand by as idle spectators while the college is applying to a few wealthy individuals. Their share in its labor now consists in simply rejoicing in its good luck when it succeeds. A *popular* effort which should seize upon the indebtedness of these men to the institution and their interest in it, and make it yield money, would be a step in the right direction. We are familiar with popular efforts of this kind for other causes. It is time that we applied it here. If every graduate who could afford it should give the college ten dollars, and others should give more in proportion, we should enter upon a plan whose financial soundness is unquestionable. We should be paying a debt which we all owe. We should be applying principles which are thoroughly in sympathy with the ideas of this popular and democratic age, and we should reach results which we can never attain by waiting for the tardy generosity of a few men of extraordinary wealth.

The second aspect of the business plan which Sumner outlines is to have the men who enjoy the benefits of the institution pay for them in money all that they cost in money. The prevailing theory at present, he says, is that it is desirable that every man should have a college education and so we *give* it to as many as possible as a free gift. It is true that if the price of tuition were raised so far as fully to remunerate the college, especially on the supposition that the college should secure the best talent available and pay for it, it would become a serious burden to many. The number now compelled to secure remission would be increased.

But why make the pride or the impecuniosity of some fix the rate of payment for all? Why should not those who can, pay fully? The normal principle of the institution should be to ask those who enjoy its benefits to pay for them. When men come who want the benefits and cannot pay for them, express provision should be made for them by the beneficence of individuals. Why inter-

fere with the business methods of the institution, for
sentimental reasons, to accomplish sentimental ends?
Business should be the rule, and sentiment the exception;
not sentiment the rule, and the consequent financial and
business weakness a constant source of complaint. In the
financial statement of the college, the income from room
rents, tuition, etc., should stand over against the running
expenses, and present a balance on the right side. If,
then, any persons step in and make the payments for
those who are unable to pay themselves, so much the better. It is the best form which their benevolence can take,
and it is earnestly to be hoped that there may be so much
generosity of its kind that no proper and deserving person need ever lose the benefit of the institution.

Sumner's connection with the "Young Yale" movement brought him to the favorable notice of many
Yale alumni. His clear thinking, his ability to go
directly to the roots of a matter and to express his
views tersely and vigorously, aroused their respect
and admiration. His utterances also called forth
some of the strong opposition, and even abuse, which
in after years he was to experience so continually.
In these earlier days they stung him deeply and he
was quick to resent them. On the fifteenth of March,
1871, Hon. William M. Evarts entertained the members of the New York Yale Alumni Association at
his home, 231 Second Avenue. At this gathering
Sumner was called out by acclamation to speak upon
the subject then "in agitation among the graduates
of Yale." He spoke principally upon the loyalty of
the alumni, and said that the puzzling question was
whether it was loyalty to the corporation, to the
faculty, or to the institution. The speech called forth
a sharp editorial in the *New York Standard* of March
18, 1871, entitled "Revolutionary Yale."

The meeting of the Yale graduates at the house of Mr. Evarts on Wednesday evening was professedly social, and nothing else. With the exception of one or two incidents, and perhaps owing mainly to the determination and the adroitness of the most genial of hosts, the meeting did not lose this character. This was undoubtedly a disappointment to many, for there was a large predominance of the younger graduates present, and there is at this time a degree of fermentation among the younger members of the Yale family that is much more easily perceived than described. Mr. William Walter Phelps, the Achilles of the myrmidons now invading the renowned citadel of learning, was loudly called for, even before the alien notabilities had exercised their time-honored prerogatives of uttering conventional compliments to deferential ears. Through some prearranged policy, and, as we must believe, fortunately for the harmony of the oyster supper, Mr. Phelps failed to be produced. It remained, therefore, for the Rev. William G. Sumner of Morristown, N. J., to provide a vent for the sentiments of the company, to raise the standard of aggression and defiance on behalf of Young Yale.

Young Yale is to be congratulated upon having secured the championship of this gentleman. With a variety of natural gifts, he combines some rather unusual exterior qualifications for the delicate and arduous service upon which he has entered. He is relatively a very young graduate. His recent experience as a member of the Faculty of Yale College must enable him to bring to his side of the controversy considerations obtained from an entirely new point of view. Furthermore, he is a clergyman practically and conscientiously devoted to the duties of his sacred avocation. It may be hoped that he will therefore be preserved from the absurd and fatal error into which some of his allies have fallen, of attempting a general crusade against ministers as being 'inferiors as a class.'

The Rev. Mr. Sumner, with all these fair auspices,

nevertheless, commenced his leadership with what we must consider a serious mistake. It is a mistake for those who would have Yale reformed somewhat and improved, to make indiscriminate war upon the men whose wise and faithful labor has made that institution what it is. It is a mistake to denounce the Faculty of Yale. It is a mistake to say that the body of Yale graduates, more especially of the younger graduates, are not loyal to the members of the Faculty. It is not only a mistake, it is rather sophomoric to talk so.

Any reform conceived in the spirit of hostility to the gentlemen who now have the discipline of the institution in charge; who are of necessity more profoundly interested in the welfare of the institution than any vaguely discontented outsiders; who have studied the necessities of the future in the light of familiar experience, can hardly fail to be a failure. The discussion has, in fact, been carried on in that spirit already long enough. It is time now, if ends are to be achieved, to think of co-operation.

The alumni of Yale in New York and elsewhere feel that they are too far removed in interest from their Alma Mater for their own good and perhaps for that of the college itself. So far, well. They do not well, however, to propose a general revolution in the management of the college.

It is rather to be wished that President Woolsey might be persuaded to remain at his post to guide the institution he has helped to rear, through the changes that are to come. It is a matter of congratulation that Professor Porter, a gentleman so like to the acting president, is generally considered likely to succeed him.

Let Yale men seek as much as they will the introduction of new plans, new men and new energy into their cherished institution. Let them beware how they throw aside its veteran defenders. Samson threw down the entire temple by displacing only two of its pillars.

In the *Standard* of March 22, 1871, Sumner published a reply in which he defines what he conceives to be loyalty to an institution in its relationship to loyalty to its officers. After stating that he was pushed upon the floor without a moment's warning, and placed in an embarrassing position by the necessity of uttering something which should do justice to the strong suppressed feeling that animated a large part of those present, and at the same time not violate his obligation to his host, or mar the occasion, he goes on to say:

In your editorial I appear as a thoughtless and noisy agitator, who made a silly, clap-trap speech to gain applause and popularity. I repudiate any such character. Nothing could be more distasteful to me. I did not 'raise the banner of aggression and defiance.' I did not make 'indiscriminate war upon the men whose wise and faithful labors have made the institution what it is'; nor do anything else equally vulgar and (as you say) 'sophomorical.' I agree with all that you say about the necessity of a sober reform and of respect for the faculty, and of coöperation with them, and of a careful and moderate criticism. I am only astonished to find that I furnish the data to which this moral is appended. Was I not a member of the faculty a little while ago? Do I not know what difficulties they have to contend with? The public is continually asking them to make bricks without straw.

I have therefore dissented from very much of the 'Young Yale' criticism of the last year. No one appreciated better than I did the clean process of dissection to which 'Young Yale' was subjected by his adversary in *The Nation*.

The point which I made in my remarks is a very important one at this crisis. Although the observation is, in itself, thoroughly commonplace, yet it corrects one of

those ambiguities which are most mischievous at a time
when it is all-important that every man should know
where he stands, and should work in this place. In a
time of peace and prosperity the loyalty which we feel
toward an institution attaches also indifferently to its
officers. If a question arises as to whether the officers
are pursuing a wise policy for the best interests of the
institution, then it becomes very important to discriminate. There is always an attempt to warp the loyalty
and devotion which is felt toward an institution, so as
to cover the officers and make it seem disloyal to criticize
them. This is a time-honored method of frustrating reform. Very many of our Alumni seem to feel that all
these questions which are in dispute ought to be passed
over in decorous silence. It seems then unfair and unbecoming and disloyal to talk about these things in public,
and to find fault with the administration of the college.
They are especially fond of closing the subject by reminding us what poor salaries the professors live on. That is
very true, but the only way to get better salaries and a
better policy and general improvement, is to discuss these
matters boldly. Want of money makes a cramped and
unsatisfactory administration, and an unsatisfactory administration causes the supplies of money to fail. Which
is the cause and which is the effect? They are so inter-
dependent that nothing can bring improvement but an
energetic determination to amend both together, and
nothing but discussion can produce this. The consequence of the policy of silence is that the 'fermentation'
grows year by year. 'Young Yale' frets under it more
and more, and becomes only more certain that things are
not going as they should, while it is less definite in its
perceptions of the faults, and more wild in its criticisms
and attempts at reform. I thought that I should clear up
at least one ambiguity which obscures the situation, and
I did not know any better way to do it than to touch
boldly on the very subject which is being ignored with
such great pains. 'Young Yale' is complimented on its

loyalty, but it is well that it should be understood that this party distinguishes the true object of its loyalty from the false, and will not allow its feeling to be misconstrued in such a way as to bribe or disarm its criticism. That is what I mean when I say that 'Young Yale' is loyal to the institution, but that it is not loyal to the faculty or the corporation.

This was the only application of the idea which I followed out at all on Wednesday evening, but it has also many others.

The matter of admitting the alumni into the corporation has been summarily settled by the assertion that the constitution cannot be changed without the consent of the present fellows, and that they will never give. Of course *discussion* is no longer possible when one party has reached *this* attitude. If the reform goes on it must take the form of a *revolution*. Here, again, it is important to notice that a collision with the corporation on this point does not involve disloyalty to the college, but may be imposed by it.

Many of the Alumni think that the corporation is impregnably intrenched in an obstructive policy, and they accordingly despair of the future of the institution and lose interest in it. These persons also ought to be reminded that it is the institution which commands their allegiance. Any one who has enjoyed the advantages of an institution which was founded in labor and patience, and which has brought to his education the strong traditions and noble reputation of 170 years, is bound to sustain it and see that it does more for the next generation than it did for him. He ought not to give it up because the corporation and the faculty do not act to suit him. Such a policy would soon throw the college into the hands of a clique. He ought to see clearly that it is the institution that commands his allegiance, and that he must labor for its interests, even against the officers, for the time being, if that be necessary.

The 'Young Yale' cause has thus far been lost by the

extravagance of its friends, and so it will be as long as those who are interested in it persist in making a sensation of every insignificant demonstration, while no genuine work is done for the solution of the questions involved.

From out all this travail, in the course of time, the new Yale was born. In July, 1871, the General Assembly of Connecticut passed an act consenting to the substitution in the membership of the Corporation of six of the graduates of the college for the six senior senators of the State. The alumni began to take a livelier interest in the affairs of the college and to give it a more generous financial support. A fund, known as the Woolsey Fund, was established early in 1872, and Sumner was one of the committee designated to promote its collection. He was one of the first alumni nominated for a place on the Corporation, and received one hundred and thirty-four votes, according to the *College Courant,* one hundred and forty-eight, according to the *New Haven Register.* The fact that he was a clergyman, and that when the election was held he had already been chosen for a professorship in the college, made his election impossible. At the Commencement of 1872, he delivered a most forceful speech, "showing conclusively," says the *College Courant,* "that Yale was ready to move forward, but that money was necessary to do so." It was his ninth year out of college, his sixth since his return from Europe, and he was already one of the most prominent of Yale's younger alumni, and generally regarded as one whose influence would steadily increase.

The strife of parties and sects will cease in view of a life of truth, which is worth more than all the questions about which they are wrangling. Differences about doctrine will fade into insignificance before a holiness which is seen to be greater and more valuable than all dogmas.

Sermon.

CHAPTER VI

EDITOR

THE ecclesiastical conditions which Sumner found in the United States upon his return from Europe dampened his desire to enter the ministry at the first possible moment. Old-fashioned orthodoxy was still in the saddle. "I speedily found," he says, "that there was no demand at all for 'biblical science,' that everybody was afraid of it, especially if it came with the German label upon it. It was a case in which if a man should work very hard and achieve remarkable results, the only consequence would be that he would ruin himself."[1] In the Episcopal communion all was strife. High Church and Low Church were aggressively arrayed against each other. The church papers were full of the polemical spirit. The conflict often waxed bitter and was marked by many personal animosities. With the views of neither party was Sumner in full accord. With their spirit he had no sympathy. Apparently, doubts began to arise in his mind as to whether the ministry was the field he ought to enter. He tarried on at Yale.

All the time, however, he was engaged in religious work and "biblical science." Upon coming to New Haven he immediately associated himself with Trinity Episcopal Church, where he directed the work of the Sunday School and engaged in other parish activities. Here he came under the influence of Reverend Edwin

[1] "Sketch of William Graham Sumner," "The Challenge of Facts and Other Essays," p. 8.

99

Harwood, D.D. Dr. Harwood was a man of striking personality and more than ordinary intellectual power, virile, and fearless. He belonged to the new school of preachers and theologians which was to become known as the Broad Church, of whose representatives, Dr. Alexander V. G. Allen, in his life of Phillips Brooks, says:

One common characteristic belonged to them: they were fearless men, unterrified by the discoveries of science or the results of Biblical criticism. They had not joined in the panic caused by the famous 'Essays and Reviews'; they refused to join in the cry that the 'church is in danger!' Rather did they see a larger opening for true religion in the fruits of an awakened intellectual activity. They held with Hooker and Bishop Butler that the human reason was the God-given faculty for verifying the divine revelation. They aspired after a larger freedom, and were interested in all methods for bringing the influence of the church to bear more directly upon the people in the upbuilding of Christian character. In a word they were the new generation of Christian thinkers. There had come to them alike an inspiration from Coleridge and from Maurice, from Arnold and from Stanley. They found satisfaction in Kingsley and in Robertson and Bushnell, begetting a new enthusiasm for proclaiming the gospel of Christ and the kingdom of God.[2]

With this attitude and spirit Sumner was in hearty sympathy. In Dr. Harwood he found a wise advisor and a warm friend, and to the older man the younger must have been a refreshment and inspiration.

Under his rector's guidance Sumner took the steps preliminary to entering the priesthood. Reverend

2 "Life and Letters of Phillips Brooks," Alexander V. G. Allen, New York, E. P. Dutton and Co., 1900, Vol. I, p. 447.

E. Edward Beardsley's "Book of Day," now in the possession of his nephew, Reverend William A. Beardsley, contains this entry for December 28, 1867:

> Went up to Trinity to be present at an ordination by Bishop Williams. William G. Sumner, tutor in Yale College, was admitted to the Diaconate. Dr. Harwood preached and several clergymen were present and took part in the service.

Dr. Harwood was one of the contributors to the Anglo-American edition of John Peter Lange's "Commentary on the Holy Scriptures," and through his influence, doubtless, young Sumner, fresh from his biblical studies in Germany and England, was assigned the task of translating and editing "The Second Book of Kings," in Lange's series. With increasing frequency he was called upon to preach, supplying at Trinity from time to time, and in other churches of New Haven and vicinity. Dr. Harwood's influence probably did much to remove Sumner's doubts about entering the ministry. He was just the type of man the broad churchmen sought to enlist.

Among Dr. Harwood's intimate friends was Reverend E. A. Washburn, D.D., rector of Calvary Church, New York, another representative of the best scholarship and more liberal spirit. To become his assistant, Sumner left New Haven in March, 1869. While he was to render such service to the church as its rector might require, his main work was to be the editorship of a church paper soon to be started. For some time there had been a growing feeling among many in the Episcopal communion that a periodical of literary and intellectual merit, embodying the point of view and spirit of the Broad Church, but free from narrow partisanship, was highly desirable. Accordingly, a small group of clergymen, of whom Dr. Washburn was one of the leaders, decided to try the experiment of issuing such a publication monthly, with the hope that later it might become a weekly. A prospectus was sent out which announced that:

The LIVING CHURCH is designed to speak to all thoughtful minds among both clergy and laity, and to deal frankly and temperately with the living Christian issues of the time. It is because such a want has been long and deeply felt by many in our communion that we seek to supply it. Those who are responsible for the editorial conduct of this paper, faithfully hold the creeds and formularies of the Protestant Episcopal Church, as embodied in its Prayer Book. Beyond this standard they acknowledge no school or party as master; but their chief purpose is to draw the best minds and hearts into that truly Catholic unity which all party organizations are apt to dwarf.

The columns of the LIVING CHURCH will be open, within due bounds, to the manifold questions of Biblical criticism, doctrinal and Church history, and worship. It will strive to give the ideas and principles that lie at the basis of a positive Christianity, with a generous allowance of any truth even in partial systems; to find harmony between Revelation and science; and aim at the rare excellence of defending the cause of Christ against error with candor and good temper. If the growth of this manly spirit can be helped hereby, this paper will do no light service. As it is more than an ecclesiastical organ, it may freshen our Christian literature by contributions from able pens in England and the Continent, as well as at home. But above all, it is sent forth in the hearty hope that it may meet the practical and social problems of Christianity at this day, and prove the reality of the Kingdom of God in its work.

According to a memorandum in Sumner's handwriting the capital for the enterprise was furnished by a small group of clergymen and two laymen. Reverend H. C. Potter guaranteed two hundred and fifty dollars, Dr. Washburn and Phillips Brooks, two hundred dollars each, and Dr. Harwood, one hundred and fifty dollars. When the preparations for publication were completed an announcement was sent out stating that the paper would be issued on the first Thursday in each month, and that all literary contributions or communications should be sent to Reverend William G. Sumner, 103 East 21st Street.

The Living Church survived just one year. From its inception, its originators had grave doubts of its success. Under date of March 1, 1869, Reverend Edward C. Porter, of Racine, Wisconsin, wrote Sumner:

> Permit me to say I am glad that you are to be editor in charge. I have heard of you from Dr. Rylance and also from Frank McVeigh. . . . Dr. Washburn writes me as if he regarded our effort almost as a forlorn hope. I trust at least it may prove a gallant one. But I have faith in a generous response on the part of our laity to any attempt to talk plain, English common sense free from the bondage of Traditionalism. (Perhaps I ought to say *American* common sense.)

The response from the laity, while it was cordial, even enthusiastic, was discouragingly meager. The paper was of too high an order to be popular. In November, 1869, Mr. Porter wrote less optimistically, expressing the wish that it were possible to make the periodical a weekly, with more general church news, so that it might compete with *The Churchman* and the *American Church*. "It would be much more easy," he says, "to press its claims upon a large proportion of our congregations who are hardly literary enough to appreciate it in its present form. We ought to reach the common people as well as the *thinkers,* who, I fear, are hardly numerous enough to support a paper in any denomination of Christians.'' In July, Charles F. Roper, the business manager, reported to Sumner six hundred and forty-one subscribers, about one half of them being in New York, Philadelphia, and Providence. Between then and December, there were only sixty-two additions to the list. The delivery of the paper seems to have been inexcusably poor, for complaints on this score came into the office in large numbers.

In addition to lack of popular appeal and proper business management, the failure of *The Living Church* was due to two other reasons. As a matter of financial policy it formed a semi-alliance with *The Protestant Churchman.* This periodical was a low church, evangelical publication, intensely partisan, and in bad repute with just the people whose support *The Living Church* hoped to gain. Under the agreement made between them, the former was to be published on every Thursday except the first Thursday of each month. On that day, the *Living Church* was to be published and furnished gratuitously to the subscribers of the *Protestant Churchman.*

This arrangement aroused a storm of protest. Dr. J. H. Rylance wrote to Reverend Edward C. Porter:

St. James' Rectory,
Chicago, May 1.

MY DEAR PORTER:
I returned yesterday from Cincinnati, where I saw Richards of Columbus, who filled me with grief by what he told me of a certain arrangement of the *Living*

Church. It is to be in some way conjoined with the *Protestant Churchman*. And that's the pitiful end of all our hopes!! I have done, for myself, feeling no interest in a concern that must all along in the minds of the other projectors have a purpose so different from what I myself conceived. That's what the large representation of the low brethren meant, or that's what it has come to. The *Living Church* is to take the fourth week in the month, the *Protestant Churchman* not appearing that week. I will be no party to such an alliance. We could have had an honest, clean, strong, independent organ if it had been well managed. I shall probably subscribe for a copy, but that is all. I dare not tell my friends of the miserable compromise. I am a low churchman, but not of the *Protestant Churchman* type and school, or of the 'Prayer Book versus Prayer Book' party.

I can write about nothing else this time, I am so full of sorrow. Will you tell me what *you* think?

Yours ever,

J. H. R.

Mr. Porter told both Dr. Rylance and Sumner what he thought. He wrote immediately to the latter, enclosing Dr. Rylance's letter, and asking for further information.

Racine, Wis., May 4th, 1869.

MY DEAR MR. SUMNER:

I have just received the enclosed from Dr. Rylance. I beg that you will assure me that there is no truth in the report he heard from Richards. I do not know what sort of an arrangement he refers to, but I am sure it would be ruinous to us to be made in any way responsible for the crazy utterances of the *Protestant Churchman* and its supporters. It would be an alliance of the no party men with the bitterest partisans.

I want to understand this matter thoroughly before I make any more efforts to interest my people in the paper.

I suppose that in my views about orders and the Sacraments I am as 'low' as the *Protestant Churchman,*—but I have no sympathy with the unscrupulous dishonesty and narrowness with which the paper upholds its views. Only a few weeks ago they committed a wicked wrong toward my friend, Dr. DeKoven. Those men do not seem to care to inform themselves even, in regard to the opinions and practices of those whom they denounce. I took the paper for a time and found it so full of 'wrath and clamor and anger and evil speaking' with a good deal of apparent 'malice,' that I stopped reading it and declined to take a gratis copy from the Post Office. I stopped it as I did the *Church Journal* when Hopkins was its editor because it stirred up too much unchristian feeling in my heart.

I can see that we have many points in common with the 'Evangelical' party but we cannot safely make ourselves partakers of their methods of supporting even those views.

I cordially sympathize with Dr. Rylance in the feeling that such an union as he understands you have made is a virtual betrayal of our cause. I cannot believe that it has been made by the men who have this paper in charge. I will not say as he does that my interest ceases or that I will do nothing for the paper, even in that case. But I shall be grievously disappointed if we who ought to be free to speak with no partiality of narrowness on either the side of ritual or of doctrine should have our tongues tied by a sort of reciprocity treaty between ourselves and one narrow school of opinion in the church.

Hoping to hear that my alarm has been groundless, I am,

Sincerely yours,

EDWARD C. PORTER.

Sumner was stung by these rebukes and imputations, but he succeeded in keeping the friendship and support of those who uttered them. He convinced them that the only hope of the paper's continued existence depended upon this alliance. Dr. Rylance wrote him a semi-apologetic letter saying that he never suspected that the cause had been "betrayed," since he knew that those who had the paper in hand were incapable of betrayal or compromise; but that though he may have spoken too strongly in his letter to Mr. Porter he still doubted the wisdom of the arrangement. The latter wrote that sober second thought had led him to countenance the arrangement, but that he regretted its necessity. It proved to be a constant source of embarrassment, however. The supporters of *The Living Church* were unable to show the same enthusiasm for the paper, and those who sought to increase its circulation found the alliance a constantly re-appearing obstacle.

Desperate efforts were made to prolong its life. It was finally agreed that the connection with *The Protestant Churchman* must be severed. An attempt was made to form a stock company. But every endeavor failed. Consequently, the editorial column of the May, 1870, issue was headed with the gloomy announcement: "This number completes the first volume of *The Living Church*, and is the last which will be issued until further notice." That some of the original subscribers had to make good a deficit is revealed in this letter from Phillips Brooks.

MY DEAR MR. SUMNER:
 I inclose my check for $150 for the obsequies of the *Living Church*. I should have sent it before, but have only this evening returned to town and found your note.

If, as the other contributors to this melancholy fund are
heard from, the amount shall fall short, I will send more.
Please let me hear if it is needed. At present this would
seem to be about my share.

Most sincerely yours,

PHILLIPS BROOKS.

Boston,
April 27, 1870.

The meteoric career of *The Living Church* is now
an almost forgotten episode in ecclesiastical history.
The only complete file of the publication known to
exist is that in the library of Yale University. It
contains six articles signed with Sumner's initials.
They show a maturity of mind unusual in one barely
thirty years old, and a grasp on fundamental principles which gives them lasting value.

The first appears in the issue of September, 1869,
and deals with *Ecclesiastical Trials*. Reverend Charles
Edward Cheney, the popular rector of Christ Church,
Chicago, later one of the organizers and bishops of
the Reformed Episcopal Church, had recently been
arraigned before a church tribunal for the omission
of the word "regenerate" in the baptismal office, and
the sentence of suspension, and subsequently of deg-
radation, had been imposed. When the ecclesiastical
officials attempted to prevent Mr. Cheney from further activities as a rector and to oust him from the
rectory, he appealed to the civil courts, and through
the brilliant handling of his case by Hon. Melville W.
Fuller, later Chief Justice of the United States Supreme Court, he won a complete victory. His appeal
brought forth a loud protest from many outside the
church, who were opposed to its coming into civil
affairs in any form or forcing any civil authority to
take cognizance of it; and also from the extreme

church party, whose theory was that the church should
prosecute its ends in its own way without responsibility to any outside power.

Sumner's article states the relationship existing between ecclesiastical disciplinary machinery and the
secular authority, and sets forth the principles
upon which such machinery should be formed and
used.

Dogma for dogma, he says, the separation of
Church and State, if it is to be elevated to a dogma, is
no better than their union. They certainly are not so far
separated, even under the 'American system,' that to go
into the Church is to go out of the State, or that one
who enters the Church withdraws himself from that
protection to person and property which the State guarantees to every citizen by its statutes and courts, even if
the menace to them should come from ecclesiastical authority. The court, at Chicago, took the ground that
the Church stood before the law simply as a voluntary
union of men. The basis of a union is a contract. The
laws of the society, its disciplinary code, the usages of
its tribunals, are known in advance. The terms of admission are distinct. Any man who enters it understands the responsibility which he incurs. It may be,
however, that an attempt is made to enforce the terms
of the contract unjustly against him. If so, the courts
of justice seem to be a refuge for him, as well as for any
other citizen who finds himself aggrieved in the execution of a contract. A clergyman who takes Orders in the
Church, undertakes definite responsibilities and incurs
definite risks; but he does not put his livelihood, and the
fortunes of his family, at the mercy of bigoted and tyran-
nical men, in case he should by any combination of circumstances fall into their hands. . . . It is a most humiliating state of things, if a clergyman of the Church
really feels that he can expect more impartial justice

from a civil judge than from a tribunal of fellow-clergy-men; and if such a feeling be well founded, then the inference is, not the wickedness of the man in seeking to save himself from wrong, but the necessity of moving in the case with such judicial calmness, impartiality, and justice, that the necessity or possibility of such an appeal shall not arise. Ecclesiastical courts have only to proceed in this manner, so that their action may stand review by anybody, to defy interference.

A church must have disciplinary machinery, Sumner continues. It is essential to its dignity to have the power to say when its fundamental principles have been violated. It must be able to punish immorality if it should become necessary. It must be in a position to enforce conformity to its standards. Nevertheless, courts and trials are a painful necessity, inevitably bring scandal and harm to the church, to be used as seldom as possible.

With respect to dispute about a doctrine, furthermore, it is little that they can do, for two questions are always involved: first, is it a doctrine of the church? and second, is it true? The former question an ecclesiastical court can decide; the latter, it cannot decide. To assume that it can, is to be governed by a theory which is Romish.

We are disputing about the truth, and no one will be convinced or corrected by a judicial decision, though he may be by reason and argument. The most that can be accomplished by judicial decisions is to establish the fact that no man can stay in the Church and teach certain things; and before we proceed to narrow the Church into such a select conventicle of men, who can and will pronounce just such shibboleths in just such a way, let us determine what things these are which are to be taught in it, just how far we are willing to go in defining the line of demarcation all about us, and what kind of men those are likely to be, who will be found enclosed in the 'ring' when it is completed. Yet this is the direction in which we are traveling, and the church is leaning more and more on these authoritative decisions, which are the weakest of broken reeds, while it is leaving the attacks of various kinds made upon it from one side and another, by argument and reason, unanswered, to make their way, slowly but surely, by their own innate force into the public mind, until they are generally accepted as unanswerable, and win, by a bitter sarcasm, the force of 'Catholic consent.'

.   .   .   .

To regard an ecclesiastical trial as a means of settling controversy, or extinguishing theological difference, is, therefore, an entire mistake. It is only available for keeping intact the basis of communion, and excluding persons whose life is immoral, or whose teaching is at variance with the received standards of the society. In this application, however, recourse to an ecclesiastical trial, in a particular case, ought to be regulated by two considerations; first, by the extent to which it is necessary to limit the basis of the communion, or, in other words, by the amount of liberty which it is considered wise or possible to give, inside of the necessary limits; and secondly, by the expediency of incurring the unavoidable scandal for the sake of the end to be gained. It must be clearly understood, moreover, that the only real way to battle with error is by reason and argument, while for any man or 'body of men' to condemn it, will not avail. If men preach falsehood, we must expose it, and set up the truth against it, and fight it. The battle is not to be won by a council of generals who meet and 'vote' a victory to themselves or condemnation to the enemy. It has got to be won by hard blows, and by brave champions who believe in the truth, know how it is learned, and how alone it can be carried on to victory.

For the October issue Sumner wrote an article on *The General Theological Seminary,* in which he .sets forth the fundamental failings of that institution, and makes some pungent remarks about the character of the students then entering the ministry. A large number of these, perhaps the majority, are men of moderate or inferior ability. They have no proper preparation in the way of education. Such men are prepared to be the victims of isms, superstitions, and selfish theories. They have not the breadth of information and the mental culture which protect men from delusions. They find themselves set with a task for which their powers have not been trained. Since they cannot magnify their office by their own worth, they seize eagerly upon a theory which will bolster them up. They have never been taught to put their faith upon what they believe fairly and honestly to be true, nor do they understand what truth is, or what belief is.

A recent conference of the Evangelical party had called for a revision of the prayer book, the repeal or modification of one of the canons, and the trial of certain prominent persons. A crisis in the Church had arisen, and in the December issue of *The Living Church* Sumner discusses it coolly and logically under the title, *The Evangelical Conference and the Crisis.*

The succeeding number contains a four-column editorial in which he states his views on "The Public School Question." For some months the propriety of reading the Bible in the schools had been widely discussed, both in secular and in church papers. In considering the controversy, Sumner, as was his custom, penetrates at once to the main, underlying issue. What is going on, he points out, is not a squabble between Romanists and Protestants. The principal

question involved is not a religious one at all; it is
one which goes to the roots of our American social
and political system; one which every man in the
community, "who believes in public education as the
surest safeguard of the public welfare, whether he is
Protestant or not, must take sides against every man
who seeks to overthrow the common school system,
whether he be Roman Catholic or not. The question
whether the Bible shall be read is only the opening
skirmish in the campaign." That which lies at the
root of the opposition, Sumner declares, is sectarianism.

The principle at the root of all sectarian education,
whether Jewish, Anglican, or Roman Catholic, is the
same. It is, that the parents hold so tenaciously to their
sectarian peculiarities that they withdraw their children
from the prevailing culture of their generation for fear
that these peculiarities may be obliterated. Sectarianism is the spirit which takes one-sided views of truth,
and looks at these through a magnifying glass, which not
only exaggerates them, but also shuts out all others. Its
errors and its wickedness consist in this, that it withdraws its adherents in order to maintain and conserve
these partial and exaggerated views, from the organic
life of the whole church and the entire human society.
This is the true spirit and the true definition of sectarianism, whether it be practiced by those who are avowedly
sectarian, or by those who declaim most loudly about
Catholicity. Over against this is the broad stream of intelligence, investigation, discovery, enlightened interest
in all things which promise wider knowledge, or higher
development of human faculties. This stream is the aggregate of the best thought, and the highest endeavor of
the time. It carries in its bosom much food for the satire
and the invective of those who love to turn up the reverse side of things. It brings terror to all who hold to

traditions and not to ideas; to them it is undoubtedly 'Destructive,' in the strictest sense of the word. It brings broad and generous standards of judgment, so that to those who have fixed a procrustean bed on which everything must be stretched, it seems 'latitudinarian.' It gives to those who once drink of it a thirst for knowledge and truth and thought which increases with every draught, and so, to those who have never felt this thirst, it seems to be a 'poison.' The man who has once plunged into it, never is willing to come out again, and so, to those who inhabit the sheep-folds upon the shore, it seems a tide which bears on to 'ruin' and 'death.' They cannot, therefore (to keep up the metaphor), permit their lambs to wander freely on its shores. They stand, themselves, aghast at its mighty force, and at its incomprehensible fascination, and so they hasten to construct strong barriers to restrain the little ones, and are eager to indoctrinate their young with their own wholesome horror of what is 'modern' and 'progressive.' This is sectarian education. It withdraws any religious earnestness which the sects really have from the prevailing current of opinion, where it is most sorely needed. It separates religion from civilization, and divides religion into the creeds of a hundred discordant communities. It teaches men to swear by the traditions of that little community in which they were born, and to pronounce all its petty watchwords, instead of teaching them to be open, unprejudiced, and free, in their consideration and judgment of all the contributions which each can bring to the sum of our best convictions. It aims to perpetuate and accentuate religious differences instead of bringing about unity of conviction by an unprejudiced examination of evidence. It is a confession of weakness for any Church or sect to adopt this policy. It can only do so upon admitting: 'We find that, if we leave our children to grow up without strictly inculcating our doctrines upon them, they never adopt those doctrines, upon a free conviction, in after life.'

The difference between the two parties contending over the public school question, Sumner continues, is at bottom a radical difference as to the fundamental principle of secular education. Shall we teach children to do certain things, because their teacher commands them, and not to do others, because they are forbidden: or shall we teach them to see and think for themselves what may be allowed and what cannot be permitted? Shall the teacher exercise discretion with regard to the pupil, doling out such measure of knowledge to him as is thought will fit him for his station in life, or shall he lead the pupil as far as he is able to go? Shall the teacher exercise discretion in the study of history, as to the things which it is wise for a pupil to learn, or teach him to seek historic truth, with a single and unfaltering purpose, no matter what men or what institutions suffer by it? This is the real question at issue. "The public schools are committed, as the American people are committed, to the second alternative. The hostility of all, of whatever Church or party, who aim first of all at the perpetuation of a traditional system, to the common school, is natural and necessary. There is a conflict here which is inevitable, and which can only end in a decisive victory for one policy of education or the other, and every man in the community has got to take sides upon it."

To the final number of *The Living Church*, April, 1870, Sumner contributed two articles. One is a lengthy review of Reverend William R. Huntington's book, "The Church Idea; an Essay Toward Unity," which he criticizes as vague in its statements, uncertain in its analysis, and imperfect in its grasp of the subject. "It touches about all over the subject of it, but does not pierce to its center and marrow." The other article is on "The Study of the Bible." In it he deplores the fact that we put the Bible freely into the hands of the laity, read it in our churches, refer to it in our Prayer Book, in our Articles, and in our sermons, teach it to our children, but do not dare to study it critically. A candid study, free from superstitious reverence, he declares, would produce an intelligent knowledge and appreciation of the Bible, which would remove the uncertainties and inconsistencies that prevail, and make its true character as a revelation of God to man in the history of the world apparent; for inspiration "is not a postulate of biblical study, it is the last and highest result of it."

Sumner's year in New York was a busy and varied one. Although trials seem to have predominated, it was not without its joys. As always, he worked with indefatigable industry. Besides carrying the burden of *The Living Church,* with its many annoyances, and assisting Dr. Washburn in the duties of Calvary Parish, he gave all the time possible to the exacting task of translating Lange's "Second Book of Kings." He found relaxation chiefly with old college friends, and especially in the home of the Whitneys, where he dined regularly once each week. In spite of his published strictures upon the General Theological Seminary, and perhaps because of them, for they were constructive and revealed capacity for leadership, that institution, in November, 1869, called him to its chair of Hebrew. "I have, I acknowledge," Dr. Washburn wrote him, "mentioned you to the powers that be, as the proper person for that chair, but did not know that they would have common sense enough to put the right man in the right place, but am only too happy if they have done so." A friend in New Haven, Miss

Hattie Russell, wrote in different vein. "I do not congratulate you," she said, "not knowing whether you have accepted, nor how it is possible for *any* one man to do the work of three. Most people would get confused with such a multiplicity of duties and there would be sermons in the class room, Hebrew in the newspaper, and, most horrible and not to be endured, *politics* in the pulpit." This additional honor and task, however, Sumner declined.

That for a period in February, 1869, his work was interrupted by an attack of smallpox is disclosed in letters written by Mrs. William C. Whitney and Dr. Washburn. From the former it is clear that some of William's boyhood characteristics had not disappeared. He still took everything very seriously, including himself, and he was proud, sensitive, and not always in the sweetest of humors.

Dr. Washburn's letter, sturdy and kindly, offers him any assistance possible.

DEAR MR. SUMNER:

I was sorry indeed to hear of your illness, and only relieved by hearing from your friend, Mr. Hopkins, that it is not likely to prove a long or hard attack. If there be anything which I can do to make you more comfortable, pray let me know it. I have no fears of this or any sickness, and not to fear is the best preservative. Mrs. Washburn sends, too, her kindest regards, and begs to say that if you need a nurse, she will come and take care of you. She is a very brave sort of Christian. I trust you have the best nursing, for it is of more importance than even the physician.

I beg you not to be anxious at all about the Calvary duties. I can attend to them, although I shall personally miss you. There is not much just now to do, and before Lent I do not doubt you will be in fine health. Perhaps indeed this ailment will clear away all the sickly humors, and leave you stronger than before.

I find this number of our paper very readable, and well spoken of. I will be laying by this week what I find in the newspapers and magazines, so that your task may be lightened for next month. So keep yourself untroubled, and say, Apage Satanas, to the varioloid.

Yours ever,
E. A. WASHBURN.

Thursday, 10 Feb.

An incident which marred the year greatly was an unfortunate break in Sumner's relations with his rector. What the rock was upon which their union went to pieces is not altogether clear. Apparently Sumner's independence, outspokenness, and brusqueness had much to do with it. He showed on this occasion, however, as more than once he did in after life, that he was big enough, when he realized that he had been in the wrong, to acknowledge it frankly, whatever struggle it might cost him.

407 W. 22d St.
March 14, 1870.

DEAR DOCTOR:

On thinking over coolly our difficulty of last evening, I am constrained to confess freely, and of my own notion, that I was in the wrong. Your reply to my question exasperated me, but I feel sure that it was a result of weariness on your part and not what I interpreted it to be. I then acted hastily and foolishly. I confess this, of course, with shame and regret, but I desire you to understand that I do it *for my own satisfaction*. I feel that I was wrong and I desire to put this confession and the accompanying apology in the direct form and not as a mere adoption of an opinion of yours as it was last night. What disappointed me at the close of our interview was

that you did not accept my apology with the generous
cordiality which I expected. I don't even blame you for
that when I look at it this morning, for it was not a spon-
taneous apology. There remain two points. You say
that I have failed in courtesy in time past. I wish to
express my astonishment and deep regret at this charge
and to beg you to overlook it and to call my attention to
this in the future. You refused to do this last evening,
but as my rector and elder friend, is it not your duty?
You say that I have serious faults. Brusqueness and
rudeness are among them. I thank you for telling me,
and I will try to correct it. I am proud and independent to excess. I imagine harm where none is meant and
I am hasty and touchy. In this case these faults have
brought me into a humiliating position. I claim, however, to be frank and sincere and to mean to do right,
and if it is not improper I beg to ask of you something
of that indulgence for my faults which you have not
thought it beneath your dignity to ask of me for yours.
If I were to tell you the real reason for last night's scene,
so far as I can explain it to myself, you would laugh.
I have stopped smoking and am nervous and agitated
and 'blue.' You saw how excited and unstrung I was.
I was for a moment the victim of that intemperance you
talked about which is half a disease. I am now satisfied
that I have put myself right in this matter and you may
take any course you choose. I doubt if we can ever be
on cordial terms again, and I have already taken steps
to secure a place. I will give you full notice so as not to
embarrass you. I write because I do not want to open
this subject in words again.

Yours sincerely,
W. G. S.

To this remarkably frank and self-abnegating letter, Dr. Washburn replied in generous spirit and with
a spontaneity and grace which one misses in his
assistant's letter.

New York, 15 March.

DEAR MR. SUMNER:

I thank you very heartily for your manly letter. Although I had no personal ill feeling, yet I honor you for your frank self-confession, and I wish with as full generosity to say that whatever in my talk may have wounded you, I most truly regret. You were quite right in your afterthought. I was very weary, as I have been of late, and unable to think or talk of any annoying business. But you call out a very lively sympathy when I learn that you, too, are a victim of Lange's Commentary. I shall have Dr. Schaff seized as a modern Thug.[3] To my certain knowledge this man has killed one Dutch Reform minister, brought a Presbyterian to the brink of death, given one congestion of the brain, and is now torturing young clerks on his Biblical rack.

Let us say and think no more, my friend, of the matter. I am too old and vexed with cares, and anxious, God knows, with griefs at home, to have any quarrel with men like you. I have a cordial honor, not only for your talents, but your manly and honest nature. Nor will I ever give you any advice. I know both myself and you well enough to know that such a temperament must cure itself by a few hard battles of experience. But I am glad to see that you perceive with me the expediency of giving up the place of assistant. We can be better friends without it. It is a case of incompatibility, or perhaps, as you suggest, of too great likeness of temper; and divorce is the best way. I beg you, dear Mr. Sumner, to take this as kindly as I mean it. I most sincerely thank you for your friendly work during the whole year. I thank you for the many times when you have borne patiently with an impetuous and weary invalid. And I wish you to arrange for the future in just the way that shall be most convenient for you. You will make me truly happy if you will not only stay through the year

[3] Dr. Phillip Schaff, who was the general editor of the American edition of Lange's Commentary.

of our engagement, but until you find whatever may be agreeable for you elsewhere. In anything, where I can serve you, I beg you to rely upon me as an unchanged and hearty friend.

As to our paper, I hardly know what to say. I shall be pained if it lose your brain and your pen. We all, I am very sure, prize your genuine work in this good cause: nor is there any necessity because you give up Calvary parish that you leave the editorship. But this I must leave to future conversation. I am in truth so situated, with all my cares and anxieties now at home, that I hardly feel able to do my share in this common work. Others must resolve what is to be done, but I only wish to impress on you, whatever the plan, that I truly appreciate your own efforts. We have got to battle together in the years to come for the Christian truth we both love better than self; and I know that in such a cause we shall be found heart to heart.

Forgive my long answer; and receive it in the sincere spirit that prompts it.

Yours very faithfully,
W. A. WASHBURN.

To the Rev. W. G. Sumner.

Amid all the duties of the year, Sumner had time to woo and win the woman with whom he was to find his greatest happiness all the rest of his life, Miss Jeannie Whittemore Elliott, daughter of Henry Hill and Elmira Whittemore Elliott. Mr. Elliott was a New York merchant, born in Guilford, Connecticut, where his ancestors long had lived. He was a direct descendant of John Eliot, apostle to the Indians.

The announcement of his engagement came as a great surprise to the most of Sumner's friends and associates. They had thought him too serious, too much absorbed in intellectual pursuits, and too unemotional, to have an affair of the heart. In a letter from Reverend Henry C. Potter, in which he incloses his contribution to meet the deficit of *The Living Church,* this surprise is humorously expressed.

Grace Church Rectory,
June 13, 1870.

MY DEAR SUMNER:

I have your note of the 10th, and inclose my check to your order for One Hundred Dollars ($100).

I had heard of your engagement, but couldn't credit it. I still find it difficult to associate so much emotion as an engagement involves, with a being whose composition I have hitherto supposed to consist only of *pure thought.* I suppose you read to her Hegel, with airy digressions into Kant and Fichte, instead of Longfellow and Mrs. Browning, and that of course she wears spectacles and writes for the *North American Review.* At any rate I can't conceive it possible that she is that very pretty girl next to whom I saw you sitting, so cozily, at the Sheltering Arms Concert on Easter Thursday night.

I will certainly bear you in mind and let you know if I hear of any opening of which you would care to avail yourself.

Faithfully yours,
HENRY C. POTTER.

To the Rev. W. G. Sumner.

After Dr. Washburn and Sumner had agreed upon the fact of their "mutual incompatibility," the latter, as indicated in the letter above, began to seek a parish. In anticipation of its duties, he sought full ordination, and the diocesan records of New York state that

The Right Reverend Horatio Potter, Bishop of New York, on Thursday A.M., July 15, 1869, at a special ordination in Calvary Church, New York, preached and admitted to the Diaconate Mr. Joaquim de Palmer and

Mr. George Herbert Watson; and advanced to the Priesthood the Rev. William G. Sumner and the Rev. Gou-
venour Cruger.

True to his word, Reverend H. C. Potter wrote
Sumner, under date of June 21, 1870, asking him to
telegraph immediately in case he was open to over-
tures in regard to the Professorship of Hebrew in
the Philadelphia Divinity School, with a salary of two
thousand dollars. Professor Packard inquired if he
would consider returning to Yale as a tutor, saying:
"Few men make so thorough work of teaching as you
did, even though you despised the office more or less."
A parish seems to have attracted him more strongly,
however. His old friend who had urged him so
strongly to come over to the Episcopal Church, Mr.
Whitney, called his attention to the Church of the
Redeemer in Morristown, New Jersey. In reply to a
letter asking information regarding it, Mr. George L.
Wright, a resident of Morristown, but not a member
of the church, wrote Sumner this description of the
parish:

You ask me to tell you something of the church. The
parish is small, but made up of first class people. The
senior warden is John Hone, formerly of New York,
now in Europe; his wife, daughter of Commodore Perry
and sister of Augustus Belmont's wife. The junior
warden is a Mr. Taylor, also of an old New York family.
The remaining members, among the gentlemen, are, for
the most part, men of culture and means. Among the
lady members are Miss Decatur and sister, grand-
daughters of the old Commodore; Miss Slidell, sister of
John Slidell, of rebel notoriety. From these names you
will recognize that the Parish is made up of people of
standing and refinement. So much for the members; as

to the church, it is what we call low church, thoroughly opposed to ritualistic forms, though, I believe, they in no wise sympathize with such radicals as Stephen Tyng, Jr., but they like all the services conducted in as simple and unostentatious a manner as possible. When you come I can talk more fully concerning it. I am not a member, but attend every morning, and as you know, looking in on the most of the game, I can tell you about how everything is. One thing, the work is easy and they don't demand much of the Rector.

In many respects this was the kind of field for which Sumner was looking. It was near New York and he would not have to break his connection with the men with whom he had been working; its congregation was one to whom thoughtful preaching would appeal; with extreme ritualism he had no sympathy; and the fact that the duties were not exacting would permit him opportunity to finish Lange's Commentary. Accordingly, in September, 1870, he began a two years' rectorship there.

The church of Christ is a church militant. It is aggressive by its very nature. There is evil and ignorance in the world with which the church has a combat which knows no compromise or truce. Its mission is to conquer them, to drive them out, and to occupy their place. It was founded to inherit the earth, and it is fighting for its birthright.

Sermon.

CHAPTER VII

RECTOR

His thirtieth birthday found Sumner a full-fledged clergyman, with a parish of his own, favorably known to many of the leaders of the church, recognized as a scholar of varied attainments who combined sound learning with practical common sense, keenly interested in public questions of every kind, and respected by all for his vigor of mind and ruggedness of character. Upon April 17, 1871, he was married to Miss Elliott, and the two established themselves modestly but happily in Morristown. Here Sumner preached twice each Sunday and with characteristic fidelity performed the other duties of his office, all the while working diligently on the somewhat dreary task of translation, which had come to be a burden from which he was eager to be free.

He found opportunity, however, to coöperate actively with his former co-laborers in efforts to develop a liberal churchmanship and an interest in the intellectual and social problems of the day, in which the prevailing party animosities and pettiness should be forgotten. In this connection he was one of the founders of "The Club," a more or less informal association of clergymen, which has survived to the present time and, directly and indirectly, exerted no little influence. The other original members were Drs. E. A. Washburn, C. S. Henry, H. C. Potter, J. H. Rylance, and Messrs. George D. Wildes, D. R. Brewer, Arthur Lawrence, R. Heber Newton, and Samuel

Osgood. To these were quickly added such men as Bishop T. M. Clark, Dr. Edwin Harwood, Dr. William A. Muhlenberg, Dr. John Cotton Smith, Dr. Thomas M. Peters, Phillips Brooks, Charles C. Tiffany, William R. Huntington, John William Payne, C. A. L. Richards, Elisha Mulford, and George Nicholls. In the beginning the club convened in the different rectories of New York, but later Dr. Washburn's library became its permanent meeting place. The most of the members were not averse to the use of tobacco, and the smoke would grow so dense at these gatherings that it became a custom in the rector's family to remove all the library hangings whenever the club was to assemble. When it was found that J. Heber Newton and J. H. Bush were absenting themselves because their sensitive throats were irritated by the smoke, indulgence during the reading and discussion of papers was forbidden. To the smoke cloud, as well as to the emanations of wisdom and criticism, Sumner no doubt contributed his full share, for the relinquishment of the weed, which caused his irritability of temper in the unfortunate interview with Dr. Washburn, was but temporary. His final abjuration of it was to come later.

The influence of "The Club" was exerted upon the general public chiefly through the publication and distribution of essays, first read before the members, and through Sunday evening addresses on correlated subjects, certified as under the auspices of an association of clergymen. Its greatest achievement, however, was its successful leadership of the movement which resulted in the establishment of the Church Congress.

If, in the face of the numerous demands which were made upon him, the young Morristown rector found it necessary to slight anything, it was not his sermons which suffered. Preaching he considered the most important function of the ministry, and his discourses were always carefully planned, written out in full, and corrected before delivery. Many of them he found good enough to repeat, and finding one so he did not hesitate to give it again from the same pulpit. Thoughtful, analytical, expository, and dependent largely upon facts and logic for their appeal, they made heavy demands upon the attention. There was little rest in them for the weary, little consolation for the distressed, no food for the sentimental, no leniency for the sinner. They sound the note of strong conviction, they glow with moral passion, they call to battle.

With characteristic frankness, Sumner declared from the pulpit his views regarding the ministry, his methods, and his aim. In his farewell sermon, preached at Morristown, September 8, 1872, he sums up convictions previously expressed, and pictures vividly his own temperament and tendencies.

A church would have no interest for me if it did not fill an actual and important function in the midst of existing society, and I never should take the office of a minister of Christ if I did not perceive that I could, in that capacity, perform a most important work for my generation. The ministry has never seemed to me to be a function or an office or a routine practice. It is not a trade or handicraft or profession. I described it very fully some months ago as a prophetic office. The minister of the Gospel must be a free, original, bold and energetic instructor if he is to be a power in our modern society. But free, original, bold and energetic instructors are just what the old Hebrew prophets were, and therefore I cannot find a better name to describe it in one word than as a prophetic office. Certainly I could not find my calling in it if it were anything else than this. If a clergyman is to be merely a man of fine esthetic culture, with an amateur or dilettante knowledge of music, architecture and decoration, or a gentleman of elegant leisure, petted and admired within a certain wealthy circle which he and his handsome church serve to ornament; or, if he is a functionary, drilled to a certain ecclesiastical routine; or if he is a man who has only chosen one trade instead of another in order to earn his bread; or if he is only a mouthpiece of tradition set to recite by rote a certain formula which he has learned, then I could certainly find no calling or duty in this office, for God has given me no gifts to fit me for any such position. On the contrary, so far as I can judge of the sort of work which I ought to do in the world, I must strive by study, reflection, and thought to vindicate and enforce the facts and laws which constitute truth upon the minds and consciences of men. If the Christian ministry, or Christian priesthood, for I am indifferent to the name, did not allow room for the exercise of this calling, then I could have no place in it. If it did offer room for such a calling then that must be my especial form of activity.

Now I believe that the Christian ministry offers manifold forms of activity to its members. I think that we even lose greatly in the efficiency of the ministry in this country from the fact that its separate functions have not been properly separated. In the older countries the preacher, the pastor, and the teacher are almost always distinguished. The preacher must be a student, that is, a man of reading, thought, reflection, eloquence. The pastor must be a man of social instincts, of genial disposition, of out-of-door tastes. It is impossible to unite the two, for no man can be in his study enriching his mind with thought and learning, or reflecting, digesting and adapting what he has read, at the same time that he is walking abroad, cultivating acquaintances and practicing social virtues. I have never known or heard of a

man who embraced excellences in these two directions,
and I believe that it is impossible to do so. . . . It is
inevitable that any man who attempts to fulfill any such
expectation should degenerate into commonplace and
drivel. . . . I will not disparage any other form of labor
in the Christian ministry, but I insist upon this, that the
duty of preaching, that is, of persuading men's minds
and informing their consciences by acute thought and
living speech, is second to no duty of the Christian minister. A church may have long rolls of communicants,
numerous and splendid edifices, proud traditions and a
glorious history, but so soon as it ceases to teach and
preach, to lead the thoughts of men and influence their
judgment on living issues, it begins to die and nothing
can save it.

Believing now that the Christian ministry includes a
teaching office, and that I might properly devote my
efforts to the instruction of so many as I could reach, I
made this the form and type of my efforts. Believing
also that the attempt to include much more would only
impair all my efforts and usefulness, I have made other
things subordinate to this. One of my great regrets, in
looking back upon my service among you, is that I have
not been able to devote myself to this portion of my work
still more exclusively. When I came here I was engaged
on a literary task of considerable magnitude which I was
obliged to complete, and I have also been obliged by circumstances to undertake much outside work which occupied my time and exhausted my energies. But I always
looked forward to the time when I should be free from
old engagements, and when the parish should be large
enough and strong enough to enable me to devote all my
time to this department of my work.[1]

Important as are the requirements and ceremonies
by which religious teachers are formally authorized,

[1] "Farewell Discourse," Morristown, N. J., September 8, 1872.

not through the laying on of hands, or any other rites, does the authority of the preacher come.

> If we maintain that these ceremonies give the authority to teach, which without them would be wanting, we assert a doctrine which is contrary to all common-sense and reason, and which never can be maintained in the face of the experience and observation of men. The authority to teach is the ability and gift to do it. The man who can discern truth and can help others to discern it is a teacher to whom God gave his authority when He gave him those gifts.[2]

Sumner never strove after effect in his preaching, and the tendency to sensationalism which was conspicuous in pulpits about him, he fiercely denounced on the grounds that it was fatal to truthfulness and destructive of the pulpit's reputation and proper influence.

> We have those who boast of a kind of preaching 'which is in sympathy with the spirit of the age,' and so, indeed, it is in sympathy with its worst faults. The Sunday morning sermon is a résumé of the topics which have engrossed public attention during the week. The newspapers have followed public events from day to day and have fulfilled their function of commenting and criticizing. They have brought the news of the crimes and accidents, the deaths among celebrated men, the battles and the diplomatic contests of the week. The restless hurry and worry of thought and business have come to a cessation. We are weary of the ceaseless demands upon our attention and interest. In the house of God, at least, there will be rest. We have turned away from the hurry and bustle to rest and peace. We shall give up business and fashion and turn to religion and charity. We shall

[2] "The Authority of the Preacher," Morristown, N. J., August 21, 1870.

forget all these things that absorb our attention one day
and are forgotten the next, and shall turn to things
eternal and unchangeable. We shall not be vexed with
the follies and crimes and shortcomings of men, we shall
contemplate the goodness of God and the love of Christ.
But is it so? Not at all. The preacher descends to
rivalry with the popular literature of the day and uses
the same arts of meretricious display to captivate, to interest, and to amuse. The question is not how to impress
upon the hearers something which the speaker believes
to be true, nor how to correct their faults, nor how to
lead them to devout worship of God and to purity of
life, but how to attract and captivate them, how to please
them and win their applause. Here, also, you see the
instinct of truth is lost. The aim is not to be true, but
to be popular, but the truth accepts no divided loyalty.
A man must be all for her or she wants none of his
homage, and so whenever a man puts popularity by her
side and tries to serve truth and popularity both at once,
you may be sure that sooner or later he will fail, and
that truth will be forgotten. So instead of pursuing
true and high convictions, teaching them boldly and uncompromisingly, the pulpit also follows the flitting and
changing sensations of the week; instead of leading the
hearers out of and above the interests in which they have
been absorbed, the Sunday sermon turns their minds back
again into the same channel. Instead of using the Sunday rest as a time for looking upon life from the vantage ground of communion with God and reflection upon
things eternal, and, from this standpoint, judging worldly
interests by calm, sober and lofty standards, men are
thrown back again into the same eddying and resistless
tide of external and human interest. The institution
which ought to be the great landmark of what is permanent and eternal in the midst of changing interests,
changing people, and changing times, becomes a mere
ornamental appendage dragged hither and thither to
grace the triumphs of successful mercantile life. The

pulpit which ought to win success by deserving it, cannot expect to be more highly esteemed than the other institutions to which it condescends to become a rival. If it is flippant and smart and descends to small wit; if it borrows the false style of the popular literature of the day; if it shows the same lack of conscience; if you feel, when it speaks, that it is only stating cleverly a certain view of a subject, but that, so far as any sincere conviction is concerned, it will probably state the opposite view just as cleverly a few weeks hence; if it depends upon sensational exaggerations and personalities to attract attention, and not upon the truth and sense and thoughtfulness of what it propounds—then it will not be respected and will not deserve to be respected, for it will stand upon the level of the other institutions which have prostituted their high calling for the sake of popularity and worldly success. The public conscience is awake to this fact. Although it may not find distinct expression for the feeling, still it has a sound instinct that popular preaching is a base truckling to popularity, and a departure from the first principles which ought to control the pulpit, namely independent conviction and fearless expression. If it be true that the pulpit is losing influence, then it is mainly due to the fact that so many men have yielded to the seductions of popularity, have abandoned the true field and calling of the pulpit, and have descended into the popular arena to vie with the magazines and newspapers in their proper functions. If the Sunday sermon has no other office than to supply the place of the ordinary editorial in the morning paper, then it will not be long before men will see that it is entirely superfluous.[3]

High functions carry with them special responsibilities. The teacher and minister cannot escape a scrutiny and criticism from which the ordinary per-

[3] "Sensationalism in Religion," New York, August 6, 1870.

son is free. They are under special obligation to exemplify the truths and precepts which they declare.

In regard to the clergy it is sometimes said that the popular criticism of their actions is censorious and captious, and that the popular standard of the severe rectitude which it is becoming in them to practice is absurd. It is asserted that if a thing is right it is right for both priest and people, and that if it is wrong it is just as wicked for a layman as for a clergyman. To this last proposition no one can take exception. As a rebuke to those who seem to hold that it is the duty of a clergyman to undertake the task of 'being good' on behalf of his entire people, it certainly applies with complete force. Some people seem to demand austere manners and morals of their clergymen in proportion as they assume license for themselves, and the more they plunge into frivolity and folly the more they demand of *him* to keep aloof from these things. He serves as a kind of anchor to windward to hold them back while they see how near they can sail to the rocks of folly and vice without actually suffering shipwreck. To such, I say, it is a valid answer to reply that there is only one moral code and that that applies to clergy and laymen alike. But, on the contrary, it is wrong to deny that a man who assumes a position as a public teacher must be under greater responsibilities than others. If he grasp at high public functions and step into a position of great public influence he must take the responsibilities as well as the honor of the position. Men always must compare precept and practice, and he who inculcates precepts most earnestly and most frequently must expect that his practice will be most continually and most searchingly scrutinized. A man in any such position courts criticism. He cannot avoid it. . . . It cannot be said, therefore, that the popular standard which imposes a stricter rule in these matters upon public teachers is unjust or wrong.[4]

[4] "Communicants of the Church Set in Evidence Before the World," Morristown, N. J., August 7, 1870.

Sumner's religious and theological views were as clear-cut and as forcefully expressed as were his ideas regarding the function and responsibility of the pulpit. From the standpoint of the modern liberal, he was extremely conservative. Biblical criticism had not then been applied to the New Testament with the fearlessness and rigor with which it was being applied to the Old. The doctrines of Darwin, Huxley, and Spencer, he had not yet been able to accept. It was not until 1875 or 1876 that Professor Marsh's horses definitely converted him to the evolutionary hypothesis. He had read Spencer's "First Principles" as a tutor, but it had not impressed him. In a series of sermons on the philosophies of the day, he points out the weaknesses of Rationalism, Individualism, Materialism, and Skepticism, and argues that the Christian doctrine of Faith best satisfies the mind and heart of intelligent beings. He believed firmly in God as the ultimate explanation of human history, in a divine revelation, in special providences, in the deity of Christ, his vicarious atonement, miracles, and the physical resurrection. The Apostles' Creed in its literalness summed up his convictions.

To the leaders of the Unitarian movement he makes this explicit reference.

To speak for myself, I do not see how the Christian religion, meaning by that neither more nor less than the religion which Jesus Christ taught on earth, can be retained and believed if his Divine Character and personality be given up. He taught as the most remarkable feature of his religion that he was the Son of God, who had come down from heaven to reveal the truth, to redeem mankind from sin and error by showing them what was true and right, that he would give his life to that end, and that he was such a proper incarnation of God that he could claim worship. Of course it is possible for a man to say, 'I do not believe that he was what he said he was, and therefore I see no guarantee that what he taught was true,' but to accept his authority, to adopt his religion, and to eliminate the most remarkable feature in it as compared with the systems of great philosophers is unreasonable and inconsistent. It cannot be done with success. It is accepting Christianity with one hand and rejecting it with the other, and in every instance in which it has been tried from Arius, who was a good man and a sincere man, to Channing, who was a holy man, the result has been a gradual loss of all hold on Christianity and a gravitation down first to rationalism, then to theism, then to deism, and finally to atheism. Channing was able by force of his devotion and his strong spiritual instincts to stand where he stood. He had a grasp of divine truth which he had won by the insight of his own pure spirit, and the most devout worshiper of Jesus Christ may sit at Channing's feet to learn to know his own Lord. Many know no more about him than that he was a nominal 'Unitarian,' and sneer at him accordingly, but Jesus Christ has had few greater champions on earth since St. John and St. Paul than he. . . .

When Channing was gone others arose who did not hold it as he did. Emerson and Parker made a very different thing of it, and they have found direct and legitimate successors among men now living, to whom Christianity is a by-word, religion a delusion, God a dream, for whom the whole welfare of humanity hangs on a few misty fancies.[5]

The same acuteness and vigor which Sumner displayed in opposing rationalism, materialism, and skepticism, he exercised boldly in criticizing the Church of Rome.

[5] Sermon on "The Trinity," Morristown, N. J., May 24, 1872.

It is charged against Protestantism that its logical conclusion is rationalism. 'Rationalism' is one of those terms which is glibly used, but rarely defined. It certainly has various shades and grades. But taking it even in its worst meaning, it cannot be denied that Protestantism, when pushed to an extreme, ends in doubt, negation, and faith only in the dictates of the human reason. This cannot be denied. The answer lies, however, in this, that almost any other doctrine or idea when pushed to an extreme ends in a similar falsehood. The opposite view, that of Romanism, ends in spiritual death and irrationalism. Democracy, if pushed to an extreme, ends in anarchy. The authority of government, if pushed to an extreme, ends in tyranny and absolutism. Freedom of speech, if pushed to an extreme, ends in insult and slander. Restraint of the press, if pushed to an extreme, ends in ignorance and slavery. That Protestantism sympathizes with rationalism rather than with irrationalism is certainly true. It seeks that presentation of religious truth which appeals to the reason and conscience of men. It is in sympathy with that scientific spirit which systematizes things and brings them into an orderly arrangement according to the processes of the human reason, and which seeks always the cause behind the effect. It believes in education and culture. It regards the reason as the high endowment of mankind in distinction from the brutes, which enables him to understand religious truth. It appeals to the conscience of mankind as the organ of faith by which they attain to a conviction of spiritual realities and lay hold on God. It regards man as endowed with native nobility and born to a high destiny, and it believes that it best prepares him for that destiny by stimulating him to the highest thoughts of which the reason is capable and the highest faiths which the conscience can receive. It hopes more from his thirst for knowledge than from his contented ignorance. In the view of Protestantism none of the good powers of man are to be repressed or constrained; on the contrary it is

held a shame for a man to fall below the best that is conceivable for him. It is not enough that he should repeat
creeds, his reason was given him that he might understand them. In this sense, and in so far, Protestantism
is rationalistic.

But there are some who, believing that this path in
which Protestantism is moving can only end in rationalism, propose to abandon it. We are forced to ask, if
this path is not right, what is the alternative? The
alternative which they offer us is to turn and go back, to
undo all that our fathers have done, to give up the
prospect of the Promised Land and to turn back into the
wilderness, or to take up once more the burdens which
'neither our fathers nor we were able to bear.' It is
said that all the evil comes from the schism which once
was made in the Catholic Church from which we started
in this path. It is proposed that we return to the
Catholic faith if not into the bosom of the Catholic
Church. The answer to any such proposition is plain and
simple. *The Catholic Church lies before us, not behind
us.* The doctrine which divided the church was the doctrine of the sacrament and if ever it were possible to lead
the Christian church back to the medieval doctrine of
the sacrament we should reconstruct medieval society.
When men believe that the mere formal act of partaking
of the elements in the sacrament can make them good
and save their souls, then they will believe that the relics
of saints may cure diseases of the body, that two men
may engage in battle and that the guilty one will fall in
the contest, that a divining rod can detect hidden
treasure, that an amulet which has been blessed by a
priest can avert danger from the wearer, that the lives
of men are written in the stars, or that in a thousand
other ways matter has control over men. Can you make
men give up astronomy and return to astrology? Can you
make them give up chemistry and return to alchemy? Can
you make them give up modern artillery and wear armor
once more? Can you make them abandon faith in knowl-

edge and believe in ignorance? Will they give up political economy and sanitary and surgical science and go
back to the law of force and robbery, to walled cities and
to the rude medical treatment of the Middle Ages? [6]

To Sumner, however, theology was one thing and
religion quite another. The two belong to different
departments of man's nature; they involve the exercise of two different faculties. Theology pertains to
the realm of reason; religion to that of the conscience
and faith. In the former the scientific method is demanded; in the latter it is out of place. Through the
conscience man perceives intuitively spiritual and
moral truth. "It is a mysterious power which stands
at the helm of character. It discerns truth and steers
towards it with greater or less accuracy. . . . It is
capable of deep and frightful perversion, but it is
capable also of the highest and most delicate cultivation, so that it may become a subtle and sensitive instinct to discern right and truth. It is not an infallible guide, for conscience in one man or generation
often sees reason to review and correct the judgments
of conscience in other men, or other nations, or other
generations, but it is the power of the soul by which
truth and right are learned and perceived." By faith
the individual lays hold of the verities which conscience reveals, and they lay hold of him and possess
him, and a union with God, which is personal religion,
results.

Although Sumner's sermons were religious in the
best sense of the term, and seldom failed to make a
definite spiritual appeal, they display a lively interest
in history, sociology, and economics. Sometimes
this is revealed in titles such as "Ill-gotten Wealth,"

6 "Protestantism," Morristown, N. J., October 16, 1870.

"The Ordeal of Prosperity," "The Responsibility of the Individual for Public Opinion," "The Solidarity of the Race," "The Relation between Public and Private Morality." More frequently, however, it appears in statements made in connection with other subjects. Often these are interesting in that they show that ideas which later became prominent in his teaching were already formulating themselves in his mind. His basic theory that all social phenomena are the result of the interplay of the unchanging tendencies of human nature and the facts of the external world is clearly foreshadowed in the following:

History is nothing but the story of the results which have followed from the action of certain human passions. The passions, the appetites, the desires, and the weaknesses of mankind are the same in all generations. They produce the same results over and over again with slight modifications of external circumstances. The task of the wise student of history is to detect the same causes in spite of these modifications, and to learn and profit by the lessons they teach in regard to the wisdom or folly of certain lines of policy, the truth or falsehood of certain doctrines, and the prosperity or the ruin which follows upon certain lines of conduct.[7]

That social prosperity depends in the last analysis upon the disposition and character of the individual, was a conviction at which Sumner early arrived and never abandoned.

We live in a good land which is richly supplied with all the means to produce a great and happy and virtuous commonwealth. We have no old traditions or

[7] "Protestantism," Morristown, N. J., October 18, 1870.

rusty institutions to hamper our free use of all that is placed in our hands. We have political institutions which, if properly administered, might give us strong, vigorous, independent national life, but it all rests upon the fidelity, the self-control, and the conscientiousness of the individual man. Its safety and success depend upon the serious conviction which each one has of the duties of a citizen, and the sober determination which he has formed to fulfill them. Its danger lies in this, that neglect or carelessness or disgust may make the individual indifferent to his responsibility. Some have an almost superstitious confidence in a republic or a democracy as a divinely instituted political system, and seem to think that it can never fail or fall, but this lesson is plainly written on every page of history, that no political system can stand when those upon whom it depends become negligent or corrupt. Our political system stands upon the individual citizen and when the citizen is either careless of his duty or false to it, when he throws away his conscience as a citizen or as a man, then we shall have a society which will reek with vice, a trade which is organized gambling, a government which is the football of adventurers, a state which is only a machine by which a few plunder the many, and a church in which a few victims of superstition will still hug the barren forms handed down from the day when men had a conscience and strength to obey it. It is on the conscience of the individual that our whole social and political fabric rests, and the task of the school, the church, and the press is to bring home to the individual his responsibility for that public opinion which makes or destroys, corrupts or reforms, condemns or approves all things in our political and social order. If the conscience of the individual citizen is pure and clear then public opinion will be strong and correct and righteous, and the state which is built upon it will have self-sacrificing and devoted citizens, wise and upright legislation, a faithful administration, a pure judiciary, and

men will shun the taint of financial dishonesty as they
would the contagion of a loathsome disease.[8]

Sumner always viewed the home as of the highest
social significance. Only through its affection and
care, he maintained, can the best human beings be
produced. There alone can true education be obtained, "for it does not come from books and schools,
it comes from tireless watching, patient training,
persistent restraint, at the fireside and at all moments
of life weaving a tissue of unconscious habit into the
fiber of the life of the future men and women." In
the circle of the family, therefore, men and women
find their first social duty and one of their greatest
social opportunities.

Many a woman seeks a calling of some sort while
she fails to keep her household in neatness and order,
and many a one is devoured with ambition to care for
neglected children while her own, or those who are so
near to her that they may justly claim her care, are
neglected and forgotten. Yet in that sacred family circle
you have that simplest form and miniature of the kingdom of God. There God has placed others of His crea-
tures under your immediate influence and care. No one
can estimate the opportunities to make happy and useful
men and women which lie in home influences, and any
man or woman, however humble may be their station,
has in the family relation the opportunity to pay the
richest service to God by making a peaceful and happy
household. . . . When you see a family bound together
by affection and respect and concord and mutual help,
you have before you the most faithful picture of the kingdom of heaven. Who is there so poor or so humble that
he cannot bear his share in the family life and therein

8 "The Responsibility of the Individual for Public Opinion," Morristown, N. J., November 24, 1870.

serve his God, or who is there so rich and so great that
he can do more than to train up his children in the fear
and admonition of the Lord, to be blessings and orna-
ments in the circle in which they live? [9]

The instrumentality by which, from the beginning,
man has won and held every step in the advance of
civilization, Sumner declares, is capital. The savings
bank depositor, he says in one of his essays, is a hero
of civilization, for he is helping in the accumulation
of that capital which is the indispensable prerequisite
of all we care for and all we want to do here upon the
earth. The power and beneficence of this instrumentality he did not hesitate to set forth in his
preaching.

The enlightened pursuit of wealth is one of the
strongest forces in society for elevating the individual
and for advancing the civilization of the State. We have
only to observe the status of nations where the ambition
for worldly success is dormant, or that of races in whom
the desire and endeavor for wealth has to be awakened
by painful exertions, and compare it with the condition
of others where this instinct is active, to be checked in
any sweeping condemnation of the pursuit of wealth.
This pursuit is the animus of that sustained industry and
energy which creates values and speeds culture and civilization, and promotes peace, and enlightens men as to
the meaning of human brotherhood.[10]

In 1870 the Franco-Prussian War was in progress
and interest in the struggle led Sumner to make certain observations about peace and war which disclose
how keenly he felt even then that conflict is fundamental in life, and how, at the same time, he was

[9] "Faithfulness in Little Things," Morristown, N. J., October 2, 1870.
[10] "Ill-gotten Wealth," New York, October 3, 1869.

hardly able to find words sufficiently strong to express his feelings with regard to the evils which necessarily accompany war.

War is not altogether an invention of man. It is something that he finds all about him in the world, nay even, something which he experiences in himself. There are evil forces at work in human society and in human nature, and there are good ones, and they have a bitter and endless conflict with one another. This war has always waged and, as far as we can judge, it always must wage as long as mankind remain upon the earth.[11]

God forbid that we should apologize for war. No orator, or poet, or painter can describe its horrors and its desolation and woe. But there is something worse than war, and that is peace in the face of vice and wrong and injustice. The sword which our Lord sent upon earth was the firm and high conviction which he taught us that there were things which were worth more than life and property, that is, truth and justice and righteousness, and things more horrible than blood and tears, that is, compromise with wrong and vice. Men sometimes go into raptures about the blessings of peace when peace is selfishness, when men look with indifference upon wickedness and injustice so long as it does not touch themselves and they can continue to heap up riches. They sigh over war when war only proves that there is a cause or an idea for which men are ready to die, and that they have a deeper horror of falsehood than of bloodshed. This is the sense in which our Lord sent upon the earth not peace, but a sword, for where such a faith and conviction come there is no peace or rest while men serve the ends of evil, and while they own allegiance to the dominion of Satan. The weapons with which the soldiers of Christ have to fight in their aggressive war-

11 "Christ's Peace." Christmas sermon preached at the Church of the Redeemer, Morristown, N. J., 1870.

fare are meekness and patience and mercy, and wherever they have been true to their calling they have fallen indeed, but they have conquered. Their great and terrible mistake has been where they have borrowed the weapons of violence and have thought that they could serve God with the instruments of evil. But, on the other hand, when those weapons are used against them they cannot turn and flee; they cannot abandon the field; they cannot even surrender their lives without a struggle, and there comes what men call war, with all its woes and calamities, and with all its bitter fruits of estranged brethren, enthroned hatreds, and hot desires for vengeance lasting through generations. War is a terrible and unjustifiable resource. Even if the right conquers yet the attendant evils which follow from war go far to destroy the power of its victory. One can imagine the devil gloating over even the battlefield on which the most righteous cause is victorious, because he knows that though his kingdom suffers harm, yet the means employed are such as to secure him many compensations for his defeat. The responsibility for war, however, rests with those who provoked it, not with those who stood by the right. It is only an instance of the power of evil to annoy and harass, even if it cannot conquer, good. In the conflict which ensues, whether it be war on the battlefield or the conflict of thought and discussion, the soldiers of Christ must be ever on the alert. The Master sent them into the conflict not to bear a weak and vain exhortation to peace, but the sword of truth and right and justice.[12]

As a young preacher, furthermore, Sumner had already perceived the folly and harmfulness of headstrong reform, and recognized the truth that the great stream of time and earthly things sweeps on in spite of us, so that all men by their puny arts can do is to

[12] "Christ's Peace." Christmas sermon, Morristown, N. J., 1870.

modify slightly some of the forces at work in the faith that, after a sufficient time, their action may be changed a little and slowly the lines of movement may be modified.

There is a great amount of cant about progress, and a great amount of platform declamation in regard to it. In words that I quoted here a few weeks ago, there are many who say, 'Forward! let us make progress, yet who know not whither they would go.' Progress in itself is not a thing to aim at. It is only one of the glorious circumstances which attend the accomplishment of faithful work. What would you think of the schoolboy who should lay down his books and cease to learn his lessons, saying that he would devote all his time to making progress? Yet he would be doing nothing else than what many of these modern apostles of progress do when they turn away from the hard drudgery of making men better to glorify and worship progress. I also believe in progress, but I believe in it as one of the results of faithful, laborious, and humble effort, and not otherwise. If we would make progress we must take heed *whither* we are striving to go; we must have our aim directly before us; we must choose our means with care; we must use them with diligence.[13]

Neither be led astray by that specious doctrine of progress which seems to worship movement, and which exhausts itself in a feverish hunger for change. When we move let us move slowly and soberly. The traditions of centuries have a true *moral* authority. No wise man will disregard it. They form for us at any rate the point of departure from which we must start in all our efforts for the benefit of mankind. We must begin with the world as we find it, that is, as it is handed down to us from the past. This gives us our starting point. We

[13] "The Creation of Man in the Image of God," Morristown, N. J., June 4, 1871.

must also think well what we aim at and rather wait for the movements which naturally develop themselves in the life of the race, than proceed to invent an ideal world and try to realize it by rash innovations. You may know that if a man endeavors to cross a trackless prairie keeping his eyes fixed on his feet, he will make a very devious path and it is entirely uncertain whither he will go. If he wishes to cross it on a straight and certain path he must look up and observe the bearings of such landmarks as there are, and must correct the little errors of each step in the succeeding one, that he may thus arrive at the point which he has chosen. Much of our modern progress is like the path of a man who keeps his eyes fixed on his feet. It has cut loose from the past. It does not start on any given lines. It has not any trained foresight to choose the point at which it would arrive. It starts at hazard and proceeds only step by step and it is uncertain whither it will go. On the other hand, the illustration may serve to show what is the true use of tradition as distinguished from traditionalism. Our progress should be like that of the man who looks up and around with a free observation and a firm intelligence. It should proceed from the past, not throwing away, but rather retaining and preserving with care the inheritance of truth which has come down to us. It should make use of this inherited wisdom to choose its objects of aim and pursuit; to discriminate between truth and falsehood, the wise policy and the foolish. It should thus guard itself against the repetition of old errors, and against the delusions of worn-out falsehoods. It should correct its own errors step by step by means of the landmarks which it sees about it. Such a progress would be real and true, for it would be a natural and normal growth.[14]

Certain personal characteristics which contributed largely to Sumner's power reveal themselves in his

[14] "Tradition and Progress," Morristown, N. J., January 14, 1872.

sermons. His own struggles had convinced him of the worth of self-restraint, self-denial, perseverance, and unremitting labor. They had become habitual with him and had carried him far. They were to carry him still further. The faith in a man's power to achieve a chosen goal, expressed below, was an outgrowth of his own experience.

Instances are numerous where men have overcome apparently insurmountable difficulties which hindered them from accomplishing their objects. The secret is to adopt one's aim exclusively enough, and to bend one's energies undividedly enough to the accomplishment of it. If a man determines to be rich and makes that the aim of his life, sacrificing to it pleasure, recreation, present comfort, perhaps even health itself, the result cannot be doubtful. If he is ambitious for fame he can win it in any profession or calling. If he determines to have influence, he can gain it. If he wishes to be useful, he will find opportunities enough. If he wishes to be a good man, that aim too can be accomplished, at least approximately. Almost any man can become an athlete by continued and intelligent exercise of his body. We must be convinced of the intrinsic worth of the aim; we must adopt it with a complete determination, and persevere in our devotion to it against the allurements of every other object which in a particular instance might draw us away. Life is a succession of little acts and little incidents, and if a man has made up his mind to accomplish one aim in his life, the result will depend on the inflexibility with which he makes every case as it arrives subserve the great end. If he perseveres and never loses sight of his grand object, whatever temptations may draw him aside, then the result is not very doubtful. This is the way in which men become great poets, artists, merchants, statesmen, saints. They set their whole lives to be one thing, and that they are with all their might.[15]

[15] "Religion," New Haven, January 5, 1868.

Devotion to principle, even in the face of misunderstanding and persecution, he held to be among the most glorious traits of human character.

If you have formed your own convictions of duty and right, be not shaken in them by the popular judgment which will call you mad. It is so certain that you will be thus misjudged that the Gospel says: 'Woe unto you when all men speak well of you,' for it is a very probable sign that you are pursuing the aims and using the means and bowing down to the idols which the world approves. Finally, when you see cases in which faithful and earnest men are unpopular and are derided as fools and insane, be at least cautious how you join in the verdict against them. I do not say that such men are always in the right or are always wise. St. Paul was as zealous when he persecuted Christians as when he preached Christ. But look well into the motives of zeal and self-sacrifice, and if they are founded on faith, and principle, and conviction, treat them with all respect. Faith may be perverted, and zeal may be great for a mistaken conviction, but, as compared with worldly policy, there is a glory in fidelity to honesty and sober conviction which no error can destroy, and wherever this virtue appears it demands the respect of all conscientious and truth-loving men.[16]

No one probably ever agreed more unreservedly with Lord Bacon's famous declaration: "Truth, which only doth judge herself, teacheth that the inquiry of truth (which is the love making or wooing of it), the knowledge of truth (which is the presence of it) and the belief of truth (which is the enjoying of it) is the sovereign good of human nature." Few, if any, ever demonstrated more practically or more valiantly

[16] "The Judgment of the Man of the World upon the Man of Faith," Morristown, N. J., August 6, 1871.

their faith in this creed. In one of his sermons, while deprecating the tendency to limit the truth to what can be perceived through the senses and verified by the methods of science, in language of great beauty, he portrays science itself as a religion.

The true votaries of science regard themselves as clothed with a certain sacred office. They serve in the temple of truth. They are striving to reach, from one side, the truth which is nothing more nor less than the word of God, while others strive to reach it from other sides. . . . They have to practice self-sacrifice and self-denial and magnanimity just as the other votaries of truth. They must hold the truth all and themselves nothing. They may not selfishly rest content to learn without ever teaching. They learn in order to teach mankind. In these last days true science has become a religion, as it is a service of truth, a revelation of truth to the mind of man.[17]

In line with this view is a quotation made in a much earlier sermon.

It has well been said that 'every scientific investigation is a prayer to the God of nature, of which the discovery is the fulfillment.' [18]

Sumner's devotion to truth was that of such votaries. His allegiance thereto he pledges in the following words:

I simply say here, in parenthesis, that for my part I am only anxious to know the word of God, by which I understand the truth, in regard to anything whatsoever that man may know. I stand ready to accept and believe

[17] "Bread Not the Chief Thing," Morristown, N. J., February 25, 1872.
[18] "Truth," New York, February 21, 1869.

anything which can be established as true, matters of science being established by science, matters of history by history, matters of philosophy by reflection, and matters of religion by the testimony of the spirit either historically in the Bible or directly in the heart, and I am also ready to adjust the various departments of my knowledge to one another, that they may be consistent.[19]

Again he says:

I know of no instinct which it is more desirable to render strong and clear and infallible than this one of truth, and I know of no habit of mind which I would rather cultivate in any person whom I could influence than that of a delicate and infallible appreciation of truth and an unswerving allegiance to it.[20]

Fichte's declaration, "I would not break my word even to save humanity," Sumner probably never would have made. It borders too much upon the sensational. Without doubt, however, he was in thorough accord with the conviction that intentional untruthfulness is to be condemned, even though it be for a seeming good.

Truthfulness is opposed to expediency and policy. You will sometimes hear certain doctrines advocated on the ground that they will have a good effect if people can be led to accept and believe them. It is argued that such and such doctrines will bring people to church more frequently, or will make them more devout, or will lead them to support more liberally all sorts of benevolent undertakings. But all such arguments, in so far as they leave out of sight the question whether these doctrines are true or not, and in so far as they are founded upon

[19] "Bread Not the Chief Thing," Morristown, N. J., February 25, 1872.
[20] "Truth and Falsehood," Morristown, N. J., September 25, 1870.

considerations of expediency and not upon truth, are disloyal to the spirit of the religion of Jesus Christ. Again, you will sometimes see certain parts of the truth held in reserve from considerations of policy. It is not judged well to make known the whole truth and a part of it is kept back by what is called a system of accommodation. But again we detect a departure in principle from that right line of fidelity and allegiance to truth which is inculcated by the whole spirit of the Gospel. A teacher of truth who allows himself to follow such a policy has abandoned the very first principle of his calling, truthfulness, openness and honesty. It is immaterial whether his motive be one of money, or what he believes to be the interest of a good cause, he has slipped into that policy of doing evil that good may come, which is a pitfall ever yawning by the side of the most earnest laborers for the best causes. No! there is but one consideration of expediency, and but one policy which is open to the apostle of truth, and that is unswerving and complete devotion to the truth and the whole truth down to the utmost letter. So when we see religious movements going on which, for any motive whatsoever, whether good or bad, have turned aside from this one simple policy, we may be sure that they have in themselves the seeds of their own failure and ruin.[21]

Since it is of the highest importance that one's sense of truth should be kept unimpaired, even falsehood in jest is not to be countenanced.

We cannot express opinions which we do not honestly entertain, even in jest, without straining our sense of truth, and losing the delicacy of our sense of right. So it is also with exaggeration, eccentricity, and love of notoriety. They have very different degrees, but they one and all set before the mind something else to be sought for than mere truth and right, and herein is their

[21] "Truth and Falsehood," Morristown, N. J., September 25, 1870.

mischief. They pervert the conscience. They leave it out of the account, although it is necessary to its sound and healthy action that it should rule continually and in all things. In time, and by the force of habit, the sense of truth and right may be greatly perverted by this means, and we may forget that these, and not what is amusing or popular or astonishing, are the things to be aimed at.[22]

Not out of regard for the dead must one compromise with truth. It is to be spoken at all times and with the utmost baldness.

There is one popular maxim which we inherit from antiquity which seems to me false and pagan and which I should like to see amended at once and forever, and that is the maxim that we should say nothing but good of the dead. It is a false and heathenish maxim, for which Christianity teaches us to say nothing but *truth* of the dead. Calumny and hatred and even just antagonism may cease at the grave, but falsehood and false sentimentality ought not to begin there.[23]

Copious in content, closely woven in structure, appealing primarily to the intellect, unrelieved by fancy or humor, unlightened by any picturesqueness of illustration, yet brilliant in analysis, irresistible in logic, frequently epigrammatic and sometimes eloquent, impressive in loftiness of conviction and nobility of spirit, Sumner's sermons were not such as to make him a popular preacher. Nor was it in the character of the man to offer the slightest concession to principle in order to become one. After hearing him at Calvary, one Sunday, William C. Whitney, with all the liberty of an old friend, wrote him a letter in

22 "Perversion of Conscience," Morristown, N. J., November 5, 1871.
23 "Bread Not the Chief Thing," Morristown, N. J., May 12, 1872.

which he points out what were probably the two greatest defects in his preaching,—lack of vividness and too little concreteness of application. The sermon was on "Practical Atheism," and had for a text the words: "That in times past ye were without Christ, being aliens from the commonwealth of Israel and strangers from the covenant, having no hope and without God in the world." In it he describes the condition of the Ephesians before they embraced Christianity and compares it with that of those in recent times who, though they may believe in God, are practically without him, because he does not enter into their daily thought or affect their daily actions. He points out that this condition is due to the intensity of modern life and its many pressing demands, which tend to make men forget God and ultimately to lose all consciousness of him.

72 Park Ave.,
Sunday Eve.

DEAR BILL:

That sermon was the best I have heard from you by far, the best in two ways—the most practical and the most vivid. Is it clear that those two things are the great things to aim at? Judging by that sermon, you see it. The great work your profession has to accomplish among professing Christians is to save the world from being overwhelmed by worldliness, and the ministry must not be satisfied with logical statements of truth, but has got to *awaken* and arouse men. Why didn't you draw a graphic picture between the Ephesians and the Calvarians, descending to particulars, so as to startle people? Here is want and suffering and sin all around. I am getting scattering and fragmentary. What I want to say is, Bill, that you *can*, if you *will*, be a great pulpit orator and do lots of good; but you must begin the writing of every sermon by reflecting on the question—How shall I impress this by figures, by illustrations, by startling language on these indifferent, listless people? Don't cover so much ground in one sermon. Take just one point and use all the arts of the orator in enforcing it. Leave the logical sequences and the train of thought it starts for some other time. A sermon to be effective must not be essayical, exhaustive, but must catch up salient points and impress them. For instance, *this sermon*—the synopsis—a graphic picture of the Ephesians without God—from ignorance. The statement of the fact that man is a creature capable of rejecting its Creator. (It couldn't be better put than you put it.) Then show them so that they will *see* how they exercise that choice and thrust God aside. (Descend to instances and take up any charity in the city and depict it struggling along and crying out for help to rescue people from want and sin and how they close their ears and never pay attention to it—or choose any one of a Christian's duties and spend time on the picture.) Then show as you did the horrible tendency of society, and show in closing up how weak a thing is our ordinary life and how magnificent a thing is goodness—or in your own way enforce it.

Now, Bill, you may have two thoughts in reading this; first, that volunteering criticism and advice is presumptuous. To that I say I want to see you do *yourself* justice. You never have yet and this last looks most like it and I must indicate my thought. You know a looker-on often sees best. Your great tendency is to cover too much ground and to *essay*. You must have in mind *impressing* the idea. It should cut out nearly all between the passage 'The man as a worm' and the passage that begins 'God is the flower?' or something of that kind. Your other idea may be that it is poor business for me to see all this terrible condition of things that is destroying Christianity and do nothing myself, but of that more some other time. If you've got a place where you want a layman—but, no—well, let us know where people are needed and we'll see if we can do anything. My wife—the dear good girl—was very much gratified, and it had the effect, let me say, of making her feel mean, and that's a slight testimonial to the sermon, and, if you care for it, for myself, I offer my congratulations on it, for it was a success. I only say it was so good it showed it ought to be better. Here's a little book that is apropos. Read it and see if it don't impress its idea. It is easy to criticize this book as a work, but it serves its purpose of arousing people to real Christian conduct. It may suggest some practical things.

Yours,

W. C. W.

One very keen sorrow came to Sumner during his stay in Morristown. A son, born March 2, 1872, died in July of the same year. His farewell sermon he closed with these words:

Probably my only experience of parish life will be that which I have gained amongst you. I am sincerely thankful that it was my lot to make experience of parish life under such pleasant circumstances, and, whatever fortune may yet be in store for me, the two years spent amongst you must remain, I am sure, amongst the happiest in my life. Certainly one imperishable recollection of a life that opened here to close again must render this spot of earth forever sacred to my memory.

There is no field of activity which now calls so urgently for the activity of honest and conscientious men as the enlightenment of the American public on the nature and inevitable results of the financial and industrial errors to which they are committed.

Introductory Lecture to Courses in Political and Social Science.

CHAPTER VIII

CALL TO YALE

In 1872 a new era was opening at Yale. The agitation for a broader curriculum, a more liberal spirit, and a policy of greater aggressiveness was beginning to bear fruit. That year, for the first time, the alumni elected members of the Corporation. The summer before, Theodore Dwight Woolsey, then seventy years old, for a quarter of a century president of the college, who himself had done much to stimulate the changes which were under way, had resigned; and Noah Porter reigned in his stead. Money was beginning to come in; new professorships were being established. In addition to his other duties President Woolsey had given instruction in political philosophy. Upon his retirement it was decided to create a chair of Political and Social Science, and among those proposed for its first occupant was William Graham Sumner.

That an Episcopal rector in a New Jersey town should have been urged for what was likely to become one of the most prominent and important places on the faculty, was not so surprising as at first it may appear. Earlier at Yale he had made a decided impression as a teacher. Like a breath of clear, cold air from without, enlivening the dullness and drowsiness of a crowded and over-heated room, had been the coming of his spirit and methods into the lifeless atmosphere in which the instruction of those days went on. Under his touch minds awoke and interest in knowledge kindled. His aim had been, not simply to communicate facts, but to reveal those facts in their manifold relationships and significance. To the subject he had taught he had given a world background, linking it up with the social and intellectual movements of the race. He represented the kind of teacher which it was felt the new era required; the kind that was being sought, but was hard to find.

He was known, too, as one whose scholarship was broad and thorough. His general training had been the best America and Europe afforded. From boyhood he had been a diligent reader in many different fields. Always, his chief interest had been in life, its laws, conditions, and problems; and in living, its requirements, principles, and opportunities. All who had come into intimate contact with him recognized that his intellectual powers were much more than ordinary. In keenness of analysis, logical deduction, appreciation of practical demands, and ability to express ideas clearly and forcefully, few excelled him. The objection that he had not had technical training in the field of political and social science could not be raised then as it would be now, for the training available was meager. As a distinct department of academic research and application it was practically new.

Those who had known him as a student, moreover, and all who had followed his career as a writer and preacher, appreciated how strongly social conditions and public questions interested him. More and more they were coming to occupy the foreground of his mind. His power to penetrate to fundamental causes and to ultimate significance, and his independence and fearlessness in dealing with whatever he discussed, was equally well known. He himself says that it was the expression of his notions regarding the effects of the Civil War, with paper money and high taxation, in college compositions, which laid the foundation for the career which afterwards opened to him.

In addition to all this, he had the confidence and admiration of the younger alumni. His activities in connection with the "Young Yale" movement had brought him into prominence as one who had sound and progressive ideas regarding educational matters. He had worked in the interests of Yale with some of the most prominent of the alumni just elected to the Corporation. His aggressiveness, sincerity, and courage had secured him wide respect. That he would prove himself a good fighter was never questioned. Altogether, therefore, he was regarded as just the kind of man needed on the faculty for the difficult work of re-construction which was to go on in the years immediately ahead.

His election was not achieved without some difficulty, however. Another candidate of exceptional gifts and superior training was put forward. Under date of June 27, 1872, the records of the permanent officers of Yale College contain the following entry:

> The Faculty were found to be equally divided on the names of Prof. J. L. Diman and Rev. W. G. Sumner as candidates for the chair of Political Science, etc.

Each faction held stubbornly to its man, and a compromise by which both candidates might be brought to Yale was suggested. An entry in the records, dated July 3, 1872, states:

> The Faculty were variously divided on the subject of appointing Prof. Diman to the chair of Political Science, etc., and of nominating Mr. W. G. Sumner for a chair of Greek and Ancient History.

Regarding the situation, President Porter wrote Sumner the following letter:

YALE COLLEGE,
New Haven, Connecticut,
July 3, 1872.

MY DEAR MR. SUMNER:

I think I ought to apprise you that your name has been prominently mentioned as a suitable person to fill the chair of political economy and political science. I have said that I believed you would be willing to accept the post and to give your energies to this class of studies. One other person has been urged who is not a graduate of the college. Those who urge him urge very strongly and those who object to him are very decided in their objections. All the members of the Faculty would like to have you here in some capacity. The proposition has been made to have you here as a third professor of Greek and Ancient History, and to raise what endowment you feel is necessary. The probability of an endowment provided you were appointed conditionally is questioned, as the argument for a third professor would not be strong. There is a question whether the Corporation would appoint your competitor in the other chair against a strong opposition, even if you should prefer the chair of Greek. If you do not wish the chair of political science, and do not think that you should like the studies and duties as a life work, the question is settled. We shall not urge you. If you do wish it, it is not certain that the Corporation may not appoint the other person against the opposition to him as a man. No such opposition is urged, or exists, against you as a man, but some prefer you for another post and think it practicable to secure another post in Greek for you. I prefer that if any communication is made of the facts and probabilities, it should come from me, and depart from my usual line of entire silence in similar cases that you may act if called to act or to express a preference with a clear understanding of all the contingencies in the case. I think that there is a possibility that some approach may be made to you by other members of the faculty and that their sanguine views for your appointment as a third professor in Greek might be stimulated somewhat by their desire to secure another person for the other chair and might not be fulfilled in fact. I owe you more than usual confidence and think that an understanding of all the facts and relations in the case should be brought before you, if anything at all comes before your mind. Hence I write that you may act intelligently. Believe me

Most truly yours,

N. PORTER.

Professor John Lewis Diman was nine years older than Sumner and occupied the chair of history and political economy in Brown University, of which institution he was a graduate. He was a man of aristocratic tendencies and high-bred reserve. His father had been governor of Rhode Island and his mother was a grand-niece of Benjamin Franklin. He had studied at Andover and in Germany, and was a Congregational clergyman, having held two pastorates in Massachusetts. His intellectual powers were very great and he was a brilliant lecturer. Princeton and Johns Hopkins offered him professorships, and Harvard sought three times to secure his services. Like Sumner, he was a free-trader, and had the courage to teach the truth as he discerned it amid the smoke and din of Rhode Island's manufactories. In candor and fidelity to principle he and Sumner were also alike; but Professor Diman was more polished and subtle, less rugged and dogmatic. Graces were his by birth and early associations, of which Sumner had been deprived. His appreciation of the truth in each of opposing schools and doctrines, and his breadth of

sympathies, sometimes made him seem inconsistent
and lacking in positiveness of conviction. It used to
be said of him that he was both a Roman Catholic and
a Unitarian. There never was any danger of such a
statement being made about Sumner. He was
against both distinctly and emphatically. Although a
Congregational clergyman, Professor Diman is listed
as one of the contributors to *The Living Church,* and
he was even proposed for membership in "The Club."
Dr. C. C. Tiffany, in his reminiscences of that organization, characterizes him as "a Congregational divine
of profound learning and churchly leaning."

How much opposition to Sumner as a man underlay
the stubborn support which was given to Professor
Diman, it is impossible to state. One suspects, in
spite of President Porter's assurance to the contrary,
that some existed, though it may have been cleverly
concealed. Certainly the desire to have Sumner a
member of the Faculty, on the part of those who objected to his filling so important a chair as that of
political and social science and would have relegated
him to a third professorship of Greek which did not
yet exist and whose establishment was problematic,
could not have been overwhelming. The old conservative party which had been anything but cordial
to him when he was a tutor was still influential in
college circles. The educational views which he had
expressed later, and his criticisms of prevailing conditions and methods, had not met with unqualified
approval. It is not improbable that there was some
opposition to him born of personal dislike and fear.
When a tutor, as has already been indicated, he had
displayed a militant and uncompromising disposition.
His brusqueness, independence, and assertiveness

some had found offensive. Professor Thatcher is said to have remarked once that Sumner was a good man if he could only have his own way. It would have been strange if there had not been those who felt that he would be a hard person to work with, provocative of faculty dissension and personal animosities.

How the deadlock was finally broken is not recorded. Sumner wanted the chair of political and social science, and that is what he got. Professor Diman retained his position at Brown, from which even offers of college presidencies were never able to dislodge him.

Why Sumner left the active ministry, the work of which he had contemplated from boyhood, is clear. Certain it is that this act was not due to any change in his theological beliefs or in his opinion of the importance of the church. That a great task lay immediately before it he was more conscious perhaps than most of his contemporaries.

Our modern society is deeply infected by philosophical skepticism and philosophical indifference. The number of men who are falling into a doubting position with regard to traditional religious doctrines is increasing every day. . . . A conflict is impending between the traditional dogmas and modern speculation and science in which it is possible that all religion may be lost. A chaos threatens the world of mind and spirit. Not two or three, nor a score, but a hundred claimants wrangle for the faith of men. It is to be apprehended that utter ruin may come upon all our universal ideas and spiritual faiths. The great question is whether there is an historical revelation of spiritual and universal truths which has authority for man, or whether each man and each generation must reason out the whole problem afresh, or rest contented with so much knowledge of the shell of things as he can win through the senses.

I say that this conflict is impending, and I believe and have always believed that it was the duty of the pulpit to prepare for it, to enter into it, and to win a victory in it. It is certain that every tradition and every inherited faith of mankind is to be stated on a re-examination of authority and evidence within the next fifty years.

To the above statement, made in his farewell sermon, Sumner added an expression of personal convictions which leaves no doubts as to where he then stood.

I believe that we have a true revelation of spiritual and universal truths and that it is recorded in the Bible, and I believe that if men would study the Bible faithfully, taking it for just what it is, and, above all, if they would stop 'defending' it, it would be apparent to the consciences of men that the truth in regard to the transcendental order has been perceived so much more closely and recorded so much more faithfully in the Bible than anywhere else that it alone is justly entitled to authority as a Divine revelation. I have devoted much time to a close, critical, and fearless study of the Bible, and this is my conviction. When it is reached, the various systems of traditionalism, dogmatism, and rationalism, seem to be so much lumber. We have in the Bible the record of doctrines won by men of the purest spiritual insight, graven on the history of nations through centuries, wrought out of the vicissitudes of generations, developed under the undisturbed progress of moral forces for long periods of time, and ratified again and again in the experience of families and individuals.

Although Sumner's views had undergone no serious change, it is probable that experience had disclosed that in some important respects at least he was temperamentally unfitted for the work of the ministry. The preaching function of his profession appealed to him, and little else. It had been his inborn desire to teach, to battle for the truth, and to reform, that had led him to enter it. For calling and afternoon teas, however, for the petty details of parish work, for the incessant demands for all kinds of service, he was endowed neither with the taste nor the patience, and he could not but have been irritated continually by the amount of time which they took from study, writing, and pulpit preparation. His independence and outspokenness also, while they may have been admired in the pulpit, were not helpful to him in the delicate work of comfort, counsel, and admonition, nor did they make it easy for him to work with others, or others with him.

But at the root of his uneasiness in the ministry, was the fact that the topics in which he was becoming increasingly interested he could not discuss from the pulpit, nor could he battle there for the principles which at that time, he felt, called imperatively for bold and intelligent support. Currency and the tariff he considered matters of most urgent importance, threatening all the interests of the nation, moral, social, and economic. About these it was impossible to preach, "But I got so near to it," he confesses, "that I was detected sometimes, as, for instance, when a New York banker came to me, as I came down from the pulpit, and said, 'There was a good deal of political economy in that sermon.'" Moreover, he had recently read the essays of Herbert Spencer, which were afterwards collected into the volume, "The

Study of Sociology.'' The conception of society, of social forces, and of the science of society there offered were just what he had long been groping after. ''It rescued social science from the dominion of the cranks, and offered a definite and magnificent field of work, from which we might hope at last to derive definite results for the solution of social problems.'' [1] This was the field to which Sumner felt himself most loudly called. An academical career would offer him the opportunity to enter it and at the same time teach, preach, and fight for righteousness and truth. He left the ministry because he was persuaded that he could best employ his capabilities elsewhere.

No one probably ever undertook a professorship in political and social science with a preparation and spirit quite like Sumner's. His chief departments of study had been theology, philosophy, and church history. He was an authority in Hebrew and had twice been called to make instruction in that language his life work. His proficiency in Greek and ancient history was such that half the Yale faculty were willing to have him come to the college as professor of those subjects. As foreign to what ultimately became his life pursuit as these branches of learning may seem, to one whose underlying interest was the development of human society and the solution of its problems in the light of history and natural laws, they could not fail to contribute material of inestimable value, and make possible first hand research of which few sociologists are capable.

In the general principles of economics and government he was well grounded, and with prevailing sociological views and tendencies, thoroughly ac-

---

[1] "Sketch of William Graham Sumner," "Challenge of Facts and Other Essays," p. 10.

quainted. His study of history had been much more than a survey of men and events; it had penetrated to laws and forces. But his preparation for the work which now lay before him had come as much from observation as from books. Since boyhood, both in this country and in Europe, he had been watching what was going on. The underlying causes of conditions and happenings, the necessary outcome of ruling motives and methods, the practical problems of the day, the direction in which things were tending, the errors to be combated, the only way of making society better, these were the matters which had all the time been occupying his mind, and regarding them he had arrived at well grounded and firm convictions. Freed from the shackles of the ministry, he was eager to speak and to act concerning them.

His personal experience, furthermore, had been such as to make the human side of social and political science appeal to him strongly. His parents had been immigrants. He had known poverty and struggle. Life in the shops he had heard discussed as far back as he could remember. By birth and early association he was of the common people. Appreciate the value of capital and capitalists as he might, his sympathy was always with the hard-working, self-respecting wage earners, the great productive force of society, who minded their own business and paid the bill incurred by the loafers, meddlers, and reformers. These forgotten and wronged appealed to Sumner's chivalry. The remembrance of them was with him always.

It was with his interest chiefly in the practical bearings of economics and sociology, therefore, that he took up his duties at Yale. All his research into social origins was to be prompted and sustained by the hope that there might be discovered that which would help solve present problems and make living together upon the earth a more rational and satisfying experience. He came to be a champion of truth, liberty, and justice, and to strike with all his might at the follies, errors, and crimes, under burdens imposed by which so many clean, quiet, virtuous, domestic citizens, giving no trouble and exciting no admiration, were living. He came not to be an academic recluse, but a public servant, participating as actively as possible in civic and political affairs. As a teacher he was not to introduce his students to the theories of text books merely, or spend the bulk of his time in subtile analyses of values, the problem of changing prices, or other economic phenomena, but to acquaint youth with the laws and principles governing the social body of which they were a part, and ought to become an intelligent and influential part. His great text book was world conditions. He began one of his first lectures by contrasting the industries of Europe with those in the United States, and calling attention to the unscientific methods of taxation in the latter. It was to be his aim in teaching not simply to give his students facts, but to make them men, and inspire them to go forth to be wise and patriotic citizens. In his "Introductory Lecture to Courses in Political and Social Science," he so declared it.

My aim will be to give to those who visit this university faith in science, in thought, in training as applied to politics. I desire to use the opportunity given me to furnish the country with citizens of sterling worth, and to give to the professions men whose public influence will tell in the cause of liberty, industry, and honesty. I hope that those of you who become lawyers will learn how to legislate far-sightedly for the permanent welfare of a free people, not to follow the clamor of a noisy faction. I hope that those of you who become editors will learn to wield honorably the immense power you will enjoy for the instruction and molding of public opinion. I hope that those of you who become clergymen will teach that no one can be a righteous man in our time and country unless he is also a faithful citizen. I hope also that the career of politics may open in the future in such a way as to tempt the ambition of the best youth of the republic. Republics learn only by experience, but the bitter experience will not be wanting. The men of this generation are not doing their duty by the men of the next. They are putting off hard duties and are shirking responsibilities and are relaxing the political virtue of the country. In one way or another the results will inevitably come. When they come, I am of the opinion that the American people will find that it does not pay to be ruled by small men. They will look about in their need for men who know what ought to be done and how to do it. It is my duty here to try to provide that when such a time comes the men may be ready; and to you I say that, whether you are in the ranks of the citizens—where you will need to know how to choose your leaders—or whether you are called to fulfill the responsibilities of office yourselves, the course of study upon which we now enter deserves your most careful application.[2]

[2] "The Challenge of Facts and Other Essays," pp. 402, 403.

I dislike to hear politicians sneered at and the career of politics tossed aside as if it were the career of a swindler, for I hold politics—or, if we must abandon the degraded word, statesmanship—to be the grandest calling open to men; and yet, if a young friend of mine goes into politics I feel misgivings for his future, not lest he may not get rich, for that is probably enough, but lest he may lose the manliness and honor of a gentleman and may acquire the character of an intriguer and a gambler.

Introductory Lecture to Courses in Political and Social Science.

CHAPTER IX

ALDERMAN AND POLITICIAN

No sooner was Professor Sumner established in New Haven than it became apparent that he had come, not to be a member of the college circle merely, but to be a citizen, expecting, both as a duty and as a privilege, to give time, thought, and labor to the interests of the community and the state. Before a year had elapsed, he had begun to take an active part in local affairs and was preparing to make himself widely heard on national issues. Without regard for precedent, he entered the field of practical politics, affiliating himself prominently with the Republican party. The reception which he received was more than cordial; it was enthusiastic. Here was a new type of college professor, hard-headed, aggressive, with a large fund of information about government and finance, as much interested in the concrete problems of the day as in books and theories, and not above joining hands with his fellows in the actual work of municipal management and political combat.

On the sixth day of October, 1873, he was elected alderman from the sixth ward, his opponent being Mr. Richard T. Merwin, who received three hundred and twenty-nine votes as against four hundred and ninety-nine for Sumner. His willingness to take the office was hailed with warm approval both by the city and the college press. A few days before his election the *New Haven Daily Morning Journal and Courier* made the following congratulatory comment:

Professor Sumner is Professor of Political and Social Science at Yale. This is the first time a Professor in old Yale has been nominated to sit in the halls of the Common Council in our recollection. We ought to have Yale represented each year on both Boards. As the sixth is such a strong Republican Ward, he, with the other gentlemen associated with him, will probably be elected. Professor Sumner lives in his fine residence on Edwards Street, near Whitney Avenue, recently completed.

The comment of the Yale *Record* was still more commendatory.

We recognize herein an act of Professor Sumner's which rightly entitles him to the praise and honor of the University. In it he has shown his readiness to share the burden of that theory of government which he so ably teaches. There can be no denial that Professor Sumner will exercise a strong influence over the action of the Board of Aldermen. The contrary is scarcely supposable. Nor is it an ignoble sphere of action. It is at the base of the edifice of city government, and hence gives tone to every department.

The *Record's* conviction was well founded, and its prophecy, fulfilled. With characteristic fidelity and thoroughness Sumner applied himself to the duties of his office, and was soon one of the most trusted and influential members of the Board. October 5, 1874, he was reëlected for a term of two years, receiving one hundred and seven votes more than his opponent, Mr. Colin M. Ingersoll. Apparently ward lines had been changed, for now he represented the ninth. The Republican aldermen that year gave him all their votes for president, but since the Democrats were largely in the majority, his opponent, Mr. Edward W. Hotchkiss, was elected.

Throughout his three years of service Professor Sumner was chairman of the Committee on Claims, and for a part of the time a member of the Committee on Ordinances. In the former capacity, especially, his ability to get at facts, his sense of fairness, and his personal honesty, were of great value. His keenness and carefulness are said to have saved the city considerable sums of money. At the beginning of 1874, according to the address of Mayor Henry G. Lewis to the Common Council, New Haven had a population of about sixty thousand. The number of dwellings were over seven thousand, and the number of carriages, horses, etc., it was impossible to ascertain, but they were to be estimated by the thousands. Some of the principal streets were being paved, and to Alderman Sumner, principally, fell the important task of determining what should be the city's policy toward the street railway companies with regard to payment for such improvements. Through a bill proposed in the legislature the companies had sought exemption from pavement assessments. This bill Sumner had stoutly opposed on the ground that the state had no right to take from the city the power to lay such a tax. What the legislature finally did was to pass an act giving to boards of aldermen the power to abate assessments on street railway companies if they judged that justice and public interest required. The companies in New Haven at once appealed to the Board for exemption. At a hearing, representatives of the roads argued that they got no benefit from the pavement, except relief from keeping the dirt between the tracks repaired, and that if the wear and tear on the horses was taken into consideration, they lost by it. Furthermore, they had no money wherewith to pay. Sumner declared that a horse railroad was a necessity and a nuisance at the same time, and that in his opinion the companies ought to be taxed. The matter was finally turned over to a special committee of three, of which he was chairman. His report, which was adopted, shows his carefulness, precision of statement, and scrupulous regard for justice.

To the Honorable Board of Aldermen:

Your committee to whom was referred the petition of the State Street Horse Railroad Company beg leave to report. Your committee felt a great responsibility in considering the first of a large and important class of cases which were placed by a recent act of the Legislature under the jurisdiction of the Board of Aldermen. The importance of the present case as tending to shape the policy of the Board toward this class of cases seemed to the committee so great that they beg leave to place on record the general principle which they had in mind in connection with the recommendation which they offer and the special reasons which influenced their decision. Your committee are of the opinion that the right of the City to lay assessments for pavements upon street railroads, as well as upon any other property benefited, is clear and ought to be maintained. The act under which this petition is brought does not curtail that right, but only gives to the Board of Aldermen a power hitherto possessed by no department of the City government to abate assessments on street railroads whenever justice or public interest may so dictate. It follows in the opinion of your committee that each application for abatement under this act ought to stand on its own merits and that in each case specific grounds in justice or public interest ought to be alleged and established before any abatement should be made.

In the present case your committee has found that the State Street Railroad was built substantially according to the order of the Board of Road Commissioners and that the proprietors thereof have been forced to take up and relay a large portion of the track on account of improvements ordered by the City and in obedience to the orders of the City authorities, whereby they have been put to such loss and damage that the sums now due the City from them may with propriety be remitted.

Your committee therefore recommends the passage of the following resolution. All of which is respectfully submitted.

WILLIAM G. SUMNER, Chairman.
New Haven, Aug. 17, 1874.

The petitions of the other companies were considered with equal thoroughness, and partial abatements were made according to the facts revealed.

Another report, somewhat amusing, which is recorded in full on the minutes of the Board, has to do with a claim for damages. One Pewtriss had requested compensation for injury done to his property. Apparently the claim had not been approved, and friends of the gentleman thought to get the better of Sumner by petitioning the Board to appoint a special committee to consider the case. This petition, too, was referred to the Committee on Claims, and Sumner presented the following report behind every word of which one can feel indignation and hot contempt.

To the Honorable Court of Common Council:
Your committee on claims to whom was referred the petition of J. C. Bradley and others for a special committee to consider the claim of S. L. Pewtriss beg leave to report that said petition assumes and implies as the ground of the prayer of said petitioners that your honorable body has passed an order refusing to allow or consider the claim of Samuel L. Pewtriss, Esq., for damages to his property. In this respect said petition is in error. Your honorable body referred the petition of said Pew-

triss to this present Committee on Claims who gave to
the same full consideration. Your committee heard said
Pewtriss and all the witnesses whom he presented on several occasions and in full. The petitioner appeared before your Committee four or five times. Your Committee
also appointed a sub-Committee to visit the premises and
they summoned before them the City Surveyor and other
City officials and they also summoned the persons who
laid the concrete sidewalk. The case was complicated
and difficult and occupied the attention and consideration of your Committee longer than perhaps any other
which has come before them and they did not act until
they understood it in all its details. Your Committee
had every reason to believe that the petitioner was satisfied that his case had been completely heard, for he was
present and urged a decision one week before your Committee acted on his case.

Your Committee do not see any occasion for appoint-
ing a special committee to revise their decision in this
case which would not apply to every other case upon
which they have acted. They cannot therefore recommend your honorable body to take that action, but respectfully recommend that said petitioner have leave to
withdraw. All of which is respectfully submitted.

W. G. SUMNER, Chairman.

New Haven, Oct. 27, 1875.

For the practical application of the moral and economic principles in which he believed Sumner contended vigorously. In 1875 the country was going
through a period of great industrial depression.
Many in New Haven were out of work. The question
was raised in the Board of Aldermen whether any of
the $14,000 for the grading of streets and the $18,000
for ordinary labor would be used to afford work to
the unemployed and needy. The head of the Road
Department stated that no such policy was antici-

pated. Alderman McGrath, a prominent Democratic
politician and something of a demagogue, insisted
loudly that some portion of these funds be used to
assist the poor laboring man. Sumner opposed the
project on the ground of its injustice, since it would
result in benefiting a selected few at the expense of
all the rest. Incidentally he had a little fun with Mr.
McGrath.

> Mr. McGrath said that if the money could go to
> laborers, the town would have no one to provide for but
> poor widows.
> Mr. Sumner asked if the appropriation was to be
> used to employ seamstresses and sewing women.
> Mr. McGrath said he did not expect any of it would
> go toward building a shirt factory.
> Mr. Sumner asked, 'Why not?' and further asked if
> there was any account of the employment of clerks who
> were suffering from want of work.
> Mr. McGrath spoke in favor of working men.
> Alderman Sumner further discussed the topic, speak-
> ing as to the *propriety* of making a distinction as to
> classes to be provided with work in hard times. If the
> people were to be taxed $20,000.00 to have it spent in
> just one spot, it would be unjust to the taxpayers and
> unjust to all working people who needed employment.[1]

As generally happens in such cases politics were
victorious over principle. The laborers got city
work, and Mr. McGrath, popularity and votes.

In addition to the duties which fell to him as a
member of the committees on claims and ordinances,
other tasks calling for special intelligence and attention to details were frequently assigned to Sumner.
In 1874 Mayor Lewis and Alderman Sumner headed
a committee to consider the establishment of a public

[1] *Journal-Courier*, December 9, 1875.

library, the other members being Councilmen Baldwin
and Countryman, Messrs. James E. English, N. D.
Sperry, James D. Dewell, and Morris F. Tyler. He
was appointed on a committee to revise the rules of
the Court of the Common Council and the Board of
Aldermen. He was made chairman of a committee
to determine the legal powers of the city in regard to
railroad bridges, and presented a carefully prepared
report taking up the questions of law involved. In
anything regarding finances he was likely to have a
hand, and served on a committee, in 1876, to consider
and report concerning such reduction of public expenses as might be necessary in order to prevent an
increase in the rate of taxes.

Although these many responsibilities must have
made no small demand upon the time and energies of
a young professor building up a new and important
department, Sumner found opportunity to take an
active part in the work of his party organization. In
1874, with General E. S. Greeley, he was a delegate
from his ward to the Republican representative convention, of which convention he was elected chairman.
In September of the same year he presided over the
ninth ward primary, and was chosen one of the delegates to the town convention at which also he presided. He is said to have written the Republican
state platform in 1874.[2] At the Republican congressional convention, held in New Haven, March 3, 1875,
he was delegate from the fourth district, and took the
floor to re-nominate Hon. Stephen W. Kellogg. In
1876, with Henry Farnam, H. B. Harrison, and Theodore D. Woolsey, he wrote a letter to Hon. Henry C.
Robinson, inviting him to speak in New Haven, cordially endorsing the Republican ticket for state of-

2 *New York World*, September 15, 1876.

ficers, and approving the party platform. That he had a hand in its framing is indicated by the following letter from Hon. N. D. Sperry.

Post Office, New Haven, Feb. 24, 1876.
Prof. Wm. G. Sumner,
My Dear Sir:
Would it be too much for me to ask of you to propose a Resolution on finance for our State Convention? I suppose several will be presented. Still I am anxious to get your views on paper and all the light I can. I know you have made finance a study of your life thus far, and I hope I am not asking too much of you at this time.
Very truly your friend,
N. D. Sperry.

Invitations to speak at public gatherings during this period were numerous. His utterances on such occasions show that he had already taken up the cudgel against what seemed to him to threaten every interest of the nation, "soft money," and protection. At every Chamber of Commerce banquet he was a popular speaker. On his first appearance he had declared that his sympathies were for "a grand, close, living union between the colleges and our mercantile and manufacturing interests," and that to this end he hoped to be able to contribute. A newspaper report of a meeting of the Chamber, held March 31, 1875, says that a most interesting discussion sprang up in which "Professor Sumner of Yale threw down the gauntlet as an advocate of free trade in frank and friendly spirit, which drew out the chairman, Mr. Trowbridge. Mayor Lewis and Hon. Charles L. English also dissented from the views of the learned professor." [3]

[3] *Journal-Courier*, April 1, 1875.

The currency question was at this time a vital one. The panic of 1873 had created an insistent demand for more money. To this Congress had yielded in 1874 by passing a bill for increase of currency to $400,000,000. This pernicious inflationist measure President Grant had vetoed, and early in 1875 Congress passed a resumption act. The promulgators of the greenback philosophy were everywhere active, however, and were loud and bitter in their denunciations of their opponents. Professor Sumner felt no duty more urgent than that of educating the people, so far as he was able, with regard to currency and the laws governing it. The respect which was accorded him in this endeavor in his home town is reflected in the following newspaper items. Under date of January 1, 1875, the *New Haven Journal-Courier* offers this comment:

The Chamber of Commerce has done a good thing by requesting our distinguished fellow citizen, Professor Sumner, to address the Chamber on the great subject now before the people, viz., the currency question. We are requested to invite our citizens to attend the meeting which will be held at Loomis' Temple of Music, Tuesday evening, 5 inst. Professor Sumner being high authority on this important subject, our citizens will be well repaid in hearing the address.

In its issue of January 6 the same paper gives a full report of the meeting, in which it says:

Professor W. G. Sumner delivered a lecture at Loomis' Temple of Music last evening, by request of the Chamber of Commerce, on the subject 'The Currency.' Owing to his knowledge of and familiarity with this difficult subject, so puzzling to men throughout the nation, the hall was filled with citizens of high intelligence, prominent in business and educational circles. He was introduced by Thomas R. Trowbridge, Esq., and spoke extemporaneously and without notes. His flow of language was copious, direct, and incisive.

In his address Sumner carefully defined currency, and with the aid of plain, illuminating examples pointed out the evils of inconvertible paper money. Illustrative of his method and also of how injustice and the wrongs of the poor were ever one of the incentives that made him go forth to battle with error and selfishness, is this extract:

Take the sewer laborer. He bargains to work one day, we will say, for one gold dollar. . . . He gets, we suppose, his gold dollar and gives it to his wife to buy calico. She lays the coin on the counter. It has to the seller a defined fascination, and he sells as low as he can possibly afford. The poor woman gets in return a fair equivalent for her husband's money. The value of the coin offered has a determined value, for gold has the most inflexible value known to man. Now take the other case. Her husband has received a piece of paper of uncertain value and with the highest possible value placed upon it by the employer—for that is human nature. She places on the counter the paper dollar, and the price of the commodity given in exchange is just as high as possible. Here you see the principle of combination comes in. The dealers stand together to look out for one another. As Cobden said, 'Wherever combination is possible, competition is impossible.' Wherever combination comes in, it is a principle of a band of robbers, and forsooth we have a system which drives men into this system of combination and warfare. Here then is an illustration from everyday life. It is a great mistake, a wrong to the poor man, and therefore, I plead, let us have done with this system.

The report of the meeting ends with the statement that "the speaker concluded amid great applause."

Again, a little more than a year later, he addressed
the Chamber of Commerce on the currency question.
Apparently his aggressiveness, vigor, and the sting
which not infrequently he put into his remarks, had
already begun to call forth the hostility and personal
abuse from which thereafter his efforts in behalf of
truth and righteousness were never to be free. On
this occasion he aroused the ire of the New Haven
Currency Club, which seems to have represented the
local greenback faction of the Democratic party. At
a meeting held February 29, 1876, one of its members,
Dr. J. P. Phillips, took this shot at Sumner:

> How can we expect the people to understand us im-
> mediately when a professor in Yale College whose duty
> it is to understand finance is so profoundly ignorant of
> the questions now before us as Sumner has shown him-
> self to be. A friend of mine has requested me not to
> reply to the pitiable exhibition that was made here last
> Saturday night. I shall therefore leave that to him and
> dismiss Sumner with the remark that every citizen of
> New Haven should feel humiliated to know that Yale
> College has in its employ a young clergyman who makes
> malicious attacks upon the private character of his op-
> ponents.[4]

Sumner's activities in behalf of sound money were
not confined to the local arena, however. The circum-
ference of his influence was steadily widening. In the
fall of 1873 he published in the *Financier* four or
five historical sketches instructive in regard to doctrines of currency. Their aim was to let the his-

[4] *Journal-Courier*, March 1, 1876.

torical facts tell their own story without comment. "It succeeded so far," he says, "that many persons who do not believe that financial laws vary with the period, the climate, or the continent, read them with interest, and drew the inferences of which it seemed to be important that we should all be convinced." These sketches he expanded and published early in 1874 under the title "A History of American Currency with Chapters on the English Bank Restriction and Austrian Paper Money." This field of enlightenment and warning had not been opened up before, and the book had a ready sale.

It contains a great number of significant facts gathered from many different sources. How in connection with his work as professor, alderman, politician, lecturer, and occasional preacher, Sumner managed to get together this material, almost passes comprehension. Only the self-discipline to which he had always subjected himself, and the power of application and capacity for incessant toil which through years of struggle to achieve his aims he had developed, can account for it. It is evident that the work had been done under pressure and with haste. The writer frankly states in the preface that he would not have published it if he had not felt that at that particular juncture it had great practical importance. It was a club thrown out to be picked up and used over the heads of those who were advocating what over and over again had been proved to be foolish and disastrous doctrines. Facts are given in profusion, but judicious selection and due subordination are lacking. The reader is left to make his own inferences, something that a limited number only could do with accuracy and assurance. Sumner's own information was so broad and his perception so keen that he always tended to assume in pupil and reader more background and understanding than they possessed.

The public received the book with gladness and with regret. It both pleased and exasperated them. Those competent to criticize it seem to have felt as Mr. Whitney did regarding the sermon about which he wrote to Sumner, that it was so good it ought to have been better. The remarkable slovenliness of style and composition, said a writer in the *North American Review,* may perhaps be forgiven under the circumstances, but "no exigencies of publication can justify an author in the use of language which is often obscure as well as incorrect, and in the heaping together of bald and disconnected statements, for which the reader is to discover for himself some principle of cohesion." [5] The hearty contempt and even hatred, which frequently appears, were thought to display an attitude not altogether judicial and scientific, likely to inspire distrust in the minds of a class of readers whose confidence it was desirable to win. There was general agreement, nevertheless, that in spite of all deduction to be made from the worth of the book, it was still one of great value and that the inferences to be drawn from its facts were scientifically conclusive. "Considered as illustrations of certain principles," said the *Atlantic Monthly,* "the work is of great merit; and its immediate and practical use is proved by its rapid sale. Whoever turns to it with the expectation of finding a complete history of American currency will be disappointed; but whoever looks within to find new arguments against the expediency of inflating the present currency will not scan its pages in vain. It is preëminently a book for the times; a light set up to warn inflationists of the in-

[5] *North American Review,* October, 1874, Vol. CXIX, p. 408.

evitable peril that will follow the adoption of their financial creed.'' [6]

The immediate cause of Sumner's withdrawal from practical politics was the attitude which he took in the Hayes-Tilden campaign. Some person signing himself "Enquirer" wrote a letter to the *New Haven Palladium* asking him whom he intended to support for President. In the same paper, September 11, 1876, he published a frank and detailed reply. He prefaced it with an interesting statement of what he considered his responsibility to the university and the limitations which he felt that responsibility placed upon him with respect to politics.

I want to promise one thing. My first responsibility is to the University, and I propose to be true to that before anything else. I shall not compromise that for political influence, and if, as 'Enquirer' says, a student and teacher of political science may fairly be asked to give his opinions and his reasons, it is also true that a man who occupies a university chair must be careful, in political activity, whether he pulls down the university or pulls up politics. I have therefore carefully limited my practical action in politics to such duties as are incumbent on *every* citizen, such as will not interfere with my university duties, and such as an independent scholar can pursue without any selfish interest or danger to that broadest influence which he ought to seek to obtain. I therefore write now the simple, frank opinion of an independent man, whose ambition and career lie entirely inside the sphere of the university teacher. Such a man is bound to be honest, dispassionate, and unprejudiced; to seek no friendships and fear no enemies. His opinion, if it is worthy of himself and his position, must be calm, broad, fair, and sincere.[7]

[6] *Atlantic Monthly*, August 1874, Vol. XXXIV, p. 238.
[7] The letter is printed in full in "The Challenge of Facts and Other Essays," p. 365.

The letter then goes on to state that, for the writer, the assertions made about the antecedents and acts of parties have no force at all. To him the good sense, sound patriotism, and correct intentions of the masses of the people in both parties, and the evil elements as well, seem substantially equal. He turns, therefore, for his ground of judgment to men. Parties as such cannot be trusted or held responsible; men can be. For the candidature of Mr. Hayes he does not see how any one can have respect. He is the creature of the machine and seems to have no other public claim to the Presidency. Mr. Tilden's nomination was opposed by all the worst elements of his party and supported by as honest, pure, and intelligent men as ever led in any political convention in the country. His nomination was wrested from the convention by the conviction that he was the real leader of the party, the champion of its best principles, the embodiment of its hope. With regard to the currency he has shown a more correct, detailed, statesmanlike knowledge of the evil, the remedy, and the process of cure than any other public man that is eligible. As the governor of the state which has led in the demoralization of our politics, he has made positive and successful steps toward reform at the risk of his own political fortunes. Furthermore, the future policy to be employed in relation to the South is at stake, and the writer is unqualifiedly against any further administration of the affairs of the South by the North acting through the general government. Finally, whatever hope of free trade there is lies in the election of Tilden.

The utterance of such sentiments brought down upon Sumner all manner of reproach. The *Palladium* letter was reprinted in New York papers and given

wide publicity. Democrats all over the country hailed
it with delight, but Republican publications, which
formerly had displayed great respect for the professor's opinions, were now unable to find words to
express adequately their distrust of his mental processes and their contempt for his views. On the other
hand, a flood of letters came to him, both from the
North and the South, commending his independent
and courageous stand, and expressing gratitude for so
concise and logical a statement of the issues. After
the election the Democratic national committee asked
Sumner with others to go to Louisiana and determine
what were the facts regarding the election there.
Upon his return, at the request of Governor Charles
R. Ingersoll of Connecticut, he made a public statement of the impressions he had received. In this he
so favored the Democratic side in the election dis-
putes and showed such sympathy with the South that
he was again subjected to a storm of newspaper abuse.

In the meantime his term as alderman had expired.
Regarding him as a renegade, the Republicans did not
renominate him. The Democrats did, but his opponent, Mr. James E. Stetson, defeated him by more
than two hundred votes. This was the end of his
excursion into politics. "I found," he says, "that
I was likely to do more harm in politics than almost
any other kind of man, because I did not know the
rules of the game and did not want to learn them.
Therefore the adepts could play with me in more
senses than one." [8] To this statement a very adroit
politician of the day replied: "He may not have
known the game, but he knew that one was going on,
and that is much more than most college professors

[8] "Autobiographical Sketch," "Earth Hunger and Other Essays,"
p. 4.

would have known." Sumner was no doubt sincere in
the reason he gave for getting out of politics; nevertheless, his retirement was not altogether voluntary.
His influence in public life was to continue, however.
The "young clergyman employed by Yale," had become a national figure.

The one thing which justifies popular education for all children is the immense value of men of genius to the society.

Folkways.

CHAPTER X

STATE OFFICIAL

ALTHOUGH Professor Sumner withdrew from active politics in 1876, his services as a public official did not end. Early in 1882 he became a member of the Connecticut State Board of Education and continued such until his death. Thus during the thirty-eight years he was a professor at Yale there were only about six in which to class-room duties, research, administrative work as a member of the faculty, and continual writing and lecturing on public questions, he did not add arduous labors as a director of community and state affairs.

For one of Sumner's views and characteristics the Board of Education offered a congenial field for service. There was no game going on there the rules of which he did not want to learn. Anything in the interest of children appealed to him strongly, not only because of its societal significance, but even more because he loved children. It was in connection with them that the softer side of his nature came most into evidence. A neighbor relates that when in his walks he passed Sumner on the street, he was generally greeted with a brief and gruff salutation, but that if he had his little grandchild with him Sumner's face would light up immediately and he would invariably stop and converse with the child. As a member of the Board he visited the schools about the state and enjoyed talking to the pupils, speaking to them about their "sums" and what school signified. Those who heard him say that he was always simple, clear, and sympathetic. At one of the first teacher's meetings he attended he spoke on increasing the happiness of little children.

Sumner was too conscious of his own indebtedness to the public schools not to appreciate their worth. Speaking to a company of citizens gathered in the high school at Hartford, he uttered these significant and emphatic words: "You must regard this institution as one of the boasts of your city. Guard it well. You may not boast of it only. You owe it a debt which you must pay. Every boy and girl who has graduated here owes a debt to the common school system of America. Every man for whom this school has opened a career which would otherwise have been beyond his reach, owes a tenfold debt, both to the common school system and to the class in which he was born. Sectarian interests, private school interests, property interests, and some cliques of 'culture' falsely so called, are rallying against the system a force which people as yet underrate. There is no knowing how soon the struggle may open, and you may be called upon to pay the allegiance you owe."[1]

Highly as he valued the public school system Sumner had no illusions regarding it. He did not expect to see any social miracle wrought thereby. "The faith in book learning," he says in his essay on "The Teacher's Unconscious Influence," "is one of the superstitions of the nineteenth century and it enters for a large part into the bequest which the nineteenth century is about to hand over to the twentieth. On the wall of our school room our teacher had pasted up in large letters: 'Knowledge is power.' Yes, that is

[1] "Integrity in Education." "The Forgotten Man and Other Essays," edited by Albert Galloway Keller, Yale University Press, 1919, p. 416.

what knowledge is. It is power and nothing more. As a power it is like wealth, talent, or any power, that is, it is without any moral element whatever.

"The moral question always comes in when we ask in respect to the man who has power: what will he do with it? . . . If he so chooses, he may, by virtue of it, be far more useful to himself, his children, and his country than he would be without it, but if he choose otherwise, he may simply be a far more efficient and harmful rascal. This is why it is simply a crude and empty superstition to believe that a knowledge of reading, writing, arithmetic, and geography makes good husbands and fathers and citizens. It does not. There is no connection of cause and effect." [2]

Though regarding the theory that education is the panacea for all the ills of society as utter nonsense, a modern manifestation of the medieval belief in magic, Sumner found ample social and economic justification for loyalty to the public schools. They increase the chances for individual self-realization and so make for a richer social life; they transmit the gain of the past; they cultivate social instincts in the young; and they can contribute to the formation of the right kind of character. As a nation, he says, we "believe that every man has a full right to make the most of himself and that the commonwealth will gain by making the most of every individual born within its limits. Our common schools are an institution framed to give practical efficiency to this conviction." [3] They tend also to perpetuate valuable traditions and the achievements of past generations. "As for the schools and churches we know that society

2 "The Teacher's Unconscious Influence," "Earth Hunger and Other Essays," p. 10.
3 "Memorial Day Address," "The Challenge of Facts and Other Essays," p. 357.

must pay for and keep up its own conservative institutions. They cost capital and do not pay back capital directly, although they do indirectly, and in the course of time, in ways which we could trace out and verify if that were our subject."[4] A school, moreover, is a miniature society and thus one of the principal agencies for affording necessary discipline and creating the ethical energy which society requires. A school has an atmosphere of its own, its members make a code of their own, and a public opinion of their own. "What a position the teacher holds in this little community. What a dangerous and responsible eminence he occupies. What criticism he undergoes. What an authority his example exerts. So, in this little society, general motives of conduct are unconsciously formed, principles are adopted, habits grow. Every member in his place gives to, and takes from, the common life. It may be well doubted whether there is any association of life which exerts greater influence on character than does the school, and its influence comes, too, just at the formative period, when impressions are most easily received and sink deepest."[5]

Convinced as he was of the value of the public schools as a social institution, and keenly interested in anything that was for the well-being of the child, Sumner found the State Board of Education with its comparative freedom from political intrigue a field where he could serve the public good with freedom and satisfaction. Even here, however, he felt the heat of political animosities. "It was not always easy to get Sumner re-appointed," says one of his friends whose influence at the Capital was considerable.

[4] "Protectionism," "The Forgotten Man and Other Essays," p. 38.
[5] "Integrity in Education," "The Forgotten Man and Other Essays," p. 413.

"The Legislature was consistently republican, and Sumner's free trade views were most obnoxious to many of the members. Objections to his continuance on the Board were always made and it was sometimes hard to overcome the opposition, but in the end recognition of his ability and the worth of his services always won out."

The immediate occasion of his appointment was the retirement of General Francis A. Walker, who in 1881 left the state to become president of the Massachusetts Institute of Technology, after having been for some time professor of political economy and history in the Sheffield Scientific School. His distinguished career in the Civil War, and, later, as Chief of the Bureau of Statistics in the United States Treasury Department, Special Commissioner of the Revenue, Supervisor of the Ninth and Tenth Censuses, Commissioner of Indian Affairs, and Commissioner to the International Monetary Commission in 1878, caused him to be regarded as one of Connecticut's most notable citizens. It was felt that his successor on the Board of Education ought in a respectable degree at least to measure up to his standard. Sumner was chosen as one who met the requirement.

There was a more concealed but none the less flattering reason for his selection, however. The public schools of Connecticut were in a deplorable condition. Large numbers of the teachers were unfit for their duties. The one normal school of the state was in ill-repute; the business of the Board was laxly administered, and its work to a considerable extent was ineffective. Those in close touch with conditions felt that a thorough reorganization of the system was imperative, and that there was needed on the Board a man of independence and fearlessness in whom knowledge and common sense were joined. Among those immediately interested in the matter was Hon. Edward D. Robbins, a graduate of Yale in the class of 1874. Mr. Robbins represented the town of Wethersfield in the Legislature and was house-chairman of the Committee on Education. Professor Sumner seemed to him to be just the type of person the occasion called for, and through his influence the former consented to serve, and was appointed. The following year Mr. Robbins himself became a member of the Board, and changes of widespread importance began to take place in the effecting of which these two men played a large part.

The following letter from a colleague on the faculty expresses the feeling regarding Sumner's appointment which was general, and also discloses the fact that at this time he was working hard on mathematics in order that he might be thoroughly equipped for every phase of economic study.

120 High St.,
New Haven, Feb., 1882.

My Dear Professor Sumner:

When shall I see your face again? I hope before very long. I am getting lonesome. Am panting to take up some more Mathematics with you.

I write this note in particular to congratulate the State of Connecticut on getting the man on the State Board of Education who of all other men it has been my desire to see on said Board—and that man is yourself.

Truly your Friend,
A. W. Phillips.

In notifying him of his appointment the Reverend Birdsey Grant Northrup, secretary of the Board, intimated to Sumner that he would not find the duties of his position numerous or exacting:

Hartford, Feb. 9, 1882.

Prof. Sumner,

MY DEAR SIR:

You have probably learned from the papers that you have been unanimously elected in both houses of the Legislature as a member of the State Board of Education, to succeed Gen. Walker, who, so long as he held his residence in Connecticut, took a deep practical interest in the State Board.

I write to express the hope that you will not decline this appointment and therefore add that the duties are not burdensome. During the past year, while fixing plans for the State Normal School, we have had frequent meetings of the Board, but as that matter is now arranged and settled, I see no probability of having more than the usual three or four meetings in the course of the year. The sessions are never lengthy. I shall be happy to do what I can to welcome you most cordially to the small but pleasant circle of gentlemen on the Board.

Most truly yours,

B. S. NORTHRUP.

Much to his sorrow, Mr. Northrup was to discover that whatever William Graham Sumner undertook was likely to develop into a considerable job before he was through with it. The "small but pleasant company of gentlemen on the Board" were soon to be awakened to the fact that they had been complacently neglecting their responsibilities. With his customary thoroughness he gave himself unreservedly to the fulfillment of the obligation he had assumed. Those who worked with him say that he seemed to feel in an exceptional degree that the welfare of the children of the state was in his keeping, and that there was something suggestive of religious devotion in the spirit with which he gave himself to their service. The number of Board meetings increased far beyond the secretary's expectations, and Sumner attended them faithfully, even coming from his summer resting place if occasion required. Once he went up to Hartford from New Haven in a blizzard, and was greatly disgusted to find that none of the other members had ventured forth. His comments on their flabbiness are said to have been explicit and vigorous.

Having been put upon the Board to arouse it to greater activity and to help bring about a much needed reorganization of the school system, Sumner insisted at the outset that there be a change in policy. From 1867 to 1882 the work of the Board had been directed by Reverend Mr. Northrup and his clerk, Reverend John G. Baird. Neither of these men had any business ability and they kept no books. Northrup was a man of the best intentions and much public spirit. He was greatly interested in the promotion of Rural Improvement Associations, the object of which was to quicken the intellectual life of the people by the support of schools and the founding of libraries, the improvement of roads, parks, and village greens, and the furtherance of good fellowship, public health, and wholesome home life,[6] and he spent much time lecturing on these matters. He also assisted in the supervision of Chinese and Japanese students who had been brought to this country for college education. There was a strong feeling in some quarters that he was neglecting the schools and also that he was careless in the handling of school funds. The General Assembly of 1882 appointed a commission to investigate certain charges made against him. This commission in its report declared that Mr. Northrup was not justly open to criticism for neglect of his

6 See report of State Board of Education for 1880.

duties, and that he ought to be relieved from any imputation of intentional dishonesty or fraudulent violation of law, but it made clear that he had been most unbusinesslike in his methods. On the whole, however, the report was as much an indictment of the Board as of its secretary, implying that it had exercised little supervision over Mr. Northrup's activities, omitted to audit and approve his accounts, failed to see that laws were properly interpreted and complied with, and neglected its duties generally.[7]

No condition could have been more repugnant or challenging to Sumner. Indifference to responsibility on the part of public officials intrusted with the interests of their fellows, and carelessness in the handling of public funds, were to him among the worst of offenses. Immediately upon becoming a member of the Board he insisted on three things: first, that its administration should be put upon a thoroughly businesslike and efficient basis; second, that it should confine itself to strictly educational matters; and third, that it should become much more active throughout the state. Mr. Northrup offered his resignation in October, 1882, to take effect at the close of the year, and it was accepted with undiminished confidence in his integrity and with a deep sense of the good work he had done to the cause of education.[8] Professor Sumner was appointed one of a committee to secure a successor. The choice fell upon Mr. Charles D. Hine, a graduate of Yale in the class of 1871. Under his direction the work of making the Board a strong constructive force in the state was begun, and in all his efforts, he says, Sumner was his constant advisor and supporter. The revolution which took place in

[7] Report of the Commission on the State Board of Education, Hartford, Lockwood & Brainard Co., 1883.
[8] Report of State Board of Education, 1883.

the administration of the Board is only faintly suggested in its report of 1884, which was written by Sumner. In its introductory paragraph he says: "Mr. C. D. Hine entered upon his duties as Secretary of the Board at the beginning of the year. The Board believes that he has already made his influence felt in the work of education throughout the State. The work done by him has been very practical and straightforward in its character; nothing being done for effect, but all tending to deserve and win the confidence of the people. By changes in the office of the Board, as regards personnel and methods of business, the whole work of the Board has been embodied in systematic and adequate records, so that full information can be obtained at any time in regard to work done and money expended."

Sumner's activities were directed particularly toward the development of normal school instruction and the improvement of the country schools. To the great progress made in these important directions during his stay on the Board, no one, according to Mr. Hine, contributed more than did he. Almost as soon as he came upon the Board he was appointed committee on normal schools, and "at the first meeting which I attended, in 1883," Mr. Hine says, "a policy with regard to the normal school was outlined. This policy included the preparation of teachers by actual training in model practice schools." "It is believed that an art like teaching must be learned, at last," Sumner wrote, "by doing it, and the question is whether the children in the schools of the State ought to be subjected to the blundering of beginners, who learn how to teach at the expense of their pupils, or whether it is the function of the Normal School to lead the young teachers through the first period of actual

experience under trained guidance, so that there may
be no blundering. It is in the latter view that the
School of Practice has been established."[9]

Previous to this time the normal school, located in
New Britain, had been scarcely more than a state high
school, and had given its pupils little practical training for what awaited them. Graduates secured situations with difficulty, especially in the country districts,
partly because previous graduates had failed, and also
because committee men preferred to give the positions
to their daughters and friends. Sumner had not been
on the Board six months before the principal, who
had held the position since 1869, and was hostile to
the changes proposed, resigned. Mr. C. F. Carroll
was appointed, one of the local schools secured for
teacher training, and the new policy put into effect.
There had been model schools before, and practice
schools, but the union of the two was an innovation.
It attracted attention outside the state, and many
educators, including General Armstrong of Hampton
Institute and General Morgan of Rhode Island came
to inspect it. The experiment proved a great success.
Confidence in the Normal School was reëstablished
and the number of its students increased rapidly. A
larger appropriation was asked of the state and was
received. In 1890 it was necessary to build an annex
and Sumner was the building committee. In 1899 the
Willimantic Normal School was established, under the
direction of Professor Arthur B. Morrill, who here,
and at the school later started in New Haven, was to
render notable service to the educational interests of
the state. Thus under Sumner's influence began the
development of modern normal school instruction in
Connecticut, which has done so much to raise the level

[9] Report of State Board of Education, 1884.

of teaching and increase the advantages received by pupils.

Sumner's activity in regard to the country schools was equally great. In the report which he wrote in 1884 he states that the Board believes that the special field in which it can be most useful is in the country districts. "The organization and supervision of the schools in the cities and larger towns is such at least that this Board could not hope to improve it much, but in the scattered country districts, there is great need of active assistance, information, and encouragement, which it is the province of this Board to provide. The Board proposes to devote its energies to this branch of the work, selecting particular parts of it for especial effort from time to time."

It was Sumner who proposed the examination of the schools of the state, the public reports of which created such a furor. The conditions it disclosed were almost unbelievable. In one county about fifty school houses were found unfit for use. In the same county two-fifths of the children over ten years old could not write, although they had been attending school three or four years at least, and some of them much longer. Out of 1,827 pupils tested 787 misspelled "which" and 699 "whose." In another county, 649 out of 1,031 children over ten years of age failed to begin sentences with capitals. In still another, 659 out of 1,205 children twelve years old failed on the following problem: "Henry had 40 cents. His sister had four-fifths as many. How many had his sister?"

That country children should be at such a disadvantage in comparison to city children seemed to Sumner a great injustice. In the most of the towns "district management" prevailed, and Sumner supported heartily the movement in behalf of the consolidation of districts and the assumption of responsibility for the schools by the towns as such. He was also a strong advocate of state examinations for teachers and the awarding of certificates according to the facts revealed, believing that such a practice would "stimulate the ambition of those whom it was most desirable to reach and encourage, that it would enable those who had not had good advantages, but had tried to make up for it, to prove that their attainments were as high as those of Normal School graduates," and that it would be a welcome service to certain school visitors, who might prefer to trust a certificate rather than to make an examination for themselves. Although the plan encountered much hostile criticism and prejudice, the state finally authorized the board to hold such examinations. One hundred and forty-three took the first examination, of whom only twenty-four were granted certificates.

Not only by such projects, but also by personal visitation, suggestions to the teachers, and talks to the children, did Sumner seek to improve the condition of the country schools. In company with Secretary Hine he took long trips into the more isolated districts. They traveled by horse and buggy, slept together in cold spare-rooms, and ate what was set before them. Such expeditions could not have been agreeable to Sumner and he must have disliked at times to turn from other important matters, but he fulfilled this responsibility as he did every other without any shirking or complaint. "On one of our trips," Mr. Hine relates, "we had a vicious horse. He kicked, bit me, tore my trousers, and attempted to do the same to Sumner, but the Professor was too quick for him. Having been brought up in the city, and knowing little about animals, Sumner was frightened, and refused to get into the buggy. It took considerable persuasion to convince him that he must either ride after the beast or go on foot, and that the danger would not be serious if he kept out of the animal's way. He was as serious and clear in his objections and criticisms as if he had been dealing with an anthropological topic."

Sumner's advocacy of town rather than district management of schools, and of increased state aid and influence, was in spite of his firm belief in individualism and local independence. To all national aid for education purposes he was strongly opposed. "It is a very serious question," he writes, "whether State aid to town and district schools does not demoralize them. Would not the people act for themselves if they had no other reliance? If the State sends money into towns, and towns apportion it to districts, no other result can fairly be expected than that towns and districts will hold back their own contributions until they have drawn the last cent which they can get elsewhere, and that when any new or special effort is called for they will throw the burden on somebody else instead of coming forward to meet it themselves.

"The immediate practical interest of this question now is in connection with proposals which are made to distribute federal money to the States for educational purposes. An invitation was extended to this State to send a representative to a conference which was held in September last at Louisville, Ky., at which this proposition was advocated. This Board had cognizance of this invitation. Without taking upon themselves to speak for the State of Connecticut in the matter, they were unanimously of the opinion that the project was a mischievous one, and that this State ought to hold aloof from it, unless it could oppose it elsewhere than in a meeting whose apparent object was to combine strength to push it. They therefore declined to recommend to the Governor any person as a suitable delegate. No delegate was sent and Connecticut was not represented. The State of Connecticut has been trying ever since it was founded, at its own expense, to reduce the illiteracy of its inhabitants. It has succeeded so well that now if the Federal Government should distribute fifty million dollars among the states on the basis of illiteracy, Connecticut would get about eighty thousand. This is not the argument against the scheme, for the smaller our share the greater our glory, but all experience teaches us that such distributions of public money are wasteful, that they give opportunities for jobbery and corruption, that they kill the very interests which they are planned to promote, and that they end in debauching the people with their own money." [10]

Throughout his career Sumner was insistent that education should be such as to conduce to a useful life. Against what he termed "sensationalism" he reacted with great vigor. "Its motto," he said, "is that seeming is as good as being. It deals in dash, flourish, and meretricious pretense. It resides in the form, not in the substance; in the outward appearance, not in the reality. . . . I see it in common-school education as well as in the universities. It attaches to methods as well as to subjects. It develops a dogmatism of its own. Men without education, or experience as teachers, often take up the pitiful rôle of another class

[10] Report of State Board of Education, 1884.

which has come to be called 'educators.' They start
off with a whim or two which they elaborate into
theories of education. These they propound with
great gravity in speech and writing, producing long
discussions as to plans and methods. They are continually searching for a patent method of teaching, or
a royal road to learning, when, in fact, the only way
to learn is by the labor of the mind in observing,
comparing, and generalizing, and any patent method
which avoids this irksome labor produces sham results and fails of producing the mental power and
discipline of which education consists." [11] "A classmate of mine," he said in an impromptu address at a
teachers' meeting in Hartford, "became interested in
discovering the best method of studying. He tried
studying sitting down, lying down, standing up, walking. At the end of the term he was dropped. Like
a good many educators he was so interested in method
he accomplished nothing."

In his later years Sumner regarded with much
disfavor the extent to which sentimentalism was
creeping into common-school management, and viewed
with anxiety the ever-increasing burden which public
education was laying upon the taxpayer. Before his
death he prophesied that if the extravagance then
existing continued, the schools would soon bankrupt
municipalities, a prophecy whose fulfillment in many
instances seems near. The debt that the state of Connecticut owes Sumner for his nearly thirty years of
hard work in behalf of her schools, and especially for
his sound counsel during an important period of reconstruction, cannot be estimated. "I was glad to
have been associated with him," said Mr. Hine, who

[11] "Integrity in Education," "The Forgotten Man and Other Essays,"
pp. 409, 410.

had leaned on him heavily through all these years,
"and proud to think that, employing the great qualities we all recognize, he revived and left more sacred
the great traditions of Connecticut public school education which are to-day threatened by mawkish sentiment."

The reason why I defend the millions of the millionaire is not that I love the millionaire, but that I love my own wife and children, and that I know no way in which to get the defense of society for my hundreds, except to give my help, as a member of society, to protect his millions.
The Family and Property.

CHAPTER XI

PUBLICIST

The ability and courage which Sumner displayed in discussing the intricate problems of the day early brought him into national prominence. The extent and variety of his information, and the mastery of economic laws and principles, revealed by the articles in *The Financier*, won him respect in banking and business circles, while his publication of the "History of the American Currency" secured for him still wider recognition. Thereafter he was regarded as one of the leading authorities of the country on questions of finance, and letters from bankers, industrial leaders, legislators, writers, students, and editors poured in upon him in an unending stream.

Nor was it in this field alone that he was prominent. His keen analysis of political conditions during the campaign of 1876 had been given wide publicity. That his knowledge of history and government was as extensive and thorough as his acquaintance with finance, was apparent; that he had profound convictions with regard to prevailing needs and policies, and could support them with abundance of facts and with pitiless logic, was equally clear.

Not only what he had to say, but the way he said it, attracted attention. There was a terseness and vigor to his utterances which held the interest of the hearer or reader to the end. They were fraught with the prophetic denunciation and the prophetic appeal. Though a college professor, he spoke as one having

217

authority and not as the scribes. Hundreds of letters still in existence show that calls for lectures and speeches came to him incessantly from all sections of the country, and that to a surprising number of them he responded. Newspapers importuned him for his opinions on current events. His talks to his classes on questions of the day were reported fully in the New York dailies. Magazines, well known and obscure, begged him for articles, frankly confessing that his name would be worth much to them, and often telling him to state his own terms. As a result, during the last quarter of the nineteenth century, not only was Sumner shaping the thoughts of college youth, and privately giving counsel to men in high places politically and industrially, he was also speaking to the country at large, and, indeed, in some measure to the world, for his utterances were heard in England and perhaps even more attentively in some portions of the Continent.

When he began his public activities, the country was suffering the consequences of past mistakes and beholding new and complex problems rise above the horizon. The Civil War had left behind it, as Sumner declared, "a heavy load of unsettled questions . . . and mistaken notions, and I must add, also, some disordered enthusiasms and deeply rooted prejudices. We have got to deal with these now, with no passion, or pride, or enthusiasm, or common impulse of any kind to help us through."[1] A great business revival was soon to begin involving the development of trusts and labor unions, with all the questions regarding rights and public welfare which these created. The relation of the government to business was to become a matter of increasing concern. With the expansion

[1] *Journal of Social Science*, No. VI, July, 1874, p. 188.

of the country and the rapid improvement in the means of communication, the question of the attitude of the United States toward the rest of the world was to present itself in very practical forms.

Sumner's presence in the public arena in the face of these conditions was not due to desire for prominence or to love of combat primarily, though the latter unquestionably was present, but to a sense of duty. Both the cause of righteousness and the good of the nation, he felt, demanded whatever wisdom and influence he could contribute. Speaking to the American Social Science Association, in 1874, regarding the need of working zealously against prevailing errors in the political life of the times, he said: "The task is a tiresome one for us who would gladly take social science as it stands to-day, taking the world over, and apply its principles to our circumstances and pursue investigations as to what yet remains to be learned; but here we are with the practical task before us, and the most useful work we can do is to demolish these foolish errors." [2] With reference to protectionism he wrote: "The moral indignation which it causes is the motive which draws me away from the scientific pursuits which form my real occupation, and forces me to take part in a popular agitation. The doctrine of a 'call' applies in such a case and every man is bound to take just so great a share as falls his way." [3] In his earlier days Sumner may not have felt it his duty to interrupt his career and go forth to war, but all the time he had been arming for service. Now he was ready to spend himself without stint, sacrificing comfort and health even, risking reputation and position, and enduring ridicule and abuse.

2 *Journal of Social Science*, No. VI, July, 1874, p. 189.
3 "Protectionism," "The Forgotten Man and Other Essays," p. 11.

In "empiricism," by which he meant unintelligent experimentation and reckless resort to chance remedies, he saw the great enemy which must be destroyed. Over the whole social organization, penetrating to the private interests of every individual, its curse was spread. The surplanter was to be science. The common idea that social and economic phenomena constitute a domain of arbitrary and artificial action and are subject to chance and control was to be driven from people's minds, and they were to be made to realize that all social life is governed by unchangeable and merciless laws, and that the only way by which such prosperity and progress as is possible can be enjoyed is by discovering these laws as they are revealed in history, and by obeying them. The difficulties of the campaign that must be waged, Sumner did not underrate. "Who shall tell the man who has bought and sold all his life that the facts of his experience bear a correct interpretation totally opposite to those which he has reached? . . . Who shall stop a passionate man at the moment of resorting to violence, to enforce cool measures and long and patient means? The facts are open to all eyes. The means to the end seem patent to everybody. That these social and economic circumstances are subject to universal natural laws which we cannot alter seems to be a strange doctrine which people are slow to understand. That there is anything here to be wrought out by study and investigation, or by scientific process, is not popularly believed or understood. Those who so assert are easily dismissed as theorists. Those, then, who do not look upon the problem as governed by any natural, universal, and inevitable laws, set to work to invent some plan for convertible bond redemption, or for mixing up bonds, greenbacks, and bank notes in some new way, and believe that they have solved the problem. The greatest financier on this theory is the man who, in the freest contempt for human history, and statistical facts, invents an apriori theory on which he is willing to stake the finances of a great nation, with all the vast physical and moral interests which the finances affect. If these men had to manage a locomotive they would find out the laws of construction of the machine and would conform to them. They would not expect to make it go by ringing the bell, although the bell is always rung when it starts, and they would not believe that they improved its working qualities by making it more complicated. If they saw boys at play under a dam which they were weakening by their operations, they would interfere, because they would say that ignorance was bringing down loss of life and ruin of property; but they lay hands on the widest and most delicate interests of forty millions of people without a compunction." [4]

The weapon by which, if at all, empiricism is to be overthrown, according to Sumner, is education. "A legislature strong in the compulsion of sound principles, bold in the assertion of them, ready to stake individual interests for the public good, might no doubt lead and remold public opinion; but we all know that we have not got this, and we cannot get it until we work lower down on the creative power which makes legislatures." [5] Out of constant agitation and discussion through the press and in assemblies must the education of the masses proceed. Whether the battle for scientific procedure can be won is a serious question. "It has sometimes been said that Democracy was on trial during the war; but Democracy is

[4] *Journal of Social Science*, No. VI, July, 1874, pp. 182, 183.
[5] *Ibid.*, p. 182.

going through a trial more severe and searching than any that comes under the enthusiasm and passion of war. To educate millions of voters to sufficient knowledge of a technical and scientific subject, involving self-denial, firmness, and perseverance, in the presence of dull and passionless peace, and for a good which is not immediate, but remote, involves the severest test to which popular institutions have ever been put, one which hitherto they have never endured.''[6]

On the firing line of this hard battle Sumner took his stand. In the lecture room, in private classes formed by thoughtful people in various cities, at clubs, through the press, and in popular assemblies, he struck lusty blows at unsound policies and set forth the facts which long, painful experience and honest study had established.

During most of the years of his public activity the fight for a sound monetary system had to be maintained. While the carrying out of the Resumption Act in the Hayes administration had been a victory won, the pernicious philosophy which found expression in the Greenback Party was by no means conquered. From the West and South particularly views and demands radically at variance with confirmed economic principles were to issue, challenging the most intelligent and vigorous opposition. The farmers in these sections were heavily in debt. With reference to their crops the purchasing power of the dollar had increased. The producer was compelled to give much for a very little money in return. The realization that, favored by no such support from the government as the manufacturers enjoyed through the tariff, he was at the mercy of the Eastern capitalists, who

[6] *Journal of Social Science*, No. VI, July, 1874, pp. 181, 182.

controlled the railroads upon whose policies his prosperity so largely depended, and of the banks from which he had to borrow the money which his enterprises required, embittered him. As a result loud and often angry demands arose for different banking arrangements, legislation affecting the railroads, and changes in the currency.

Most insistent of all was the demand for more and cheaper money. If the purchasing power of the dollar decreased, argued the farmer, the producer would get more dollars for his crops and experience some of the prosperity which was his during the war when paper currency was plentiful. With cheaper money, furthermore, he could pay off his debts with considerable gain to himself and a corresponding loss to the eastern capitalist, whom he considered unworthy of the slightest consideration.

From greenbacks the inflationists turned to silver. Preparatory to the resumption of specie payment, when there was no silver or gold in use at all, Congress had very wisely codified all the laws of the United States regarding coinage into a statute. By this act silver was demonetized. No particular comments, hostile or otherwise, were provoked at the time, although later the advocates of silver dubbed the Act "the crime of 1873." Subsequently the price of silver fell, and the miners of this metal and those who wanted cheaper money joined forces in demanding the remonetization of silver. These two classes found support in the views of a few theoretical bimetallists, who believed that gold and silver could be made to circulate concurrently by international agreement. Having by virtue of the Act of 1873, "the best system of coinage yet devised," Sumner says, "and having no lot or part in the silver difficulty," the

United States willfully plunged into it, "and, moreover, came forward to tell those who were in silver difficulty how to get out, and volunteered to lead the way."[7] In 1878, Congress passed the Bland-Allison Bill, which provided for the purchase of not less than two million or more than four million dollars' worth of silver each month at the market price, and restored the full legal tender character to the silver dollar. This act was not satisfactory to the silver men, but it was something gained. When introduced into the House by Mr. Bland, it had called for the free coinage of silver. Upon its return from the Senate with Mr. Allison's limitation upon it, Mr. Bland shouted with a good deal of heat: "Let us take what we have and supplement it immediately on appropriation bills (i.e., by riders) and if we cannot do that, I am in favor of issuing paper money enough to stuff down the bond holders until they are sick. I protest this bill while I vote for it under protest."[8] "This piece of legislation," Sumner declared, "was extraordinarily perverse and senseless," and arose out of the "notion, born of the paper money period, that 'legal tender' means a device for making currency pass at a nominal value differing from its true value. This notion is false and pernicious."[9]

The agitation for free silver continued. In 1890 the Sherman Act was passed, requiring the Secretary of the Treasury to purchase each month at the market price four and a half million ounces of silver bullion, using treasury notes in payment. The currency

[7] "Bimetallism," "Essays in Political and Social Science," New York, Henry Holt and Company, 1885, p. 11.

[8] Quoted from the Congressional Records, 45 Congress, 2 Session, p. 1251, in "The American Nation, a History," A. B. Hart, Vol. XXIII, "National Development," Edwin E. Sparks.

[9] "Our Country for the Last Twenty-five Years," *Harper's Weekly*, February 7, 1885, Vol. XXIX, p. 91.

movement was now fast approaching a crisis, however. In 1893 a panic occurred, "absolutely unnecessary," said Sumner, brought about by the policy of our legislation in "scrambling the currency of the country."[10] To save the situation the Sherman Act was repealed. The campaign of 1896 found the agricultural areas of the South and West in great distress. Prices had fallen so low that the farmers were desperate. They believed that they were being crucified on a cross of gold. The Democratic and Populist parties united on a platform of free coinage, and the silver men made their last great stand. The Republicans were victorious, and the gold standard was assured.

Few contributed more to the final outcome of this long battle than did William Graham Sumner. Throughout the struggle he was one of the most conspicuous opponents of bimetallism, noted both as an effective popular lecturer on the subject, and also as a keen exponent of its scientific aspects. The Bland-Allison Bill he assailed vigorously before its passage, and its folly he pointed out relentlessly after it had become a law. Large audiences listened to him wherever he went. On the evening of January 25, 1878, he spoke before the Manhattan Club of New York. The following day, the *World* gave a three-column report of his address, which it prefaced with this statement: "Professor Sumner, of Yale College, lectured last evening before the Manhattan Club of this city on the remonetization of silver. There was a large gathering of club members and invited guests, the clubroom being filled in every part. Among those present were noticed Mayor Ely, ex-Mayor Wickham,

[10] "The Currency Crisis," Lectures at the home of Mr. J. E. Parsons, New York. Lecture VI, p. 10. Typewritten report, Yale Library.

David Dudley Field, A. J. Vanderpool, Ferdinand de Luca, the Italian Consul-General; Judge Curtis, H. M. Meigs, President of the Stock Exchange; Augustus Schell, Judge Shea, Charles H. Marshall, Lawrence Turnure, Judge Barbour, Henry L. Clinton, Erastus Brooks, and others." Sumner was introduced by Augustus Belmont, who said concerning him that "nobody, throughout the extent of our country, is a more trusted authority on questions of political economy."

In the East Sumner had sympathetic hearers, but he was not at all averse to carrying the campaign into the enemy's country. A little more than two weeks previous to his lecture before the distinguished audience in New York, he had spoken on "Honest Money" to a crowd in Farwell Hall, Chicago. The audience here was inclined to heckle him, and he met their comments and questions with the utmost skill and good nature. According to the *Chicago Times,* of January 8, 1878, which gives a very full report of the meeting under the caption, "Pictures of Silver, Words Fitly Spoken on the Remonetization Question by Professor Sumner," the address began as follows:

Gentlemen: A man talking to me the other day about silver shook his clenched fist and declared: 'The people have determined that they will have silver, and there is no use of any further talk about it.'

A Voice: 'That's the business.' (Laughter.)

They say that the first thing a speaker ought to try to do is to find out the state of mind of his hearers. (Laughter.)

Upon raising the question whether matters had really come to such a pass that the debtor was at war with the creditor, each ready to spring at the throat of the

other, and calm discussion no longer possible, Sumner
got a second response from the audience:

A Voice: 'Yes it has. We are prepared to fight
them.'
Another Voice: 'No, No!' (Confusion.)

Further along in his speech Sumner stated that the
money broker would like nothing better than that the
scheme of the silver people should be carried out.

A Long-haired Lunatic in the Crowd: 'What are
they against it for?'
Professor Sumner: 'They are not against it.'
Long-haired Lunatic: 'They are.'
Professor Sumner: 'I beg pardon. Take the most
reckless class and they are not against it at all.'
Lunatic: 'It don't look like it.' (Hisses.)
Professor Sumner: 'Never mind this thing. I enjoy
it. (Applause.) I always tell my boys at New Haven
to stop me and ask me questions, and all that, just as
much as they have a mind to.' (Applause.)
Voices: 'Go on. Don't interrupt the speaker.'

As Sumner proceeded, his candor, fearlessness, and
graphic presentation of the evils threatened by the
proposed legislation, won the attention and respect of
the listeners. There were no more interruptions and
applause was frequent.

From time to time, after the passage of the Bland-
Allison Act, Sumner would call attention to the
trouble it was creating, and whenever the advocates
of free silver became especially active he would rise
up and smite them. He assailed the Sherman Bill,
through *Frank Leslie's Illustrated Newspaper,* in
articles entitled: "Can We Get More Money?" and

"Proposed Silver Legislation." During the Bryan campaign, twenty years after he had entered the fight, he was hammering away as relentlessly as ever. Another series of popular articles from his pen appeared in *Leslie's Weekly*, which included "The Policy of Debasement," "Prosperity Strangled by Gold," "The Free-Coinage Scheme Is Impracticable in Every Point," "Delusion of the Debtors," "The Crime of 1873," and "The Single Gold Standard." In the *New York Evening Post* he published "A Free-coinage Catechism," and gave a course of six lectures on "The Currency Crisis," at the home of Mr. John E. Parsons in New York.

When addressing popular audiences Sumner avoided the technical aspects of the subject as much as possible and confined himself to its practical bearings. His aim was to make his hearers feel that the re-monetization of silver would be a bad thing for them individually and especially for the honor and welfare of the country. In his Chicago speech he showed with great concreteness of detail what the carrying out of the project would mean to the indebted farmer—something quite different from what he supposed; what it would mean to the laborer and manufacturer; what it would mean to the real estate owner; and to the money broker, who alone would win. Every sentence was a blow straight from the shoulder. It always landed and frequently hurt. As was to be expected of one whose ethical sense was so keen and whose standards were so high, what stirred him most was the fact that the proposition was morally wrong, and would tend to destroy the character of the nation and respect for it abroad. Speaking of public credit, he said: "You must understand that it is like the honor of a man. There is never but one grade in it and that is perfection. When a man gives up, in regard to his honor, the standard of perfection, and that he will be an honorable and honest man right straight through, then there is no depth of infamy to which he may not fall; and when a nation gives up, not only the letter, but the spirit of public credit, then its credit may fall to depths which you cannot measure.''

In summing up his address at the Manhattan Club, he gave very succinctly the practical grounds upon which both his written and spoken arguments were commonly based. ''There is no reason plainly and rationally put forward for believing that the proposed measure will benefit any but a small number of persons, exceptionally situated, and some employments which do not need or deserve favors at the public expense. If the gains hoped for by certain parties could be gained they would only be gained by transferring property from the industrious, prudent, and economical, who to-day have something, to the idle, reckless, and extravagant, who to-day have nothing. The means by which it is proposed to accomplish this transfer are such that they would destroy the prosperity and endanger the peace of the country for an indefinite future, because they would destroy the public credit, establish a fluctuating currency as a permanent institution, put the industrious and economical permanently at the mercy of the crafty, and make it impossible to practice forethought, energy, and thrift in business, which latter methods of business are the school in which sterling national character is developed. It is only by studying history that men learn prudence. It is by looking back that they learn to look ahead, and when we hear men scout the lessons of history we need not be astonished to see them pushing ahead without knowing or caring whither they are going, and without appearing to ask themselves what consequences must be expected from the course they propose. Our experience for sixteen years has been one long proof that when we once abandon the real standard of value we flounder from one calamity to another, and that the only hope for rest, peace, and security is to return. The return from a mistaken course always costs pain and loss. There is no such thing possible, either in morals or economics, as to slip easily back from a mistaken course into the right one. It is always a costly process. It is that which we are now going through, and in all common sense and right reason there is nothing to do but to struggle on until we emerge once and for all on solid ground.''

Sumner presents a thoroughgoing treatment of the scientific aspects of the monetary question in his article on ''Bimetallism,'' published first in *The Princeton Review* of November, 1879, and later in ''Essays in Political and Social Science''; and in ''A Concurrent Circulation of Gold and Silver,'' an address given before the Connecticut Academy of Arts and Sciences, and printed for the first time by Professor Keller in ''The Forgotten Man and Other Essays.'' He declares the notion that two metals can be joined together in the coinage by any human artifice or device whatsoever just as false in science as that of perpetual motion is in mechanics. The experiment has been tried over and over again, and it has always failed. The reason for such failure is to be found in the fact that the value of a thing is controlled by supply and demand and by nothing else. Supply and demand are natural forces and act under natural laws. Gold has its own conditions of supply and demand and silver has its own conditions of

supply and demand, and they are both independent
of each other. Legislation can effect these conditions
in no respect whatever. "It cannot increase or de-
crease the amount of the metals within the reach of
man, or his willingness to labor to produce them
according to the profit of such production. It cannot
make men want what they do not want, or cease to
want what they do want. Economic phenomena are
due to economic forces, and one of the first lessons
the student has to learn is not to rest from his
analysis until he has reduced economic phenomena to
economic forces and laws."

The Bland-Allison Act contained a section stipulating that the President should invite the governments
of the countries composing the Latin Union, and
those of other European nations, if deemed advisable,
to a conference for the purpose of establishing inter-
nationally the use of bimetallic money and securing a
fixity of relative value between these two metals. This
proposition Sumner discusses thoroughly and shows
to be impracticable. The notion of a concurrent circulation is one "snatched from the air." It could never
be realized until we could extinguish economic forces
by human energy. "But we can no more extinguish a
force than we can create one, so that this scheme is
in economics what perpetual motion is in mechanics."
A conference was held, and Sumner could not refrain
from casting a gibe at it, and especially at one of its
members, General Francis A. Walker, then professor
in the Sheffield Scientific School, one of the most
prominent of the theoretical bimetallists, for whose
economic opinions Sumner did not have unqualified
respect. "The American delegates," he says, "began
by slandering the legislation of their country, and it
was left for a foreigner to show (1) that the historical

232 WILLIAM GRAHAM SUMNER

facts about the legislation of 1873 were incorrectly
stated by the American delegates, and (2) that the
United States is a constitutional country, not ruled
by plebiscites, and that we cannot plead ignorance on
the part of 'the people' against legislation constitutionally adopted. General Walker endeavored to sustain the allegations of his colleague by saying that he,
although a professor of political economy, engaged,
at the time, in lecturing on money, did not know what
was going on. It does not appear that this argument
elicited any reply. Perhaps it was thought that its
force all lay in the recoil, and some wonder may have
been excited whether all American economists would
have been obliged to say the same.'' [11]

Vigorous as was the battle which Sumner waged
against false notions about money and the pernicious,
immoral propositions growing out of them, the warfare he carried on against protectionism was characterized by even greater strenuousness and intensity
of feeling.

The establishment of protectionism as a welfare
doctrine and national dogma was another of the consequences of the Civil War. Previous to 1861 a moderate tariff had been in effect. To carry on the war
it was necessary to have more funds, and one of the
means of securing these was through a very comprehensive and severe internal revenue system. In order
that it should not put domestic producers at a disadvantage as compared with foreign, the tariff was
greatly increased. After the war reductions were
frequently proposed but, for one reason or another,
were not made. ''Gradually,'' Professor Taussig
says, ''as the organization of industry in the country
adapted itself more closely to the tariff as it was, the

[11] "Bimetallism," "Essays in Political and Social Science," p. 12.

feeling that no reform was needed obtained a strong hold. Many industries had grown up, or had been greatly extended, under the influence of the war legislation. As that legislation continued unchanged, still more capital was embarked in establishments whose existence or prosperity was in some degree dependent on its maintenance. All who were connected with establishments of this kind asserted that they would be ruined by any change. The business world in general tends to be favorable to the maintenance of things as they are. The country at large, and especially those parts of it in which the protected industries were concentrated, began to look upon the existing state of things as permanent. The extreme protective system, which had been at first a temporary expedient for aiding in the struggle for the Union, adopted hastily and without any thought of deliberation, became accepted as a permanent institution. From this it was a short step, in order to explain and justify the existing state of things, to set up high protection as a theory and dogma."[12] As a welfare doctrine its hold on the nation strengthened.

Against this general trend a relatively small but resolute group fought stubbornly. David A. Wells, of Norwich, Connecticut, was one of the early leaders of the opposition. With him, upon coming to New Haven, Sumner, who had become a free trader because, as he said, he didn't believe in magic and considered protectionism immoral, entered into close intimacy. Tariff reform associations were formed, and an attempt was made to organize one in every state. In January, 1876, Sumner was a member of the Boston Free Trade Club, and serving on the ad-

---

[12] "The Tariff History of the United States," F. W. Taussig, G. P. Putnam's Sons, p. 174.

visory committee with Wells, Edward Atkinson, William C. Bryant, William Lloyd Garrison, Carl Schurz, and Professor Perry, of Williams College. Later he was on the executive committee of the Connecticut Free Trade League, and a vice-president of the American Free Trade League. In the early days not much popular literature on the subject was to be had, and Sumner was called upon to furnish a good deal of the ammunition used by the various clubs. He also lectured extensively in the East and throughout the Middle West. A series of five addresses on "Protectionism in the United States," delivered before the International Free Trade Alliance, in New York, were published and widely circulated. His contributions on the subject to newspapers and magazines were voluminous.

The fight was an unpopular and discouraging one. Not until 1883 did Congress undertake a general revision of the tariff, and this made practically no reduction in the high level of duties which obtained during the Civil War. The McKinley Act of 1890 expanded the protective system. The hopes born in the reformers at the beginning of Cleveland's second administration were short lived. Protectionism held its ground, and the year before his death Sumner saw it still more strongly entrenched by the Tariff Act of 1909. To the end, however, he fought it uncompromisingly and often bitterly. It was in connection with this more than with anything else that the moral passion conspicuous in him from his youth found expression. The battle was one which demanded great patience, power of endurance, and faith. "As long as I can remember," he said at a dinner of the committee on tariff reform of the Reform Club, in New York, June 2, 1906, "and as long as I have had any share in it, we have got along without any encouragement in it at all. We have done what we could without that. We got so we did not expect it. We knew that we should be neglected and treated as persons whose opinions in these matters were not of any importance or worthy of any attention, and so we went on and kept up our arguments, as we considered them, to the best of our ability and without very much result." [13] In one of the closing speeches of his life, an address on "The Effects of Tariff Policy on Agriculture and Commerce," given at the International Free Trade Congress, held at London, August 3-8, 1908, he remarked that for forty years he had talked free trade to gatherings which probably did not hold a single man who agreed with his views, and that it was a pleasant novelty to speak before a sympathetic audience. While much of the old fire is lacking, the address shows no weakening of conviction.

Sumner's intense antagonism to protectionism, "the ism which teaches that waste makes wealth," was based on three grounds. In the first place, he was convinced that all its pretensions are both false and foolish. At a student who once asked him for the arguments in support of protectionism he thundered: "There are none." It "seems to me," he writes, "to deserve only contempt and scorn, satire, and ridicule. It is such an arrant piece of economic quackery, and it masquerades under such an affectation of learning and philosophy, that it ought to be treated as other quackeries are treated." [14]

Protectionism is a quackery, according to Sumner, because without any scientific foundation or method it promises to further the industrial prosperity of the

[13] "Protectionism Twenty Years After," "The Forgotten Man and Other Essays," p. 137.
[14] "Protectionism," "The Forgotten Man and Other Essays," p. 10.

state. Free trade, on the other hand, is only a mode
of liberty. It is not an innovation or an experiment.
It promises nothing. "No free trader will affirm that
he has a device for making the country rich, or saving
it from hard times, any more than a respectable
physician will tell us that he can give us specifics and
preventives to keep us well." Free trade is commerce
in its normal condition. It always irritated Sumner
greatly to be asked what he would propose in place
of protection. The implied assumption that a welfare policy of some kind is essential to social well
being was one with which he had no patience. "Cease
the empirical process," was his plea. "Institute the
scientific process. Let the state come back to normal
health and activity so that you can study it, learn
something about it from an observation of its phenomena, and then regulate your action in regard to it
by intelligent knowledge." [15]

The vain pretensions on the basis of which protectionism assumes to interfere with freedom, Sumner
takes up one by one in his essay on "Protectionism,"
and discloses their emptiness. The contention of its
advocates is that through means of a tax they can
produce national wealth and prosperity. They would
set up certain duties to act as bars to importation, the
result of which would be the creation of a wall, enclosing the domestic producer and consumer, and pre-
venting the latter from having access to any other
source of supply for his need, in exchange for his
products, than that which the domestic producer
controls. At the port of entry the government lays a
tax which it does not collect. It says to the producer,
"I do not need to tax the consumer for myself, but I
will hold him for you while you tax him." From such

[15] "Protectionism," "The Forgotten Man and Other Essays," p. 15.

an arrangement, it is asserted, various benefits will
accrue to the country.

Assuming, says Sumner, that there is something in
this prosperity scheme, and that good might really
be accomplished by it if we had an agency capable of
putting it into operation, have we as a matter of fact
any such agency? If Congress can do this thing, and
is going to try to do it, ought not the legislators to
have a distinct idea of what is to be aimed at and the
forces with which they must deal? Would it not be
in line, with common sense to apply some test to the
experiment after a term of years to see whether it is
really doing what was expected? None of these conditions has Congress ever met. It has never had any
plan or purpose in its tariff legislation, but has simply
"laid itself open to be acted upon by the interested
parties, and the product of its tariff legislation has
been simply the resultant of the struggles of the interested cliques with each other, and of the log-rolling
combination which they have been forced to make
among themselves." There is nothing in the legislative machinery which indicates that it could make
such a device effective, even if there were the remotest
possibility of benefits issuing therefrom.

But all the assurances of protectionism are false
promises. The blessings which are said to accompany
its reign dissolve when keenly scrutinized, and gross
evils appear in their place. A tax is a burden, and
in the nature of the case cannot be anything else. It
should always be regarded as on the defensive. "I
have been studying political economy almost exclusively for the last fifteen years," Sumner says, "and
when I look back over that period and ask myself
what is the most marked effect which I can perceive
on my own opinion, or on my standpoint, as to social

questions, I find that it is this: I am convinced that
nobody yet understands the multiplied and complicated effects which are produced by taxation. I am
under the most profound impression of the mischief
which is done by taxation, reaching, as it does, to
every dinner-table and to every fireside. *The effects
of taxation vary with every change in the industrial
system and the industrial status,* and they are so complicated that it is impossible to follow, analyze, and
systematize them; but out of the study of the subject
there arises this firm conviction: taxation is crippling,
shortening, reducing all the time, over and over
again." [16] People, it is true, make mistakes and fail
of the highest prosperity under freedom, but more
taxes cannot correct their errors and lift them up.
On the contrary, *"all taxation, beyond what is necessary for an economical administration of good government, is either luxurious or wasteful,* and if such
taxation could tend to wealth, waste would make
wealth."

The statement so often made to the effect that protectionism produces industries is utterly false. "An
industry is an organization of labor and capital for
satisfying some need of the community. It is not an
end in itself. It is not a good thing in itself. . . . If
we could satisfy our needs without it, we should be
better off, not worse off." The only way an industry
can be produced is by finding in nature some power
to supply human need hitherto unknown, or by invent-
ing some better way of doing what has been done.
The telephone has given rise to a comparatively new
industry. The gain from it is not in the employment
of certain persons in telephone offices, but in increased
ease of communication. Brains and energy and not

---

[16] "Protectionism," "The Forgotten Man and Other Essays," p. 32.

taxes create industries. What protectionism really
does is to take one industry and set it as a parasite
to live upon another, and the mill which is not an
independent and profitable establishment, but has to
be supported by a sixty per cent tax on cloth, is not a
benefit to a country, it is a nuisance.

Nor, if protectionism has to be resorted to in order
to accomplish it, is the development of natural resources a benefit. Natural resources have sometimes
become national calamities. "We had the misfortune
to find emery here. At once a tax was put on it which
made it cost more wheat, cotton, tobacco, petroleum,
or personal services per pound than ever before. A
new calamity befell us when we found the richest
copper mines in the world in our territory. From
that time on copper cost us five (now four) cents a
pound more than before. By another catastrophe we
found a nickel mine—thirty cents (now fifteen) a
pound tax! Up to this time we have had all the tin
we wanted above ground, because beneficent nature
has refrained from putting any under ground in our
territory. In the metal schedule, where the metals
which we unfortunately possess are taxed from forty
to sixty per cent, tin alone is free. Every little while
a report is started that tin has been found. Hitherto
these reports have happily all proved false." [17]

That protectionism raises wages is another mistaken notion regarding it. "The wages which are
paid to the men who make an article have nothing to
do with the price or value of that article." Value is
determined by the supply and demand of a commodity; prices by the supply and demand for labor.
Between the two there is no connection. "If taxes
are to raise wages, they must be laid, not on goods,

[17] "Protectionism," "The Forgotten Man and Other Essays," p. 42.

but on men." It is the fact that the country is new and land available which creates the high scale of wages in America. The non-capitalist class has another chance besides the job he holds, and the chance is near and easy to improve. It is not necessary that all or any large number should use it. That it exists is enough to keep up wages. If employers told the truth, they would confess that one of the reasons why they want a tariff is because it tends to lower wages. They have found that the laborer is provided and maintained by the economic circumstances of the country. This is against the interests of those who want to hire the laborers. From the point of view of the employer, therefore, the fortunate circumstance of the laborer is an obstacle to be overcome. It is this and not the "pauper labor" of Europe that troubles him. Even from the latter protectionism does not save the laborer, as is commonly declared. The real condition is this: A tax is laid to protect the American woolen operator from the operators abroad. This tax the American wheat grower has to pay. As a result the evil effect of competition with "pauper labor" is simply transferred from one class in the community to another.

The second of the three convictions out of which Sumner's opposition to protectionism sprang was that it is a political evil. In the first place it is a system of graft and encourages graft in general. It teaches a man to believe that a "pull," or something of the kind, is necessary to make an industry profitable. "People are told that tariff taxes are a rightful gift to the beneficiary. Those who do not get that gain seek another one of the same kind somewhere." Furthermore, the protected interests gain great power in Congress and determine the course of legislation.

As a result democracy gives place to plutocracy. In 1906 Sumner affirmed that the country was being governed by a combination of interests which had got control of the machinery of government and of its personnel to such an extent that it was almost impossible to make any breach in the system they advocated. Protectionism was to blame, also, he believed, for much of the evil which civil service reformers sought with scant success to remove. Although in a form more or less disguised, he points out, protectionism is socialism and tends to encourage that theory of government. "Socialism is any device or doctrine whose aim is to save individuals from any of the difficulties or hardships of the struggle for existence and the competition of life by the intervention of 'the state.'"[18] The demand of the protected interests is that "they shall be saved from the trouble and annoyance of business competition, and that they be assured profit in their undertakings by 'the State,' that is, by their fellow-citizens. If this is not socialism, then there is no such thing."

But what gave power and heat to Sumner's opposition was his conviction that protectionism is legalized robbery. "The biggest job of all," he says in his essay on "The Forgotten Man" is a protective tariff. . . . "When you go to Willimantic they will show you with great pride the splendid thread mills there. I am told that there are sewing women who can earn only fifty cents in twelve hours, and provide the thread. In the cost of every spool of thread more than one cent is a tax. It is paid to get the Willimantic Linen Company, which is not worth having and which is, in fact, a nuisance, because it makes thread harder to get than it would be if there were no such

[18] "Protectionism," "The Forgotten Man and Other Essays," p. 79.

concern. If a woman earns fifty cents in twelve hours, she earns a spool of thread as nearly as may be in an hour, and if she used a spool of thread per day, she works a quarter of an hour per day to support the Willimantic Linen Company, which in 1882 paid 95 per cent dividend to its stockholders.'' Some one once tried to get Sumner to debate the question of free trade with a manufacturer who had made half a million under protection. ''What chance have I,'' Sumner replied, ''against a half a million dollars? The people I want to talk to are the five hundred thousand who have each given this man one dollar.'' In one of his letters on the tariff to working men published in the *New Haven Register,* he writes under date of October 14, 1880: ''I am no socialist or demagogue. I do not flatter 'workingmen' so-called, or tell them that they have any better right to that title than bankers, merchants, and professional men. I deny that they have any more right to government care, help, and protection than any other class. I deny that the state should pet 'the poor' or 'the weak' or 'the laborers.' I deny that it is the special duty of the economist and social philosopher to find out means of 'helping' the poor, or the laborers, and I do not pretend to do any such thing. I am not a 'friend of the poor man,' as the phrase goes. But when a man without capital is trying by his own industry and economy to better his condition, to educate his children, and to put them in a better condition than his own, I say that any legislation which stands in his way, makes his task harder, and robs him of advantages which he might have for the struggle, is the worst abomination I know of in politics, and I will make every effort to break it down. The most ironical political action I know of is the exhortation of the protected employers to their men to come up and vote for protection on the ground that they—the workmen —benefit by it. It is as if a slave owner should arm his slaves to fight for slavery, on the ground that he feeds them, and that, if slavery is abolished, they will get no food.''

Perhaps the most condensed and pungent remarks that Sumner ever made on the moral aspects of this ism were in a discussion at a meeting of the Church Congress, held in New Haven, October 20-23, 1885. Many of the most prominent Episcopal ecclesiastics of the country and a goodly representation of the laity were in attendance, together with Canon Farrar and some other notables of the English Church. On the evening of the second day's session "The Ethics of the Tariff Situation" was the subject assigned for consideration. "Despite the storm," says the *New Haven Register,* of October 22, "a large audience assembled at the 3rd session of the Church Congress. Tho audionce was troated to a discussion of tho tariff question which rivaled those of political meetings in heat and intensity. The interest steadily rose until it culminated in the climax when a clergyman in polite terms called a layman a liar. At that point the excitement was intense." The trouble was started by Charles Heber Clark, Esq., of Philadelphia, who said that free trade was responsible for the poverty-stricken condition of the people in Ireland and India. This statement aroused the ire of Reverend Frederick Courtnay of Boston, who jumped to his feet at the conclusion of Mr. Clark's speech and said that he was an Englishman and gloried in free trade. He resented the misinterpretation of conditions in connection with it. "It is not becoming," he added, "for one to break the Ninth Commandment in discussing the ethics of the Tariff. If the gentleman will go home and think this question over, I think he will be a man and apologize for bearing false witness against his neighbor." Mr. Clark retorted by saying that though he was not as widely known as Dr. Courtnay, he thought his reputation was as good as far as it went. Courtnay at once raised a point of order on the ground that Clark was making a personal attack on his character. Immediately the meeting was in confusion. Some cried, "Order! Order!" and others, "Go on! Go on!" Finally Mr. Clark was silenced on the ground that his time had expired and with some difficulty quiet was restored.

In this heated atmosphere Sumner made his speech. As he arose, we are told, there was great applause in all parts of the house. It cannot be said truthfully that his address was as oil on troubled waters. Referring to Mr. Clark, he declared that the gentleman had recited again the complete catechism of Pennsylvania protectionism, no two propositions of which could stand along side of each other without destroying each other. The matter under discussion, he said further, was a distinctly domestic one. It did not affect any Englishman. It was not the question of any East Indian. "You can let the woes of Ireland rest for to-night. The question of to-night is the woes of the American. When you lay on this tax, you lay it on an American, you don't lay it on anybody else. It is that man over there who is paying the tax to that man over there; and that is all there is of it. It is right here in our own family." The ethics of the question are "just what old Dr. Bacon, of New Haven here, once said to me about it: 'I don't see anything,' said he, 'in your tariff question but just 'Thou shalt not steal.' ''

Now then, if you take the ethical effect of the tariff on the Government, I maintain that it all the time demoralizes the Government. It lessens the dignity of the Government in the eyes of the people. It has been said that the Government ought to watch over the people. It ought. But how difficult to do any such thing! Because who is the Government with the big eye? It is nothing but ourselves. . . . We have got to take care of ourselves. We are orphans, we American people are. What is the ethical effect of the tariff on your Congress? It is demoralizing it all the time. It is teaching them the business of lobbyism and log-rolling all the time. The biggest and most shameful case of log-rolling in this country is the tariff. Over and over again, I say that with the figures in my hand to substantiate it. Take the effect upon a Congressman. The effect is all the time to teach him bad ways of carrying on the Government, bad ways of doing business, to go against good ways of carrying on the Government, to sacrifice the true public interests of the People of the United States. What is the effect on your laws? Under all right theories of government the object of government is to repress every selfish interest, not to let any of them come up, because they will do it if they get a chance. But under the tariff principle your government gives license to one set of interests to go out and oppress the rest. What is the effect upon the people who are the beneficiaries of it? It takes away correct ideas of business. It takes away the business enterprise and energy of the American people, and teaches them, instead of relying on themselves, and economic power, and national character, and the advantages that nature has given to this country, to rely on lobbying and special legislation in the halls of Congress. (Here the bell struck.) [19]

[19] "Papers and Speeches, Tenth Church Congress of the Protestant Episcopal Church in the United States," p. 113.

Although Sumner fought protectionism as one of the great social evils of the time, varied, widespread, and penetrating in its corruption, he did not, as did many of his free trade allies, join in the hue and cry against big business, which was raised in the eighties and continued with greater or less vociferousness for some years. As the railroads and other means of communication developed, the field in which an industry could operate expanded. Competition ceased to be local and became nation wide. Under the circumstances the cost of rivalry and the gain to be derived from consolidation became so obvious that concerns began to combine under the management of trustees. The tendency of these trusts was all in the direction of monopoly. Competitors were bought out or forced out. Those who could get special rates from the railroads had an almost insuperable advantage. Soon strong opposition to the movement began to manifest itself. The trusts were attacked on the ground that they could control prices and dominate legislation. Finally, in 1887, the Interstate Commerce Act, forbidding discrimination in rates and creating a commission with power to investigate and regulate, was passed. Three years later the Sherman Anti-Trust Law was enacted, making illegal "every contract, combination in the form of trust or otherwise, or conspiracy in restraint of commerce among the several states or with foreign nations." During the latter part of the nineteenth century the tendency to monopoly, which had been somewhat checked by business depression, became active again, and President Roosevelt prosecuted some of the trusts under the Sherman Act and made the force of the government strongly felt in industrial relations generally.

Against all this meddling by the state Sumner vigorously protested. The popular clamor against trusts he deemed unwarrantable. In August, 1887, he published a forceful article on "State Interference" in the *North American Review,* and the following year, a series of articles on "Monopoly" in the *Independent,* replete with brilliant analysis and trenchant statements,[20] showing that monopoly is in the nature of things, that it always has existed, and must always exist. Perhaps his most thoroughgoing treatment of the whole situation, however, was that printed in the *New York Journal of Commerce,* June 24 and 25, 1901, under the titles, "The Economics of Trusts," and "Policy in Regard to Trusts."

In these phenomena Sumner saw an inevitable phase of industrial evolution. They were the necessary accompaniment of the remarkable improvements made in the facilities of communication, and the development of organization and leadership. What gives man power over nature is wealth. Its production is "vital to the nearest and dearest interests of every man of us." Science, education, religion, charity, reform, are all dependent upon it. Human welfare requires that it be increased to the utmost limit possible. The enterprise requires two things, improvement in the arts, and personal training, talent, and skill. The latter are of the utmost importance. Business management of the highest order becomes more valuable at every stage of advance. "Routine is worth less at every stage, because routine can be superseded by machinery, or never ending change makes routine worthless. . . . There is a doctrine abroad that handicraft produces all the wealth, and ought to own it all, and another doctrine that society, by simply existing around the master of industry,

[20] These are reprinted in "Earth Hunger and Other Essays."

enables him to get wealth, which, therefore, the society may take away from him. The industrial army in the face of the tasks of to-day would be doomed to destruction without its generals. It is quite as true that society owes its wealth to the captains of industry as it is that the latter owe their opportunity to the society. Vanderbilt's wealth was trifling compared with the wealth which his enterprise enabled people of the Mississippi Valley to win." [21]

Popular fears regarding the trusts Sumner deemed unfounded. Where there is no monopoly, or only a weak one, a trust cannot arbitrarily raise prices. Experiment has shown that successful management of more or less absolute monopolies is in accord with, and not hostile to, cheapness and abundance. If the public has arrived at the conclusion that trusts are a peril which it would be wise to check, the one reasonable and straightforward method of doing so would be to abolish the tariff and patent systems which create artificial and legal monopolies. "It is obviously most absurd to establish a protective system and a patent system and then to denounce patentees and protected interests for availing themselves of the advantages which have been granted them. The proposal to abolish patents and tariffs, however, is proposing to the public to throw away two of its idols in which it believes most religiously. It seems far more inclined at present to accept the new fetish of 'State control' for the natural monopolies." [22]

The remedies proposed Sumner regarded as more dangerous than the disease. "There is no evil or danger in trusts," he said, "which is nearly so menacing to society as the measures which are proposed

[21] "The Economics of Trusts," *New York Journal of Commerce*, June 24, 1901.
[22] *Journal of Commerce*, June 25, 1901.

for destroying trusts. . . . No one can devise any law by which it can be made a crime for any number of persons to unite their capital and efforts for the production of wealth in a lawful enterprise. When, however, popular clamor is aroused for or against some ill-understood societal movement, legislators make laws and judges interpret them along lines of compromise between popular notions and jural principles. The result is to load the statute book with laws, parts of which have been set aside, and other (unknown) parts of which may be in force. The net result is anxiety and uncertainty in wealth production. We are obstructing ourselves in what we all want to do.''

It was inevitable that, holding these views, Sumner should have condemned both the Interstate Commerce Law and the Sherman Anti-Trust Act. Writing in 1888, he said: ''In our country the most remarkable piece of paternal legislation which has ever been passed is the Interstate Commerce Law. . . . It is certain from so much experience of the Act as we have yet had that it was not based on any clear analysis or correct solution of the problem. However, when such an act is passed, the effort of all concerned is to conform to it if they can; and here commences the evil effect I have described. In so far as they conform to it, the phenomena which subsequently present themselves are mixed products of the economy of railroading and of the law. Not only this, but the law also has its imposing effect upon the imagination of all concerned with the matter, and it affects all the assumptions with which they come to the study of it. This is a very common experience. After a law has been in existence for ten or twenty years, and a generation has grown up which can hardly remember anything else, it is almost impossible for them to understand what it would be to be without it. The worst ills from which civilized nations suffer to-day come from just that kind of law, unwisely adopted in the first place, but now regarded as a 'bulwark of society.' The Interstate Commerce Law is on the way to become just such another.'' [23] He pointed out also that such an act of paternalism would not fail to have its offshoots, and that an extension of the same type of legislation must be expected.

As a publicist Sumner was also conspicuous among those who waged the battle for civil service reform. The spoils system had been under attack since the Grant administration, during which some attempts to correct it were made which failed of success principally through lack of whole-hearted support on the part of the President. As Secretary of the Interior, under Hayes, Carl Schurz, Sumner's associate in the free-trade campaign, was able to put some of the ideas of the reformers into practical operation. The various branches of the Civil Service Reform Association kept the matter in agitation and at their call Sumner lectured in various parts of the country. Regarding the impression made by him an Elmira paper states: ''The opera house was quite well filled by a very fine audience last evening, on the occasion of the civil service reform lecture by Professor William G. Sumner of Yale College, who spoke under the auspices of the Elmira Civil Service Reform Association. 'The Democratic Theory of Public Offices' was announced as the topic, and the learned speaker was introduced to the audience by Vice-president Hall of the local association. The former is a tall gentleman

[23] "The State and Monopoly," "Earth Hunger and Other Essays," pp. 275, 276, 277.

of fine appearance, and not advanced beyond middle age. His manner of address is very clear and logical, and one interested in his theme must listen attentively while he is speaking.'' In 1883 the Civil Service Act was passed. This, unlike the Interstate Commerce Law, Sumner deemed within the proper scope of legislation because it raised up a commission merely for the administration of executive business, while the latter endowed a commission with discretion to pass upon interests of free and equal citizens, ''not being itself either executive, legislative, or judicial.''

The views regarding the causes of the evils associated with the civil service which Sumner set forth in the above mentioned address, are given more fully in articles originally published in the ''Princeton Review,'' and later in ''Essays in Political and Social Science,'' entitled, ''The Theory and Practice of Elections,'' and ''Presidential Elections and Civil Service Reform.'' These evils he regarded as symptoms of political disorder. They are not the object upon which attention should be focused. The faulty system from which they rise is that which requires correction. Until this is altered, there is no hope for their permanent removal. ''The corruption of the civil service,'' he says, ''is a historical product of the forces at work in American political life, under the conditions set by American political institutions. It is not an artificial product. No one brought it about. It was in no program. It is a growth. Its origins and its laws are to be sought in the facts of human nature, and of the political order, together with historical conditions. It follows that no artificial remedies will correct the abuses of the civil service unless they are such as reach to the remolding of political institutions. The elective system as employed by us, especially the system by which the President is elected, is the institution most in question." [24]

This declaration is preceded by a most brilliant analysis and criticism of the democratic-republican state. Accepting Alexander Hamilton's definition as one which goes to the very heart of the matter, he views a republic as a form of government in which power is conferred by a temporary and defeasible tenure. It is not a dogma, but a device, an arrangement for getting necessary work done. The test of its value is whether it produces good government. How the depositories of power are chosen, by heredity, by natural selection, or by vote, is not important, provided the purpose of the arrangement is realized.

Democracy, on the other hand, is a set of dogmas in which equality and the rule of the majority are supreme. Its tendency for a century has been to identify "the people" with the populace. The notion has gained control that the power which has been wrested from monarchs, oligarchies, and aristocracies has now reached its true place, and that error is corrected when the divine right of the majority is put in the place of the divine right of kings.

A widely extended electoral system is a natural accompaniment of the democratic-republican form of government. This puts into the hands of the masses the patronage which is an element of political power. The sovereign majority uses it as autocrats have used it, to win adherents, "to reward flatterers and parasites, and punish the recalcitrant." There has grown up the notion that there is greater rationality and propriety in the electoral system of selecting officials than in any other. The mere suggestion of a different

[24] "Elections and Civil Service Reform," "Essays in Political and Social Science," New York, Henry Holt and Company, 1885, p. 158.

method is regarded as a reflection upon the wisdom of the people.

For the successful operation of elections, parties are necessary. In this country these are highly organized and well drilled. They form, as it were, nations within the nation. Party fealty takes the place of patriotism. Elections become struggles for power. The successful party seizes upon the state and deals with it as formerly a conquering nation dealt with the conquered. In this struggle a private citizen may enlist only as a private soldier. "He must then look on while the boys and idlers amuse themselves, and the serious interests of the country are disturbed and injured, and, after all, it is a matter of very little importance to him which group wins, since either will serve the public interests equally ill. The contempt and weariness which most men over forty, not in politics, feel for politics is fully accounted for." In spite of all these evils, however, parties are a necessity. There is no possibility of active political life without them, and in its absence representative institutions cannot exist. Without parties there will be factions and personal cliques. The party system must be preserved, but it must be perfected.

The extension of the electoral system is a poor device for getting good government. Its basal assumptions are false. It assumes that the voter has a "will," or an opinion formed on great political issues, whenever the election day arrives. This he never has, however, except in instances where the issues appeal strongly to his feelings, or widespread debate has been carried on. That the voter, when asked to record his opinion, will respond directly and independently is also a false assumption. He may be frightened, or cheated, or bribed. He may let some one else make

up his mind for him, and then the former has two
votes instead of one. The theory of elections, furthermore, assumes that each voter will aim only at
the public good, a postulate which the facts do not
warrant. Self-interest, class interest, and other considerations, repeatedly determine men's attitude on
political questions. The theory that the ballot with
majority rule is an adequate mechanism for getting
a clear expression of the public will is unsound. The
truth of the matter is that the popular feeling regarding these is superstitious. "It attributes to elections causative force which they do not possess. This
false notion of causation is the essence of superstition. The popular notion is that we have a free country because we select our political officers by elections,
that our 'free institutions' center in and depend upon
elections, that our prosperity is due to the political
methods of which elections are the most important,
that our 'rights' depend upon and are guaranteed by
elections, and that the right of voting is the most important civil right we possess. . . . Woman's suffrage
is almost entirely a product of the superstition of elections. The crudest statements of it which I have ever
heard have been given in woman's suffrage meetings.
Upon analyzing the institution of elections, and exam-
ining the operation of this institution in practice, we
have found that, if we disregard the halo of sentiment
and humbug which has been thrown around elections,
elections are only a clumsy and inefficient apparatus
for the political purposes they aim to serve, and that
they are rather a disgrace to our civilization, so imperfect and inadequate are they. . . . Elections are
not a gift from heaven or from nature, as a source of
good government, or a means for getting it. They are

a burden or a task. They demand energy which we have to expend out of the store at our command." [25]

The frequency of presidential elections is especially fraught with evils, Sumner held. There is a growing dread of their recurrence. The increasing use for money drives the party in power to political assessments. They are chargeable with most of the worst errors and mishaps in our history. Their "intrigues cost us the war with Mexico, the repeal of the Missouri Compromise, the Kansas-Nebraska Act and the civil war in Kansas. Presidential intrigues wrought up the sectional misunderstanding until 'Yankees and Southerners' formed legendary and fabulous notions of each other. . . . Presidential intrigues in Johnson's administration frustrated the most peaceful and promising efforts at reconstruction, and brought about the carpet bag era with tyranny on one side and Ku-Klux outrages on the other. In 1876 we had a very narrow escape from another civil war." These elections must also be charged with corrupting the public men of the country. They have made them ambitious, and their desire for the highest honor in the country has forced them to do what they preferred not to do and to leave undone that which they would like to have performed. "To offset this evil we have the proud boast that any American may be President. Do we not pay too dearly for this bit of clap trap? How many of us want to be President? How many of us would surrender our reversion in the office if we could only be sure that no American could become President unless he were fit and competent?" Local politics, also, are corrupted by these elections, and

[25] "The Theory and Practice of Elections," "Essays in Political and Social Science," pp. 133, 134.

they act upon "timid reforms and newly planted improvements as a storm acts on sprouting plants." [26]

It is out of the election system which characterizes our adherence to the dogmas of democracy, therefore, that the corruption of the civil service springs. "As far as I can judge from conversation with experienced politicians, it is because they know that, in fact and practice, what is called the abuse of the civil service is just as essential to the system of elections as steam is to the locomotive, that they cannot understand what the civil service reformers are talking about. I am so far in accord with the politicians that I do not see how civil service is to be reformed so long as the chief executive office is put up to be struggled for every four years." [27]

The remedies Sumner proposes for existing conditions are the substitution of correct knowledge and loyalty to the institution of civil liberty for political dogmatism; more political sense and a higher civic virtue; and great curtailment of the use of elections for the selection of officers, especially those whose function is administrative. "Appointment pure and simple, by an Executive who would be solely and directly responsible to public opinion for his selections, is far more suitable for the selection of this class of officers. The power of removal should be equally absolute under the same responsibility."

Through magazine articles, furthermore, Sumner was continually throwing hot shot into the ranks of the socialists. Their dogmas he found to be utterly without foundation and their proposals among the most glaring examples of that empiricism which at

[26] "Elections and Civil Service Reform," "Essays in Political and Social Science," pp. 151, 152.
[27] *Ibid.*, p. 145.

the beginning of his career he had gone forth to fight. One still turns to his writings for the strongest refutation of socialistic doctrine available.

That the state of which the socialists dreamed, or anything like it, would ever be established Sumner had little fear, though he did not doubt that they would put society to the expense of some very foolish experiments. He had too much faith in the strength of the property interest to hold any different view. Writing in the *New York Herald* of January 1, 1906, he says: "Property is the earliest, broadest, and most invincible of all the interests of men. They will rally to its defense against any project or theory, no matter how alluring it may seem. Nothing has ever been, or will be, so strong a bond of union between men in society as the interest of property." In the same paper on January 2 of the following year he declared: "Property is an essential condition of education, religion, and science, and it is essential to the family. We may therefore have discussions about many societal propositions, but where any serious proposition is made to alter the rights of property, or to diminish its guarantees, the men will all go back to the old ideas and institutions." In support of this view, Sumner much enjoyed telling the following story: "Some time ago I heard a socialist orator say that he could get along with an audience except 'these measly, mean-spirited working men, who have saved a few hundred dollars and built a cottage, with a savings bank mortgage, of which they rent the second story and live in the first. 'They,' said he, 'will get up and go out, a benchful at a time, when I begin to talk about rent.' If he had been open to instruction from facts," Sumner would add, "he might have learned much from the conduct of those measly workingmen. They will fight far more ferociously for their cottages than the millionaires for their palaces.''

An article in connection with socialism, which occasioned comment all over the country and brought Sumner many letters commendatory and otherwise, is ''The Fallacies of Socialism,'' which appeared in *Collier's Weekly*, October 29, 1904, and is reprinted in ''The Challenge of Facts and Other Essays,'' under the title, ''Reply to a Socialist.'' It was an answer to an article which Mr. Upton Sinclair had written for the same periodical on ''The Socialistic Party: Its Aims in the Present Campaign.'' The assumptions and arguments of the latter Sumner shakes and tears to pieces, like a bulldog playing with a rag, and when he is through nothing but shreds remain. Apparently Mr. Sinclair never forgave the Yale professor, for in the ''Goose-step,'' published in 1923, he refers to him as the ''prime minister in the empire of plutocratic education.'' ''I doubt if there has ever been a more capitalistic economist than Sumner,'' he says, ''a man who took a ghoulish delight in the glorifying of commercialism. . . . Of course to such a man there was no person so irritating as a reformer of any sort, and he never wearied of pouring out ridicule upon the man who imagined he could do anything to make society better. . . . Such a man is worth many billions of dollars to the plutocrats; they pay him a few thousand a year, and tickle his vanity with solemnly conferred degrees and an academic robe to wear, and at the end of his thirty years of service the editors of the *Yale Review* celebrated him in a series of articles as 'Pioneer'—'Teacher'—'Inspirer' —'Idealist'—'Man and Veteran.' ''

With regard to international relations, Sumner expressed opinions in his later years which won for him

both friends and enemies. Sometime during the
Roosevelt administration he went back to the town
where as a young man he hád preached, for the purpose of giving an address. What happened is thus
described in an undated newspaper clipping.

A dozen members of the Friday Evening Club at
Morristown, N. J., left their lecture room last night while
Prof. W. G. Sumner, of Yale, was addressing them on
the subject, 'The United States as a World Power.'

They were angered at opinions expressed by the professor, condemning the attitude of the Administration in
favor of a large navy, and casting ridicule upon the
Monroe doctrine.

The objectors gathered in the lobby and became so
loud in their denunciations of the lecturer, who was still
speaking, that he was forced to stop several times. The
most outspoken of the angry ones was United States District Attorney, J. B. Vreeland.

The remarks which stirred up the small tempest were
these:

'We have a constitution and laws which we are supposed to obey, but we have that which is called a doctrine
thrust upon us. We cannot find any statement concerning it in any public document. It just seems to be
floating about in the air. But it binds us or gives us the
liberty to put our fingers in all the quarrels in this continent. It is a preposterous, ridiculous, and dangerous
doctrine.

'We have no reason to maintain a powerful navy
because no Power dare attack us. The only possible use
of such an institution would be to send it abroad where
we have no business.'

Sumner had no respect for the Monroe doctrine for
two reasons. He objected to it, first, on the ground
that it was a *doctrine*.

History contains instances enough to show us the frightful burden which a doctrine may be. It comes with prestige of tradition, antiquity, and perhaps a great name, to take away from the living generation the right to do their own thinking and to compel them to sacrifice their lives and happiness against their will and without the consent of their reason and conscience.

In his message of December 17, 1895, President Cleveland referred to the balance-of-power doctrine as a parallel of the Monroe doctrine. The example was unfortunate if the parallel had been true. What oceans of blood and mountains of treasure have been spent for the balance-of-trade doctrine! And what result is there to show for it all? We have had in our history many doctrines: America for the English; no taxation without representation; state rights; separation of purse and sword; manifest destiny; the self-expanding power of the Constitution; God's purpose to civilize the earth by African slavery; and I know not how many others. Some of them are obsolete or forgotten. Others it has cost us frightful sacrifices to set aside. Inasmuch as a United States Senator has referred to the doctrine of Washington's farewell address as the 'Washington fetish,' I may perhaps be allowed to call the Monroe doctrine the 'Monroe fetish.' We should do our best to declare our emancipation from all doctrines, to do our own thinking on all our own questions, and to act according to our own reason and conscience, not according to anybody's traditional formula. . . . If I were an educated young man now growing up, I would not allow anybody to entail any formula on me that would fetter my judgment of questions and cases which may arise.[28]

An even greater objection to the Monroe doctrine in Sumner's view is that it implies the division of the globe into two independent halves. This aspect of the

[28] "Earth Hunger," "Earth Hunger and Other Essays," pp. 58, 59.

doctrine he set forth in *The Popular Science Monthly* for August, 1906, under the title, "The Proposed Dual Organization of Mankind," [29] saying that under it

> Instead of the old notion of a world-unit ruled from Europe as its head, we should have a dual world-system, one part under the hegemony of Europe, the other part under that of the United States. Is this a rational or practicable plan of future development? Is it not fantastic and arbitrary? If the United States pretends to hold aloof from a share in the affairs of the Eastern continent, and to demand that all European states shall abstain from any share in the affairs of the Western continent, is that anything more than a pose and an affectation? Have we not within a year or two been forced to take action in protection of our citizens in China and Armenia? If Africa is opened up to commerce, do we mean to hold aloof from a share in it? Are we not already deeply interested in it so far as it has advanced? We have interests in Madagascar which have already drawn us into the proceedings there, and which promise to involve us still further. We accepted a rôle in the war between China and Japan which was by no means that of an uninterested stranger. Will any one maintain that we could carry out the policy of abstention in respect to that part of the world? [30]

Such a course as the doctrine implies, Sumner goes on to state, is contrary to the general trend of evolution. The modern conception is that "the states of the world are all united in a family of nations whose rights and duties toward each other are embodied in a code of international law. All states may be admitted into this family of nations whenever they accept this code, whether they have previously been

[29] Reprinted in "War and Other Essays," p. 271.
[30] "War and Other Essays," p. 276.

considered "civilized" or not. The code itself is a
product of the reasoning and moral convictions of
civilized states, and it grows by precedents and
usages as cases arise for the application of the general principles which have been accepted as sound,
because they conduce to peace, harmony, and smooth
progress of affairs. . . . This is the only conception
of the relation of parts of the human race to each
other which is consistent with civilization and which
is worthy of the enlightenment of our age. Any
"doctrine" which is not consistent with it will sooner
or later be set aside through the suffering of those
who adhere to it." [31] The only part of the Monroe
doctrine which, according to Sumner, has any soundness in it, is the determination which it expresses
"that the social and political systems of Europe
should not be extended over any part of the American continent, lest people who were weaker than we
should lose the opportunity which the new continent
gave them to escape from those systems if they
wanted to." [32]

Sumner was prominent among the unpopular few
who opposed the strong sentiment in favor of imperialism aroused in the people of the United States
by the events associated with the Spanish-American
War. Although for reasons of health he had been
making but few speeches for several years, on January 16, 1899, in the old College Street Hall, New
Haven, with every seat filled and aisles jammed, he
delivered an address under the auspices of the Yale
Chapter of Phi Beta Kappa, upon "The Conquest of
the United States by Spain." Standing like a rock,
his head slightly thrust forward, conscious that prac-

[31] "War and Other Essays," p. 280.
[32] "The Conquest of the United States by Spain," "War and Other
Essays," p. 333.

tically every person in the audience was on the side
he was opposing, Sumner delivered what was probably the strongest statement of the grounds for anti-
imperialism made in that eventful period. Such was
its logic, its force, its striking phrases, and its comprehensiveness of view, and such was the power of
the speaker's personality, that in spite of themselves
the hearers' minds moved in sympathy with him.
Applause broke forth repeatedly, and at the close of
the address this fighter of so many unpopular battles
received an ovation.

The address was widely circulated and commented
upon throughout the country. Like almost all of
Sumner's important utterances, it was both highly
praised and hotly condemned. It argues that expansion and imperialism are at war with the best traditions, principles, and interests of the American people, and will plunge them into a net-work of difficult
problems and political perils which offer no compensating advantages in return. "We cannot govern
dependencies with our political system, and . . . if
we try it, the State which our fathers founded will
suffer a reaction which will transform it into another
empire just after the fashion of all the old ones, . . .
and the democratic republic which has been will stand
in history, like the colonial organization of earlier
days, as a mere traditional form." [33]

Except as alderman of New Haven and member of
the Connecticut Board of Education, Sumner held no
public office but one. On May 19, 1885, William C.
Whitney, then Secretary of the Navy, appointed him
a member of the Board of Visitors to the Naval
Academy at Annapolis. In that capacity he served

[33] The whole address is printed in "War and Other Essays," pp.
297-334.

as chairman of the committee on Subjects of Study
and Standard of Scholarship, and was a member of
the committee on English Studies, Modern Languages,
and Drawing, and on that of Final Report and Selection of Orator to Address the Cadets. He is credited
with writing the annual report of the Board, dated
June 6, 1885. The Secretary of War, William C.
Endicott, in 1886, asked him to serve as Visitor to
West Point, an honor which he seems to have declined.

Through all this long period of active participation
in public affairs, Sumner maintained the attitude of
independence with respect to parties which he had
assumed in the Tilden-Hayes campaign. Speaking to
the students of Yale shortly before the election of
1884, he made these blunt statements: "An independent voter is not an office holder or a candidate for
an office, but a man who proposes to do his duty conscientiously at every election. I hold that is the only
kind of voting. There is no other kind that becomes
a free man and a sovereign. . . . To me both parties
seem equally bad. The independent voter has had to
do what he can. I don't know the time that I ever had
the satisfaction of voting for an ideal candidate, and
I never expect to have. An independent voter can't
withdraw himself. The whole case of politics is of
choosing the best and the most available. . . . Nothing tells on a party but defeat. Scolding won't do
any good, growling won't do any good. Defeat is the
only thing to dispose of politicians. To make party
men understand that if they make their arrangements
to dispose of us, they can't deliver the goods, is our
duty."

Although in espousing the candidacy of Mr. Tilden,
Sumner had said rather harsh things about Mr.
Hayes, he was big enough and frank enough, later, to

confess that he had been wrong in his estimate. "If I had been asked just what I wanted done," he writes, "I should have described just what Mr. Hayes did do after he got in."[34] He also gave him high praise for his efforts in behalf of civil service reform. "It is said that Mr. Hayes has done very little. In fact when we consider the nature and difficulty of the task, he has done a great deal. He has not been supported as he deserved in what he has done. Those who believed in the reform and desired it were bound to understand the difficulty of it, to welcome little beginnings toward it, to take what they could get and nurse it carefully, in hopes of more, to appreciate the President's efforts, and to support and encourage him. They have, on the contrary, taken the position of spectators and critics."[35]

In the campaign of 1880 Sumner opposed both General Grant and Mr. Blaine, who were the leading candidates for the Republican nomination. With many others in Connecticut he favored Senator Edmunds. General James A. Garfield was nominated by the Republicans and General Winfield S. Hancock by the Democrats. Apparently the former's record did not satisfy Sumner, while the latter, who is remembered chiefly for his remark that the tariff is a local issue, had had no political experience to fit him for the Presidential office. Sumner did not vote. He supported Cleveland in 1884 and attacked Blaine in acrimonious terms. "All the rings and jobbers in the United States," he said to the students of Yale in the speech on independent voting already referred to, "are around Mr. Blaine, and their hopes are in his

[34] "Sketch of William Graham Sumner," "The Challenge of Facts and Other Essays," p. 12.
[35] "Elections and Civil Service Reform," "Essays in Political and Social Science," p. 154.

election, and what crowd could be worse than the southwestern politicians that are managing his campaign? People have good forgetfulness, but they can't forget that dinner at Delmonico's when 'in vino veritas' certain politicians bragged of the wholesale bribery of a state. Mr. Blaine is under charges that touch his personal integrity. I have carefully examined these charges and I believe that Mr. Blaine has acted as no president of the United States has acted or should act. His friends have tried to explain away his deeds, but the explanations are vague and insufficient." In the following election Sumner supported Cleveland on the tariff issue. Mr. Roosevelt aroused his ire. The views and ways of this man of action had not the scientific background which Sumner deemed requisite to a true statesman, and he regarded Roosevelt's attitude toward big business, when he was President, as unsound and pernicious. In a speech on "War and Its Effects on Civilization," delivered in Indianapolis in April, 1903, Sumner hit out right and left at Roosevelt's militancy, calling forth this comment upon himself from the *New Haven Register:* "We shall look in vain for the characteristics in that gentleman which make a coward. Mr. Sumner may not always be right, but we submit that he is not second even to the courageous President in stating his convictions."

I warn you that if you pursue what is good, you will find yourself limited by the stupidity, ignorance, and folly of the society in which you live; and I promise you also that if you hold on your way through the crowd or try to make them go with you, you will have ample experience of self-sacrifice and as much martyrdom as you care for.

Discipline.

CHAPTER XII

SOME REACTIONS

SUMNER's speeches and addresses were of a temper to call forth bitter opposition. In the open minded they awakened respect; from those in general agreement with their point of view they received enthusiastic commendation; but in the rank and file of the opposition they stirred up anger, wrath, malice, and evil speaking. Seldom was there anything conciliatory in Sumner's words or attitude, and never was he troubled by anxiety to keep the peace. The terms which he applied to men and conditions were not the pleasantest available, and from his conviction that there must be no concealment or withholding of the truth he never swerved in the smallest degree. It is said that a colleague once remonstrated with him mildly for putting something "butt end foremost." "Well, it's the truth," Sumner answered. "But the truth is not to be spoken at all times," suggested his critic. "That," retorted Sumner, "has never been my policy."

Not only what he said and the way he said it, but his appearance and manner irritated Sumner's opponents. An interesting picture of him in action, as seen by an unsympathetic observer, which in spite of some exaggeration and unfairness has a modicum of truth in it, is given in a letter in the *Brooklyn Times,* dated February 25, 1885, and signed, James A. Skilton.

As to person, tall, strong and vigorous, with a large brain well piled up, and a forehead so extensive that it reached nearly to the back of his neck. As to manner, bold, self-asserting and aggressive—would have made a good soldier—might have done good service as an aide to General Gordon in the Sudan, fighting El Mehdi, and might possibly have been taught a lesson or two by the Arabs, except that the whole air of the man was, for a professed teacher, singularly unteachable. To all these was added an underlying, alternately serene, or arrogant, cocksureness of expression, typical of the entire tribe. The moment he opened his mouth, the voice—that revealing index of character—shot out like a charge from a gun, combining a growl with its roar, and ending the sentence with a peculiar snarl from the throat, as if he would rivet his statement in your mind past all removal or dissent. This last peculiarity combined the comical with the startling, and continued throughout, producing an irresistible impression that in occupying the chair of a teacher he had missed his vocation. Then there was a strong nose which, from its commanding central position in his face, constantly took part, as if swiveled for the purpose, in an extraordinary series of smirks and grimaces, some vicious, some sardonic—all mischievous and threatening. In both manner and method he seemed to be intent on filling up each person in the audience with his free trade ideas, as if with a stomach pump and with the jaws of the victim pried open. Then there were such pleasant convincing words as 'thief,' 'steal,' 'robbery,' 'crime,' etc., applied to protectionists and protection. In fact, so far as manner, method, and temper were concerned, no better man could be found and let loose in a promiscuous audience for the purpose of making or confirming protectionists than Professor Sumner.

Because of widespread and careful investigation, combined with hard thought, Sumner considered himself an authority on the matters which he discussed and had no hesitancy in saying that he knew more than most men about them. It was difficult for him to conceal his contempt for those who wandered in fields other than their own and presumed to declare what was true and right there. In his "Pictures of Silver" speech in Chicago, in 1878, he said: "I have been studying the question for years to find out what I know about it. Many of you may be very much smarter than I am, but I may, without impropriety, say that you cannot outstrip me here. Furthermore, I cannot put what I know about it in a few simple sentences and teach it to you in a single lecture. I propose to discuss the question in its popular aspect and in no other." Further on in the address he held up to derision a statement of a local paper and declared that whenever he read the newspapers he was struck with the fact that the persons writing for them on the silver question knew little about the facts involved in it and misconstrued those with which they were familiar.

As a consequence the newspapers pictured him as conceited and inefficient.

Professor Sumner of Yale College was invited to lecture in Chicago on the silver question; he has delivered his lecture, and the silver question remains unsettled. Prof. Sumner was introduced as a man who was master of the subject; and, on the principle that if a man wanted a good dinner he should employ an educated cook to prepare it, so it was advisable that information on an economical question could be more certainly obtained from a philosopher like Prof. Sumner. The address, regarded as the production of an expert, as the product of a person who modestly announced that no one knew more about it than did he, was about the weakest and thinnest soup ever got up by a professional cook. The lecture was written and spoken in dogmatic style, the author assuming that he knew all about the question and that his hearers knew nothing, and that his assertions were to be accepted as conclusive. Taking his lecture as embodying all that can be said in favor of demonetizing silver, the very weakness of the case presented by the man who declared he had made it a life study and knew it all, will probably confirm the friends of silver in the justice of their cause.

A somewhat similar picture is given in a clever bit of parody published in 1883 in the *New York Tribune*.

ODE TO A YALE PROFESSOR

(After reading his letter on Mr. Evarts's speech)

Abou Ben Sumner, may he curb his ism,
Awoke one night from dreams of dogmatism,
And saw within his own apartment fine,
Where Free Trade pamphlets make a rich moonshine,
An angel writing in a book quite scrumptious;
Exceeding self had made this Sumner bumptious,
And to the presence in his room he said:
'What writest thou?' The vision raised his head
And, with a look sweet as candied jam,
Replied: 'I am writing of the great I Am.'
'Meaning myself?' said Sumner. 'Nay, not so,'
Answered the vision; Sumner spake more low,
But cheerily still and said: 'I'm sore afraid
You never listened while I talked Free Trade.'
The angel blushed and vanished; the next night
He came again with a great wakening light
And said to Sumner, while he wiped his eyes,
'I've seen your letter—I apologize.'

The letter referred to was one written to Mr. Abraham L. Earle, of the American Free Trade League,

February 2, 1883, expressing Sumner's views regarding a speech made by Hon. William M. Evarts at a meeting called by the New York Association for the Protection of American Industry, held at Cooper Union, February 1, 1883.

New Haven,
February 2, 1883.

DEAR MR. EARLE:

I have been reading Mr. Evarts's speech. The first reflection suggested by it is, What would be Mr. Evarts's comment on me if I should go into court and argue an important case with only a popular and newspaper knowledge of law? Little as I know of law, I doubt if I should make such an exhibition of myself as Mr. Evarts made in his attempt to discuss a matter of political economy. He assumed all he had to prove, affirmed what was of no importance, and had back in his mind theories of political economy which are puerile and absurd in the extreme. Mr. Evarts ought to know that, although this sort of argument passed for powerful in the days of Henry Clay and Horace Greeley, we have got a great way beyond it now, and a man who comes into the tariff debate to-day has got to come with a great deal bigger outfit than an ability to sound the tom-tom about 'British anxiety' and a 'wall of peaceful duties.' Mr. Evarts has obviously never given himself the trouble to clear up his own ideas about what free trade would be. He conceives of it as if one nation would absorb all the trade of the world. What would that mean? If that nation really 'traded' with others it must give its products for theirs. They would not make this exchange unless it was advantageous to them. Such a state of things, then, must be advantageous to them. If that nation gave its products to them and got nothing back from them it would be their tributary and slave. If it took from them and gave them nothing in return it must first conquer them in war, which it could do as well without as with 'a wall of peaceful duties.' Mr. Evarts said that the time for us to have free trade would be when we could sell to other nations everything and they could sell us nothing. From this it appears that his idea is to get us into the second position.

The doctrine that you must buy to sell and sell to buy is the hardest easy doctrine in the world. Mr. Evarts could not do any better than the most vulgar protectionist. He goes off to talk about England and Englishmen when his subject was America and Americans. 'Do not let us do it,' says he, 'because Englishmen want to have us do it,' when the question is, 'Is it for the advantage of Americans to do it?' If we do it we shall do it because we think it is for our advantage, not because Englishmen or other men want to have us do it. If you go down the main street of any town the shop windows are full of goods displayed with the most tempting art. Behind the windows are men who want to sell you something—just like the wicked Englishmen. I never heard that any man wanted an armor of iron or of taxes to protect him against the man who wanted to sell him something. On the contrary, we regard it as an advantage to have a chance and a choice of good things offered to us, which we can take if we want it, and which does us no harm if we let it alone. The anxiety of foreigners to sell us goods is an advantage of just the same kind.

Yours respectfully,

W. G. SUMNER.

Upon the appearance of this letter the protectionist press, under the leadership of the *New York Tribune,* opened all its guns on Sumner. That a young college professor should assume such an irreverent, not to say insolent, attitude toward a much older and greater man, one who had been both Attorney General of the United States and Secretary of State, was not a thing to be tolerated. It determined to drive him from his seat, and by argument, ridicule, and false report worked for years to do so. In the *Tribune* of February 11, 1883, appeared this angry editorial:

UNWORTHY OF YALE

There are gentlemen among the leading advocates of Free Trade in this country; gentlemen who, however mistaken their opinions, are able to state them with sufficient courtesy toward opponents to command a respectful hearing, and to defend them with enough fairness to convince a hearer of their sincerity, even if he cannot assent to their conclusions. But among such gentlemen Professor Sumner cannot be classed. His manners in discussion are precisely those of the cheap Tombs Shyster when he knows that a case is so bad that he cannot afford to treat adverse witnesses with decency. His coarse dogmatism tends neither to instruct nor to convince; it repels doubters and disgusts friends. Assailing the matured convictions of men who are and will be regarded by the intelligent as superior to himself, Mr. Sumner calls them 'vulgar protectionists.' A comparatively young man, who has hardly achieved the right as yet to set up for intellectual Pope of the universe, he thinks it quite enough to say of Ex-Secretary Evarts that his theories of political economy 'are puerile and absurd in the extreme.' This is not argument, nor is it decency. The theories thus assailed have been held and powerfully advocated by many of the world's greatest statesmen, and by not a few of its profoundest thinkers. If they have been in error the fact is hardly established past controversy by mere insolent dogmatism from a man of the mental stature of Mr. Sumner.

. . . .

Men who are really able are not often inclined to substitute insolence for argument. Men who are fit to teach others, especially, stand much in need of minds large enough to comprehend that those who dissent from them are not necessarily fools. It is not to the advantage of Yale College that shallow and one-sided dogmatism directs its instruction in a science of the highest practical importance. . . . The sort of Free Traders who are apt to emerge from instruction of the sort suggested by Mr. Sumner's letter about Ex-Secretary Evarts will not go far to revolutionize the world, nor will they gain great weight among practical men of the world who have minds large enough to see both sides.

In order, if possible, to lower Sumner in the estimation of his students, marked copies of the *Tribune* in which this editorial appeared, together with an assortment of protectionist literature, were sent to every member of the senior class. Before such an attack Sumner could not remain silent, and he retorted immediately in the following letter to the *Times*.

To the Editor of the *New York Times:*

Some one has sent me an article from the *Tribune* of yesterday, in which that journal tells the public its opinions of my age and mental capacity, apropos of a criticism which I made and justified about Mr. Evarts's speech. I am charged with 'assailing the matured convictions' of men who are my superiors. It must be, then, that certain economic opinions are sacred and above criticism. It is said that I 'say of William M. Evarts that his theories of political economy are puerile.' This is not even grammatical, for it does not affirm that I have said anything about Mr. Evarts, but about his opinions. I have criticized opinions about public questions. I have never learned that it was a personal aspersion on any man to criticize his opinions on a public question. If it is, then there are some privileged persons in this protectionist controversy, some people who can say what they like, who, for various pious reasons, are not to be criticized as I would be if I ventured to speak in public. I am willing to have it understood once for all that I recognize no sacred doctrines in economy and no privileged persons in public discussion. I am so lost to decency that I do not respect the opinions of Henry Clay and Horace Greeley on an economic question, and I do not admit that anybody could make a public speech on protection without exposing himself to any criticism which I choose to make over my own signature, and such that a respectable newspaper will publish it.

I have never been guilty of any personality in any public discussion, but it certainly is my right to say whatever I have to say about any public question and to participate in the debate in any proper manner, and what I say is to go for just what it is worth, without reference to my age, academical position, or other personal consideration. The article in the *Tribune* is an outrageous personality, for which there was no occasion or excuse. It does not deal with the merits of the subject matter at all. The protectionists would do well if they could secure a privileged position for their doctrines and their speakers. They need such extraneous support. 'Dogmatism' is a big word. It is easy to sling it about. It answers no facts of arguments. The protectionists fall back on authority. Henry Clay believed in protection. Lincoln signed the Tariff bill. Charles Sumner voted for it, etc. I have never debated all that rubbish. The tariff question is not to be settled by any such considerations as that.

The protectionists get lachrymose. They are grieved that there is not more respect for antiquity. They begin to whine as soon as the debate gets hot. They sigh to think that young men are growing up who assail the theories of old political saints and economic quacks. Their tenderness is violated that any of the most ignorant and prejudiced among their number should be called 'vulgar protectionists.' They are shocked that any free trader should declare 'puerile' and 'absurd' dogmas which Greeley used to defend by chaste and scientific reasoning. They weep over the unworthiness of a young professor who will not respect old humbugs. They run to protect Evarts with the names of Lincoln and Sumner. I am old enough to wish that I was younger. In the course of my life I have picked up one or two observations. I have noticed that whenever a big newspaper thinks it worth while to spend half a column to tell a man that he is of no account, he may be sure that he counts for his full share; and he may fairly believe that he has reached a certain altitude when it is worth half a column to try to put him down. I do not doubt that I shall get all the credit that I deserve from the public, without regard for what the *Tribune* may try to tell them about me. As for poor old Yale, she has lots of friends. They have called her 'Black Republican,' 'Beecherite,' and all sorts of things besides. They all wag their heads at her and tell her what will happen to her if she does not take their advice, support their interests, and defend their notions. She seems to stand it pretty well so long as she pays no heed to any of them. There is only one thing which could do her any harm. That would be to get some Professors who believed at the same time in 'both sides' of a scientific question, or who, having scientific convictions, could not, or dare not express them. She is safe—too safe. That is what is the matter.

W. G. SUMNER.

New Haven, Monday, February 12, 1883.

How intense the rancor displayed by the Republican press was is shown by a story in the *Bridgeport Standard,* so absurd that its only effect among Sumner's friends was to provoke a laugh.

It is said that when Sam Tilden was running for the presidency Professor Sumner, of Yale College, met

him at Saratoga, and old Sam gauging his size, picked
him up and put him in his pocket, making him believe
that if he, Tilden, should be elected Sumner would be
his prophet at the court of St. James, or any other place
he might select. Sumner's vanity was tickled and he at
once became a Tildenite. This explains why Sumner left
his duties at the college, went down to New Orleans and
intruded his presence among the strong men there assembled, to see about the disputed count of votes. He was
looking after that foreign appointment through Tilden's
chances. How that sly old fox must have laughed to see
his bait so quickly swallowed by Sumner, to whom of
course he never thought of giving anything except an
implied promise. Still, if any foreign appointment will
take Sumner away from the college and out of the
country, we do hope something of the kind will be
squeezed out of him.

In pursuance of this attempt to drive Sumner from
Yale a report was widely circulated that the students
were up in arms against his dogmatic teachings. It
first appeared in the *Tribune*.

New Haven, February 15th.
Yale College students have written a letter to William
M. Evarts, urging him to come to New Haven to combat
the free trade utterances of Professor Sumner. Yale is
in a ferment over the recent attack of Professor Sumner
on Mr. Evarts, and it is probable that a demand will be
made upon the college authorities to provide more liberal instruction in political economy. At present only
free trade is taught. Protectionist documents are being
eagerly sought and read by the students. There is something like a little rebellion not improbable.

The only effect which these attacks had was to call
forth rebuke from other newspapers and to rally the

students to the defense and praise of one of their most liked and trusted professors. Regarding the story in the *Bridgeport Standard,* the *New Haven Register* remarked, "as Professor Sumner is not only one of the most talented, useful and popular men in Yale College, it is hardly likely that his services will be spared just yet. Yale has a right to be proud of him." The *Waterbury American* hastened to disabuse the *Hartford Courant* of the idea that the former had ever stated that Sumner was offending patrons of the college and injuring its interests.

There would have been something decidedly inappropriate in the *American's* giving expression to any such idea. But the *American* never entertained and therefore never expressed such a thought in relation to Professor Sumner's teachings. The item to this effect which is referred to by the *Courant* and which is being circulated in the papers and credited to the *American* is wrongfully so credited, as nothing like it ever appeared in these columns. In fact within a week the *American* stated that in spite of his dogmatism Prof. Sumner was the most successful and most popular instructor on the Yale faculty and referred especially to the respect and trust in which he is held by all who know him and are associated with him in college work. The statement that he is offending the patrons of the College and so injuring its interests is so far from the truth that we are especially strenuous in denying all responsibility for it. Yale College has taught the same doctrines for years and Prof. Sumner is treading in the footsteps of his universally respected predecessor, Ex-President Woolsey.

The general point of view and feeling at Yale with regard to Professor Sumner is well stated in this letter written by a Yale student who was a protectionist.

To the Editor of the *Evening Post:*

Sir: In the opinion of the students of Yale there is at present much smoke over so small a fire in the matter of the Sumner-Evarts controversy. The statement has been made in the metropolitan press that the senior class has invited Mr. Evarts to address them on protection, and this statement having found recognition in your editorial columns, it is the general desire here that the real facts in the case be made known, and, as both free traders and protectionists express it, this misrepresentation cease. It is a serious misrepresentation of the sentiments of the vast majority of the class to say that they have done so puerile a thing as to send a letter to Mr. Evarts asking him to come here to refute Professor Sumner's free trade arguments. The writer has been at much pains to ascertain the full opinion of the class upon the subject. In the first place, the class, as a class, have sent no such letter, and not only that, but no one seems to know who could have taken it upon himself to do such a presumptuous thing. Indeed, the general tone as to the action—if it has really been committed by some over-zealous classmate—is in the highest degree condemnatory. While there are many of both views who would like to hear some prominent protectionist champion, there can be found scarcely one who wishes this as hostile to Professor Sumner. The statement is made that the class are opposed to the one-sided instruction of this gentleman, that his resignation may be called for, indeed that 'a small rebellion is probable.' Nothing is more improbable. Few instructors in the University give the general satisfaction that Professor Sumner does and as to his one-sided method of instruction on free trade there is only this to say: During the year he has expressed himself to only the most limited extent on the subject; the chapter in the textbook—Fawcett's—which bears upon international trade was passed over with less attention than many of the others, and this fact was a matter of comment at the time by those who had been taught to believe in the rabidness of the Professor. His free-trade utterances as made before the public are never thrust upon young minds which have two paths open before them to choose between in the classroom. No more dictatorial is his instruction than that of President Porter in ethics. Only until the recent charges have been made against him, and then not until his pupils had asked him questions, has he made any decisive statements before us, and they have been made outside of the regular recitation.

As an instance of his worthiness as an instructor, the class is now studying the national bank system. Day after day the Professor drops the routine of the Yale style of question-and-answer recitation to go into the minutest and most lucid explanations of this difficult subject; without tiring, he prepares extensive schedules and charts to illustrate his explanations; and, to show the appreciation of his powers as an instructor, all the graduate students in the city who can find time, as well as members of other departments, come to his recitation room. Outside of the regular course he gives lectures, nominally to the Senior Class, but in reality to all of the University who can attend, several times a week, and yet constant demands are being made for more. To judge by outside talk, one would think that the Professor spoke only on free trade, but in reality that is one of the things which he touches least upon. His subject is political economy, and he realizes as well as any of his critics the breadth of it, the necessity of brevity with individual departments in order to go over it all in one year.

While personally I may be of that part of the class who are said to be opposed to the Professor's views, and also one of the number who would like to see the suggestion of the *Evening Post* that the Union League Club send some man to speak in New Haven, adopted, yet I share the desire of the College to see the matter stated correctly. . . . As to the means adopted by the free traders in marking certain articles against Profes-

sor Sumner in the metropolitan press, and sending the
papers containing them to all the members of the Senior
Class, it is necessary to make no comment in this connection. Those who understand student nature will be
able to appreciate how strongly such conduct must and
does react upon the agents of it. It is tolerably safe to
predict that, if the present misrepresentations are indulged in, there will soon be not a protectionist in the
college.

A YALE SENIOR.

New Haven, Connecticut, February 17, 1883.

The *New York Tribune* did not cease its assaults
upon Sumner. In 1885 it reviewed his essay on "Protectionism" in an abusive article which it entitled
"An Unworthy Teacher." The writer of it declares
that Sumner's intellectual dishonesty and lack of decency are of public consequence only because of his
place. "His is not the mode of reasoning to which
the father of any Yale student would wish his son to
be trained." The review closes with this statement:
"Yale should not thrust a 'Professor' like this upon
the attention of persons who are in the habit of telling
the truth and behaving decently." With grim sense
of humor Sumner wrote over a clipping containing
this attack: "This answers the question, Why is Yale
falling in public estimation?"

During this period of persecution Sumner sent the
following letter to some person who was aggrieved
because "Yale was teaching" free trade.

New Haven,
Feb. 25, 1883.

DEAR SIR:

'Yale College' has never 'taught' anything about
free trade so far as I know. Dr. Woolsey did not teach
protection in 1863, and so far as I have learned his

opinions from conversation with him they agree with mine. Yale College has appointed a man to teach political economy, who is supposed to be a man of integrity of mind and character, and he teaches the science as a science, seeking what is true in it, without prejudice or interest. So long as he does this he does his duty by the college, whether his convictions suit one party or another. The science of political economy points to free trade, all the free trade we can get, as a blessing to the human race, the non-capitalist class especially. 'Moderate' protection and protection to 'promising industries' are mere figures of speech to save a lost cause.

I participate to some extent in public discussions on questions of public interest, many of which are now economical. I appear on the platform and in private as an advocate of free trade. The college is not responsible for me and has no authority over me when I address my fellow citizens on a public question. I distinguish between my work in college and my public work according to my own sense of propriety. I send you some of my pamphlets.

Yours sincerely,

W. G. SUMNER.

The onslaught upon Sumner which his Evarts letter occasioned was augmented by the feeling which his statements about the Willimantic Linen Company created. These were made in a lecture on ''The Forgotten Man,'' delivered in Brooklyn, January 30, 1883, and gave rise to the famous controversy between Sumner and Colonel W. E. Barrows. Colonel Barrows was the president and general manager of the Linen Company, and is described by the *New Haven Palladium* as the gentleman ''who in one day at the Atlanta Exposition, in 1881, picked, spun, wove, dyed and made into clothing Georgia cotton, worn by Governors Bigelow and Colquitt at a reception held the same evening in that city. During the Commencement at Yale last year the degree of A.M. was conferred upon him,—the first mechanic, not a graduate, upon whom that honor has been bestowed. He is regarded by many as a man who more thoroughly understands the relations of capital and labor than any other man in New England.''

How the trouble began between the manufacturer and Professor Sumner is best told by Sumner himself:

New Haven, Conn.,
Feb. 10, 1883.

To the Editor of the *Register:*

In my lecture on the 'Forgotten Man' I said: 'All the burdens (of philanthropy, social quackery and jobbery) fall on him or on her, for it is time to remember that the Forgotten Man is not seldom a woman. When you go to Willimantic they will show you, with great pride, the splendid thread mills there, and challenge you to say that a policy is not good which has produced such results. They say that those mills would not exist but for the protective tariff. If that is the case, let us look at the Forgotten Man. I am told that there are sewing women in this country who earn fifty cents a day of twelve hours and provide the thread. On the cost of every spool of thread more than one cent is a tax. It is paid, not to get the thread, for that could be got without it, but to get the Willimantic Linen Company's mill, which is not worth having, but is a nuisance because it makes thread harder to get than it would be if there were no such concerns. If a woman earns fifty cents in twelve hours, she earns a spool of thread, as nearly as may be in an hour. If she uses a spool of thread per day, she works fifteen minutes every day to support the Willimantic Linen Company, which in 1882 paid ninety-five per cent dividends to its stockholders. If you go to look at the mill it will captivate your imagination, and if you

see its operatives you will be gratified by their prosperity, until you remember all the sewing women in all
the garrets, and all the laborers' wives and daughters
scattered in the tenements and cottages of the country,
spending their hours of labor, not to get goods, but to
pay for a system which makes it harder for them to get
the goods, a system of which, at Willimantic, you are
seeing the beneficiaries and forgetting the victim.'

On Saturday, February third, I received a long dispatch from Mr. Barrows, giving statistics of wages paid
at Willimantic. Later I received another, inquiring if
I had stated that hundreds of women at Willimantic were
paid fifty cents a day. I replied that I had never in my
life made any statement about the wages paid at Willimantic. On Monday I received a letter from Mr. Barrows complaining that his establishment had been singled
out, and saying that I ought to correct the erroneous
report of my lecture. I replied that I had learned to
economize my equanimity by never reading reports of
any of my lectures or speeches; that I could not afford
to correct, either for my own sake or that of others, all
mistakes made in reports; that I would correct any mistakes made by me, but not one made by a reporter. I
then said that I had stated that the dividend in 1882 was
ninety-five per cent; that I did this on the authority of
a newspaper slip taken from a Willimantic paper; that
this was the only statement of fact made by me, and that
I was willing to be corrected. Up to this writing I have
not heard from Mr. Barrows. He telegraphed me what
the wages are, but he has not yet replied as to the
dividend.

I always want to be right on my facts, and so I applied
to an ex-stockholder for facts about the dividend. They
are given to me thus:

January, 1882, 10 per cent. dividend on $1,500,000.
July   1882, 10 per cent. dividend on $2,000,000.
January, 1883, 8 per cent. dividend on $2,000,000.

In July, 1882, or just before, the stock was increased by $500,000 distributed to stockholders at par, viz., 25 per share, when the market quotation was $75, and none offered. The profit on this stock dividend was, therefore, $1,000,000. The first dividend in 1882 was $150,000, and the second $200,000. Other authorities put the stock dividend earlier and make these dividends $400,000. The total profit to stockholders in 1882 was, then, at least $1,350,000 on the old capital of $1,500,000. On these figures then I will own a mistake. It was not ninety-five per cent. It was ninety per cent.

I am very glad that I have been forced to publish this. I have no spite against the Willimantic Company any more than any other company. Who will say that I am not right to try to make people understand the truth about this tariff system? Who will say that I am not right to expose the fallacy which is involved in all the arguments drawn from the wages of the operatives and the beauty of the mills? Who pays the wages? The Linen Company—out of its ninety per cent, perhaps? The people who use thread pay the wages, the expenses, the dividends, and all the rest. Now every soul uses thread. The babies' first garment and the dead man's last one use thread. That is one reason why the thread mill is one of the cases which ought to be used. My chief reason for using it, however, was to get a case which would bring in the women.

The whole point of my lecture on the Forgotten Man is to bring out the forgotten, scattered, neglected classes, who pay, and to attack the fallacy of fixing one's attention on the big crowds, the large interests, the petted classes. I affirm that there is always somebody who pays, and that it is always the sober, honest, industrious, economical men or women, who attend no meetings, pass no resolutions, never go to the lobby, are never mentioned in the newspapers, but just work and save and pay.

I see it stated that the Linen Company have invited people to go and see their mill. They want to work the

fallacy over again. I hope that people will go, but I
hope that they will, when they get there, try to call up
the Forgotten Man and the Forgotten Woman; the bigger the mill the bigger the load those persons have got
to bear.

I suppose that it is too much to expect that people will
take in, without considerable study, the notion that when
we want thread, we want thread as cheap as we can get
it; we do not want a thread mill. If a mill does not get
us thread cheaper than we could get it elsewhere, what is
it for? It is not an industry; it is a public institution
like a poorhouse or an insane asylum supported by taxation, and the more sad the bigger it is.

Very respectfully,
W. G. SUMNER.

For a month or more the controversy continued
with much sparring back and forth regarding dividends and the cost of thread here and in Canada.
Colonel Barrows invited the faculty and the senior
class of Yale to visit Willimantic and see for themselves the protective side of the argument as exemplified by the company's mills, their operatives, and
their conditions and surroundings. The senior class
accepted the invitation because, as one of them said,
it was an offer of a free ride and what they expected
was an interesting trip. That is what they got.
Alighting from the train, according to the *Willimantic
Journal,* they marched to the mill, where all were introduced to Colonel Barrows, who shook hands cordially with each. After eating an excellent luncheon
served by a well-known Hartford caterer they were
approached by a bevy of young ladies from the wind-
ing room, wearing the traditional blue of Yale, and
bearing baskets of souvenirs which they "attached by
their deft fingers to the coats of the not unwilling col-

legians.'' After the plant had been thoroughly inspected the students reassembled in the packing room. There Colonel Barrows, stepping upon a table, announced that he was ready for questions. Some were asked, and the Colonel used them as a basis for a lecture on the advantages of protection; after which the boys returned to New Haven with as much regard for Billy Sumner as ever.

This controversy with the Linen Company occasioned much interest and newspaper comment throughout the East, and the *New York Tribune* published the following article:

HOW TO FIND A WHITE ELEPHANT

Advice Tendered to Mr. Barnum—The Yale College Jungle

It is rumored in the menagerie and circus circles of the country that the irrepressible and indefatigable Mr. Barnum has announced his intention of rendering the Greatest Show on Earth still greater by climaxing and cap-stoning its manifold attractions with an elephant fair of complexion as one of Oscar Wilde's lilies. Rumor further has it that Mr. Barnum has been striving for many months to secure such an elephant, but all to no purpose. In the plenitude of his resources of experience, ingenuity, enterprise and hard cash he is unable to possess himself of a white elephant. . . . It is understood that he has scoured India in pursuit of his object. But we have yet to see it stated that he has gone to white elephant hunting in the United States. It must be, therefore, that he is laboring under the impression that the fauna of North America is not inclusive of the white elephant. So in order to correct such an absurd preconception we have a suggestion to make to Mr. Barnum. Phineas T., the first spare day you have just you take a run up from your native Bridgeport to New Haven and

290 WILLIAM GRAHAM SUMNER

see if you do not find what you wish. Obviously it never occurred to you that white elephants were indigenous to your own Connecticut; but never mind—try the experiment. Arriving at New Haven, take a hack for Yale College, and reaching that institution, ask to see the authorities and tell them what it is you yearn for. If you follow this advice the chances are you will return home the proud proprietor of your long-sought-for white elephant. For the public begins to suspect, Mr. Barnum, that Yale College now harbors in one of her professorships a white elephant which it stands her in hand to part with. It is rather a bumptious and self-conceited elephant, and it has acquired, after much practice, a swagger as colossal as it is comical. If the animal passes into your hands, Mr. Barnum, you may find it necessary to keep a sharp watch upon its movements to prevent it from endeavoring to sit down upon the rest of the menagerie in case the rest of the menagerie does not roar in harmony with its own tones. That is the sort of elephant it is. And still it is hardly to be regarded as dangerous. Its bark is simply immense, but its bite is comparatively harmless. It is also a trick elephant. It has taught itself to stand upon its capacious ear and call the royal Bengal tiger, the Numidian lion and the gray forest eagle 'Puerilities,' 'trash,' and 'tariff-built frauds.' This program is always voted very amusing—by sub-Freshmen. It is but fair to mention, Mr. Barnum, that it is a spavined elephant. Sad but true. Some days ago it had the misfortune to entangle and rupture itself in the meshes of some Willimantic thread with which it was recklessly fooling. Since this casuality it has not been so handsome as it was before, but it is believed that it knows more.

A word to the wise is sufficient. We have always regarded you as a wise man, Mr. Barnum. And if the moment you finish reading this article you do not at once proceed to pack your gripsack for New Haven, you are not the enterprise incarnate we have taken you for.

So disturbed by Sumner's free-trade teachings did some become that in 1886 Professor R. E. Thompson, of the University of Pennsylvania, was secured by them to deliver a course of lectures on protectionism at Yale. His coming seems to have been with the knowledge and consent of Professor Sumner, for previous to it President Porter wrote him the following letter:

Yale College, New Haven, Conn.
1886.

My Dear Sir:

I go to Washington for two or three days and for this reason I write the following, not being certain of finding you and being very much driven by work. Several gentlemen, mostly if not entirely from Hartford, propose to the Corporation to defray the expense of a course of lectures in exposition and defense of the protective system, to be open to the students of the University, stipulating only that they shall be given in a proper fashion and asking the privilege perhaps of being consulted in the nomination of the lecturer. On several occasions within the last ten years, when a similar project has been suggested to me, I have uniformly met the proposal with a certain favor as likely to be agreeable to yourself and all parties. I presume so at present, but do not think it proper to proceed any further till I have your consent and sympathy and that of Professor Farnam. I have made some inquiries and find that Professor R. E. Thompson, of Philadelphia, would willingly give such a course. If the plan and demand are acceptable to the heads of the departments in the college and scientific school, I will call a meeting of the Prudential Committee to authorize the giving of the course, it being scarcely worth while to call the Corporation.

In great haste,

N. Porter.

P.S. I presume that the course will consist, if given,
of ten to twelve lectures, one or two a week.
Prof. W. G. Sumner.

Professor Thompson came and delivered his lectures. After hearing them, it is said, the students
were more strongly committed to free trade than ever.
An attempt was made by some of Sumner's friends to
arrange a debate between him and Professor Thompson in Philadelphia. The plan did not succeed for the
reason stated in a letter to Professor Sumner from
Mr. George G. Mercer. "I went to the University
yesterday," he says, "and, on my own responsibility,
asked Professor Thompson whether he would debate
with you under the auspices of the Pennsylvania Club.
He said no, that he had never been able to discover
in himself any adaptability for debate, and for that
reason had already declined two or three like invitations from Clubs in Brooklyn and New York to debate
with you. In my humble judgment the Professor's
head is level. I think our best chance to arrange such
a debate is to find some one who has never met you,
and who does not know how much it hurts."

Among those whose criticism of him awakened
Sumner's ire was the Reverend Thomas Kinnicutt
Beecher, brother of Henry Ward Beecher. This gentleman made the mistake of charging Sumner, in a
rather sneering way, with looseness in the use of
terms. If there was anything upon which Sumner
prided himself, it was in knowing what he meant,
saying precisely what he meant, and always having
abundance of facts to substantiate his statements.
Consequently, Mr. Beecher received the following
reply which suggests why some people came to hate
Sumner.

New Haven, January 12, 1883.

To the Editor of the *Gazette and Free Press:*

I am not surprised that my remark that 'the United States has rarely been governed by its best public opinion' should provoke comment. It looks as if it assailed one of the great orthodox political sentiments. It has an air as if it might cover the heresy that educated men know more than uneducated men. What is 'the *best* public opinion'? There are those faithful servants at the altar of political dogmatism who are sure to prick up their ears at such an expression.

I suppose that any man accustomed to give spiritual and moral advice to his fellow men will know what is meant by a man who does not live up to his best convictions.

When I speak of the United States as not having been governed by its best public opinion I mean that its acts and fortunes have not always been guided by the sober, deliberate judgment of those among the people who work and think. I do not believe that the political history of the United States in regard to slavery between 1836 and 1860 was controlled by the sober judgment and good sense of the people, but by party spirit and sectional prejudices. I do not believe that the Mexican War was brought about in accordance with the good sense and intelligent will of the American people, i.e., 'the best public opinion' of 1844-5. I do not believe that the Kansas-Nebraska act was an expression of the sober, intelligent judgment of the voting population of the whole country. I think it was a political move which was dictated by selfish ambition and passed by chicane. I do not believe that a protective tariff has ever had the support of the good sense and better judgment of the American people. The old Jackson party was opposed to the protective theory. The whole history of the tariff is a repetition of fraud, chicane, and corrupt bargain, from 1816 until to-day. The reënactment of the protective law by the republicans when they came to power was the result of a corrupt bargain to carry Pennsylvania in 1860, and the present excessive protection was forced on the country during the war by a fraud on the patriotic willingness of the people to endure high taxation for the sake of the war. If a man votes for a tariff because he thinks that it enables him to levy taxes on his neighbors when he sells them goods, I do not count his vote into 'the best public opinion' of the country. I do not believe that reconstruction was guided by the sober good sense of the people. I think that men who ought to have been wiser and better gave way to vindictiveness and party spirit when questions of reconstruction came up. I do not believe that the river and harbor act of 1882 expressed the sober judgment and will of the mass of the people. I do not believe that the good sense of our people or their best public opinion reached a correct expression in the pension act, which now taxes us on an average two dollars per head, man, woman, child, and baby, including pensioners, to squander gifts among ourselves. I think that the last two named laws, even, are plainly due, not to the 'best public opinion' of the nation, but to vulgar political ambition and party cowardice. Yet both are laws and have passed into history.

I am often mistaken in my views of opinion, but I am under pretty heavy bonds (such, for instance, as very few preachers lie under) to know what I mean by anything I say, and to know by what facts and authorities I mean to justify my assertions if they are questioned. I have said enough above to show what I meant by the remark which has been criticized, and to show that I had some facts in mind which deserve sober consideration from any one who aspires to give a vote in 'the best public opinion' of his time. Some men, I know, when their pet dogmas are questioned, hop over a fact like a bird over a twig,—shake your wings and over you go. It is rarely my fortune to please such people.

Yours very respectfully,

W. G. SUMNER.

Much notoriety came to Sumner because of a statement made in the classroom regarding marriage and ideals. In calling attention to the fact that ideals in the nature of things rarely come true, and that under the vicissitudes of life they constantly change as one grows older, he remarked that "only ten per cent of the married couples can say at the end of their lives that their ideals of married life have been realized."

The newspapers, however, very generally represented him as saying that ninety per cent of marriages are failures. In this error they persisted in spite of repeated corrections by the Professor's friends. A flood of letters came to him from all over the country, varying in character from courteous discussions of the statement to such notes as the following:

New York, February 16, 1900.

Prof. William G. Sumner,
New Haven, Conn.
DEAR SIR:
    You should see a doctor at once, as your stomach must be in a very bad condition.

Respectfully,

. . . .

People wrote to the newspapers on the subject and editors commented upon it at length. A "Happy Wife" called upon the women of Brooklyn to shame the Professor, and "A Bachelor, Thank Goodness" called for cheers in his honor. President Eliot didn't believe Sumner had said so ridiculous a thing. The incorrigible optimist, Colonel Thomas Higginson, who later said that he had seen the world go to the devil a dozen times without arriving, cried, "Oh! he's wrong, very wrong!" Alice Freeman Palmer hoped the Professor had not made the statement, and Julia Ward Howe declared that marriage was an institution of such value to society that "it is not to be spoken of in so trivial a way." A priest in South Bethlehem showed his resentment of the Professor's ungallant remark by announcing that whenever his parishioners desired to marry he would perform the ceremony free of charge. Finally it became necessary to assure the general public, unfamiliar with Sumner's history, that he was not a fool or a misanthrope, one disappointed in love or unhappily married, but a man of attainments and distinguished career, regarded as one of the closest reasoners on the Yale Faculty, with a delightful home and two children.

Sumner's strictures upon socialism and his hostility to the imperialistic policy of the late nineties again subjected him both to harsh criticism and to abuse. From a San Francisco socialist came the following:

San Francisco, November 4, 1904.

MR. WILLIAM G. SUMNER:

Sir: I have just finished reading your article in reply to Mr. Sinclair's article on socialism, and hasten to write this that you may know what at least one socialist thinks of you and your kind.

You have in no wise answered Sinclair's article, not even in one particular, but you have begged the question throughout and shown that you are incapable of answering the simplest questions in industrial affairs.

In your reply the most prominent thing is an intimation that the socialists intend to shoot their way to victory. I suppose you infer this from what Mr. Sinclair said in reference to a possible revolution brought about by the vast number of unemployed that will soon be facing starvation in both this country and Europe. In this you are mistaken, for if ever there is a bloody revolution it will be by those who believe as you do, but who are not so fortunate as yourself in having gained the favor of powerful capitalists. Why, Sir, we socialists do not believe in violence and would not shoot even John D. Rockefeller, or even an insignificant intellectual prostitute such as yourself.

When we have established the coöperative commonwealth, the task of enlightening the criminals and paupers will be great and will require great labor, but it will be a light and pleasant task compared with that of making useful citizens of the present college professors, and what we shall do with them is an unsolved problem to me.

Yours without respect,

. . . .

P.S. Mr. Sinclair would be very foolish to answer such a puerile and evasive article as yours, as there is nothing in it.

In connection with the same article a letter to the editor of *Collier's Weekly* from Daniel Kisam Young concluded with this paragraph:

It is as astonishing as it is terrible that the innate brutality of the Capitalistic System should allow such falsehoods to be taught to the students of a respectable college and it is no wonder that the college is more renowned for its football team and its athletics than for its profound students in Political Economy. The brutality of Prof. Sumner's article and the brutality of modern football are correlated in the degenerate Capitalistic family.

"The Conquest of the United States by Spain" brought forth many a cry of pain. The *New York Sun* seems to have been wounded most deeply of all.

We have just received proofs of an article written by Prof. William G. Sumner of Yale University, from which, the sender informs us, we are permitted to make extracts, 'though under no circumstances' are we 'to print the entire article.'

Both the permission and the prohibition are unnecessary. We have no intention of burdening the columns of the *Sun* with either the whole or any part of an article which has for its title 'The Conquest of the United States by Spain,' though it is by a Yale Professor and is typical of the smart and shallow teaching with which that institution has suffered him so long to pervert the intelligence of its students.

Possibly college boys may be imposed on by this article's pretensions to philosophy and its cocksure assertions, but it adds nothing really deserving of consideration to the discussion of the national problems brought to us as a consequence of our swift and complete victory in the war with Spain. Perhaps, however, when the Yale students learn from their elders that this same Prof. Sumner has opposed in the same spirit the whole economical progress of this country during the last generation they will be wise enough to let what he says on the subject pass in at one ear and out at the other.

The only considerable impression the article makes on us is of the necessity for the employment of some functionary to whom shall be assigned the duty of correcting the written English of Yale professors in order that any of the students who may happen to read it shall not be corrupted by a vicious literary example.

According to an undated clipping which he carefully preserved, this same paper proposed a special degree for Sumner and men of his type.

The *New York Sun* has invented a new degree for the college professors who make fools of themselves in the treatment of questions of national or international

politics, and has already found two worthy of the honor.
The *Sun* says: 'Doctor W. S. Scott, described as a former president of the Ohio State University, has read
Prof. William Graham Sumner's history of the conquest
of the United States by Spain and has been fired to imi-
tate the gentle New Haven sage.' According to great
Scott, 'the invasion of Porto Rico was unjustifiable: the
naval battle at Manila was without justifiable excuse:
Spain should not cede Porto Rico and the Philippines,
and any argument which would justify the keeping of the
islands would justify human slavery.' Dr. Scott seems
to be fully as good as Billy Sumner. We recommend
both for the degree of 'D.Ph.' For the enlightenment
of those who may not understand the meaning of the
initial letters, we venture the information that the 'Ph.'
stands for phool.

To compensate for all this abuse, Sumner was constantly receiving expressions of appreciation and
gratitude from widely different sources. Perhaps
none of these gave him greater pleasure than such as
the following letter contains:

Mount Vernon, August 24, 1878.
Professor Sumner,
DEAR SIR:
Permit me as a laboring man to thank you for the able
and fearless manner you spoke before the congressional
labor committee. You are the only man who has *dared*
to go into the den of manufacturing lions and attack the
protection tariff, which is entailing upon us laborers and
our children more distress than any one cause, as all protection is designed to raise the price of *home* commodities. . . . Protection is only secured as foreign goods are
kept out, while revenue is increased as foreign goods come
in. I do not intend to teach you anything, but to let
you see that we as laborers understand when even a

learned man testifies whether he is guided by the inspiration of truth and justice or is the mere tool of the capitalist in disguise. With the most sincere respect for testimony, allow me to thank you. May our Heavenly Father raise up more such men who are clear upon all the topics in Political Economy which you have been pleased to bring before the committee.

With high esteem,
Truly yours,
John Newell.

That the effect of Sumner's utterances, though tending somewhat to alienate men of the capitalistic class, was not altogether detrimental to Yale's financial interest is disclosed by this interesting correspondence:

Durham, Conn., Oct. 21, 1878.

Prof. W. G. Sumner,
Dear Sir:

I send you herewith a copy of a note addressed to me in connection with a donation of $5,000 for Yale College. The donor is seventy-two years of age and a very shrewd observer of men and things. He chooses in the matter of a donation to be nameless. It is a full satisfaction to an honest and true man to be able simply to bear his testimony to the truth. But to know that his testimony has borne good fruits makes his cup to run over. May this your joy be fulfilled.

Yours very truly,
A. S. Chesebrough.

The enclosed note opens with these words:

When I saw in the *New York Times* of August 23 the excellent and wise words of Professor Sumner of Yale College before Mr. Hewitt's Committee, I concluded to double the amount before spoken of (making it $5,000

instead of $2,500); convinced that Yale College is a good
and safe place for the keeping and using of property and
the sustaining of civilization when endangered by ignorance, rascality, demagogues, repudiationists, rebels, cop-
perheads, communists, Butlers, strikers, protectionists,
and fanatics of sundry roots and sizes.

Such tokens of appreciation were no doubt highly
pleasing to Sumner, though by the outcry which his
utterances raised he was seldom greatly disturbed.
On the contrary he took a rather grim enjoyment in
it. If he was shown to be mistaken he was quick to
acknowledge the fact, but the mis-statements and misrepresentations of others regarding him he seldom
corrected. "If I tried to," he used to say, "I would
have little time for anything else." He would hit
back hard if the maintenance of his position or the
demolishment of a dangerous error seemed to demand,
but to personal abuse and attempts to undermine him
professionally he paid no attention. He strove always
to be fair, but he spared no one's feelings, and as for
himself, he asked no quarter and he bore no malice.

In regard to history it seems to me right to say that history has value just on account of the truth it contains and not otherwise. Consequently the historian who leaves things out, or puts them in, for edifying, patriotic, or other effect, sins against the critical-scientific method and temper which I have described. In fact, patriotism is another root of non-reality, and the patriotic basis is hostile to critical thinking.

The Scientific Attitude of Mind.

CHAPTER XIII

AUTHOR

SUMNER was a prolific writer. Letters, book reviews, and magazine articles flowed steadily from his pen, and now and then a book appeared. For the copiousness of this output there was a twofold reason. In the first place he felt it his duty to express his convictions on public questions; and in the second place he needed the money which his writings supplied. As was the case with all college professors his salary was small, and he always felt himself hampered by the scantiness of his material resources. He once amused William C. Whitney greatly by the gratification he displayed over an increase in the compensation granted him by the Yale Corporation. "How much did they boost you, Bill?" asked Mr. Whitney. "Two hundred and fifty dollars a year," replied Sumner. And Whitney, to whom at that time two hundred and fifty dollars was as the small dust of the balance, roared with laughter.

The amount of writing which Sumner did would have been impossible for most men cumbered by the same cares and subject to a like number of calls. He himself was equal to it only because of the fact that he wrote with extraordinary ease. The manual labor involved was the chief tax upon him. His ideas arranged themselves in his mind, he says, faster than he could transfer them to paper. There was never any hesitation as to what to say; there was never any time lost waiting for inspiration. To the niceties of

305

rhetoric he paid little attention, especially in his later years. A pedant might point out many infelicities of composition. With respect to facts, he exercised the most scrupulous care; regarding form, he was not so punctilious.

His major writings may be divided roughly into three classes; histories of an economic nature, biographies, and essays. One work, and that the most important of all, "Folkways," falls outside these categories. "Folkways" is an exhaustive and convincing study of the sociological importance of usages, manners, customs, mores, and morals. In a subsequent chapter its main thesis will be outlined. It contains Sumner's particular contribution to sociological investigation and theory, and its influence is likely to have an extent and permanence greater than that of anything else he produced.

In the field of economic and political history, his more ambitious works include the "History of the American Currency" of which mention has already been made; "Monetary Development," a study incorporated in "The First Century of the Republic" written by T. D. Woolsey and others; "The Financier and the Finances of the American Revolution"; and the "History of Banking in the United States." For the most part these are books for the specialist rather than for the general reader, and the former will often find them tedious. They show vigor, thoroughness, and industry in their author, and great skill in expounding financial laws and conditions. The abundance of historical detail which they contain makes them valuable for reference, but confusing and wearisome. Due proportion, proper subordination, and logical form are wanting, and there is no color or charm of style.

The biographies are but three in number and these, biographies of a special kind, for they are as much studies in the political conditions amid which their subjects lived, as portrayals of the men themselves. The life of Andrew Jackson might well be described as a history of his times with special reference to their effect upon him and his influences upon them. Regarding the life of Hamilton, Sumner states: "I have undertaken to show *how, and in what sense, Alexander Hamilton was one of the makers of the American State.* I have constructed my book with just that and nothing else in view." Robert Morris he first buried beneath the many details of the finances of the American Revolution. Later he resurrected and separated him in some degree therefrom, but even in the "Life" one feels that the author's main interest is in the finances rather than in the financier. All three are biographies properly speaking, however, for one leaves them without complete knowledge of the careers of those with whom they deal perhaps, but with a distinct impression of the kind of men they were, the chances that came to them, and what they did with them. Material to which Sumner did not have access has since become available, but his "Alexander Hamilton" and his "Andrew Jackson" still remain authorities. Regarding the former, Samuel E. Morison, Professor of American History in Oxford University, England, has recently remarked, "It is, in my opinion, the best life of Hamilton that has ever been published"; and of the latter, Professor John S. Bassett of Smith College, one of Jackson's later biographers, says, "It is a remarkable summary of the career of this remarkable man," and "I cannot fail to express admiration for the succinct, calm treatment in Professor Sumner's book."

"Andrew Jackson as a Public Man" was published in 1883 in the American Statesman series. It is a keen, unemotional study made, not by a partisan, nor by a proud American, but by one who sets forth the facts unexaggerated and unsoftened whether they please or hurt, indifferent to the cherished traditions which they may destroy. In the cold northern light which Sumner throws upon him we see Jackson as a product of the frontier life in which he grew up. The qualities which it bred were his qualities; its code was his code. Like the most of his contemporaries he was of a quarrelsome disposition. "Instead of making peace he exhausted all the chances of conflict which offered themselves." He kept alive feuds and fought duels. He was neither better nor worse than the general run of men in his time, but he was greatly favored by chance. Among his worst misfortunes was the lack of that discipline which a good home affords. There is no warrant in his case for the picture, so familiar in political biography, "of the orphan boy hewing his way up to the presidency by industry and self-denial. If the information is trustworthy, Jackson was gay, careless, rollicking, fond of horses, racing, cock-fighting, and mischief." He studied law for a while, but soon fell back into the position of a farmer and storekeeper. "There is no evidence that he was dissatisfied with his circumstances, and set himself to work to get out of them." He was not an ambitious man. It was his military operations which gave him fame and popularity. In these he displayed "energy, perseverance, and skill of a high order"; but all his personal acts show him "ignorant, perverse, quarrelsome, and astonishingly indiscreet." Everything that interested him took on some relation to his person, and in this fact is the keynote to his character. "An opinion or a prejudice became at once for him a personal right or interest. To approve it and further it was to win his gratitude and friendship. To refuse or oppose it was to excite his animosity." He was swept into the presidency on the rising tide of democracy. The masses felt, "He is one of us." "He stands by us." "He is not proud and does not care for style, but only for plenty of what is sound, strong, and good." "He thinks just as we do about this." As President he was skillfully manipulated by his "kitchen cabinet." Whatever he did was from some personal motive. Because Clay condemned Jackson's invasion of Florida during the Seminole War, he evermore hated and opposed him. His opposition to nullification was due to his enmity for Calhoun. He fought The National Bank because he had been made to believe that it had worked against his interests. During his administration "it came his way to do some good, to check some bad tendencies and to strengthen some good ones; but the moment the historian tries to analyze these acts, and to bring them for purposes of generalization into relations with the standpoint or doctrine by which Jackson acted, that moment he perceived that Jackson acted from spite, pique, instinct, prejudice, or emotion, and the influence he exerted sinks to the nature of an incident or an accident." [1] When Jackson died, "he had had honors beyond anything which his own heart had ever coveted. His successes had outrun his ambitions. He had held more power than any other American had ever possessed. He had been idolized by the great majority of his countrymen, and had been surfeited with adulation. He had been thwarted in hardly any-

[1] "Andrew Jackson," Houghton, Mifflin and Company, Boston, 1882, p. 279.

thing on which he had set his heart. He had had his desire upon all his enemies. He lived to see Clay defeated again, and to help bring it about. He saw Calhoun retire in despair and disgust. He saw the bank in ruins; Biddle arraigned on a criminal charge, and then dead, broken-hearted. In his last years he joined the church, and on that occasion under the exhortation of his spiritual adviser, he professed to forgive all his enemies in a body. It does not appear that he ever repented of anything, ever thought he had been in the wrong in anything, or ever forgave an enemy as a specific individual." [2]

Such is the impression of "Old Hickory" which one gets from Sumner's story. That he had virtues is not denied, but they were mostly of the negative type. He was as faithful a friend as he was an implacable enemy. He was not vain or conceited. He never showed any marked selfishness. He had a great deal of *amour propre*. "He was above every species of money vice; he was chaste and domestic in his habits; he was temperate in every way; he was not ambitious in the bad sense." [3] But in the qualities of statesmanship and the personal characteristics necessary to public service of a high character he was lacking.

Even the notoriety which Jackson has gained as the reputed originator of the spoils system, Sumner does not allow him. "It is a crude and incorrect notion that Andrew Jackson corrupted the civil service. His administration is only the date at which a corrupt use of the spoils of the public service as a cement for party organization under democratic republican self-government, having been perfected into a highly

2 "Andrew Jackson," Houghton, Mifflin and Company, Boston, 1882, p. 386.
3 *Ibid.*, p. 80.

finished system in New York and Pennsylvania, was first employed on the federal area. The student who seeks to penetrate the causes of the corruption of the civil service must go back to study the play of human nature under the political dogmas and institutions of the States named. He cannot rest satisfied with the explanation, 'Andrew Jackson did it.' " [4]

Throughout the book, as in almost everything Sumner wrote, one feels the presence of the teacher and the preacher. It was as impossible for him to appear in any other character as it is for the Ethiopian to change his skin. To warn and instruct was as natural to him as breathing. In this instance his convictions are not obtruded, but they are clearly indicated. There is "an unformulated dogma," he says, "which seems to command a great deal of faith, to the effect that if a man is only sufficiently ignorant, his whims and notions constitute 'plain common sense.' " The evil which results in public life from the practical application of this faith is one of the truths which the book sets forth. It also serves to substantiate indirectly the wisdom of *laissez faire*, for it illustrates the folly of empiricism in government and the calamities which follow arbitrary interference with the natural trend of affairs. Without any question, Sumner hoped the book would bring home these truths very forcibly to men's minds.

A less interesting study is "Alexander Hamilton," published in 1890, in the Makers of America series. Here Sumner had a greater man to portray, but not so striking a personality or so spectacular a career. This biography, like the earlier, is rich in historical background, keen in analysis, and strong in statement of situations, but it is written with less vigor, its

4 *Ibid.*, p. 147.

utterances are not so terse and pungent, and there are evidences of haste in composition.

In reply to an inquiry, Sumner once wrote the *New York Times* this statement: "I think that the three men to whom we are most indebted are Franklin, Washington, and Hamilton." For Hamilton as a statesman, Sumner had great admiration; but he did not rate him highly as a financier, declaring that in that rôle his attainments and achievements had been greatly exaggerated. "His bank was a paper money machine, and the scheme of it contained financial fallacies which he never conquered; but the boldness of the scheme, and the skill with which it was aimed at the difficulties of the situation, are most remarkable. It is the statesmanship of it which is grand, not the finance. He had seized the chief faults in the existing institutions of government. He says he wants 'system and vigor.' "[5] "His writings," Sumner declares, "show a remarkable amount of confusion in regard to money, capital and debt"[6] and he was under the dominion of the most vicious fallacies with reference to banking. His statements about trade show that he was "completely befogged in the mists of mercantilism," for they are based on the doctrines of the first quarter of the eighteenth century. Unfortunately, according to Sumner, it was Hamilton's belief that trade may be beneficially stimulated by prudent aids and encouragement on the part of the government. "It was impossible that a masterful man like Hamilton should consent to that theory of statesmanship which would have taught him to confine his efforts to an intelligent promotion of growth, with the removal of obstacles and gentle impulses at critical moments, in the direction

[5] "Alexander Hamilton," New York, Dodd, Mead & Co., 1890, p. 114.
[6] *Ibid.*, p. 150.

which his genius indicated as the path of prosperity.
. . . Herein lies the secret of the catastrophe which he
brought upon his own political theory and his own
political enterprises. He naturally could not consent
to a policy which would have dictated to him to withhold his rash hands, when his whole being was in a
quiver to seize that which he thought was going
wrong, and impress upon it at once, and with un-
shrinking reliance on his own judgment, the form and
tendency which he thought for the best."[7]

The greatness of Hamilton, as Sumner pictures him,
lies in the fact that he had some pervading ideas as
to what the stability and growth of the new nation
required, and acted upon them with such force and
success as to be one of the "makers of America."
The faults in the public affairs of the United States,
at the outset, "were indolence, negligence, lack of
administrative energy and capacity, dislike of any
methodical, business-like system, and carelessness as
to money responsibility and credit." "The Union
was from the start at war with the turbulent, anar-
chistic elements which the revolution had set loose.
. . . Therefore the contest with anarchy and repudia-
tion was the great work which went to the making of
this nation at the end of the last century, and Alexander Hamilton was one of the leading heroes in it."[8]

The life of Robert Morris, published in 1892, is an
unadorned and rather monotonous recital of such
facts as are known about Morris—how he made his
money, his plan of action as Superintendent of Finance, his public life, social standing, business ven-
tures, and bankruptcy. The fact that it is made up
of material culled from "The Financier and Finances
of the American Revolution" detracts from its effec-

7 *Ibid.*, p. 178.   8 *Ibid.*, p. 13.

tiveness. It lacks the episodes, comments, and generalizations which gave to the earlier biographies much of their interest and value.

In these writings there is considerable which readers accustomed to look at the past through the beautifying haze of patriotic tradition will not find pleasing. Sumner cuts straight through the idealization and sentimentality which have attached themselves to events and persons and reveals their character and significance in all their nakedness. The following extract from "The Financier and the Finances of the American Revolution" is an example:

> It is certain that the military service never reached any excessive or distressing demand upon the population. In December, 1776, Washington had only about 3,000 soldiers left. At Valley Forge he had only about 5,000. It is very improbable that the number under arms at any one time ever reached 40,000, and much more likely that it never exceeded 30,000. If it is true that the colonies provided 25,000 for the Seven Years' War, when their population was under two million, the strain of the war of independence seems by comparison to have been very small.
>
> Such statements as are met with in respect to the quality of the rank and file of the army forbids us to believe that it was recruited from the body of the independent class of the population. (See Vol. I, p. 306.) It was made up of the social waste of the period, which, in an agricultural community, is always large in proportion to the total.
>
> On the whole if we compare the American war of independence with the struggle of the Dutch for independence, or with that of the Southern states in 1861, the sacrifice of the Revolutionary War must be considered trivial.[9]

9 Vol. II, p. 148.

The Boston Tea Party and the Boston Massacre
are portrayed as disgraceful episodes in American
history.

> The destruction of the tea was another act which had
> no rational connection with the purpose in view. It was
> the destruction of the property itself, about which a tax
> quarrel was pending. It was an act of mob violence, and
> destruction of property. Its effect to secure an abolition
> of the tax was not apparent. The only excuse for it that
> could be made was that it was really an act of war, a
> first step in overt resistance to law, against which it was
> intended to employ all means, even military resistance.
> In that view, however, it ought to be regarded as an act
> of war, entirely outside of constitutional resistance, or
> any of the methods of peace and order, and ought not
> to be held up to our children as a laudable and glorious
> act in the heroic period of our history. It would be in-
> teresting to know how many times within a hundred
> years that act has been quoted as a precedent by people
> who were engaging in some act of lawlessness.
>
> The Boston Massacre, likewise, turns out upon cool
> examination to be anything but an incident to be proud
> of. If we should hear that some boys and street idlers
> in the District of Columbia (which is taxed without being
> represented) had insulted a sentinel of the federal army
> on duty at Washington, had forced him to leave his post
> and call the guard, and that in the resulting mêlée be-
> tween the soldiers and the mob, some of the latter had
> been shot, we should not regard the latter as victims of
> a 'massacre.' [10]

The treatment of the Tories by the patriots, Sumner
declares to be the darkest blot on the history of the
Revolution.

[10] "Alexander Hamilton," pp. 42, 43.

This revolution, no more than others, could run its course without proscription, persecution, and confiscation. . . . The abuse of the tories was not executed under martial law, or in the neighborhood of the seat of war. If such had been the case our judgment upon it must be different. If the majority had forbidden the minority to take up arms, or to give intelligence and aid, or to organize; or if their stricter measures had been reserved for times and places where there was much at stake; or if even a regular tribunal had been charged with the duty, even though it might be a military tribunal,—the case would have been far different. If the whigs had been exasperated at persons who were by turns combatants and non-combatants, some extreme measures might have been excused. But the case was that the proscription was made general. Tories were formally hunted by detachments. They were exposed to the most cruel and humiliating personal abuse. They were punished for opinions, or at most for words. The punishments were in the hands of utterly irresponsible persons or committees.[11]

Of course, such fidelity to facts, irrespective of prevailing notions and feelings, gave offense and called forth abuse. The picture which Sumner drew of Andrew Jackson made the worshipers of that popular idol howl with rage. The *New York Journal* with difficulty found language sufficiently insulting to apply to him. In an article under date of March 21, 1903, entitled "Yale's Queer Contribution to American Biography," it says:

The recurrence of Andrew Jackson's birthday has sent many a man to the bookshelves during the past week with the object of freshening his knowledge of that fiery and resolute old hero, who did so much for his country

11 "Alexander Hamilton," pp. 53, 54.

and was so well loved and hated in his time. He was
a man.

That is why William Graham Sumner can't bear him
and, though Jackson has been dead this half century
and more, gets into a bad temper over him.

Who is this William Graham Sumner that his dislike
of Andrew Jackson should be worth mentioning here?

It is Yale's misfortune that Mr. Sumner should be
her Professor of Political and Social Science. And it is
the American public's misfortune that Houghton, Mifflin
& Co. should have printed a book about President Jackson by Mr. Sumner that is included in the 'American
Statesmen' series.

. . . .

The portrait which Mr. Sumner, the pigmy, has
drawn of himself while painting a pettily malignant
caricature of Jackson, the giant, is that of an anæmic
mugwump, a mentally and morally pigeon-breasted prig.
He has not the brains to enable him to understand characters different from and infinitely bigger and more complex than his own. He has the bitterness and arrogance
of littleness, and in his conceit lacks utterly the temper
of the historian.

. . . .

No man of judgment after reading Mr. Sumner's
life of Jackson would care to have Mr. Sumner for his
son's teacher in history, political and social science, or
anything else, for in this astonishing book Mr. Sumner
has made it painfully clear that Mr. Sumner is a
whiffet.

To this outburst, the *Hartford Courant* replied:

Professor Sumner of Yale has written a life of
Andrew Jackson for the 'American Statesmen' shelf
of popular biography. The General is not portrayed
with wings and a halo. There is no absurd swinging
of the incense pot. Professor Sumner is not that kind

of biographer and he is not that kind of democrat. . . .
The New York newspaper that has a young presidential
ambition on the premises chooses to take offense at this
plain talk about one of democracy's tutelaries. It describes Sumner's book as a 'drizzle of detraction' and it
genially calls the author a 'swaggering pedagogue,' and
'anæmic mugwump,' a 'pigeon-breasted prig,' and a
'whiffet.' And William G. Sumner will be as much disturbed as is the moon by Fido's yapping.

The *Courant* was quite right.

The *Journal's* review is an extreme and vulgar
example of the irritation Sumner's writings frequently created. It was not alone the unpalatable
facts presented which produced it, but the spirit and
tone of their presentation. Unquestionably Sumner
was something of an iconoclast. The things which he
smashed were false, and as a rule it was desirable
that they be shattered, but there is no escaping the
impression that he took much delight in the operation.
Disturbing the complacency of smug traditionalists
was not unpleasant to him, and even his most ardent
admirers would find it difficult to clear him entirely
of the charge of censoriousness. His father had re-
buked him for it as a youth, and his brother and
sister had writhed under it. It was too much a part
of his nature to be eliminated. He was more quick
to see error and evil than to discern excellence; it was
easier for him to blame than to praise. One feels the
breath of hot indignation far oftener than any warmth
of admiration. The times were always out of joint,
and Sumner always seemed quite certain just why
they were and what was needed to set them right.
This censoriousness, tinged as it invariably was with
a bit of intellectual arrogance, was responsible for
many of the hard things which were said about him.

By far the major part of Sumner's writings are in
the form of essays. Here he is at his best. Their
comparative brevity reduced the importance of structure to a minimum, and in taking up a single subject,
analyzing it, and disclosing its relationships and significance, he had no superior. For effectiveness it
would be hard to find a series of essays comparable
with those composing "What Social Classes Owe to
Each Other." They have movement, clarity, distinctness of outline, compactness, vigor, and striking-
ness of phrase. Their logic is cruel in its keenness
and coldness. They cut through sentimentality, error,
and sham like a two-edged sword. They suggest a rich
and varied background of information. One feels that
the author has more in reserve than he gives forth,
and that if the circumstances demanded, he could multiply proof and illustrations indefinitely. The essays
on "Liberty," while somewhat less popular in tone,
are equally remarkable for their thoroughness of exposition, concreteness of definition, searching analysis,
and general convincingness.

For the making of phrases Sumner had great apti-
tude, and his writings are replete with crisp, epigrammatic sayings. Apparently they formed themselves
spontaneously as he wrote; they never seem forced.
The following are taken almost at random from his
pages:

The most wise and patriotic citizen is not that one
who is most jealously tenacious of his rights, but that one
who is most soberly careful to fulfill his duties.

An opportunity missed may be a mere negative loss,
but an opportunity abused becomes a cause of positive
harm or of ruin.

Civilization does nothing but open chances. It does nothing to guarantee their advantageous effect.

We all agree that he is a good member of society who works his way up from poverty to wealth, but as soon as he has worked his way up we begin to regard him with suspicion as a dangerous member of society.

Anything which has a charitable sound and a kind-hearted tone generally passes without investigation because it is disagreeable to assail it.

Whenever we try to get paternalized we only succeed in getting policed.

The men who start out with the notion that the world owes them a living generally find that the world pays its debt in the penitentiary or the poor house.

Men whose minds have once closed with a good grip on a dogma never give it up on account of facts of experience, or on account of the absurdities into which it carries them,—least of all if they think it favorable to their interests.

There is no such conception as enough when more can be had.

Torture and burning are forbidden, not because the victim is not bad enough, but because we are too good.

Government by interests produces no statesmen, but only attorneys.

The only man who is fit to govern the community is the man who can govern himself.

The lack of form and the infelicities in composition to which reference has been made were not due to any absence of structural sense, or inability to write

AUTHOR 321

with smoothness and even beauty of style. Sumner's
early work often had much grace and finish. The
sermons, for the most part, are well planned, and
show considerable attention to detail. Passages of
sustained eloquence are not infrequent. The "Memorial Day Address," written in 1873, is a model of its
kind. Its closing paragraphs ring with sincerity, and
are not wanting in rhetorical effect.

Neither are we met to-day to exult over the defeated
party or to keep alive the rancor of civil strife. That
phase of this celebration is fading—happily fading out
of the public mind. Rather, now that the heat of the
conflict has subsided, we see distinctly the sad misfortune
of civil strife. The blows which we struck were blows at
our own body; the wounds which we gave left scars upon
ourselves; the destruction which we wrought fell upon
our own interests. This is the fatal character of all civil
strife, that the one commonwealth suffers the losses both
of the victors and the vanquished. The names of places
which we inscribe on our monuments are not those of a
foreign foe; they are our own and a part of the inheritance of our children. Fifty years hence, when your sons
visit Richmond and Charleston, they will hardly be able
to find a rebel or the son of a rebel there. They will find
a new race, energetic, patriotic, and American, a race of
colonists and immigrants from the North and from foreign lands, cramped by no inherited crime, warped by no
false traditions, and demoralized by no discord between
conscience and social institutions. They will smile at the
old folly and they will not meet with a frown the sons
of the victors. Already the movements are in progress which promise to rescue the South from the unprin-
cipled adventurers who have profited by the transition
period, and to bring it into political, social, and industrial harmony with the rest of the nation. Already
nature spreads her healing hand to conceal the physical

scars which war has made. The trees spring again on the devastated hillside. The sod spreads over the half-buried cannon-ball. The shrubs and bushes obliterate the lines of the entrenchments. The industry of man assists in the same work, and new industry and new achievements spring up on the ruins of the old. It is not the province of Memorial Day to reverse or retard this process and by tearing open again the old wounds to rescue anger and hate from oblivion. Its province is to keep alive in the hearts of the people the meaning and the value of the nation, the price which it cost, and the memory of those who died to purchase it. When men go to war for glory, let them have their reward. Pay it in the booming of cannon, in the blare of trumpets, and in the tinsel and trappings which perish in the using; but when men go to war for duty, let them also have their reward. Pay it in a new devotion to the duty for whose sake they fell; pay it in a nobler zeal in behalf of our rescued country; pay it in a loftier wisdom in public policy which shall destroy abuses before they grow so strong that it shall cost the blood of your sons to root them out.[12]

It is impossible to imagine Sumner writing in this manner in his later years. As time went on, style became less and less a matter of concern with him. There was nothing in his nature which compelled him to strive after perfection of form. While not lacking in appreciation for beauty, he was sensuous in an uncommonly small degree. His intellect and critical faculty dominated his emotions, and his intense moral feeling made him hostile to all pagan joy in the loveliness of nature or of art. The type of mind which he exhibited was the Hebraic rather than the Greek. He was intuitive, rugged, emphatic, fervently and relentlessly ethical, denunciatory, prophetic. For him

[12] "Challenge of Facts and Other Essays," pp. 361, 362.

to perceive a truth was to receive a command. He must straightway go forth and speak to the people, convince them of error and force them into the right way. His purpose was not to delight, but to reveal and to awaken. Not only did he lack the characteristics which constrain some to give painful attention to form, he distrusted all rhetorical artifices or striving for effect because of their tendency to conceal or misrepresent the truth. Accuracy of statement, clearness, and force were the only qualities he deemed important, and the Lancashire strain in him made him judge superfluous and foolish, if not pernicious, anything which did not add to the sense or convincingness of one's utterances. It was inevitable, therefore, that form should always be secondary with him, and his style plain, direct, incisive, and epigrammatic.

A college which is a refuge for mere academicians, thresh-
ing over the straw of a dead learning, is no better than a
monastery. Men who believe they can meet the great
interests of mankind which to-day demand satisfaction, by
a complacent reference to what satisfied them when they
were young, are simply building for themselves a fool's
paradise.

Our Colleges Before the Country.

CHAPTER XIV

COLLEGE OFFICIAL

THE duty which he owed to the college was always Sumner's first consideration. With this, writing and public activities were never permitted to interfere. He assumed his full share of administrative work, and shirked none of the drudgery that went with his office. For years, in addition to classroom routine, he read from three hundred to five hundred test papers weekly. The humblest task which the running of the college imposed he did not feel it beneath him to perform. In the days before the executive machinery had become highly developed, there fell to him and to Professor Edward S. Dana the tedious labor of arranging the term time schedules. "Many a hot summer's night," says the latter, "did we sit under a blazing gas jet, tormented by mosquitoes, struggling until the small hours of the morning with the exasperating difficulties which arose."

Sumner had not been long at the college before it was recognized that he was a person well fitted for duties involving student discipline. Those assigned to him he executed with vigor, fearlessness, and indifference to sentiment. On November 9, 1872, the faculty voted that the Thanksgiving Jubilee might be held in Alumni Hall under the supervision of Professors Northrup and Sumner. This Jubilee was one of the cherished institutions of the college year. It consisted of a series of ludicrous acts of different kinds arranged and carried out by the students. In the early seventies it had fallen into considerable disrepute because of its roughness and vulgarity. For five years Sumner censored and policed it. Finally he killed it. In a report to the faculty, made in 1873, he criticized the exhibition severely, mentioning as grounds of objection "the disorderly throwing of beans, nuts, etc., to the injury of the windows, wall, and pictures; the admission of townspeople; and the evasion of the law against female attire." The following year, accordingly, the Jubilee was permitted only under numerous and strict conditions. All the pictures near the stage were to be removed; one professor was to attend a dress rehearsal, and one the performance; nothing was to be exhibited which had not been rehearsed to the supervisor; there was to be no evasion of the law forbidding female attire; the entertainment was to be closed before twelve o'clock, and was to be terminated abruptly if disorder such as bean throwing occurred. Evidently these rules were not sufficient to check the license which had come to be associated with the celebration, for in 1876 Sumner presented a report which caused the faculty to refuse to sanction its recurrence.

It was Sumner again who, in 1874, headed a committee "to consider the question of disciplining certain sophomores and of abolishing the sophomore societies." An outrage perpetrated by the Phi Theta Psi society, a sophomore organization, upon the Gamma Nu society, a freshman fraternity, gave rise to the question. The matter consumed much of the faculty's time for several weeks and stirred up considerable feeling. The committee recommended abolishment, but apparently the societies had strong supporters among the professors, for the report was not approved.

The business sagacity and capacity for handling

details with which Sumner was endowed were also utilized freely in administering the affairs of the college. One of the first tasks given him by the faculty was in the form of a practical business problem. Seemingly, it was as difficult to feed the students satisfactorily a half century ago as it has proved to be in recent years, for under date of December 4, 1872, the minutes of the Permanent Officers of Yale College state that Professors Thatcher and Sumner, with the treasurer, were "requested to consider the constitution of the 'College Boarding House,' and to report what regulations, if any, were necessary to separate the College from any financial responsibility for the same; also to inquire by what means the Club may be made to accomplish its purpose more satisfactorily." He was on a committee, in 1874, to recommend what should be the disposition of the old chapel. The next year he was at work devising means for improving the recitation rooms. Later we find him one of three appointed to draw up a memorial to be transmitted to the corporation regarding the division of the academic funds; and later still, presenting an analysis of the expenses of the college for a period of years, together with certain conclusions to be drawn therefrom. Similar evidence showing that for a long period he was one of the busiest men on the faculty is abundant.

It was in connection with the curriculum, however, that Sumner's chief service was rendered. During the last quarter of the nineteenth century there was a well-defined movement in American colleges away from prescribed programs of study and in the direction of the elective system. Its impulse came from the rise of the physical sciences and the general widening and diversifying of human interests. In increasing numbers there came to the colleges men who were not looking forward to the ministry, the law, the medical profession, or teaching, as their life work. These asked for courses suited to their particular tastes and ambitions. The pressure upon the colleges to widen the scope of their teaching became irresistible. One study after another forced itself into the program of instruction, long dominated by mathematics and the classics. Others clamored for admission. What were the colleges to do? The amount of subject matter which a prescribed course can include is limited. "A crowded curriculum," as Professor George H. Palmer of Harvard declared, "is a curriculum of superficialities." It was necessary either to bar the door to new subjects on the assumption that there is a given amount of knowledge which all graduates should possess, or else modify the traditional program and permit students more or less freedom of choice. The general tendency was toward the latter.

Some of the colleges yielded to it readily; others fought it stubbornly. Among the former, Harvard was conspicuous. Here, ever since the days of George Ticknor, who had watched with interest and approval the opening of the University of Virginia with a complete elective system in 1825, there had been a bent toward freedom. In his inaugural address, in 1869, President Eliot declared the development of the elective system to be the established policy of the college. Under his direction it was so extended that in 1884 seven-sixteenths of the freshman work was required, and the entire remainder of the course, with the exception of some exercises in English composition, was arranged by each student to suit his own tastes, abilities, and needs.

At Yale, on the other hand, the tendency toward freedom of choice was stoutly opposed. As early as 1828, while Ticknor was laboring to promote the elective principle at Harvard, the Yale faculty was making public declaration of its allegiance to the established curriculum and all that was therein. Demands to revise it had caused the appointment of a committee from the corporation and the faculty "to inquire into the expediency of so altering the regular course of instruction in this college as to leave out of said course the study of *dead languages,* substituting other studies therefor; and either requiring a competent knowledge of said languages, as a condition for admittance into college, or providing instruction in the same for such as shall choose to study them after admittance."[1] It was the opinion of this committee that for the "discipline" and "furniture" of the mind which a college education should give, all the studies then required were indispensable. "Why, it is asked, should *all* students in a college be required to tread the same steps? Why should not each one be allowed to select those branches of study which are most to his taste, which are best adapted to his peculiar talents, and which are most nearly connected with his intended profession? To this we answer that our prescribed course contains those subjects only which ought to be understood, as we think, by every one who aims at a thorough education. . . . What subject which is now studied here could be set aside, without evidently marring the system? Not to speak particularly in this place of the ancient languages: who that aims at a well-proportioned and superior education will remain ignorant of the various

[1] "Report of the Course of Instruction in Yale College by a Committee of the Corporation and the Academic Faculty," New Haven, 1828, p. 3.

branches of mathematics, or of history and antiquities, or of rhetoric and oratory, or natural philosophy, or of astronomy, or chemistry, or mineralogy, or geology, or political economy, or mental and moral philosophy?" [2] Least of all could the classics be spared. Regarding the importance of these, according to the committee, "the learned world long ago settled the matter, and subsequent events and experience have confirmed their decision. By the estimate in which classical literature is held in any community, its advancement in civilization and general learning may be satisfactorily ascertained." [3]

For almost half a century this conservative attitude at Yale was maintained. When Noah Porter was inaugurated as president, in 1871, President Woolsey mentioned among the gratifying achievements of the past few years the fact that optional studies had been introduced "without at all overthrowing the curriculum." At that time a student might substitute differential and integral calculus for Greek or Latin during the first two terms of his junior year, and during the third term he might take German in place of Greek. In his last year he had the privilege of continuing German for one term in place of astronomy or Latin. Truly the curriculum had not been at all overthrown. The year before his inauguration Professor Porter had published a book entitled "American Colleges and the American Public," a second edition of which was issued in 1878. In it he argues at length against the elective system, extols the classics, and refers with ill-concealed contempt to statements in President Eliot's inaugural. His own address upon assuming the presidency was upon "The Higher Edu-

[2] Report, pp. 18, 19.
[3] Ibid., p. 50.

cation of the Country," and expressed strong disapproval of the liberalizing tendency of the day.

Another obstacle to the broadening of the curriculum at Yale was the existence of the Sheffield Scientific School. This allied institution provided the opportunity for those who believed in keeping things as they were to say: "If any want the sciences and the more obviously utilitarian studies, let them go to 'Sheff.' Why should we introduce into the academic course what is taught there?" A statement made by President Porter clearly indicates that in his view the two were to be complementary departments. "We have opened," he says, "two schools for undergraduate students, the one of which is prevailingly scientific and looks more to modern and active life, and the other is especially classical, historical, and speculative."[4] Not only did this association furnish the conservatives with an argument against the introduction of new studies, it fostered jealousy and made the officers of the Scientific School resent any apparent encroachment on their preserves.

Nevertheless, Yale College did, slowly and with great pain, broaden its curriculum and afford considerable opportunity for choice. It was inevitable that it should, for such action was in line with educational evolution. Conditions had changed and different adaptation or death were the only alternatives. In the long-drawn-out and difficult labors involved and in the hostilities engendered, Sumner played a leading part. When he became a professor, as has been shown, he was widely known as one of the sanest and most competent of the younger alumni who believed that it was time for Yale to move forward. His

[4] "Address at the Inauguration of Professor Noah Porter, D.D., LL.D., as President of Yale College," New York, Charles Scribner and Company, 1871, p. 42.

associates looked to him to stimulate and direct, and
he did not disappoint them.

His own views on the subject of higher education
were given in an article in *The Princeton Review* of
March, 1884, under the title, "Our Colleges Before the
Country."[5] In it he asserts that college officials are
for more reasons than one unfitted for college management. At this conviction he had arrived after
twelve years of association with them. At the moment he wrote, there was going on at Yale a struggle
over the educational policy to be pursued. A new
program of courses was being worked out, and all
kinds of difficulties were being encountered. Every
fault to which teachers are particularly susceptible
was conspicuously in evidence. It was knowing
whereof he spoke, therefore, that Sumner said of college professors, "They are exposed to all the pitfalls
of every pedagogue. They have to guard themselves
against the vices of dogmatism, pedantry, hatred of
contradiction, conceit, and love of authority. They,
of course, come each to love his own pursuit beyond
anything else on earth. Each thinks that a man who
is ignorant of *his* specialty is a barbarian. As a man
goes on in life under this discipline he becomes more
self-satisfied and egotistical. He has little contact
with active life; gets few knocks; is rarely forced into
a fight or into a problem of diplomacy, gets to hate
care or interruption, and loves routine. Men of this
type, of course, are timid, and even those traits which
are most admirable in the teacher become vices in the
executive officer. Such men are ever fond of *apriori*
reasoning and fall helpless the moment they have to
face a practical undertaking. They have the whole
philosophy of heaven and earth reduced, measured

[5] Reprinted in "War and Other Essays," p. 355.

SUMNER AS A YOUNG PROFESSOR

out, and done up in powders, to be prescribed at need. They know just what ought to be studied, in what amount and succession of doses. That is to say, they are prepared to do any amount of mischief at a juncture when the broadest statesmanship is needed to guide the development of a great institution. Certainly the notion that any body of men can now regulate the studies of youth by what was good for themselves twenty, forty, or sixty years ago is one which is calculated to ruin any institution which they control. It is always a hard test of the stuff men are made of when they are asked to admit that a subject of which they have had control would profit by being taken out of their control and intrusted to liberty."[6]

Sumner's appreciation of fundamental laws, and the character of his studies, made him particularly conscious of the fact that all things change continually and that no institution or method is permanently good. That in the natural course of events the time had come for a readaptation of college education to altered conditions was patent. The curriculum then in force was excellent once. "At a time when the sciences which teach us to know the world in which we live were still in their infancy; when the studies by which the mind is trained to high, strict, and fearless thinking were as yet undeveloped; when history was still only a record of curious and entertaining incidents in war and diplomacy; when modern civil institutions were yet in many respects below the standard of the ancients, and still on the same military basis; when no notion of law had yet found footing in the conception of society;—at such a time no doubt study of classical types and models was valuable; ideas were obtained from an old treasure-house which could

6 "War and Other Essays," pp. 360, 361.

not have been obtained from the experience of actual life; literary culture was the only possible discipline; grammar stood first as a training in thought and expression; formal logic was a practical tool; perhaps even introspective metaphysics was not entirely a scholastic and dialectic exercise.[7]

But at the present time, Sumner proceeds to point out, the whole complexion of things is altered. History is no longer an exercise in memory, it is an analysis and investigation of relations and sequences. Constitutional history has become of the utmost importance to students of law, political science, and jurisprudence. Sociology is still in its infancy, but promises to grow into a science of the first rank as regards utility to the human race. Biology with its affiliated sciences holds the key to a number of important problems and "to a new philosophy destined to supersede the rubbish of the schools." Physics, anthropology, archæology, and a host of other sciences offer just the stimulus necessary to draw youthful energies and awaken youthful enthusiasm. In the face of all these facts how can a college hold to a program approved in 1828, or acquiesce in the views expressed in Porter's "American Colleges and the American Public"? "An American college," declared Sumner, "ought to be the seat of all the learning which would be of value to an American man in the American life of to-day. . . . It ought to offer its pupils an opportunity for becoming acquainted with all which is, or is coming to be, in the great world of thought, and it ought to offer such opportunities that those who profit by them faithfully would be highly trained men, drilled and disciplined for any of the tasks of life."[8]

[7] "War and Other Essays," p. 359.　　[8] *Ibid.*, p. 370.

No college can possibly fulfill such a function as this if it "clings to the classics." For these Sumner was not without respect. He had studied them thoroughly and had taught them. Clergymen, teachers in certain departments, professors of modern languages, philologists, literary men, and some kinds of journalists, ought, in his opinion, to have not less acquaintance with Latin and Greek, but more. No student of political economy can pass over the subject matter of Aristotle, or Demosthenes and the orators, nor the life and polity of the Greek state. But that every one desirous of pursuing a college course should be compelled to study these, Sumner regarded as ridiculous. To Mr. George L. Fox, rector of the Hopkins Grammar School, he complained with much emphasis because one of his sons, who as his father expressed it was "all for railroads," and is now an official of the Pennsylvania system, was compelled to study Greek in order to get into Yale College. Furthermore, he believed that classical culture had "distinct and mischievous limitations." "I do not doubt that I gained great profit from a classical education," he writes, but "I know that it cost me years of discipline to overcome the limitations of the classical training and to emancipate my mind from the limited range of processes in which it had been trained." Long experience in teaching political economy had disclosed to him that young men who had been trained in a curriculum based on the classics had facility in recitation without familiarity with the subject, that they hardly ever knew what a "law" is in the scientific sense of the word, but regarded it as similar to a rule in grammar and were quite prepared to find it followed by a list of exceptions, that they lacked vigor and force in thinking, and that they were content to take things and "hold them in a jumble." "In short," Sumner declared, "the habits and traditions in which men have been trained when they reach senior year in college are such that they are yet boys in responsibility, and, although they are very manly and independent in many respects, they are dependent and unmanly in their methods of study, in their conceptions of duty, in their scholarship, and in their code of conduct in all that affects the institution. It has been claimed for the classics that they give guidance for conduct. This is, to me, the most amazing claim of all, for, in my experience and observation, the most marked fact about classical culture is that it gives no guidance in conduct at all." [9]

But it was in the fact that the classical studies tend to exalt authority and to inculcate reverence for what is written rather than for what is true, and that they give a man a limited horizon, that Sumner beheld their supreme mischievousness. Men educated upon them "are apt to be caught by the literary form, if it is attractive. They are fond of paradoxes and will entertain two contrary ideas, if only each come in a striking literary dress. They think they prove something when they quote somebody who has once said it. If any one wants to keep out "new ideas," he does well to cling to classical studies. They are the great barrier to new ideas and the chief bulwark of modern obscurantism. The new sciences have produced in their votaries an unquenchable thirst and affection for what is *true* in fact, word, character, and motive. They have taught us to appreciate and weigh evidence and to deal honestly with it." With regard to the horizon the classics give, he says, "There is far more beyond it than within it." They

9 "War and Other Essays," p. 367.

teach a man "to believe that he has sounded the depths of human knowledge when he knows nothing about its range or amount. If any one wants to find prime specimens of the Philistinism which Matthew Arnold hates, he should seek them among the votaries of the culture which Matthew Arnold loves." [10]

On the other hand, Sumner was no advocate of unrestricted freedom in the choice of studies. The broadening of the curriculum and the adoption of the elective system he deemed imperative, but he regarded the Harvard policy as the elective system run wild. "Heterogeneous and nondescript electives, he says, jumbled together without coördination of any kind, and offered to the choice of lazy youth, can never command the confidence of sober teachers. A university ought to teach everything which anybody wants to know. . . . It ought to give complete liberty in the choice of a *line* or *department* of study, but it ought to prescribe rigidly what studies must be pursued in the chosen department by any one who wants its degree. A Yale diploma ought not to mean that a man knows everything, for that would be absurd; nor that he knows 'something about the general principles' of all those things which 'every educated man ought to know,' for this is a formula for superficiality and false pretense. It ought to mean that he has acquired knowledge in some one line of study, sufficient to entitle him to be enrolled amongst the graduates of the institution, and the college ought to define strictly the kind and quantity of attainment which it considers sufficient, in that line or department, to earn its degree." [11]

Guided by such convictions as these, Sumner applied his energies, so far as he was given opportunity,

[10] *Ibid.*, p. 369.   [11] *Ibid.*, p. 361.

to the improvement of Yale's curriculum. One of the first and one of the last references to him in the faculty minutes are in connection with the courses of study. As early as June 28, 1873, we find him presenting a report from the committee on senior studies. Apparently it was not of a character to be passed over lightly, for it was laid upon the table to be taken up early in the next term. In March, 1876, Professors James Dana, Newton, and Sumner were requested to bring in a schedule of optional courses. Their recommendations, which were approved by the faculty and corporation, made about one-fourth of the work of each term in the junior and senior years elective. Any student, furthermore, who could show on examination a thorough acquaintance in advance with one or more of the required studies of these years might add another optional in the place of each study thus anticipated. The following year the committee was re-appointed with special instructions to take up the requirements in French.

Some gain for breadth and freedom was thus early achieved, but it was not until 1884 that the great battle was fought. The elective system at Harvard had attracted wide attention and not a few of the smaller colleges had adopted it in a more or less modified form. The pressure upon Yale to liberalize further her curriculum became irresistible, and a committee was appointed to undertake the task, consisting of Professor Edward S. Dana, George Trumbull Ladd, Tracy Peck, and Sumner. The members were not altogether congenial. Professor Ladd was very opinionated and unbending, but he had great influence in the faculty because his department, that of philosophy and ethics, was deemed worthy of a consideration second only to that of revealed religion.

Sumner had no use for philosophy. He had studied it long and thoroughly in his youth, and had been throwing it overboard, as he said, ever since. It dealt with abstractions and phantasies, in his opinion, was altogether speculative and unverifiable, and never got anywhere. Its spirit and methods he deemed unfavorable to fearless devotion to exactness and truth. Peck, as professor of Latin, represented the classics, while Dana, whose field was physics, was naturally a friend of the sciences. Neither Ladd nor Peck were very sympathetic toward Sumner and his ideas, but Dana and he were in substantial accord.

The work of the committee was carried on in the face of great difficulties, and taxed the patience and self-control of its members to the utmost. The conservative element in the faculty was still strong, and included President Porter. All the dogmatism, pedantry, and other vices which Sumner enumerates as peculiarly conspicuous in teachers had to be combated. Not a few of those who favored a revision of the curriculum were not able to stand the test of having their own subjects taken out of their control and intrusted to liberty. Among these was Professor Ladd himself, who insisted stubbornly that psychology and ethics should be required in the senior year.

At the outset of the committee's labors, Professor Sumner presented a well-defined plan which provided for "schools" within the college. Upper classmen were to be permitted to elect one of these, that of philosophy, it might be, or of ancient languages, or some other, and specialize therein. This proved impossible of adoption, however. There were some required studies which the majority felt essential to a college education. Concessions had to be made to this professor and to that. The committee worked an

entire year with great care and perseverance. Finally
a program was agreed upon which made a little more
than one-half the junior year and four-fifths of the
senior year elective. On May 14, 1884, the faculty
approved a memorial to the corporation embodying
the recommendations of the committee. President
Porter, however, announced his "non-concurrence
with the entire scheme," and stated that as a member
of the corporation he should oppose it. The committee was dumbfounded. They had conferred with
the president throughout the year on every detail,
and apparently he had given his approval. The whole
year's work seemed likely to go for nothing. Accordingly, the committee decided upon drastic measures. They would bulldoze the president into acqui-
escence. In pursuance of this plan they went to his
office one day with the determination not to leave him
until he had consented to approve their plan. After
two or three hours' bombardment by the four professors he capitulated. "It was a brutal procedure,"
said Professor Dana, "but it was effective."

This victory decided the future educational policy
of the college. From that time, gradually and wisely,
Yale liberalized her curriculum and sought to adjust
her courses to such ends as Sumner had outlined in
his article in the *Princeton Review*. In the critical
years immediately following he was the ruling spirit
of the standing committee on electives. He continued
to fight aggressively for the introduction of more
scientific courses into the academic department, and
only a few years before his retirement we find him
the chairman of a committee on the establishment of
a chair of biology, and waging what proved to be a
bitter fight.

There is no wickedness in any disinterested and sincere opinion. That is what we all pretend to admit, but there are few of us who really act by it.

Folkways.

CHAPTER XV

THE SPENCER CONTROVERSY

SUMNER's contribution to the emancipation of Yale from the shackles of conservatism was by no means confined to his labors in connection with the curriculum. In behalf of freedom from theological control, the ascendancy of the scientific spirit, and academic liberty, he rendered service no less important. The battle waged with President Porter, which attracted attention through the country, was something more than a contest over a textbook; involved in it was the question: What principles shall rule in the government of a college?

The trouble started with Sumner's use, in his senior class, of Herbert Spencer's "The Study of Sociology." Sumner was no blind follower of the English philosopher. That for which he valued his works most is described in a review of the "Descriptive Sociology," which he wrote for the *Independent* of May 14, 1874. "It presents history," he says, "as a social evolution in which no factor is contemptible, because the social outcome of a nation's life is a resultant of a vast number of forces, each of which must be estimated for what it was in its day, not for what it would be now." It was Spencer's demonstration of the possibility of a science of society, his method and data, and not his particular ideas and general conclusions, which commanded Sumner's respect. With the former, he believed, it was essential the youthful student should become acquainted, and there was then

345

no place where they could be found save in Spencer's own writings. But Yale stood before the country as a Christian college; eleven of her corporation were clergymen; she looked for much of her support to people who were conservative in their views, and by the majority of these Spencer was regarded as anti-Christian. Should a Yale professor be permitted to use one of this man's writings as a textbook in a class of immature youth? There were those both outside the college and on the faculty who thought not.

Hostilities began with the following letter to Sumner from President Porter:

> Yale College,
> New Haven, Connecticut,
> Dec. 6, 1879.

My Dear Prof. Sumner:

The use of Spencer's 'Study of Sociology' as a textbook has made a great deal of talk and is likely to make still more. When the subject has been brought to my notice I have been able to reply that I have used his First Principles and his Psychology in my graduate classes with very great advantage. I cannot, however, think that this is or ought to be satisfactory, for the reason that the capacity of an undergraduate student when introduced to the elements of a science, to discriminate between the valid and the invalid is much below that of a graduate. A much more cogent reason is that the book itself is written very largely in a pamphleteering style, which is very unlike most of Spencer's more solid treatises. The freedom and unfairness with which it attacks every Theistic Philosophy of society and of history, and the cool and yet sarcastic effrontery with which he assumes that material elements and laws are the only forces and laws which any scientific man can recognize, seem to me to condemn the book as a textbook for a miscellaneous class in an undergraduate course. I ought to have examined the book sooner, but I feel assured that the use of the book will bring intellectual and moral harm to the students, however you may strive to neutralize or counteract its influence, and that the use of it will inevitably and reasonably work serious havoc to the reputation of the college. Having these opinions, I can do nothing else than express them, and as I am presumed to authorize the use of every textbook, I must formally object to the use of this.

Faithfully yours,

N. PORTER.

Upon the receipt of this letter Sumner went to President Porter to discuss the matter personally. In the course of the interview he put such pressure upon him that the President acquiesced reluctantly in the continued use of the book. The meeting between the two Sumner himself describes in a statement made to a reporter of the *New York Times* a few months later, when, much to the annoyance of all concerned, the press was beginning to give rather sensational publicity to the incident.

Prof. Sumner, who is passing a few days at the house of his friend, Corporation Counsel Whitney, in Park Avenue, was asked yesterday whether it was true that there had been a difference of opinion between himself and the officers of Yale College in regard to the employment of Herbert Spencer's works as textbooks. The Professor was at first reluctant to speak on the subject, but finally declared that the affair had been very much exaggerated.

'In December last,' he said, 'President Porter wrote to me calling my attention to the fact that the students under my instruction were using Herbert Spencer's "Study of Sociology" as a textbook. The book, he thought, was open to grave objections. It treated of sacred subjects in a tone that, however disguised, seemed to him sneering and flippant, and liable to give a wrong bias to the thoughts and opinions of the students using it. He, therefore, requested that, if possible, its use should be discontinued. I did not answer him by letter, but called upon him personally two or three days later and discussed the subject. I was treated most courteously, and the controversy, if you choose to call it such, was carried on in the most amicable manner on both sides. President Porter did not specify any particular passages which he considered as being of an infidel or irreligious tendency, but contented himself with a general objection to its tone of dealing with sacred things. There was an understanding between us that if the use of the book was prohibited, I should resign my position, as I did not think I could properly fill the chair of Political and Social Science if I was hedged about and restricted in such a manner. With Mr. Spencer's individual opinions upon the matter of religion I have nothing to do, but this work on sociology is the only book of the kind in the English language, and coming from as great a philosopher and student as Mr. Spencer, and embodying, as it does, the results of years of the most exhaustive and discriminating investigation into a particularly complex subject, it naturally commends itself to those engaged in the study of social science. Indeed, it would be difficult to see how English students could study social science at all if the works of so high an authority as Spencer were to be debarred them. I stated my view of the case to President Porter very frankly, and, while he did not at all change his view of the book, he yielded so far as to permit the book to remain upon the schedule, and even went so far as to announce it as one of the subjects of study at the commencement of the January term. It is only used by the Senior Class, and that during one term—from New Year's to Easter. The work was a popular one with certain of the younger students and tutors, and I have been at some pains to restrain the

hot heads among them from getting up a public controversy over the affair. As it was, the whole question was
settled between President Porter and myself three months
ago, without the intervention, to my knowledge, of a
single one of the Faculty, and it has not been reopened
since. I may add that I do not expect that it will be reopened. President Porter throughout acted in the most
courteous and kindly spirit, and while he still retains
his original opinion of the book, he has not gone so far
as to exclude it. I sincerely trust that the press will
let the matter alone, as its agitation would only call
forth useless controversy and be prejudicial to the college interests.'

Sumner's desire was not to be realized, however.
The matter was by no means settled. Its roots went
down too deep for it to be disposed of so easily. Shall
a professor be permitted to conduct his department,
at least so far as subject matter and authorities are
concerned, without interference? Shall he be free to
present, without elimination or softening the results
of fearless investigation, regardless of the effect upon
prevailing ideas and institutions? Shall he be allowed
to state what he believes to be the truth, whether it
agrees with accepted dogmas or not? Or shall the
college president or trustees supervise his selection
of textbooks, dictate what he shall teach, and censor
his utterances in the interest of sect or party, or to
insure financial support? This was the question at
issue, and Sumner recognized the fact. The matter,
furthermore, was one upon which he felt strongly.
Ten years before, in the *Living Church,* he had described the evils of sectarianism in education with
great vividness. He would rather give up teaching
altogether than teach shackled. It is doubtful if he
really believed that his interview with President

Porter had brought the incident to a close. The latter was well known to be vacillating. Sumner's politic statement to the reporter gives the impression of a person who is afraid some one will make a noise and endanger a valuable concession.

The controversy, too, was really a part of the wide-spread conflict between orthodoxy and modernism then going on. The extent to which the views of the Darwinian school were gaining acceptance had alarmed and aroused to bitter opposition those wedded to tradition. That these views should be promulgated in Christian colleges seemed to the conservatives an anomaly not to be tolerated. Two factions existed on most college faculties. At Yale the liberals were in the minority, but included some of the ablest of the professors. James Dwight Dana, and O. C. Marsh were of their number. James K. Thatcher and Henry A. Beers were also classed with them. Sumner, outspoken and aggressive, was regarded as one of the most dangerous radicals of them all. On the other side were President Porter, Ex-President Woolsey, and Franklin Carter, soon to become the head of Williams College, and accused of looking with covetous eyes upon President Porter's chair. In the same camp was Cyrus Northrup, active in politics, collector of the port of New Haven, and violently opposed to Sumner's views in general. One or two of these, unquestionably, looked upon Sumner as a dangerous teacher and would not have been sorry to see him leave. The statement of the *New York Observer* that "the resignation of any professor who has sympathies with Herbert Spencer will be a great advantage to the college," perhaps expressed their honest conviction. Sumner felt himself compelled to make the stand he did, therefore, not only in behalf of academic freedom, but also in the interest of intellectual advancement. "He was not defending agnosticism," he said: "he was resisting obscurantism."

With so much involved, it was inevitable that the matter should not be permitted to rest. President Porter, in his letter to Sumner, had intimated that it was within his province to sanction or disapprove the use of textbooks. That any such right belonged to him many of the faculty doubted, and discussion of the question waxed warm. The defenders of the faith were much disgruntled. Sumner and atheism seemed to have won a victory. Was unbelief to be taught at Yale, or Christianity? Apparently they urged the President to exercise his authority, and if this were disputed, to take the matter before the trustees.

In the spring of 1880, just as Sumner was completing the one-term course in which the "Study of Sociology" was used, the conflict was broadened and made more complicated by the fact that some one in New Haven gave out a story of it to the newspapers. On the fourth of April, there appeared upon the front page of the *New York Times* a long account of the controversy under the heading, "Yale a Battle Ground." This was followed the next day by another article entitled, "Two Parties at Yale." On the morning following, the *Times* contained a scurrilous editorial on "Yale College," intended, no doubt, to be humorous. Its main thesis was that "no intelligent man in this age of the world will for a moment maintain that there is any truth in Christianity." It then went on to defend the teaching of Christianity at Yale on the ground that among so many young men order must be maintained, and that Christianity, however unworthy of belief, is a confessedly useful instrument to such an end. Furthermore, the college was founded by men and women who intended that their money should be employed incidentally, if not directly, in the support of the Christian religion. To change Yale into an anti-Christian institution, therefore, would be perversion of the college funds. After stating that President Porter, though in other respects an able man, was really a believer in religion and would probably make a vigorous effort to preserve the Christian character of the college, an effort in which he would be supported by not a few men of comparative intelligence, the editorial closes with these words: "After all, if there is no God, no future life, no true system of religion, what real difference does it make whether Yale students are taught to believe in Christ or Herbert Spencer? We may have a desire that they should be taught scientific truth, but what is that desire except a mere prejudice? Let us rid ourselves of prejudice as well as religion, and boldly admit that nothing is of any particular consequence, and that if Christianity continue to be taught at Yale, we ought not to lie awake and groan over it."

Who was responsible for this publicity is not known. There was some suspicion that it came from the camp of Sumner's opponents, and was prompted by the desire to arouse the conservative constituency of the college against him. The *New York Evening Post,* correctly or incorrectly, stated the facts as follows: "The whole sorry business at Yale College had been known for a long time, and until some needy penny-a-liner took it in hand there was every prospect that it would adjust itself in accordance with reason and common sense. It sprung chiefly from the whisperings and doubts and fears—honest ones, perhaps—of two or three narrow-minded members of the faculty, one of whom is the devoted scholar who divides his time between his college duties and the comfortable fauteuil of a federal office, and the other not a Yale man at all, but who, nevertheless, is said to cherish hopes that some day he may be duly rewarded for his zeal by being made President of the college. Already the mischief wrought in this way has had the effect of checking the growth of the most important department of the college and perhaps seriously threatening its existence.''

The *Times* articles called forth comments on the controversy both in religious and secular papers. Expressions of approval began to come to Sumner from widely different quarters. A Rochester merchant wrote: ''A telegram in our morning paper states that President Porter of Yale College has requested you to discontinue using Mr. Herbert Spencer's 'The Study of Sociology,' and that you have refused. Although an entire stranger to you, except so far as I have become acquainted with you through your writings, I cannot refrain from expressing the wish that public opinion will support you in your position, and the desire to add what little weight I possess in sustaining you in it. That such bigotry as is here displayed by President Porter should still obtain in one of our first institutions of learning, almost passes belief.'' David A. Wells offered the following advice: ''I note your controversy about Herbert Spencer. Don't resign, if you have to give up. Your position, your influence, is too valuable to be abandoned. Protectionists, soft money idiots, damn fools generally, would shout at your retirement. *Stick,* if the world doesn't move up to your standard as fast as you think it ought to.'' Henry Holt wrote him: ''I am glad the issue has come. If theological tests are to be applied to untheological subjects at Yale, it is time the facts were clearly published. . . . Of course you will stick to your position. If you leave your chair, you can, if you care to, draw the same income from me that you now draw from the college, if you will give me the same time that you give it, and you need not change your residence."

At Yale, however, the newspaper notoriety was much deplored. It created bitterness and made a settlement of the trouble all the more difficult. Professor Lewis R. Packard came forward as a peacemaker.

New Haven, April 8, 1880.

My Dear Sumner:

I hope you regret as much as I do the publication of our affairs in the newspapers during the past week. I do not know at all who is responsible. If it was a friend of the college, he has acted, I think, very foolishly; if an enemy, he could hardly have used his time better. I am afraid it will force upon us some kind of settlement of the matter for which we may not be ready, and which therefore may not be satisfactory and final. I should be sorry to have it come up now as a question to be voted on either in the Faculty or in the Corporation. I do not know at all, I may truly say, how the vote would go in either body, but I do think it would be an unfortunate thing to have it decided either way at present in such a manner. Now I write to you without the knowledge of any one else, to ask if there is not some way in which that issue can be avoided. . . . It seems to me that the matter now lies in your hands more than in those of any one else, and I think I see two ways in one of which you may with entire propriety and dignity settle it. One way would be for you to make a statement to your colleagues and the President, orally, of course, unless you prefer writing, as to your use of Spencer's book, the criticisms you make upon it, the influence you think it has, such as you made to me at your house. You said then in addi-

tion that you would define your position on the whole
subject of your relation to Christianity when the time
came. If you are willing to go on and do that now, I for
one should be very glad. I hope and suppose you could
make such a statement on the special point and the general question as would lead to the dropping of all objection to your use of the book and establish a better feeling
on all sides than perhaps now exists.

Another way would be for you to say that, still holding the book to be proper for your use of it, you are
willing in deference to the opinion and wish of the
President and some of your colleagues to lay it aside,
though under protest. I need not urge this upon you as
a manly and dignified course. I am sure that you see it
would be so in the highest degree, if only there is not in
this particular case a sacrifice of principle involved. Of
that you must be for yourself the judge, of course, and
my opinion will not help you to decide.

You told me there was no other book you could use,
but could you not give the valuable substance of this,
without the objectionable tone, in the form of lectures,
with a full printed outline? In some way you could
certainly get around this difficulty, I should think. If
you can do some such things as these I have taken the
liberty to suggest, I believe we should find there was no
question at all on which parties could be formed among
us, whatever irresponsible persons outside the college
may say. I have written, as you know, with the friend-
liest feeling towards you, and I sincerely hope you can
take one of these ways or some other which may end the
matter. In any case, let me say, even if the Corporation
forbids the use of the book, you have no occasion to
resign. They differ from you in their judgment. What
of it? You are in danger of exaggerating the importance of it, I think, if you view it so. But you have
never said that you did in my hearing.

Sincerely yours,

LEWIS R. PACKARD.

Well meant and wise as this advice may have been, it was impossible for Sumner to act upon it. There was nothing of the conciliatory in his nature. Furthermore, in his opinion, there were principles involved which it was of the utmost importance should not even seemingly be sacrificed.

The widespread publicity given the controversy made it inevitable that notice of it should be taken in the Corporation. In order to preclude the asking of any questions, the necessity of any discussion, or the passage of any resolutions, according to President Porter, he read to that body in June, 1880, a statement of the whole matter. Ex-President Woolsey had ready for presentation, if Dr. Porter should call for it, a resolution relating to the power of the President with respect to textbooks. In his statement Dr. Porter said that Professor Sumner had yielded and given assurance that the book in question would not be used by him again. In view of this fact the Woolsey resolution was not presented.

It was not until December, six months later, just before the reopening of his course in sociology, that Sumner was informed that the matter had been before the Corporation. Knowledge of the fact came to him in a letter from President Porter, enclosing a copy of the paper which he had read before its members. Sumner was highly indignant. He felt that the President had acted unfairly in making an *ex-parte* statement. That he had ever agreed not to use Spencer's book again, he declared to be untrue. He inferred that the Woolsey resolution would have been passed had he not been represented as yielding. Under such circumstances, he considered his position at Yale intolerable. Accordingly he made up his mind to resign, withdrew from all administrative activities, and began looking about for an opening in banking or business circles.

In order that his side of the case might be known, and also, perhaps, to give some vent to his feelings, he sent the following letter to each of the members of the faculty and corporation:

A private and personal communication to the members of the Corporation and to the permanent officers of Yale College

New Haven, June, 1881.

DEAR SIR:

On the 27th of December, 1880, Pres. Porter wrote me a letter enclosing a copy of a paper read by him to the Corporation in June, 1880, about the disagreement between him and me arising from the use by me of Spencer's 'Study of Sociology' as a textbook. Up to the moment of receiving this communication I had had no knowledge or suspicion that Pres. Porter had carried that matter before the Corporation on an *ex-parte* statement, although the President stated that he had previously informed some other persons not members of the Corporation. I have, although suffering much annoyance from misrepresentation and public abuse, entered into no explanations either in public or private, not even in private conversation, until within a month, believing that public excitement and scandal could do no good. I have hoped that some change in my own position, or in circumstances, would cause the point in issue to solve itself. There are, however, very important interests at stake, as I will show in this paper, and I cannot allow the annual meeting of the Corporation to pass, and another academic year to open, without placing this matter before the college world as it stands in fact, and extricating myself from a false position. It will be seen that Pres. Porter's statement of the issue does not agree at all with my understanding of it.

The facts out of which the trouble arose are as follows: I am professor of political and social science. Four or five years ago my studies led me to the conviction that sociology was about to do for the social sciences what scientific method has done for natural and physical science, viz.: rescue them from arbitrary dogmatism and confusion. It seemed to me that it belonged to me to give my students the advantage of the new standpoint and method just as fast as I could win command of it myself, just as every competent professor aims to set before his students all the speculations, anticipations, efforts, extensions, reconstructions, etc., etc., which mark the growth of the sciences. Sociology is so new that only three or four persons in the world have written upon it as an independent science. It is so difficult that very few indeed prosecute it, or even know what it is. My studies have led me to independent convictions on certain points of detail in sociology, but I could not lecture upon it. If I should pretend to do so I could only cram a half dozen books and reproduce the material. It is a case for using a textbook. When I looked about for one, Spencer's 'Study of Sociology' was the only one which could come into account. I considered it very faulty as a textbook, and I doubted if I could use it, but after considering the matter for more than a year I made up my mind that the right and interest of the students to learn something of sociology outweighed any faults or deficiencies in the book, and that, for want of something better, I could probably use this book as a means of giving the students the instruction to which they were entitled. In this judgment I did not take into account the religious character or tone of the book, which is not, so far as I can see, open to any fair objection. Mr. Spencer's religious opinions seem to me of very little importance in this connection, and, when I was looking for a book on sociology, the question whether it was a good or available book in a scientific point of view occupied my attention exclusively. Neither did I take into account the horror of Spencer's name, which, as I have since learned, is entertained by some people. If I had known of it, however, I should not have thought that it was a proper consideration to weigh much in the question which presented itself to me. I used the book for two years with the result of interesting and instructing the students, awakening their powers of observation and analysis as to social phenomena, and suggesting to them most valuable trains of thought as to practical questions in society. I have the amplest testimony that this was the most valuable and successful course ever given by me, and one of the most valuable given in the university. I have heard no word of complaint from the classes which used that book of any harm of any kind arising from the use of it, and to inquiries made by me and by others the invariable answer has been that no harm was done.

To all this Pres. Porter opposes in contradiction of the experience of two years his *apriori* judgment that Spencer's book cannot be used without corrupting the students.

Pres. Porter asserts that the Corporation did not intend, when I was appointed in 1872, that I should teach sociology in some sense which, he says, he will not undertake to define. I was not aware that the Corporation had any intention in the matter except that I should bend all my efforts to study and teach political and social science according to the advance of sound learning in regard to those matters. I supposed that I was just as free as any other professor, no more and no less, and I did not know that I was limited by any intention. As sociology has taken shape as an independent science since I was appointed, the Corporation cannot have had any intention about it. It is not, therefore, of any importance that a definition of the kind of sociology from which I am debarred should be given, essential as such a definition would be if there were any such limitation as is asserted.

Pres. Porter affirms that sociology is inchoate and tentative. So is psychology; so are many new developments of physics, biology, and other sciences. To object to what is inchoate and tentative is to set up a closed canon of human learning.

He and I therefore came to an issue on which I was on the defensive. His position was that the students might better get no sociology than run the risk of getting agnosticism in getting sociology, and he even seems to maintain that they might better get no sociology than get it from a book by Spencer. I resisted this and maintained that they should have sociology anyhow, from the best means available, and I would not submit to a restraint the motive of which was consideration for metaphysical and theological interests. This is the only issue to which I have been a party. Pres. Porter has never prohibited the use of the book. He has never distinctly claimed authority to prohibit it. He said that, *if* he had any authority, he wanted to be understood as using all the authority he had against it. This left me to act on my own responsibility without coming into direct collision with him. I did so act and I have stood and now stand responsible for using the book.

It will be seen from this statement—

1. That I have had no controversy about the merits of Herbert Spencer's philosophy. Pres. Porter devoted a large part of his paper to stating his objections to that philosophy. This was quite irrelevant to any matter in which I am concerned, but I think it carried a suggestion that I had been teaching an infidel and pernicious philosophy, which is not true in fact. I have taught sociology as a science, from second causes only, and have not meddled with anything outside of my department. In my controversy with Pres. Porter I did not defend agnosticism; I resisted obscurantism.

2. I have had no controversy about the use of a book by Spencer, as an independent and substantive question. I should be very glad if I could obtain my ends by the

use of a book to which no one could make either reasonable or unreasonable objection, but I have refused to sacrifice my ends to a silly horror of Spencer's name, or a prejudice against his works. Pres. Porter has used Spencer's books, as he stated in his paper. I had no reason to suppose that Spencer's writings were ruled out. Pres. Porter devoted by far the largest part of his paper to an elaborate argument to prove: 1. That he is glad to have the young men study Spencer's philosophical writings with him, because he is able by using those writings to overthrow Spencer's philosophy; 2. That Spencer's non-philosophical works could not be used by another gentleman (me) without inculcating Spencer's philosophy. In this view of the matter the use of Spencer's books is a privilege of the President and his use of them does not, then, constitute a precedent for anybody else; but I confess that this view of the matter never suggested itself to me. I may add, in regard to the "maturity" of the students to whom I taught sociology, that they were the same students, at just the same point in their course (second term of senior year), as those to whom Pres. Porter taught Spencer's philosophy.

3. I have had no controversy about the merits of this particular treatise: 'The Study of Sociology.' Pres. Porter has offered me such a controversy both in public and private. I have declined to enter upon it. I have my well-settled opinion about the merits and faults of that book for my purposes, and I could give them if I saw proper occasion. I think I am also in a position to estimate the correctness and fairness of Pres. Porter's strictures on the book, but what could be gained by an argument about that question? Where should it be carried on? Who wants to hear it? I thought that it belonged to me to consider and decide the practical question on my responsibility. I did it and I take the responsibility. Will the Corporation say that Spencer's Study of Sociology is such a book that I ought to be dis-

ciplined for using it, or is it such a book that public opinion would sustain them in so deciding? It certainly is not. Cases unfortunately happen very often in life where one has to do without the unanimous approval which it would be pleasant to possess. I suppose this is one of those cases.

4. I have had no controversy on the question whether the President has a veto on textbooks. I do not admit that he has it, and I do not know of any college officer who admits it, but I have not raised that question. It is plain that if a professor is indiscreet, silly, negligent, incompetent, immoral, or otherwise unfit for his position, he ought to be disciplined, and it is plain that the President is the proper agent for bringing him to discipline. It requires no law to prove this. To use an improper textbook would simply be a case under this general principle. But it is plain also that the President can himself impose no sanctions whatever. He is only a reporting officer for that purpose. It is also plain that the Corporation cannot impose sanctions on the report of the President. They could not sustain him in a position of pure prerogative and sustain his authority at the expense of the rights of a professor. Hence if the law is asserted to mean more than that which understands itself, law or no law, it is ridiculous. If the law means only what every one fully admits, then we come back again to what I have already stated. I used the book and I take the responsibility. If called on to answer to the President's charges I will not object to his jurisdiction within the only form which it can take.

Pres. Porter, in the paper read to the Corporation, represented me as having yielded the point, and he gave assurances that the book would not be used again. Candor compels me to say that he was in error in this matter. I have never yielded the point or authorized any assurances that I would not use the book again, if I should still find myself so situated that I could not teach sociology without it. In January, 1881, the question

came up again, no book yet having been published which
I could use in the place of Spencer's book. But a new
factor now came into account. There was reason to fear
that, if I used the book, the students and the newspapers
would be on the *qui vive* to see what would happen, and
also that the students would watch and weigh every word
said by me about the book, and report the same to the
newspapers, more or less incorrectly, according to the
evil modern custom. The consequences of using Spencer's
book which I could foresee were, therefore, unedifying
and mischievous, and I could not take the responsibility
of bringing on these consequences. I suspended the use
of the book. The consequence of the outside excitement
and uproar which was stirred up in the Spring of 1880
(I know not by whom, but certainly against my most
earnest efforts) has therefore been that the class of 1881
has had no opportunity to study sociology. I appended
to my annual report the following protest: 'I now,
therefore, append to this, my annual report, a formal
and official protest against the interference with me in
my rights and duty as an instructor which has led to this
result, by which the students are deprived of a part of
the benefits to which they are entitled in their course of
study here, out of regard to metaphysical and theological
interests which ought not to come into account in this
connection.' So the matter now stands. I have made
no concession. I suspended the use of the book out of
regard to major considerations, but the matter is not settled at all. I consider that it involves rights and interests
which no honest teacher ever ought to concede.

Certain misunderstandings have, unfortunately, been
included in this matter. In his letter of December 27,
Pres. Porter said: 'The communication was framed de-
signedly so as to preclude the asking of any questions,
the necessity of any discussion or passing any resolutions. A written resolution affirming or confirming the
oldest form of the law was prepared by Pres. Woolsey,
but, at my request, was not presented.' I saw nothing

ambiguous in this statement, and I proceeded to make my arrangements according to my understanding of it. On the first of May it became evident that the plans I had in mind would not be matured at present, and, in view of what it might be necessary to do, I called on Pres. Woolsey, to find out accurately the scope of his resolution. He said he did not recollect having prepared any resolution. In answer to an inquiry from me, Pres. Porter wrote: 'The written resolution which Pres. Woolsey proposed to offer, or not, as I should prefer, related to the power of the President in respect to textbooks and did not concern either your conduct or my own.' I then wrote again to Pres. Porter as follows: 'I understood from yours of Dec. 27, 1880, that you read to the Corporation, at their June meeting, 1880, a paper containing, with other things, an *ex-parte* statement of facts about the use of Spencer's Study of Sociology as a textbook, and about conversations between you and me in that regard. I understood that, thereupon, Pres. W. proposed to offer a resolution which he had written, affirming the "old rule" (which I supposed to be, as you now state, an alleged rule that the President has a veto on the use of all textbooks in the Academical Dept.). I understood that this was intended as a solution of the subject which your paper brought before the Corporation, and that it would have been a vote of censure on me, but that you protected me from it by asking Dr. W. to withhold it. I inferred that you had done this by the assurance which you gave that the book would not be used again. . . . I politely and respectfully beg you to point out wherein I am in error in the understanding of your letter which I have above recited.' To this he answered: 'Allow me to correct what seems a misunderstanding on your part. The resolution prepared by Pres. Woolsey I am sure was not intended "as a vote of censure on you," but solely as a more explicit affirmation of the power of the President which had been questioned by some members of the Faculty, and which Pres. Woolsey supposed I might desire should be phrased in more positive terms.' To this I replied: 'I do not see the appositeness of any such resolution (as that which Pres. Woolsey prepared) aside from the sociology question, although there may have been other occasion for it (and I do not know of any member of the Faculty who admits the rule as claimed by you), but I do not see the point of informing me of Dr. W's. resolution, especially in this connection, if it had nothing to do with the subject matter of the paper of which you were sending me a copy. I do not argue, I only justify my inference.' Here the correspondence ended. It had, at any rate, corrected the impression derived by me from Pres. Porter's letter of Dec. 27 that the Corporation had reached a decision about the sociology matter which they had been prevented from recording in a formal vote framed by Pres. Woolsey, only by the interposition of Pres. Porter. My position, therefore, was by no means such as I had supposed from January to May. The case was not closed and the way was open for such further steps as I thought proper. I have seen nothing more proper than the present communication.

I have always considered that the Corporation did me great honor when they elected me, a young and untried man, to this important chair. I have tried to justify their confidence. I threw myself into the work of my department and of the college with all my might. I had no other interest or ambition. I have refused (until within six months) to entertain any proposition to go away or to go into other work. It is impossible, however, for me to submit to interference in my work. So long as I am interfered with, my relations to the college are constrained, unsatisfactory, and precarious. I have already lost ground in my work which I had won by great exertion, and I have been forced to suspend further plans on account of the interference to which I have been subjected. While my personal relations to the college are in this uncertain condition I cannot coöperate with my colleagues in planning about the institution as I have been accustomed to do. I seek no action and I deprecate none. I simply seek to place myself on the same plane in regard to this matter on which Pres. Porter placed himself a year ago, and to correct any false impressions which may exist as to my position in the minds of members of the Corporation who heard his paper. I also think that my colleagues ought to know about this matter, for I have been in a false position in respect to them for a year, and as I do not know how or why to select some for my confidence I include all.

Yours respectfully,
W. G. SUMNER.

This letter drew warm expressions of sympathy from Sumner's friends on the faculty, all of whom earnestly urged him not to resign. Professor Simeon E. Baldwin wrote:

Yale College,
Law Department,   June 21, 1881.
MY DEAR MR. SUMNER:

I have read your circular letter with much interest, though I must say that I am half sorry that you have boiled over into print. I believe that the true position of affairs was less misunderstood among your colleagues than you think, and that you have much more sympathy than was expressed.

Several of your fellows on the Academic Faculty have spoken to me lately in the kindest way of their feeling toward you, and of their hope that you would not let anything that has occurred divert you from your work here. 'Time and the hour wear out the longest day,' and there are few controversies with any one man which can justify the change of course of one's whole life.

Yours sincerely,
SIMEON E. BALDWIN.

Professor Beers expressed his opinions more in detail.

DEAR PROFESSOR SUMNER:

Your communication to the members of the Faculty and Corporation, a copy of which I received to-day, does not call for any expression of opinion on the part of individual instructors, and possibly you might regard any such expression from me as unimportant or even impertinent. But as your communication may not perhaps be made the subject of any joint action or discussion by the Academical Faculty, I take this opportunity to put myself individually on record in the matter.

You don't need to be told that my sympathies have been with you in this fight from the beginning. I don't know whether law (or custom, which in this instance is equivalent to law) lodges the power of vetoing a textbook in the President; but I know that the possession of any such power by the President would be a disastrous thing for the college, and would, if exercised, be revolting to the self-respect of every professor in the college. In case any professor uses a textbook which the President thinks mischievous, and declines to give up its use on having his attention called to it, it seems to me that the President should either give up his opposition or else should bring the matter squarely before the permanent officers of instruction where an issue might be made and the professor might have the chance to defend his choice of books. From any decision reached by the professors' body either side might appeal to the Corporation as the final arbiter. So much for the procedure in any supposed case.

In the case that has actually arisen, I, of course, see no need for any objection to the textbook that you have used. I think that no objection should have been made to it. But here, I incline to think, you would find the professors dividing on the line of their theological professions. I imagine that some of them would and do consider Spencer's Sociology (unless in the hands of an orthodox teacher) mischievous. I doubt, however, whether the most bigoted of their number would go to the length of voting against its use, after hearing what you might have to say as to your method of instruction, the purpose for which you used it, etc. The liberty of every teacher to decide on his own methods should be so jealously guarded that only a decided abuse of his privilege ought to justify interference. And I think the faculty would take that ground, could the issue be fairly presented.

One point in your statement I don't fully understand viz., why this matter should prevent your coöperation with your colleagues in planning about the college, etc. I don't believe that the occurrence of this disagreement has made your person or opinion at faculty meetings, etc., any less valuable than it was formerly, and I am sorry that it has seemed necessary to you to absent yourself from the deliberations of a body where every vote on the right side is often needed.

I hope that this thing won't result in your leaving us for other fields of work. I should regard that as the worst loss which the Academical Department could sustain.

Yours sincerely,
HENRY A. BEERS.

Among those to whom Sumner had written with regard to leaving Yale was his old friend, Charles E. Grinnell, then a lawyer in Boston. From him he received the following counsel: "I hope that you will not allow yourself to be driven out, or frozen out, or shrewdly opposed so as to be led to go out in disgust. You know we are comparatively young yet, and we shall bury most of the men who are fifteen years older than we are. Unless you have a mighty good and sure thing, not only in view, but in hand, I say, without further knowledge, stay and bury them."

In the end, the flames of this controversy died down and went out. With perhaps the exception of one or two men of little breadth or outlook, no one wanted Sumner to resign. Even those who did not like him recognized that the college could ill afford to lose him. Either he found no other place to his liking, or the voices of his friends prevailed, for he stayed on at Yale. The disturbance was a salutary one for the college, however. The theological influence there had been strong and intimidating, and there was too much silence and evasion upon the part of the liberals. If untrammeled investigation and honest teaching were to prevail, it was time that some one took a decided stand for academic freedom. In the natural course of events the call came to Sumner and he was not the type of man to shirk it. He made his fight, and thereafter every professor at Yale who was devoted to truth rather than tied to dogma had greater confidence and courage, and every boy who came to the college had a better chance of having the results of human thought and experimentation fairly presented to him.

It is by the imperceptible influence of the teacher's character and example that the atmosphere of a school is created. It is from this that the pupils learn what to admire and what to abhor, what to seek and what to shun.

Integrity in Education.

CHAPTER XVI

TEACHER

IF Sumner had carried out his intention of finding a place for himself in the industrial organization, a great teacher would have been lost to Yale. Without question he was one of the most effective instructors any American college has ever had. A fair supply of good teachers, says Dr. Nicholas Murray Butler in one of his reports as president of Columbia University, may be had. "Of great teachers there are not many in a generation, and nothing is more certain than that such are born and not made. Once in a long while there appears a Huxley, or a Du Bois-Reymond, or a William G. Sumner." [1] Not only did Sumner impart information to those who sought it, such were his character and powers that he drew the youth to him, awakened their minds, extended their horizon, elevated their aims, and molded their characters.

No analysis can adequately account for an influence like that which he exerted upon the stream of boys which for thirty-five years flowed through his classroom; but certain factors in it are obvious. His very physical appearance was in its favor. He had the outward characteristics essential to one who is to impress others which he himself enumerated to a younger contemporary in Hartford. This youth, who was being urged by his grandmother to prepare for the ministry,

[1] Columbia University Bulletin of Information. Annual Report of the President and Treasurer for the year ending June 30, 1919, p. 24.

came to Sumner, then a new-fledged rector, for advice.
The latter looked him over critically for a moment
and then with all the unmitigated truthfulness for
which he was noted declared: "You won't do. In the
first place, you are not tall enough; in the second place,
you haven't the look; and in the third place, you will
never know enough." Sumner had the "look." His
big frame, fine head magnificently bald, stern countenance, and keen unflinching eye, all gave the impression of intellectual power and rugged character. As
he sat in his chair in Osborn Hall and, leaning forward with his long finger stretched out, uttered some
emphatic statement in a deep, iron voice, you knew
in your heart that he was not one to be trifled with or
lightly disputed. You were in the presence of a man.

In a very definite sense of the hackneyed term,
moreover, Sumner was a born teacher. It was his
natural tendency to impart information and to correct
errors. How irresistible this tendency was has been
repeatedly pointed out in former chapters. When
he came into contact with ignorance or misconceptions
it was practically impossible for him not to instruct
or challenge. Teaching was a joy to him, not a burden,
and it was with the greatest delight that he got back
to his classroom after an illness. Instinctively, too,
he conformed to the laws governing the communication
of knowledge and the awakening of the mind. He detested books on pedagogy and it is doubtful if he ever
read one through, but he employed right methods. His
fame went abroad. As early as 1878, President James
B. Angell, of the University of Michigan, to whose
lot it had fallen to give a course in economics, wrote to
Sumner asking him how he taught the subject. In
1883, Dr. Nicholas Murray Butler came up from Columbia to visit Sumner's classroom and to discover,

if possible, the secret of his success. This visit President Butler describes in the following words:

When I began my teaching of logic to undergraduates in Columbia College in the autumn of 1883, I tried to find some method of presenting the subject that would be more interesting, more lively, and more practical than the old-fashioned drill in the rules of formal logic had been. A close friend of mine, William J. Forbes, who was graduated from Yale with the class of 1877, happened one day to describe the method by which Professor William G. Sumner taught economics to undergraduates at Yale. I was so much impressed with its novelty and simplicity, as well as with its effectiveness, that I went to New Haven at an early opportunity and procured from Professor Sumner the privilege of attending his class.

On this particular day he had procured a large number of copies of a daily paper, I think it was the *New York Times,* and he put a copy in the hands of each member of his class. He then had them turn to the page which contained the trade and commerce reports of the previous day and directed their attention to a dispatch from Chicago which recorded the number of cattle, of hogs, and of other farm animals that had reached the Chicago stockyards during the twenty-four hours preceding. He then began an analysis of these facts and figures and by dint of simple exposition and an occasional question he quickly had the whole class deeply interested in the details of the raising, sale, and shipment of farm animals. From this he passed to an examination and elucidation of the economic principles and economic interests involved. In short, he made the simple facts of daily trade life reveal a fascinating story of economic law, economic principle, and economic interest.

I at once proceeded to apply this method to the teaching of logic at Columbia College. I too procured a number of copies of a New York morning paper and put

one copy in the hands of each member of my class. I
then took one of the leading editorials and proceeded to
analyze it with a view to ascertaining the premises or
assumptions upon which it was based and the conclusion
to which it led and with a view to determining the form
and validity of its logical argument. Within a few days
I had my class keenly interested in formal logic and in
throwing the argument of a newspaper editorial into
syllogistic form. For the first time they began to see
that formal logic had application to the practical affairs
and daily happenings of life and that Aristotle was a
pretty modern man after all.

Without doubt, no small degree of Sumner's classroom success was due to the fact that he made life
his textbook. Not only did he begin with everyday
happenings, he ended there, showing the practical application of the facts he portrayed to social welfare
and individual duty. But his influence sprang in an
even greater measure from the view he took of his
office, and the kind of man he himself was.

In the first place, he made teaching his chief business. With him, classroom work was not an irritating
interruption of research, or time grudgingly spent between hours devoted to the writing of books. He engaged in research and wrote much, but he looked upon
teaching as his primary duty and as an opportunity
fraught with great possibilities. He was at Yale, as
he intimated in his introductory lecture, to make men,
to develop the critical faculties of the youth committed
to him, to create in them hatred of shams and love of
truth, to point out to them the laws and principles of
life, to send them out to be useful citizens. The duty
which he owed was not to the college alone, but to the
boys, to their parents, and to the state. He gave
scarcely any "cuts," and refused to make engage-

ments which would conflict with his classes. "He believed in teaching school," writes Professor A. G. Keller, "and had no sympathy with laxity of discipline. Not many years ago there occurred a heavy snowstorm, on a Sunday night and Monday morning, and the trolley cars had not yet begun to run on time for an 8:30 class. Some of us who had waded in through the drifts were wagering that Sumner had been stopped for once, for he lived a mile or so from the college, and was not very strong at the time. But when we went to his lecture room to look, he was there, in his familiar, old-fashioned boots, flushed and panting, but ready for business. He had risen earlier, in anticipation of conditions, and was feeling rather well satisfied with the maintenance of his record." [2] Suffusing all Sumner's teaching there was something approaching religious zeal. It was the medium through which he served the well-being of future generations.

Furthermore, it was obvious to all that he knew his subject deeply, thoroughly, and at first hand. He was not a mere hearer of recitations, or a subservient follower of textbooks, or a quoter of authorities. He was himself an authority. He spoke out of a wide knowledge gained by personal investigation and honest testing and comparison of facts. Nor was his knowledge confined to his own field. Much had he traveled in other realms. He knew the Bible and theology as well as the professors in the divinity school, perhaps better than some of them; he knew the classics as intimately as the teachers of the classics; he was conversant with the different systems of philosophy; he was well read in history; he was much more a man of affairs than most college professors are able to be,

[2] *Yale Review*, 1910, Vol. XIX, p. 9.

and was in close touch with many of the leaders in
the commercial and political world. He illumined subjects not his own. "To things we got in other courses,
which there were meaningless to us," says one of his
old students, "he gave meaning. In mathematics we
studied curves, and never saw any reason for studying
them. Sumner applied them practically in economics
and sociology, and we returned to our mathematics
with greater interest."

He had convictions, too, and expressed them emphatically and fearlessly. He did not so qualify and
refine and balance that the students did not know
what he believed or what they ought to believe. President E. Benjamin Andrews, in point of character not
unlike Sumner, used to startle his classes in ethics
at Brown University by saying: "If any of you men
go into the ministry, don't try to tell your people the
truth." He would then explain his statement by saying that the speaker who attempts to point out every
factor which may enter into a given case, and allows
for all contingencies, makes no impression on his
hearers and defeats his own end. Sumner never tried
to tell the truth in this sense of the phrase. Teachers
who do, only weary and confuse their pupils. He himself studied a matter from every side, with an honesty
unsurpassable, until he had arrived at a conviction.
Then he gave the students the truth as he saw it with
all positiveness, stating his reasons, but not taking
them over all the roads and bypaths which he himself
had traveled, or weighing before them all the pros and
cons whose relative value he himself had appraised.
This habit laid him open to the charge of dogmatism.
Dogmatic he certainly was, but not from any failure
to appreciate the complexity of the matter under consideration or the possibility of being mistaken to which

the most careful man is subject. His mind was always open and he was continually altering his opinions. In his notes one comes across such annotations as these: "(Look out for my use of 'force.' It is to be revised.)" "They hold metaphysical notions of law as an independent power in nature (my old notion). . . ." Neither was he dogmatic from prejudice or partisanship. His assertiveness was due to the fact that he was as much a man of action as a man of thought. He wanted to see wrongs righted and truth prevail, and if these results were to be achieved, it was essential that men should have positive ideas about laws and principles. His most thorough study and his best judgment persuaded him that those which he proclaimed were in line with what intelligent action required. Therefore, he lifted up his voice with strength.

From him, as a result, his students acquired convictions. He sent them away with clearly defined feelings about liberty, democracy, representative government, commerce, money, wealth, and interests. It used to be said that every one left his course in political economy a free trader. Certainly the tariff reform clubs in New York, from which much of the agitation against protectionism emanated, were dominated by men who had been under his teaching. Not all his students in after life adhered closely to the principles Sumner laid down, but often they would explain their deviation, in a rather shamefaced way, by saying, not that they had found Sumner wrong, but that on the grounds of practical expediency they had yielded to the exigencies of the situation in which they found themselves.

Another reason for Sumner's hold on the students was that he was of the new era just opening to which they themselves belonged. The most of their in-

structors were anxious to preserve the existing order
of things, or, if they were dissatisfied with it, were
rather timid about expressing their sympathies with
the ideas and demands of the progressives. Sumner,
however, was openly and emphatically for the new
day. "We revered and admired the old men," said
Mr. Henry DeForest Baldwin in his address at Sumner's memorial service, "but they did not altogether
meet our needs. The college had not then departed
very far from the old curriculum which characterized
institutions of learning for the three or four previous
centuries. . . . We were looking for a teacher who
we felt could free himself from the old ways of thought,
and whom we could rely upon to speak boldly, honestly,
and clearly from the new point of view. We found
our intellectual leader in Sumner."

Every one, furthermore, loves a fearless fighter;
young men, especially. This Sumner was preëminently. In the classroom he did not hesitate to assail
whatever aroused his ire. In talks to the students on
current events he would speak in the plainest terms,
irrespective of the political or social connections of
his hearers, and inflict merciless blows upon both policies and men. That he himself was being subjected
constantly to all kinds of attack the students were well
aware. His controversy with President Porter was
not a thing hidden from them, and they felt that he
was fighting their battles as well as his own. Assaults
upon him in the newspapers, and attempts to undermine him in his position at Yale, always rallied the
students about him and called forth letters from them
in his support, the most of which reveal a boyish pride
in the writer's idol and the confidence that he cannot
be overthrown.

In an exceptional degree, too, Sumner had the gift

of lucid exposition and terse, epigrammatic statement. Following his thought did not require the mental effort which it was necessary to exercise in some other class-rooms. Homely illustrations made clear his meaning, and every now and then some striking statement would be uttered which the student would later repeat with great zest to his mates and perhaps remember all his life. "He knew better than most," says one who had been under him, "the value of a paradox judiciously suggested and defended. For one thing, if used in the lecture room, it compelled instant attention. It challenged some commonly accepted opinion or custom, and probably at first gave no hint of what he meant to suggest by it before he was through. Every hearer was set at guessing instantly what it meant and how it was so applied. . . . It was of the nature of a challenge, like a slap in the face." In Sumner's classroom, Mr. Otto Bannard states, "against our will we became willing and eager, . . . and if we wanted to cut, we cut other recitations. Sumner's was not drudgery; it was stimulation."

But above all, perhaps, he commanded the respect and liking of the students because of his honesty. In arriving at his conclusions he did not allow himself to be influenced by his own preferences or prejudices, but excluded the personal equation as completely as it is possible for a human being to do so. He did not permit prevailing notions or any consideration for revered authorities to warp his judgment. He never blinked at the facts, however disagreeable they might be, or hesitated to make a frank statement of his opinions. The fact that these opinions might be contrary to the teaching which his hearers had received at home, or out of harmony with those held by the officials and supporters of the college, or the fear that

they might unsettle some and force them to make new
intellectual and religious adjustments, did not weigh
with him for an instant. All theories of accommodation he despised. Any concealment of the truth, as
he had forcefully declared long before in one of his
sermons, he deemed fatal to a teacher's usefulness,
for it entailed sacrifice of what was fundamentally
important,—the pupil's confidence. He took no delight in disturbing a man's peace of soul, but he had
too high a sense of his responsibility to countenance
ignorance and error whatever the effect of enlightenment and emancipation might be. "In the other departments of the college," says a graduate of the
eighties, "we felt that the professors hedged and modified their statements in the interests of orthodoxy and
security. From Sumner we knew we got the truth.
We could trust him."

The need for a science of life in society is urgent, and it is increasing every year.

The Science of Sociology.

CHAPTER XVII

SOCIOLOGIST

EARLY in the nineties Sumner relinquished his undergraduate work in economics, and though he continued to give courses in this subject to advanced students, and wrote and lectured frequently on economic questions of popular interest, he directed his attention thereafter more and more exclusively to the field of sociology. People generally never came to associate him with this department of study, however. To them he was always an economist and publicist. Even as late as 1907 his election as president of the American Sociological Society created surprise, not only without, but within that organization. To many of his friends and admirers his change came as something of a shock. They were accustomed to think of him in connection with the great problems of the political and financial world, a teacher whose keenness, courage, knowledge, and broad experience made him invaluable to those who were soon to be in the thick of life. It was difficult for his old pupils to picture him as living mentally in ancient times, digging through moldy layers of accretions for the roots of social institutions, concerned with the customs of primitive peoples rather than with the conditions of his own day. It was hard for them to believe that he turned from the latter to the former willingly.

The transition, however, was undoubtedly in line with Sumner's development and desires. Opposition to his views had nothing to do with it. As preceding crises had shown, Yale prized freedom of speech too highly and appreciated Sumner's greatness too well to let any antagonism which his vigorously expressed opinions may have created interfere at all with his college work. Nor was his faith in the general principles for which he had contended in the least shaken. Indeed, he was more fully committed to them at the day of his death than when he began to teach, for in his sociological research he had found much to substantiate them. The statement has been made that he became dissatisfied with the results of his work in economics. This is doubtless true. He himself said that in his youth he believed that if any one only worked hard enough he could present the facts and laws of the industrial organization in such a way as to influence perceptibly for the better the economic conditions of the country. Time disillusioned him. What experience revealed was that while the principles which he advocated were altogether right, they could not be applied absolutely and in their totality to existing conditions as he had assumed. The industrial organization had become so complex, and its errors and evils so intertwined with human interests, that concessions had to be made and partial adaptations countenanced. For such procedure he had neither the ability nor the taste. Furthermore, he had learned that human beings in general are not controlled in their actions by cold logic, and that the reasonableness of a policy, however vividly demonstrated, does not in itself impel them to adopt it. They are swayed as much, if not more, by inferior forces. Persuaded of this, he certainly lost some of his zest for the work he had been pursuing.

But most influential of all the conditions which caused him to withdraw his thought and effort from the field of economics was the fact that his chief interest was, and always had been, in sociology. Of this there is abundant evidence. We have his own testimony that with the keenest avidity, after reading Buckle, he discussed with other students at Oxford the possibility of a science of society based upon a study of history. His sermons disclose that as a clergyman his reflection was much upon social facts and forces, and that he was groping for some satisfactory explanation and classification of them. The idea of a science of society was ever in the background of his mind. His introduction to Spencer's "Study of Sociology" was an epoch in his life. It pointed out the path by which, he believed, that which he sought might be achieved. At once he formed a class for the reading and discussion of Spencer's book, which, he says, was probably the first course in sociology ever given in an American college.

The truth of the matter was that Sumner was so constituted that he could not be content to be an economist merely, but was forced to be a sociologist. In fact, he came to feel that he could not be an economist unless he was a sociologist. It was characteristic of him to see things whole. He could not narrow his vision and study a phenomenon as if none other existed. Whatever he viewed he saw in its manifold relationships. It was inevitable, therefore, that he should be especially conscious of the solidarity of human life. That there exists no one department of interests and activities wholly distinct from the rest, is a truth which it was impossible for him to ignore. Each, he perceived, is more or less interwoven with the others, and all are determined by the ruling desires of human beings living together under the conditions imposed by nature. Consequently, whenever he looked at an economic condition, what he always saw was a particular aspect of the social organization. He had, too, the analytical type of mind. It was not possible for him simply to describe the details and relationships of a set of circumstances. He must get behind them, trace back their connections, and discover the laws and forces which governed them. Pursuing this method in relationship to economic phenomena, he was all the time finding himself in the field of sociology. As early as 1881 he declared that "It is to the pursuit of sociology and the study of the industrial organization in combination with the other organizations of society that we must look for the more fruitful development of political economy. We are already in such a position with sociology that a person who has gained what we now possess of that science will bring to bear upon economic problems a sounder judgment and a more correct conception of all social relations than a person who may have read a library of the existing treatises on political economy. The essential elements of political economy are only corollaries or special cases of sociological principles." [1]

Such being the facts, it was inevitable that in the field of sociology Sumner's deepest interest should center, and that there his most painstaking efforts should be put forth. No greater ambition possessed him, it is safe to say, than that of making substantial contribution to the establishment of a science of society. While he was teaching economics and discussing public questions he was also delving into the history of mankind and the origin and growth of social institutions. He made and classified thousands of notes containing information derived from an almost incredible number of sources, many of them difficult of

[1] "Sociology," "War and Other Essays," p. 182.

access. No task the performance of which promised
to make him better fitted for the work seemed too exacting. After he was forty-five years old, on evidence of dates in his dictionaries and grammars, he
acquired a good working knowledge of the two Scandi-
navian tongues, Dutch, Spanish, Portuguese, Italian,
Russian, and Polish. In 1899 he began to write out
the results of all this study in the form of a textbook.
Desiring at a certain point in this undertaking to introduce his own treatment of the "mores," and feeling that he could not do justice to it in a single chapter,
he turned aside from the work he had begun and wrote
his great treatise "Folkways," the preface to which
closes with these words: "My next task is to finish
the sociology."

Unfortunately death came before this could be accomplished, but what he had already done makes it
certain that his reputation will rest upon his achievements as a sociologist. In the field of economics he
was a great expositor and propagandist. He set forth
fundamental principles in their relationship to history and present-day conditions with great clearness.
As one of his contemporaries, Professor F. W. Taussig,
remarks, "He expounded and clarified certain doctrines, simple enough in their essence, with a remarkable gift of phrase and with telling effect," but "he
cannot be said to have contributed anything novel to
economics." "Folkways," on the other hand, not
only contains a vast amount of data with respect to
social origins, which makes it a reference book of
great value, it also offers an interpretation of them
which is a definite advance in the development of a
science of society. The recognition accorded to it since
its appearance has steadily increased. Much higher
than the estimate of Sumner as an economist just

quoted, is an estimate of him as a sociologist by one of the best known living authorities, Professor Franklin H. Giddings, who, in one of his latest books, refers to the "teaching of William Graham Sumner," and adds, "whom, now that he is gone, we are beginning to recognize as perhaps the most consistently sociological, if not the greatest of sociologists." [2] In a private letter, Professor Giddings has this further to say about Sumner, both as a man and as a scientist: "For almost half a century I have held him in admiration and respect as one of the ablest and most useful men that America has produced. The clarity of his intellect, the transparent sincerity of his thinking, its wide range and cohesion, have rarely been equaled. These qualities stand out in all his writings as do also his hatred of humbug and his devastating wit. In the field in which I myself have worked he was a trail blazer whose 'Folkways' will, I think, for all time be recognized as having the value that attaches only to the discovery and annexation of territory."

The motive which impelled Sumner in this sociological research, as in all his labors, was the advancement of human welfare. A purely academic interest was something which he was incapable of cherishing. He never sought knowledge for its own sake or for personal satisfaction or renown. Like Comte he "united a scientific view of life with a passion for humanity." Nothing is more false or unfair than to picture Sumner as a cold, hard, crass individualist and advocate of *laissez faire*. Those who have done so reveal a very superficial acquaintance both with the man and his writings, and often, ill-temper, because of his criticism of their way of doing things. Nothing could be more contrary to fact than that he was against all attempts

[2] "Studies in the Theory of Human Society," New York, 1922, p. 293.

at reform, a scoffer at every effort for social betterment. That for years he fought protectionism almost
single-handed is in itself sufficient refutation of this
charge. The sentimental school of sociologists, it is
true, he held up to ridicule and scorn. With the people
whose sovereign remedy for social ills is to get laws
passed, and the people who try to remold this world
according to their hearts' desire, and the motley
throng of uplifters with souls afire, he had no patience.
Perhaps he did not always treat them with the courtesy and consideration due them, but if he did not, it
was because he was so conscious of the harm they were
doing, the injustice they were inflicting on the worthiest
class of citizens, and the trouble they were making for
succeeding generations, that he could not but speak
in the plainest and sternest terms. His own life
throughout, however, was dominated by the desire
to remove the ignorance and error which prevail and
the limitation and suffering which they entail. No one
was ever more obsessed with the passion to make this
a better world than was the youthful Sumner. As
editor and preacher he was a fearless rebuker and
fiery advocate. Much of his exhausting work as a publicist was inspired by a sense of duty to society. If he
attacked certain forms of idealism, so called, and
poured contempt upon the ordinary type of social reformer, it was not because he was a cynic, or one who
felt that nothing could be done, but because he deemed
these reformers and their schemes to be social evils
themselves. He treated them as the thoroughly and
scientifically trained physician treats a quack; and he
had no less sympathy for the oppressed and suffering,
and no less faith in the efficacy of proper treatment,
than has such a physician. From his point of view
they were meddling ignorantly and disastrously with

a great, complex organization, continually changing in accordance with the natural laws which control it. The harm done by such unintelligent interference is incalculable. It rolls on in ever-widening circles, and sets secondary forces to work. We lose sight of the evil effects, so many and complicated do they become, but they go on for generations. Absurd attempts to make the world over Sumner ruthlessly attacked, but his warfare was nevertheless in the interests of a better world. His own positive contribution was a whole life given in a sacrificial spirit to such an objective study of the characteristics of the social body and the laws governing it as should furnish a basis for intelligent behavior in relation thereto. To distinguish such scientific procedure from the sentimental and irrational, with which in the minds of most people the term "sociology" is associated, Sumner coined the word "societology," which, however, has never won general acceptance, and he himself regarded it with considerable philological disfavor.

In the social field Sumner was as independent an investigator and as tireless and patient a seeker after truth as any man could be; nevertheless he had his inspirers and guides. In Charles Darwin he found the spirit and method which appealed to him most strongly. The former's industry and perseverance, his honesty of mind, his unrelaxing vigilance in pursuit of facts, his painstaking verifications, kindled Sumner's admiration and gave him a concrete exemplification of the kind of person to whom truth reveals itself.

The rather widespread opinion that Sumner was a disciple of Herbert Spencer is more than half false. He neither owed as much to Spencer nor was in as close agreement with him as is generally assumed. Spencer's doctrine of *laissez faire* was never Sumner's.

The latter allowed far greater scope for legitimate state activity than did Spencer, whom we can never imagine serving for twenty-five years on a state board of education. Their conceptions of liberty and justice were similar, it is true, but there is no evidence that Sumner derived his opinions on these matters from the English philosopher. On the contrary, they seem to have been acquired from the reading and associations of his youth. From Harriet Martineau, Sumner learned that rights are legal conventions and not natural endowments, and Thomas Hooker gave him additional ideas regarding them. These were supplemented and clarified later by Ludwig Gumplowicz, from whom he gathered much also with respect to group conflict. To Julius Lippert he was perhaps more indebted than to Spencer, for in the "Kulturgeschichte der Menschheit" he found a rich mine of suggestions regarding the origin and evolution of social institutions, which were invaluable to him in the construction of his own science of society.

Spencer's type of mind, moreover, was not one with which Sumner's had affinity. One can imagine the feelings of Sumner if he ever read in the "Principles of Ethics" statements like these: "A game of skill is being played with one whose little boy is a spectator. The father's play is such as makes his antagonist tolerably certain of victory, should he put out his strength. But if he is adequately swayed by the sentiment of negative benevolence, he will, not obtrusively, but in a concealed way, play below his strength so as to let the father beat him. . . . In like manner none will doubt that one who, in a discussion or in a wit-combat, might be easily overcome, may, even though at other times unworthy of consideration, be rightly let off under particular circumstances. Say, for in-

stance, that his *fiancée* is present." The mental
processes of one who declares ethical any such subter-
fuge and betrayal of the truth, Sumner would have
found difficult to understand. Neither was Spencer
the open-minded seeker for knowledge, however disagreeable it might prove, whom alone Sumner commended. Says one of the former's biographers, Mr.
Hugh Elliot, "He often boasted how he had never
read more than a few pages of Kant, and had thrown
aside the works of that philosopher as soon as he came
upon a conclusion with which he disagreed. And he
applied the same principle, or gave in to the same
weakness, throughout." Spencer, furthermore, was
a philosopher rather than a scientist, concerned with
constructing a formal, abstract system. This there
is no evidence that Sumner ever accepted or that he
had any use for it. He was accustomed to say that the
"Principles of Sociology" was about the only part of
Spencer's work that would live, because here he was
obliged to get down to facts.

Just two things Spencer did for Sumner, but these
were of such fundamental importance that he always
felt that he owed the former a great debt. In the first
place, Spencer defined for him the field of sociology
and revealed the magnificent possibilities which it contained. This concrete vision, coming to him as a youth
eager to discover how the corporate life of human
beings could be made easier, more intelligent, and
more profitable, but confused by crude notions floating
about in his mind, was an inspiration which lasted all
his life. From it he got his conception of social forces.
It solved for him the difficulty about the relation of
social science to history, and rescued it from the domain of the cranks. Thereafter he was able to see
with some distinctness what was involved in the task

to be undertaken. To Spencer, also, Sumner felt himself and all sociologists indebted in a marked degree
for demonstrating the method which must be employed
in the establishment of a science of society, and for
revealing the governing law in the social realm. "To
win a correct method," he said in his address at the
farewell banquet given to Mr. Spencer on the occasion
of his visit to this country, in 1882, "is, as we all know,
to win more than half the battle. When so much is
secured, the question of making the discoveries, solv-
ing the problems, eliminating the errors, and testing
the results, is only a question of time and of strength
to collect and master the data." Spencer he credits
with having established the universality of the evolutionary principle by ample inductions in the experimental sciences and given it to sociology as a governing law. "It will be one of its crowning triumphs,"
he says, "to bring light and order into the social problems which are of universal bearing on all mankind.
Mr. Spencer is breaking the path for us into this domain. We stand eager to follow him into it, and we
look upon his work on sociology as a grand step in
the history of science." Sumner's relationship to
Spencer was not that of a disciple, therefore, but that
of an enthusiastic comer into a field in which the former had been a pioneer and of whose boundaries and
conditions he had made a survey.

Thus all things conspired to make Sumner a sociologist. Such was his nature that the social chaos in
which he found himself troubled him profoundly, and
the impulse to bring some measure of order into it,
and therewith greater freedom and opportunity to
mankind, moved him irresistibly. Economics he found
too narrow a department in which to confine his
thought and endeavors. The need of a science of

society broad enough to solve the ever-changing problems of the social organization he felt to be "urgent" and "increasing every year." To offer a solid, lasting contribution to such a science, he at length made his main task. The next few chapters will sketch his methods, some of the main results of his investigations, and his conclusions as to what man's attitude should be toward the conditions in which he finds himself.

Life in society is the life of a human society on this earth. Its elementary conditions are set by the nature of human beings and the nature of the earth.

Sociology.

CHAPTER XVIII

DETERMINING FACTORS IN SOCIAL EVOLUTION

As might be expected of one committed to the evolutionary hypothesis and so characteristically all-inclusive in his view, Sumner beheld societal phenomena as an aspect of the earth's history. Like geological and botanical phenomena they are the necessary accompaniment of facts and forces inherent in the natural order. The earth brought forth man, and through his reaction upon his surroundings according to the laws of his being, social relations and institutions were born. He did not think them out or consciously will them. Since fundamental conditions are what they are, their appearance, like that of mountains and forests, was inevitable. Referring to the socialists, Sumner says: "They criticize 'the system,' by which they mean the social world as it is. They do not perceive that the world of human society is what has resulted from thousands of years of life. It is not a system any more than a man sixty years old is a system. It is a product. To talk of making another system is like talking of making a man of sixty into something else than what his life has made him.[1] Nowhere can this truth be better observed than in the advancing organization of America, from the colonial settlement up to the present time. At whatever phase of it we look, the industrial, civil, social, or political, we find that it has been "a life process, a growth process, which our society had to go through just as

---

[1] "Reply to a Socialist," "Challenge of Facts and Other Essays," p. 55.

inevitably as an infant after birth must go on to the stages of growth and experience which belong to all human beings as such.''

Back of all social phenomena there are four facts or constants. They are in the nature of things and from generation to generation persist unchanged. It is the existence of these in juxtaposition which unites individuals into societies, generates social activities, and determines their direction. They are man's relation to the earth; the solidarity of the race; the presence of mystery in human experience; and the ruling motives of human nature, hunger, love, vanity, and fear.

Man is a piece of the earth. His relationship thereto is that of a part subordinate to the whole. Out of it along with other forms of life he has come. In conjunction with theirs his existence must be maintained. To the physical laws and conditions surrounding him, his well being requires that he properly adjust himself. From the earth, under the conditions it sets, he must get his means of subsistence. Toward him as he approaches her on the enterprise upon which his life depends, she turns a cold, hard face. There is no sentiment in nature, no predilection to serve man's interests. That she was made for him is true only in the sense that he may possess her if he can. Before her he has ''no more right to life than a rattlesnake; he has no more right to liberty than any wild beast; his right to the pursuit of happiness is nothing but a license to maintain the struggle for existence if he can find within himself the power with which to do it.'' [2] From her, moreover, he gets only what he extorts. Life is ever a struggle, not a feast of good things. There is no ''boon'' in nature, nor has there

[2] "The Boon of Nature," "Earth Hunger and Other Essays," p. 234.

ever been. On the contrary she presents man with a
task perilous and of appalling magnitude. He lives
and grows if he is strong enough to conquer obstacles;
if not, "then he may lie down and die of despair on
the face of the boon and not a breeze, or a leaflet, or a
sunbeam will vary its due course to help or pity him.
This is the only attitude in which we find nature when
we come face to face with her in her original attitude
toward mankind; it is only when we come to her, armed
with knowledge, science, and capital, that we force
back her limitations and win some wider and easier
chances of existence for ourselves."

Success in this struggle with nature for the means
of self-maintenance and self-realization is dependent
upon the accumulation of capital. "Capital is any
product of labor which is used to assist production."
So long as a man has to use all his time and strength
just to keep alive, all he succeeds in doing is to keep
alive. If he tills the soil with his fingers or a stick,
he gets a small crop. With a spade or a hoe he might
get a larger one. But to fashion even the rudest of
these takes time, during which the laborer must still
eat and drink and wear. Not until he achieves a sufficient surplus of life's necessities to maintain him while
he constructs his tools can he increase his power over
nature and begin the long, hard climb up the road of
progress. "The instrumentality by which, from the
beginning, man has won and held every step of this
development of civilization, is capital." First the
material and then the spiritual, is one of the oldest
and most fundamental of laws. "It is impossible to
stir a step in any direction which has been selected
without capital: we cannot subsist men, i. e., laborers,
without it; we cannot sustain study or science without
it; we cannot recruit the wasted energies of the race

without it; we cannot win leisure for deliberation without it; we cannot, therefore, undertake greater tasks,
that is, make progress, without it.''

The struggle for existence against the rough conditions presented by nature, and the acquisition of power
over nature through the securing of capital, do not in
themselves give rise to societal forces, however. They
do so only in connection with the second fact of the
natural order already mentioned—the solidarity of
the race. Whatever may be the prevailing indifference
to the practical implication of Shylock's words, their
truthfulness as a description of the relationship between human beings is too obvious to be disputed,—
''fed with the same food, hurt with the same weapons,
subject to the same diseases, healed by the same means,
warmed and cooled by the same winter and summer.''
All have the same feelings, needs, and ruling motives.
All are subject to the same fundamental life conditions. All tend to react to their environment in essentially the same way, for ethnography discloses that
primitive peoples all over the earth present a surprising similarity in their habitudes. All are working to
secure what their lives require out of the store, be it
little or much, which their portion of the earth affords.

From the fact that the struggle for existence is carried on by individuals of such oneness of nature, interests, and activities, the number of whom ever tends
to increase, the competition of life arises. Monopoly
is in nature, and what one man utilizes another, though
equally needful, cannot. For what there is to get,
therefore, individuals must compete. Competition is
a natural law and one of the principal societal forces.
Men strive with each other or with the flora and fauna
with which they are associated. The collision may be
light and unimportant if the supplies are large and

the number of men small, or it may be harsh and violent if there are many men striving for a small supply; but the fact ever remains that "every man who stands on the earth's surface excludes every one else from so much of it as he covers; every one who eats a loaf of bread appropriates to himself for the time being the exclusive use and enjoyment of so many square feet of the earth's surface as were required to raise the wheat; every one who burns wood to warm himself, appropriates in monopoly a part of the land so far as the land is of utility or interest to man. Perhaps the most fundamental fact which makes this a world of toil and self-denial is that two men cannot eat the same loaf of bread. This pitiless and hopeless monopoly is, in the last analysis, the reason for capital, and rent, for property and rights, for law and the state, for poverty and inequality."[3] It develops human powers, classifies individuals, and disciplines them. It makes the advantages of capital, education, talent and training count for the utmost. "It draws out the social scale upward and downward to great extremes and produces aristocratic social organizations in spite of all the dogmas of equality."

But if the solidarity of the race creates competition, it also makes possible coöperation. Among those who are essentially alike there can be sympathy, mutual understanding, imitation, and common effort for common gain. These in turn will tend to produce greater similarity and cohesion. The force of competition is such that in the nature of things it leads to coöperation. When one man is trying to carry on the struggle for existence in the same environment with others there arises this alternative: "He and the others may

[3] "The Boon of Nature," "Earth Hunger and Other Essays," pp. 235, 236.

so interfere with each other that all shall fail, or they may combine, and by coöperation raise their efforts against nature to a higher power." This latter method has given rise to the industrial organization. "The crisis which produced it is constantly renewed, and men are forced to raise the organization to greater complexity and more comprehensive power, without limit." Such unions always entail the subordination of minor interests, however. For the satisfaction of his most urgent needs an individual has to sacrifice the gratification of less important desires. What he gets he has to pay for with his liberty. Nevertheless, the necessity for this "antagonistic coöperation" is so great that not only among primitive peoples, but even among the plants and animals of the desert, there is combination to secure the maximum of life.

Another fact of the natural order which has had vast influence in shaping societal phenomena is that of mystery. To the man of early times this was always very close; for the modern man scientific knowledge has pushed it back, but even he comes to it ultimately. Outside of a very limited range everything was a terror to the savage. To this fact his mythology bears witness. "The civilized man is light and careless, or even merry in the face of nature, because he understands her so well; when nature, however, puts on her terrors or her mysteries, we quickly lose our spirit and come to feel our insignificance." But it was not through nature alone that the fact of life's mystery was brought home to man. "There was an element in the most elementary experience which was irrational and defied all expedient methods. One might use the best-known means with the greatest care, yet fail of the result. On the other hand, one might get a great result with no effort at all. One might also incur a calamity without any fault of his own. This was the aleatory element in life, the element of risk and loss, good or bad fortune. This element is never absent from the affairs of men. It has greatly influenced their life philosophy and policy. On the one side, good luck may mean something for nothing, the extreme case of prosperity and felicity. On the other side, ill luck may mean failure, loss, calamity, and disappointment, in spite of the most earnest and well-planned endeavor. The minds of men always dwelt more on bad luck. They accepted ordinary prosperity as a matter of course. Misfortunes arrest their attention and remain in their memory. Hence the ills of life are the mode of manifestation of the aleatory element which has most affected life policy.''[4]

In his efforts to account for these facts of experience man constructed an imaginary environment of spiritual powers. In early times he attributed all incidents to the agency of men or of ghosts and spirits. Good and bad luck were attributed to superior beings and resulted from their good will or their displeasure. The struggle for existence, therefore, had to be carried on with reference to these as well as to material objects. Religious rites became the means by which men sought to control the aleatory element in the interest of daily welfare. These and the ideas associated with them have greatly influenced social development, affecting markedly the acquiring and use of capital, men's treatment of their fellows, and nearly every custom and institution. ''The destruction of a man's goods at his death was a great waste of capital, and it must have had a disastrous effect on the interests of the living, and must have very seriously hindered the development of civilization. With this custom we

[4] "Folkways," Ginn and Company, 1907, pp. 6, 7.

must class all the expenditure of labor and capital on graves, temples, pyramids, rites, sacrifices, and support of priests, so far as these were supposed to benefit the dead. The faith in goblinism produced otherworldly interests which overruled ordinary worldly interests. Foods have often been forbidden which were plentiful, the prohibition of which injuriously lessened the food supply. . . . On the other hand, the protective taboo which forbade killing crocodiles, pythons, cobras, and other animal enemies of man was harmful to his interests, whatever the motive.'' [5] Furthermore, the mystical and practical elements blended in creating ideas of societal welfare. ''It is quite impossible for us to disentangle the elements of philosophy and custom so as to determine priority and the causative position of either. Our best judgment is that the mystic philosophy is regulative, not creative, in its relation to the folkways. They reacted upon each other. The faith in the world philosophy drew lines outside of which the folkways must not go. Crude and vague notions of societal welfare were formed from the notion of pleasing the ghosts, and from such notions of expediency as the opinion that, if there were not children enough, there would not be warriors enough, or that, if there were too many children, the food supply would be inadequate. The notion of welfare was an inference and resultant from these mystic and utilitarian generalizations.'' [6]

The fourth determining factor in social evolution is man's own nature. Sumner was not a psychologist. He attempted no subtle analysis of the human mind, and made no assertions as to how, because of its constitution, it must act. Much less was he inclined to seek there the social bond and the final explanation of

[5] "Folkways," p. 26.   [6] *Ibid.*, p. 30.

the course human relationships have taken. What he did do was to go up and down the stream of history and observe how in the face of life conditions man has always tended to respond. From a multitude of examples thus gathered he was convinced that human nature has always been controlled by four major motives— hunger, the desire for the means of subsistence; love, in the sense of sex-passion; vanity; and fear of ghosts and spirits. All man's good and all his ill have arisen from these, and to one or more of them run the roots of every social institution. How they operate Sumner illustrates with reference to war: "The four great motives which move men to social activity are hunger, love, vanity, and fear of superior powers. If we search out the causes which have moved men to war we find them under each of these motives or interests. Men have fought for hunting grounds, for supplies which are locally limited and may be monopolized, for commerce, for slaves, and probably also for human flesh. These motives come under hunger, or the food-quest, or more widely under the economic effort to win subsistence. They have fought for and on account of women, which we must put partly under love, although the women were wanted chiefly as laborers and so, along with the slaves, would come under the former head. They have fought to win heads or scalps, or other trophies, and for honor or dignity, or purely for glory; this comes under the operation of vanity. They have fought for blood revenge, to prevent or punish sorcery, and to please their gods; these motives belong under the fear of superior powers. It was reserved for modern civilized men to fight on account of differences of religion, and from this motive the fiercest and most persistent wars have been waged."[7]

[7] "War and Other Essays," pp. 14, 15.

The process of making folkways is never superseded or changed. It goes on now just as it did at the beginning of civilization. "Use and wont" exert their force on all men always.

Folkways.

CHAPTER XIX

THE FOLKWAYS

Of the elemental facts stated in the preceding chapter societal phenomena are the necessary accompaniment. Man, impelled by hunger, love, vanity, and fear seeks to adapt himself as advantageously as possible to the conditions which his relationship to nature, to his fellows, and to the mystery in his experience creates. The means of adaptation are the social institutions which have developed in the course of this unceasing struggle for adjustment. Sumner finds the beginning or germ of these institutions in the folkways. "The folkways are habits of the individual and customs of the society which arise from efforts to satisfy needs."

Their origin, like all origins, is lost in mystery. "We go up the stream of history to the utmost point for which we have evidence of its course. Then we are forced to reach out into the darkness upon the line of direction marked by the remotest course of the historic stream." If, however, "we put together all that we have learned from anthropology and ethnography about primitive men and primitive society, we perceive that the first task of life is to live." Man did not think before he acted. The pressure of need was too great and the hand of death was too near. Every moment brought necessities which had to be supplied at once. It is generally admitted that men inherited some guiding instinct from their beast ancestry, which controlled and aided the first efforts to satisfy needs. Such efforts, however, were clumsy and blundering.

The method was that of trial and failure, which produced repeated pain, loss, and disappointment. Satisfaction and pain, on the one side and the other, were the rude constraints which defined the line in which effort proceeded.

Under such a condition selection would naturally result. Men would adopt those ways of meeting the necessities of life which worked best. These would become habitual, and routine and skill would develop them. Since the struggle to maintain existence, though carried on individually, took place in groups, there would be a tendency for the ways proved best to become the ways of all. Thus habit in the individual became custom in the group, and we have the folkways. They are not, therefore, "creations of human purpose and wit. They are like products of natural forces which men unconsciously set in operation." They reach a final form of adaption to an interest, are handed down by tradition and change to meet new conditions, but within fixed limits, and without rational reflection or purpose.

Language, Sumner selects as one of the best examples of the folkways and quotes Professor W. D. Whitney's description of its development. "No one ever set himself deliberately at work to invent or improve language—or did so, at least, with any valuable and abiding result. The work is all accomplished by a continual satisfaction of the needs of the moment, by ever yielding to an impulse and grasping a possibility which the already acquired treasure of words and forms, and the habit of their use, suggest and put within reach." "Every single item of alteration, of whatever kind, and of whatever degree of importance, goes back to some individual who set it in circulation, from whose example it gained a wider currency, until

it finally won that general assent which is alone required in order to make anything in language proper
and authoritative." [1]

Not from experiment and proved efficiency alone,
however, did the folkways arise. The presence of
mystery in human experience gave opportunity for an
imaginary interpretation of events and their demands,
and the supposed control of the aleatory element by
magical rites influenced habit and custom in a marked
degree. Ghost fear produced needs which man was
as eager to satisfy as those of hunger and the family.
Irrational actions, also, based on false inferences,
played their part. "On the Nicobar Islands some na-
tives who had just begun to make pottery died. The
art was given up and never again attempted." A
great number of similar cases illustrating how the current mode of reasoning among nature people affected
their ways could be produced. History shows that
vanity, too, has been a powerful motive in influencing
men's acts. Group vanity has often been more powerful than personal, and the desire to gratify it has often
proved superior to rational conviction. Thus superstition, pseudo-knowledge, speculation, and pride, as
well as pure experimentation, have determined man's
ideas regarding what it was best to do.

It is in the nature of the folkways to become fixed
and coercive. That the customs of the older and more
experienced members of a group should have great
authority is inevitable. In former times much deference was shown the old and their practices were imitated by the younger. On the other hand, it was natural for the old to cling stubbornly to the examples of
their predecessors and to what was most familiar to
them. Ethnocentrism, too, increased this tendency to

[1] "Folkways," pp. 135, 136.

WILLIAM GRAHAM SUMNER

rigidity and permanence, for it is characteristic of a group to consider itself the center of everything, and to rate other peoples with reference to itself. Each nourishes its own pride and vanity, boasts of its superiority, exalts its own divinities, and looks with contempt on all outsiders. Contact of groups increases group consciousness, therefore, and tends to strengthen the hold which each has upon its members.

From the folkways proceed all ideas of right, morality, truth, life policy, and world philosophy. They are not of independent origin, brought to the folkways to test them. The latter, according to the primitive view, were right because they were traditional and existed in fact. They were their own warrant and not subject to verification by experience. They contained in themselves the authority of ancestral ghosts, in the former ways of whom it was well to walk since they still lived on, as it was believed, in a world like this and would visit pain and loss upon mankind. The ghosts, furthermore, had rights, and could enforce them, and these rights involved duties on the part of the living. Out of this view of things there arose a complete world philosophy from which a life policy in the interest of welfare was deduced.

When folkways come to be viewed as right and beneficial in an accepted interpretation of life and the conditions which it lays upon well being, then they become *mores*. "The mores are the folkways, including the philosophical and ethical generalizations as to societal welfare which are suggested by them, and inherent in them, as they grow." They are "capable of producing inferences, developing into new forms, and extending their constructive influence over men and society."[2]

2 "Folkways," p. 30.

In order to appreciate how the mores work within a group, it is necessary to understand the composition of a group. Each contains extreme diversity because made up of individuals no two of whom are alike; yet each has solidarity and internal correlation. "If a number of persons with different degrees of power and resistance are acted upon by the same influences, it is most probable that the greatest number of them will reach the same and a mean degree of self-realization, and others in proportion to their power and resistance." If, therefore, we take societal value as a criterion of the classification of a social group, we shall find that the masses constitute the great central portion, or core. Through the center of these runs the line of mediocrity. Above this, the individuals rise through successive gradations of steadily decreasing numbers up to the talent class. The individuals in this rise in similar fashion to the extremely limited genius group. Below the line of mediocrity, the individuals sink through successive gradations of steadily decreasing numbers into the unskilled and illiterate, the proletariat, and the defective, dependent, and delinquent classes. Thus a social group is made up of divisions within which are sub-divisions. Each of these has its own mores. "This is true of ranks, professions, industrial classes, religious and philosophical sects, and all other sub-divisions of society. Individuals are in two or more of these groups at the same time, so that there is compromise and neutralization. Other mores are common to the whole society."

In connection with the mores the masses are of great importance. They are not the base of a social pyramid, but the core of society. They are the real bearers of the mores. They accept life as they find it and live on by tradition and habit. They are con-servative, but their conservatism is not that of castes and aristocracies whose members resist change of custom and institutions by virtue of which they hold social power; it is not produced by interest, it is in-stinctive. "Change would make new effort necessary to win routine and habit. It is therefore irksome. The masses, moreover, have not the power to reach out after 'improvements,' or to plan steps of change by which needs might be better satisfied." "They may accept standards of character and action from the classes, or from foreigners, or from literature, or from a new religion, but whatever they take up they assimilate and make it a part of their own mores." The masses do not think. "Thinking and understand-ing are too hard work. If any one wants to blame the masses let him turn to his own case. He will find that he thinks about and understands only his own intel-lectual pursuit. He could not give the efforts to every other department of knowledge. In other matters he is one of the masses and does as they do. He uses routine, set formulæ, current phrases, caught up from magazines and newspapers of the better class."[3]

Furthermore, any assumption that the people have peculiar ability to discern between the false and the true, the evil and the good, is utterly without sound basis. They are not an oracle. Their voice is not the voice of God. They have no instinct which leads them to correct decisions. If any answers to the questions of life are to be obtained, they will come from the classes rather than from the masses. It is from the former that initiative and change proceed. "The historical or selected classes are those which, in his-tory, have controlled the activities and policy of gen-

[3] "Folkways," pp. 47, 48.

erations. They have been differentiated at one time by one standard, at another time by another. The position which they held by inheritance from early society has given them prestige and authority. Merit and societal value, according to the standards of their time, have entered into their status only slightly and incidentally. Those classes have had their own mores. They had the power to regulate their lives to some extent according to their own choice, a power which modern civilized men eagerly desire and strive for primarily by the acquisition of wealth. The historical classes have, therefore, selected purposes, and have invented ways of fulfilling them. Their ways have been imitated by the masses. The classes have led the way in luxury, frivolity, and vice, and also in refinement, culture, and the art of living. They have introduced variation." [4]

The masses are liable to control from elements which they themselves contain. Which part will rule the whole is always a critical question. The upper strata of the masses contain those who possess comfort without luxury, intelligence, culture, and the best family mores. In civilized states there seems to be a movement from the lower into the upper strata, so that the upper are constantly being reënforced by all the elements in the society which have societal value after they have been developed by discipline and labor. "The share which the upper strata of the masses have in determining the policy of the masses is therefore often decisive of public welfare." On the other hand, when the masses are controlled by the lower strata there is the most violent impulsiveness in societal movements. Revolutionary activities and policies have their rise in these classes, although, in

[4] "Folkways," p. 45.

other cases, these classes adhere most stubbornly to popular tradition in spite of fact and reason. "The French Revolution began with the higher strata of the masses, and the control of it passed on down from one to another of the lower strata, until it reached the lowest—the mob gathered in the slums of a great city."

Out of the mores all laws and institutions have proceeded and by them they are still conditioned. Legislation always has to seek standing ground upon them and be consistent therewith. "It is sometimes said that 'public opinion' must ratify and approve police regulations, but this statement rests upon an imperfect analysis. The regulations must conform to the mores so that the public will not think them too lax or too strict. The mores of our rural and urban populations are not the same; consequently legislation about intoxicants which is made by one of these sections of the population does not succeed when applied to the other." "Pure enacted institutions which are strong and prosperous are hard to find. It is too difficult to invent and create an institution, for a purpose, out of nothing. The electoral college in the constitution of the United States is an example. In that case the democratic mores of the people have seized upon a device and made of it something quite different from what the inventors planned." [5]

The mores are transmitted through the family and by the general education, discipline, and ritual of the group. They share the life of the individual from his birth and their authority over him is despotic. "Each individual is born into them as he is born into the atmosphere, and he does not reflect upon them, or criticize them any more than a baby analyzes the

[5] "Folkways," p. 54.

atmosphere before he begins to breathe it. Each one is subjected to the influence of the mores and formed by them before he is capable of reasoning about them. It may be objected that nowadays, at least, we criticize all traditions, and accept none just because they are handed down to us. If we take up cases of things which are still entirely or almost entirely in the mores, we shall see that this is not so. . . . Democracy is in our American mores. It is a product of our physical and economic conditions. It is impossible to discuss or criticize it. It is glorified for popularity, and is a subject of dithyrambic rhetoric. No one treats it with complete candor and sincerity. No one dares to analyze it as he would aristocracy or autocracy. He would get no hearing and would only incur abuse. The thing to be noted in all these cases is that the masses oppose a deaf ear to every argument against the mores. It is only in so far as things have been transferred from the mores into laws and positive institutions that there is discussion about them or rationalizing upon them. The mores contain the norm by which, if we should discuss the mores, we should have to judge the mores. We learn the mores as unconsciously as we learn to walk and eat and breathe. The masses never learn how we walk, and eat, and breathe, and they never know any reason why the mores are what they are." [6]

Though characterized by rigidity, inertia, persistence, and authority in an unparalleled degree, the mores are subject to variation. Children do not perpetuate them just as they received them; offspring do not feel the same ideas and sentiments that their parents felt. Furthermore, as life conditions and interests change, the mores alter. Where they do not

[6] "Folkways," pp. 76, 77.

conform to new interests and needs, crises arise. In
higher civilization these are solved by revolution or
reform. Such was the case in the sixteenth century
and in the French Revolution of 1789. Following a
revolution there is always a period in which there are
no mores. "The old are broken up; the new are not
formed. The social ritual is interrupted. The old
taboos are suspended. The new taboos cannot be
enacted or promulgated. They require time to become
established and known. The masses in a revolution
are uncertain what they ought to do." At the point
where reconstruction should begin, every revolution
collapses. Then the old ruling class assumes authority
and forces society into its old grooves once more.
"The French Revolutionists tried to abolish all the
old mores and to replace them by products of speculative philosophy. The revolution was, in fact, due
to a great change in conditions, which called for new
mores, and so far as the innovations met this demand
they became permanent and helped to create a conviction of the beneficence of the revolution. Napoleon
abolished many innovations and put many things in
the old train again. Many other things have changed
name and face, but not character. Many innovations
have been half assimilated. Some interests have
never yet been provided for." [7]

Only to a very small degree can the mores be modified through conscious effort. "It is not possible to
change them, by any artifice or device, to a great
extent, or suddenly, or in any essential element; it is
possible to modify them by slow and long-continued
effort if the ritual is changed by minute variations." [8]
Changes which run with the mores are easily brought

[7] "Folkways," p. 87.
[8] *Ibid.*, p. 87.

about, but those which are opposed require long and patient effort, if they are possible at all.

"The ruling clique can use force to warp the mores towards some result which they have selected, especially if they bring their effort to bear on the ritual, not on the dogmas, and if they are contented to go slowly. The church has won great results in this way, and by so doing has created a belief that religion, or ideas, or institutions, make mores. The leading classes, no matter by what standard they are selected, can lead by example, which always affects ritual. An aristocracy acts in this way. It suggests standards of elegance, refinement, and nobility, and the usages of good manners, from generation to generation, are such as have spread from the aristocracy to other classes. Such influences are unspoken, unconscious, unintentional. If we admit that it is possible and right for some to undertake to mold the mores of others, of set purpose, we see that the limits within which any such effort can succeed are very narrow, and the methods by which it can operate are strictly defined. The favorite methods of our time are legislation and preaching. These methods fail because they do not affect ritual, and because they always aim at great results in a short time. Above all, we can judge of the amount of serious attention which is due to plans for 'reorganizing society'; to get rid of alleged errors and inconveniences in it. We might as well plan to reorganize our globe by redistributing the elements in it." [9]

But since old mores are mischievous if they live on after the needs and conditions to which they were adjusted have passed, free and rational criticism of them is essential to societal welfare. Only the

[9] "Folkways," pp. 94, 95.

greatest and best can so react against the mores as
to alter them, however. "The trained reason and
conscience never have heavier tasks laid upon them
than where questions of conformity to, or dissent
from, the mores are raised. It is by the dissent and
free judgment of the best reason and conscience that
the mores win flexibility and automatic readjustment." [10]

Thus out of man's struggle to meet the needs of
the situation in which he finds himself, a mass of customs arise in each group which dominate it and give to
it its distinguishing character. The moral or religious
sanction which wraps itself round these increases their
authority and makes them less subject to change.
Thus they acquire tremendous coercive power, direct-
ing society along fixed lines and strangling all liberty. Individuals in a group, consequently, do not,
for the most part, form their own ideas or choose
their own actions. They think and do according to
the notions and ways which rule in their particular
time and place, acquired from the preceding generation and passed on, with some change, it may be, to
the next. There is a determinism, therefore, in the
social realm, and the force which gives it its life is
what Sumner calls the folkways or mores.

[10] "Folkways," p. 95.

The free man who steps forward to claim his inheritance and endowment as a free and equal member of a great civil body must understand that his duties and responsibilities are measured to him by the same scale as his rights and powers.

What Social Classes Owe to Each Other.

CHAPTER XX

EQUALITY, RIGHTS, LIBERTY

FROM what has preceded it appears that groups and societies arise inevitably and in prescribed ways because the constitution of the world so necessitates. It is as impossible to create them or to remold them by taking thought as it is to add a cubit unto one's stature. Each is held together, arbitrarily governed, and given distinctiveness, by the modes of doing and judging which have gripped it. In such a society what is the status of the individual? To what measure of freedom may he justly lay claim? What are his rights? In what relationship does he stand to his fellows? Are all equal and entitled to like possessions and privileges? These are questions of fundamental importance. They have given rise to a vast amount of speculation and theorizing which in their turn have created philosophies and schools and inspired disastrous empirical interference with government. They are questions which no degree of abstract reflection can settle, however. Their answer is in the nature of things, and there it must be sought. What are the facts as Sumner's investigation reveals them?

Nothing is more certain, in the first place, than that inequality is a law of life. That all men are created equal is not only not a self-evident truth, it is not a truth at all. Nowhere as we go up the stream of history do we find evidence of a golden age when individuals enjoyed the same powers, possessions, and opportunities, and those who think they see one in the future, toward which they seek to move the world, are only chasing rainbows. No two persons are ever born equal. They differ in physical characteristics and in mental capacity. Children are not equal to men, nor are old men equal to youth. The two sexes have not the same chance in the struggle for existence and never can have. The peculiar function of the woman handicaps her in the effort for self-maintenance and creates a disparity between her and the man in all the interests of human life. Not all individuals, whatever their character and training, can have the same societal value. In fact, "No man ever yet asserted that 'all men are equal,' meaning what he said. Although he said 'all men,' he had in mind some limitation of the group he was talking about. Thus, if you had asked Thomas Jefferson, when he was writing the first paragraph of the Declaration of Independence, whether in 'all men' he meant to include negroes, he would have said that he was not talking about negroes. Ask any one who says it now whether he means to include foreigners—Russian Jews, Hungarians, Italians—and he will draw his line somewhere. The law of the United States draws it at Chinamen. If you should meet with a man who should say, as I would, although I do not believe that all men are equal in any sense, that such laws are unjust and that all men ought to have an equal chance to do the best they can for themselves on earth, then you might ask him whether he thought the Bushmen, Hottentots, or Australians were equal to the best educated and most cultivated white men. He would have to admit that he was not thinking of them at all. Now if we draw any line at all, the dogma is ruined." [1]

[1] "The Challenge of Facts and Other Essays," pp. 302, 303.

Inequality, furthermore, is beneficial and necessary. Without it there could be no society at all. The latter involves organization, a division of labor in which a variety of tastes, talents, powers, and ambitions are required, and by which they are intensified and multiplied. A horde in which the only differences were those of age and sex could not long maintain itself. Superior minds and characters are needed to point out new and better ways and to inspire and direct. Both the survival and advancement of a social group is dependent upon leadership, in which term the idea of inequality is implicit.

Even when equality is interpreted to mean, not like endowment of all individuals, but equality before the law, it does not exist nor does there seem to be much hope of realizing it. Theoretically the state is no respecter of persons. "It surrounds all, without distinctions, with the same conditions and guarantees. If it educates one, it educates all—black, white, red, or yellow; Jew or Gentile; native or alien. If it taxes one, it taxes all, by the same system and under the same conditions. If it exempts one from police regulations in home, church, and occupation, it exempts all. From this statement it is at once evident that pure equality before the law is impossible. Some occupations must be subjected to police regulations. Not all can be made subject to militia duty even for the same limited period. The exceptions and special cases furnish the chance for abuse. Equality before the law, however, is one of the cardinal principles of civil liberty because it leaves each man to run the race of life for himself as best he can. The state stands neutral but benevolent. It does not undertake to aid some and handicap others at the outset in order to offset hereditary advantages and disadvantages, or to make them start equally. Such a notion would belong to the false and spurious theory of equality which is socialistic. If the state should attempt this it would make itself the servant of envy. I am entitled to make the most I can of myself without hindrance from anybody, but I am not entitled to any guarantee that I should make as much of myself as somebody else makes of himself." [2]

What people really have in mind when they put forward the doctrine of equality is equality of possessions and the privileges which they bring. They covet that which is their neighbor's, or at least as much of everything good as their neighbors enjoy, and they see many who have more than themselves. This covetousness issues in a claim based on the assertion that all should have an equal amount of welfare. For this proposition, however, there is no warrant in history, science, religion, or politics; and even if it were sound, it could not be put into practical operation. "We know of no force which could act for the satisfaction of human desires so as to make the satisfaction equal for a number of men, and we know of no interference by 'the state,' that is, by a committee of men, which could so modify the operation of natural forces as to produce that result. There is an old distinction between commutative and distributive justice which goes back to the Greeks, and which some writers of the nineteenth century have brought out again. Distributive justice is justice in which all personal circumstances are duly allowed for so that all are made 'equal' on an absolute standard. Of course equality must necessarily be carried to some

2 "The Challenge of Facts and Other Essays," pp. 44, 45.

such conception at last. It is evident that God alone
could give distributive justice; and we find, in this
world in which we are, that God has not seen fit to
provide for it at all." [3]

Inequality of possessions, furthermore, is in accordance with natural laws, and any equalization can be
accomplished only by destroying liberty and fairness.
It arises from the never-ending competition for
capital which the struggle of men with nature for the
meager supply which she offers creates. This competition develops the powers which the individuals
possess. The more intense it is, the more thoroughly
are those powers developed. If there is no restriction upon liberty, the results cannot be equal. They
will differ according to the inherited advantages,
training, industry, perseverance, courage, and good
sense which the persons concerned display. Nature
is neutral. She yields to him who most wisely and
resolutely wrestles with her. In proportion to men's
being and doing is their having and enjoying. "Such
is the system of nature. If we do not like it, and if
we try to amend it, there is only one way in which we
can do it. We can take from the better and give to
the worse. We can deflect the penalties of those who
have done ill and throw them on those who have done
better. We can take the rewards from those who
have done better and give them to those who have
done worse. We shall thus lessen the inequalities.
We shall favor the survival of the unfittest, and we
shall accomplish this by destroying liberty. Let it be
understood that we cannot get outside this alternative: liberty, inequality, survival of the fittest; non-
liberty, equality, survival of the unfittest. The for-

[3] "Earth Hunger and Other Essays," p. 89.

mer carries society forward and favors all its best members; the latter carries society downwards and favors all its worst members."[4]

Although free competition thus brings to the fore those best fitted to secure capital and to further civilization, it does not follow that it always produces results according to merit, for results are always affected by inheritance and especially by the aleatory element. Nevertheless, it does secure to merit all the chances it can enjoy for which none of one's fellow men are to blame. But whatever the merit of individuals, good and evil fortune will continue to create inequality, for they cannot be eliminated. It is frequently said that every one ought to have everything which anybody can have. "That proposition abolishes luck. In making propositions we can imply that all ought to have equally good luck, but, inasmuch as there is no way in which we can turn bad luck into good, or misfortune into good fortune, what the proposition means is that if we cannot all have good luck no one shall have it. The unlucky will pull down the lucky. That is all that equality can ever mean. The worst becomes the standard. When we talk of 'changing the system,' we ought to understand that that means abolishing luck and all the ills of life. We might as well talk of abolishing storms, excessive heat and cold, tornadoes, pestilences, diseases and other ills."[5]

Inequality is fostered also by the family. Attempts to equalize the life conditions of human beings involve its destruction. Under monogamy the family is a closed group. Special interests, privacy, and reserve are considered essential to its development, and high

[4] "The Challenge of Facts and Other Essays," p. 25.
[5] *Ibid.*, p. 57.

prerogatives are granted to parents, although it is well known that thousands of human beings are unfitted to bring up children. It follows, therefore, in a society where such an organization of the family prevails there must be great inequality. "The son of wise parents cannot start on a level with the son of foolish ones, and the man who has had no home discipline cannot be equal to the man who has had home discipline. If the contrary were true, we could rid ourselves at once of the wearing labor of inculcating sound morals and manners in our children." Associated with the family, furthermore, is the institution of bequest and hereditary property, because of which some come into life with special protection and advantages. The right of bequests rests on the sufficient grounds of expediency. The love of children is one of the strongest motives to frugality, and the state guarantees the right of bequest because it thereby encourages the accumulation of capital on which all welfare depends. "The most rigorous and logical socialists have always been led sooner or later to attack the family. For, if bequests should be abolished, parents would give their property to their children in their own life-time; and so it becomes a logical necessity to substitute some sort of communistic or socialistic life for family life, and to educate children in masses without the tie of parentage. Every socialistic theory which has been pursued energetically has led out to this consequence. . . . It is plain to see that the only equality which could be reached on this course would be that men should be all equal to each other when they were all equal to swine." [6]

Inequality, therefore, according to Sumner, is a necessary accompaniment of those fundamental con-

[6] "The Challenge of Facts and Other Essays," pp. 43, 44.

ditions in the natural order for which no one is responsible and no one can change. It exists because this is the kind of world it is. Differing degrees of ability, the competition of life, the aleatory element in human affairs, make it inevitable. It is not within human power to remove it wholly or in any considerable degree. All attempts to do so involve an injustice and despotism which would of necessity produce either rebellion or social decay.

If, then, it is in no wise true that all men are created equal, what is to be said regarding the proposition that all are endowed by their Creator with certain unalienable rights? As we look in vain for equality of human beings as we go up the stream of history, so we look in vain for "natural rights," or any "rights of man" of which all are joint inheritors. A right implies a just and proper claim upon something. Men say that they have a right to life, to liberty, to a living wage, to happiness. Against whom do they hold such rights? Certainly not against nature. It is a matter of indifference to her whether there are human beings on the earth or not. There is nothing to indicate that the universe suffered lack of anything necessary to keep it going on in a round of transformations prior to man's advent. "When he appears on earth he does not appear as one needed, but as another competitor for a place here. He is infinitely interesting to himself, and he has constructed for the gratification of his vanity whole systems of mythology and philosophy to prove to himself that the rest has sense only as used up by him. In truth he is here like the rest, on the tenure of sustaining himself if he can. The curse of the self-glorification of the human species is that it blinds them to the truth of their situation, keeps them from intelligent effort to make the best of it, and sets them to rending each other when their demands are not satisfied.'' [7]

If man has no claim upon nature, upon whom then has he a claim? There can be no rights as against God. ''A man may curse his fate because he is born of an inferior race, or with an hereditary disease, or blind, or, as some members of the race seem to do, because they are born females; but they get no answer to their imprecations.'' If men have any rights at birth, therefore, it must be against their fellows, whom it is assumed must limit themselves or expend some of their energy in the former's behalf. What then becomes of the natural rights of the ones who are to be the servants of the others? As a matter of fact, the notion of natural rights ''lends itself to the most vicious kind of social dogmatism, for if a man has natural rights, then it is clear up to the finished socialistic doctrine that a man has a natural right to whatever he needs, and that the measure of his claims is the wishes which he wants fulfilled. If, then, he has a need, who is bound to satisfy it for him? It must be the one who possesses what will satisfy that need, or else the state which can take the possession from those who have earned and saved it, and give it to him who needs it and who, by the hypothesis, has not earned and saved it.''

There is only sense in which the term has any value of importance. In medieval times the assumption was that in advance of action by the civil authority men had no rights. All were under the same constraints and restrictions until by franchise, privilege, or exemption from the ruling class some had emancipated themselves. The eighteenth-century notion of

[7] ''The Challenge of Facts and Other Essays,'' p. 113.

"natural rights" was a revolt against this theory. It embodies the idea that a man should be regarded as free and independent until some necessity had been established for restraining him. When so regarded the term has meaning, but it is not in that sense that it is now commonly used. On the contrary it stands for the doctrine that to all those things necessary to earthly comfort men by nature are entitled. It then comes to be established by easy deduction that every man has a natural right to succeed in the struggle for existence, or to be happy; and there follows the conclusion that it is the duty of the state to insure him this right.

Outside the realm of philosophical speculation and unreality, however, the only rights that exist are those which might has created in the course of human history. "They are the product of civilization, or of the art of living." The interests of individuals clashed. Some adjustment was necessary. Those who had the greater power determined what the adjustment should be. Even in the lowest form of the divisions of labor, that of the sexes, interests conflicted. The man, with perhaps the help of other men, settled the matter by force, and a precedent was established, which later, it may be, became a law carrying in itself a definition of rights between men and women. Thus have all so-called rights developed. They are not "natural" or "God-given" or absolute in any sense. They are the rules of the game which have come to prevail in the competition of life in order that the peace may prevail which is essential to group strength. Nothing but might has ever made right, and if we include in the former, elections and decisions of courts, nothing but might makes right now. Here, however, we must distinguish between the anterior and the posterior view of any matter in question. "If we are about to take some action and are debating the right of it, the might which can be brought to support one view of it has nothing to do with the right of it. If a thing has been done and is established by force (that is, no force can reverse it), it is right in the only sense we know, and rights will follow from it which are not vitiated at all by the force in it. There would be no security at all for rights if this were not so."

"When all the wrangling about rights has been exhausted on a political question," therefore, "it comes down to this: Has any one the means to prevent you from doing what you want to do? or, Have you any power at your command to prevent your opponent from doing what he wants to do?" [8] The whole history of mankind has been a struggle between individuals and classes. The actions which have issued have always been open to criticism and dispute, but "all subsequent history has been forced to take up the consequences of those acts and go on. The disputants about 'rights' often lose sight of the fact that the world has to go on day by day and dispute must end. The end always leaves some complaining in terms of right and rights. They are overborne by force of some kind." Therefore, "all the great fabric of what we now prize so highly and justly as rights, has come out of such acts of force against some defeated parties," and have been modified and revised by a better view of life.

The most essential requisite with regard to rights is that they should be in equilibrium with duties. It is not necessary from the point of view of justice that all should have the same privileges, but it is necessary that those who have more than do some should also

8 "Alexander Hamilton," 1890, p. 30.

be under greater obligations. It is through such
equilibrium alone that true liberty is realized.

"A monarchical or aristocratic system is not immoral if the rights and duties of persons and classes
are in equilibrium, although the rights and duties of
different persons and classes are unequal. An immoral political system is created whenever there are
privileged classes—that is, classes who have arrogated
to themselves rights while throwing the duties upon
others. In a democracy all have equal political rights.
That is the fundamental political principle. A democracy, then, becomes immoral if all have not equal
political duties. This is unquestionably the doctrine
which needs to be reiterated and inculcated beyond all
others, if the democracy is to be made sound and permanent. Our orators and writers never speak of it,
and do not seem often to know anything about it; but
the real danger of democracy is that the classes which
have the power under it will assume all the rights and
reject all the duties—that is, that they will use the
political power to plunder those who have. Democracy, in order to be true to itself, and to develop into
a sound working system, must oppose the same cold
resistance to any claims for favor on the ground of
poverty, as on the ground of birth and rank. It can
no more admit to public discussion, as within the
range of possible action, any schemes for coddling
and helping wage-receivers than it could entertain
schemes for restricting political power to wage-payers.
It must put down schemes for making 'the rich' pay
for whatever 'the poor' want, just as it tramples on
the old theories that only the rich are fit to regulate
society. One needs but to watch our periodical literature to see the danger that democracy will be con-

strued as a system of favoring a new privileged class
of the many and the poor." [9]

Upon the importance of liberty Sumner laid the
utmost stress, but by liberty he did not mean unre-
strictedness of action. It is as impossible to find this
anywhere in man's past as it is to find equality or
natural rights. "From one end to the other of history, from one extreme to the other of the social scale,
we can find no status in which men realize the kind
of liberty which consists in doing as one pleases."
The freedom of primitive man was limited by the
necessities of self-preservation, by the mystery and
terrors of nature, and by disease and old age. "A
wandering savage wanders to get his living, and as a
rule he finds it more than he can do; the exigencies
of subsistence hold him as tightly as they hold a factory hand, and his success is far more uncertain. If
he unites with others like himself in order, by organization, to increase his power, then he must submit to
discipline of the most severe kind, enforced by penalties of the highest severity. Instead of being lawless
he is under traditions and customs which admit of
no relaxation whatever; he who tries to revolt against
the tradition is thrust out into banishment or put to
death. There is no such thing conceivable as private
judgment or dissent. He who breaks a custom is an
outlaw." [10] Civilized man has won some exemption
from the tyranny of nature and has a power to choose
his ends which primitive man did not enjoy, but modern life, too, has its peculiar form of bondage. To get
his share in the products of civilization a man has to
do his share of the work. "The bigger the crowd,

9 "What Social Classes Owe to Each Other," pp. 36, 37.
10 "Earth Hunger and Other Essays," p. 138.

the more intense the struggle; the higher the organization, the more imperative its coercion on all its members. We cannot get our living unless we get into the organization; when, however, we once get into it, it is ruin to fall out, but if we stay in, we must submit. We must make contracts binding us to the other members of the organization, and we must keep them. But they fetter our liberty; we must spend our time at the bench, the counter, or the desk, and we cannot get away. Where is there any liberty, in the sense of unrestrained self-will, for the civilized man?" [11] He only goes and comes as he pleases who is willing to forego the respect of his fellows and many of the fruits of civilization. "The 'Bohemian' who determines to realize some sort of liberty accomplishes his purpose only by sacrificing the most of the rights and turning his back on most of the duties of a civilized man, while filching as much as he can of the advantages of living in a civilized state."

The reason why a man cannot do as he likes in human society is because he cannot get away from responsibility. This is another of those conditions imposed upon him by the constitution of things. Failure to comply with its demands is visited with the severest penalties. Responsibility to nature is enforced by want, suffering, and death. Responsibility to society is enforced by revolution, decay, or subjugation. It "rises up by the side of liberty correlative, commensurate, and inevitable."

It is the function of social institutions to make privilege and responsibility equal and coördinate. There cannot be more of the former in one section of a group without increase in the latter elsewhere. Those classes which at one time or another have got

[11] "Earth Hunger and Other Essays," p. 144.

comparative liberty to do as they please upon the earth, have got it at the expense of the servitude of others. Earth always gets its price for what earth gives us, and if we do not pay it ourselves, some one else must. When the state brings privilege and responsibility into equilibrium for all its members it has established civil liberty. This term connotes the aggregate of rights, privileges, and prerogatives which the laws and institutions of a country secure for a man as conditions under which he may fight out the struggle for existence in competition with his fellows. It "is really a great induction from all the experience of mankind in the use of civil institutions; it must be defined, not in terms of metaphysics, but in terms drawn from history and law. It is not an abstract conception; it is a series of concrete facts. These facts go to constitute a status—the status of a freeman in a modern jural state. It is a product of institutions; it is embodied in institutions; it is guaranteed by institutions. It is not a matter of resolutions, or 'declarations,' as they seemed to think in the last century. It is unfriendly to dogmatism. It pertains to what a man shall do, have, and be. It is unfriendly to all personal control, to officialism, to administrative philanthropy and administrative wisdom, as much as to bureaucratic despotism or monarchical absolutism."[12] It works as impersonally as possible, leaving a man to run his own career in life, guaranteeing to him that whatever he does in the way of industry, economy, prudence, sound judgment, etc., shall not be diverted to somebody's else benefit. "Of course it is a necessary corollary that each man shall bear the penalty of his own vices and his own mistakes."

[12] "Earth Hunger and Other Essays," p. 160.

It is only through such liberty that practical justice is assured. The individual must be left as free as possible to go up against the facts of life as they exist in his time and place, and win from them that which by the measure of sagacity and power he displays he demonstrates that he deserves; and what he thus shows belongs to him because of what he is, he should be permitted to retain and dispose of as he will. If the responsibilities laid upon some are greater than those imposed upon others, then injustice is perpetrated. "It is impossible to know whence any definition or criterion of justice can be derived if it is not deduced from this view of things; or if it is not the definition of justice that each shall enjoy the fruit of his own labor and self-denial, and of injustice that the idle and the industrious, the self-indulgent and the self-denying, shall share equally in the product. Aside from the *a priori* speculations of philosophers who have tried to make equality an essential element in justice, the human race has recognized, from the earliest times, the above conception of justice as the true one, and has founded upon it the right of property." [13]

From what has preceded, it is clear that liberty is a high and costly thing. It makes great demands, not only upon the individual, but also upon the whole mass of people. From the former it calls for self-discipline. He must accept intelligently the conditions inherent in this earthly life, conform himself to them, and manfully endeavor to succeed under them. He must fight his own battle, and not expect others to lend him aid. He must not ask the state to assist him in any way, for this would involve injustice to others. No man can live in a state of freedom, therefore, un-

[13] "The Challenge of Facts and Other Essays," pp. 23, 24.

less he be self-controlled in a high degree, and discipline should be the first object of education. Upon the whole mass of people, moreover, liberty imposes the strain of a perpetual exercise of the reason and conscience, for rights and duties must be continually reëxamined and their equilibrium readjusted, since civil liberty is not in the order of nature, not positive and objective, but historical and institutional. Liberty, therefore, is not a boon or a blessing to be had for the taking and to be enjoyed for nothing; it is a task. Men are beginning "to cry out that it is too great for them; that they cannot attain to it nor even bear it; that to be a free man means to come up to the standard and be it; and that it is asking too much of human nature. They want somebody to come and help them to be free. It has always been so. Men have failed of freedom not because kings, nobles, or priests enslaved them, but because liberty was too high and great for them. They would not rise to it; they would submit to any servitude rather; therefore they got servitude." [14]

[14] "Earth Hunger and Other Essays," p. 128.

Every age is befooled by the notions which are in fashion in it. Our age is befooled by "democracy."

Concentration of Wealth.

CHAPTER XXI

THE STATE

IN the preceding chapter reference has been made to laws and institutions, and the evolution of government and the state has been implied. All these have appeared in response to the needs to which life together on the earth gives rise. They have in no case been deliberately planned and adopted, or brought forth by declamation or resolution. "It is in utopias only that men have ever invented new political institutions. They have never put their utopian institutions to the experiment for the simple reason that every utopia begins with the postulate that the world must be made over again from what it is into that kind of a world which the utopia needs in order to be practicable. . . . Many people believe that American institutions were invented by the fathers, and I presume that this is one reason why the belief is so strong that men can invent institutions of civil government. The truth is that the fathers invented some expedients in governmental machinery, all of which have failed of the objects they aimed at or have been distorted to others; but American institutions are striking illustrations of the doctrine that political institutions which endure and thrive always are the products of development and growth, that they grow out of the national character and the national circumstances, and that the efforts of men to control or limit them are restricted within very narrow limits and even at that require an immense exertion of force for the results attained." [1]

[1] "The Challenge of Facts and Other Essays," pp. 243, 244.

Regarding the nature and function of the state there are many misconceptions which frequently lead people into wrong actions and unwarrantable expectations. In the idea of some German writers that "The State" is an "entity having conscience, power, and will sublimated above human limitations and as constituting a tutelary genius over us all," Sumner's keen, practical mind could discover no truth. "I once lived in Germany for two years," he says, "but I certainly saw nothing of it there then.[2] My notion of the State has dwindled with growing experience of life. As an abstraction, the State is to me only All-of-us. In practice—that is, when it exercises will or adopts a line of action—it is only a little group of men chosen in a very haphazard way by the majority of us to perform certain services for all of us. The majority do not go about their selection very rationally, and they are almost always disappointed by the results of their own operation. Hence 'the State,' instead of offering resources of wisdom, right reason, and pure moral sense beyond what the average of us possess, generally offers much less of all those things. Furthermore, it often turns out in practice that 'the State' is not even the known and accredited servants of the State, but, as has been well said, is only some obscure clerk, hidden in the recesses of a Government bureau, into whose power the chance has fallen for the moment to pull one of the stops which control the Government machine. In former days it often happened that 'the State' was a barber, a fiddler, or a bad woman. In our day it often happens that 'the State' is a little functionary on whom a big functionary is forced to depend."[3]

[2] "What Social Classes Owe to Each Other," p. 9.
[3] Ibid., pp. 9, 10.

"The little group of public servants who, as I have said, constitute the State, when the State determines on anything, could not do much for themselves or anybody else by their own force. If they do anything, they must dispose of men, as in an army, or of capital, as in a treasury. But the army, or police, or *posse comitatus,* is more or less All-of-us, and the capital in the treasury is the product of the labor and saving of All-of-us. Therefore, when the State means power-to-do it means All-of-us, as brute force or as industrial force."[4]

Originally, as we have seen, human beings were drawn together into coöperative groups, because in the nature of things there was advantage to be gained from such union. In these, customs and regulations arose and became coercive. Internally a group was peaceful and orderly, but toward all other groups its relation was that of war and plunder. Indeed, it was the exigencies of war more than anything else that enforced orderliness within. The nearer and greater the danger from outsiders, the more intense was the internal order and discipline. The common interest was at variance with individual interests and tended to crush individualism, prescribe dissent, produce uniformity, and make private judgment a special offense.

Authority in the group was exercised by the individuals or classes which were powerful enough to enforce it. Naturally, they used it so far as possible for their own advantage, employing the power of the organization for their own satisfactions. As a result, conflict of classes and control by the strongest became an inevitable condition of society. In medieval times warriors and ecclesiastics were in the saddle, and

[4] "What Social Classes Owe to Each Other," p. 11.

they used all their power to divert social effort to their services and gain. Now the middle class is in the ascendancy. The only safeguard against class aggrandisement is institutions which call into play opposing interests and forces. The motive of constitutional government is to devise such institutions, which, operating at critical moments, will prevent abusive control of the powers of the state.

Until comparatively modern times an individual's opportunities and restrictions in his group were determined by his status. Into this a man was born, from it he could not escape, and by it his rights and duties were defined. Under such circumstances it was impossible for persons to develop to the full the possibilities which might be in them. "Status holds down individual energy and power. If a black man is told that the only status allowed by social institutions to him is that of a slave, no black man can work out into realization the powers which he may possess. If the status of women is fixed by custom and law, no woman can show her power to do anything outside of the limits. The social arrangement which sets free individual energy is liberty; for under this each one may prove what he is by what he does, and the society profits by the expansion and evolution of all the power there is in it." [5]

The whole drift of the world for five hundred years has been toward democracy, in which contract under liberty replaces status. The latter condition marks a great advance in the history of mankind, for a society based upon contract is made up of independent men and women who form ties without favor or obligation, and coöperate without cringing or intrigue. It makes possible the highest realization of

[5] "Earth Hunger and Other Essays," p. 308.

individual powers and opens to the world the gain that resides therein. "That a society of free men, coöperating under contract, is by far the strongest society which has ever yet existed; that no such society has ever yet developed the full measure of strength of which it is capable; and that the only social improvements which are now conceivable lie in the direction of more complete realization of a society of free men united by contract, are points which cannot be controverted." [6]

This appearance of the free state as a societal phenomenon has been due entirely to the working of economic forces. There were few facts which Sumner emphasized so strongly and so repeatedly as the fact that the ratio of population to land, and the status of the arts, determine the institutions of society and government and the prevailing mood and habit of thought. The drift of the world toward democracy during the past five centuries he attributes in "Folkways" to the opening of new continents, the application of new inventions, and the expansion of commerce, which has made it easy for men of suitable talents to increase wealth. These changes have cheapened luxuries, they have made land accessible to all, they have lowered rent, they have raised wages and the standard of living and comfort, they have lessened the competition of life and made the struggle for existence less severe, they have made slavery impossible, and extended humanitarian sympathy. In short, "they have lessened social differentiation (that is, they have democratized)." Political ideals and philosophies have shaped themselves accordingly.[7]

That political democracy should have prevailed in

6 "What Social Classes Owe to Each Other," p. 26.
7 See "Earth Hunger and Other Essays," pp. 41-43.

America, therefore, was inevitable. The idea that it was established because the men of the eighteenth century were wise enough to choose and create it is wholly without foundation. The original colonists were on a substantial equality with respect to property and social antecedents. Land was abundant. All were proprietary farmers. There were few traditions or prejudices or vested interests to prevent the freest possible organization of society. The English government was unable to establish a colonial aristocracy, as much as it may have desired to do so. Had the settlers so chosen and worked ever so hard and wisely, they could not have built up any but democratic institutions, for no other were consistent with determining conditions.

Pure democracy, however, is possible only in small and homogeneous communities. As soon as a town increases in physical size difficulties arise and multiply. "The division of labor and the introduction of diverse occupations break up the old simplicity and uniformity; the requirements increase so rapidly that public affairs become far more important; universal acquaintance no longer exists amongst all townsmen; supervision is not close or continuous and responsibility declines. As soon, therefore, as the town meeting reaches a certain size, it becomes an arena for chicanery and faction. Busy citizens cannot attend so as to make the meeting full, and the opportunity for 'packing' a meeting is offered; the town is therefore the prey for any energetic faction with a well-defined purpose which it is determined to accomplish. Private and special interests find an arena of conflict in the town meeting and in their conflicts with each other the conception of public interest is lost. The notion that the people desire to have only the public good provided for is a delightful political dogma which it would be pleasant to believe, but which is contradicted by the observation of town democracies. The people do not positively want what is for the public good; they want, in a positive and active sense, what is for their interest. The vague and benevolent preference for the public good which men feel when their own interests are not involved does not rise high enough to produce self-sacrifice, work, and conflict." [8]

To avoid the difficulties which come from physical size, representative government is finally adopted. The representative of a democracy is only a delegate, however. He is not selected because he represents and is endowed with independence and responsibility. The rather is he an agent employed to perform a specific duty, for a democracy does not part with its sovereignty. It pledges and instructs. Representatives, furthermore, are likely to be the agents of interests, sent into an arena where interests are lost or won to fight for those intrusted to their care. "They do not, therefore, form a great council of the nation, but a body of struggling and scrambling attorneys. The public interest is a vague notion which finds little expression amongst them and has little chance of prevailing except so far as the local and private interests may neutralize each other."

Democracy is in the American mores. It is accepted as a matter of fact and regarded with almost superstitious reverence, so that its nature, limitations, and possibilities of evil are not candidly considered and understood. It does not in itself insure liberty and social well-being, however, and there are perils associated with it which ought not to be overlooked. It is characteristic of democracy, in the first place, to

8 "The Challenge of Facts and Other Essays," pp. 257, 258.

dread executive power, and it knows no better means of weakening it than to divide it among independent officers. "It fears above all 'one-man power' and sacrifices to this fear the efficiency of the administration. It insists also on electing all officers, or as many as possible, by popular vote, although it is impossible that the mass of voters can ever form any judgment as to the qualifications of candidates for purely administrative offices. . . . Official discretion is jealously forbidden, although, as a nation grows and its interests become diversified and complex, it must be that occasion will often arise for action on the part of executive officers which may be most timely and beneficial, although it has been ordained by no act of the legislature; and such action ought to be taken under responsibility to the representatives of the people. This, indeed, is what government means; it does not mean the mere mechanical execution of routine functions."[9]

In a democracy, furthermore, the idea of equality leads to the notion that the public functions are within the power of every citizen, and thus stands in the way of the best government possible. "The doctrine of equality, which no one believes in anywhere else, is supposed to be the great principle of politics. I presume that the great popular indifference to or dislike of civil service reform arises from the fact that the notion of comparative fitness or unfitness for office sins against the doctrine of equality, and the sincere inability of many to comprehend what is meant when it is said that civil appointments ought to be made on business principles comes from the long tradition that politics belong to another sphere from business and ought to be controlled by other principles. As

[9] "The Challenge of Facts and Other Essays," pp. 261, 262.

the people have not yet learned to apply the test of fitness to elected officers, they can hardly complain that it is not yet applied to appointed ones. The right to be chosen to office, or the passive electoral right, is valued by every citizen, and if rightly understood it ought to be valued. A moment's reflection will show, however, that there is no absolute right of the kind. The only right which exists is that of every man, without regard to birth, wealth, or other conditions of life, to qualify himself for public honor and trust, and to be privileged of election or appointment if he be qualified. If the absolute right be affirmed without the condition, the state must continually suffer from bad service simply to gratify the vanity and ambition of certain men. It is only natural, however, that men should forget or ignore the troublesome condition, and when they do the dogmas of rotation in office and of frequent elections naturally follow. Those men, therefore, who said there were a thousand men in a certain county who were as good as the incumbent of a certain office, and that he ought to be turned out on that account, spoke with perfect good faith; the same notion has prevailed in all democracies and it has always led inevitably to the distribution of offices by lot."[10]

The rule of the majority is another aspect of a democracy which is irrational and fraught with dangers. It does not express the wishes or the will of nations, but is the assumption by the part of the prerogatives which belong to the whole. It is an imperfect practical expedient for turning public opinion into a determination as to what shall be done. It is not a permanent form of government, and it is quite probable that some other device for the same end

[10] "The Challenge of Facts and Other Essays," pp. 262, 263.

may be conceived. ''No fallacies in politics are more pernicious than those which transfer to a popular majority all the old claims of the king by divine right, and lead people to believe that the notions of arbitrary and irresponsible power are not wrong, but only that they were wrong when applied to kings or aristocracies and not when applied to popular majorities. This fallacy of course inheres in democracy by its definition. The majority profits by the subtlety of the conception of the sovereignty of the people and enjoys power without the responsibility which always follows any king, however absolute he may be. The majority cannot be called to account, not because, like a constitutional king, it has no power, but, first, because it cannot be found or seized, and second, because, like an autocrat, it will submit to no accountability. It has often been remarked that the sovereign people has clothed itself with all the old prerogatives and is as tenacious of them as any other depository of political sovereignty ever was. The sovereign majority will not submit to criticism; it punishes criticism more harshly than by any press laws; it is as eager for flattery as any monarch and as inaccessible to harsh truths; it will not be sued for its debts; it claims the prerogative of deciding on its own obligations and sometimes shows an obliquity of conscience in this regard as great as that of some of the absolute monarchs of history. It is as tenacious of its honor, in the sense of demanding all due respect, as any other form of the state, but it is not always careful of its honor, in the sense of responsibility to itself, to do and to give all which may fairly be demanded of it— it is not always sensitive to its international reputation.'' [11]

[11] "The Challenge of Facts and Other Essays," pp. 264, 265

Political organization is indispensable in a democracy and with it comes the party manager and the spoils system. There follows a combination between the organizer and the civil officer. The claim is made that the government cannot be carried on unless we have men to work up interest, arrange the machinery, and do the drudgery, and that the civil offices should be given to such. It must be conceded that this class is necessary to the working of representative democracy, but it would be wiser, according to Sumner, to have such functionaries appointed and regularly paid than to have the spoils system which now exists. "It is not self-government to have Congressmen appoint local civil officers and civil officers secure the election of Congressmen in perpetual reiteration. I call it a self-perpetuating oligarchy. It is not civil liberty to walk in processions and cast ballots once in a while under such a system. When we are told that we cannot govern ourselves except by this machinery, it seems a worse insult than to say that we cannot govern ourselves without a king, or a privileged class, or titles and ribbons, or pensions and parliamentary corruption. The people who make such assertions pique themselves on being 'practical' when they are only base and vulgar; but it remains to be proved that the people need to be debauched with their own money and by their own servants, in order to carry on a government whose boast it is that it has thrown away all the old instruments of political debauchery. If it is true, then let us try to govern ourselves a while or do without government until we have better. We may, at any rate, hazard the experiment." [12] Parties in a democracy, moreover, are despotic. They carry on their contests as if there were no limits upon the

[12] "Challenge of Facts and Other Essays," p. 268.

privileges of victory, "hardly those which humanity imposes in war." "Majorities strike down opposition as criminal and allow little room for the conception of constitutional opposition." When it is established that the legal right to do a thing exists, it is deemed weak or cowardly not to exercise the power. "Such notions are hostile to the true conception of party, and they lead to those victories to win which parties destroy institutions."

Still another and one of the greatest weaknesses of such representative government as prevails in the United States is that it is unable to give support to public welfare in the face of sectional demands or strong cliques. Agents of special interests, as representatives on the whole are, naturally look upon the defense or victory of these as of primary importance. The conflict of politics ceases to be one of argument, to be decided by reason, and becomes a contest of wills, influence, and money. In the face of a strong sectional demand, therefore, or the short-sighted desire of a large number, or a powerful array of corporations, the real needs of the moment, the establishment of a permanent policy, or provision for a distant good, have no chance whatever. "The deepest disgrace which has ever come to us as a nation has come from this source, and we are threatened with more."

Even in a modern democracy, therefore, the strife of classes and the tendency of the strongest to employ the machinery of the state in its own interests still goes on. In recent times the wealth-power has steadily increased and democracy is threatened by plutocracy. After the great discoveries and inventions had raised the middle class out of the servile class, the former in alliance with the crown crushed the feudal classes. Later the middle class turned upon the crown and with the help of the handicraftsmen and peasants conquered it. The next conflict which must come is that between the middle capitalistic class and the proletariat. "If a certain construction is put upon this conflict, it may be called that between democracy and plutocracy, for it seems that industrialism must be developed into plutocracy by the conflict itself. This is the conflict which stands before the civilized world to-day, and it is big with fate to mankind and to civilization." [13] "A plutocrat is a man who, having the possession of capital, and having the power of it at his disposal, uses it, not industrially, but politically; instead of employing laborers, he enlists lobbyists. Instead of applying capital to land, he operates upon the market by legislation, by artificial monopoly, by legislative privileges; he creates jobs and erects combinations which are half political and half industrial; he practices upon the industrial vices, makes an engine of venality, expends his ingenuity, not on processes of production, but on 'knowledge of men,' and on the tactics of the lobby. The modern industrial system gives him a magnificent field, one far more profitable, very often, than that of legitimate industry." [14]

"It is the supreme test of a system of government whether its machinery is adequate for repressing the selfish undertakings of cliques formed on special interests and saving the public from raids of plunderers. The modern democratic states fail under this test. There is not a great state in the world which has not been democratized in the nineteenth century, there is not one of them which did not have great financial scandals before the century closed. Financial scandal is the curse of all the modern par-

[13] "War and Other Essays," p. 204.
[14] "Earth Hunger and Other Essays," p. 298.

liamentary states with a wide suffrage. They give liberty and security, with open chances for individual enterprise, from which results great individual satisfaction and happiness, but the political machinery offers opportunities for manipulation and corrupt abuse. They educate their citizens to seek advantages in the industrial organization by legislative devices, and to use them to the uttermost. The effect is seen in the mores. We hear of plutocracy and tainted money, of the power of wealth and the wickedness of corporations. The disease is less specific. It is constitutional. A disease of the mores is a disease of public opinion as to standards, codes, ideas of truth and right, and of things worth working for and means of success. Such a disease affects everybody. It penetrates and spoils every institution. It spreads from generation to generation, and at last it destroys in the masses the power of ethical judgment." [15]

It was Sumner's belief that the only reasonable and hopeful course to pursue under the circumstances is for the state to confine its activities to its one essential function, that of maintaining civil liberty through such laws and institutions as secure an equilibrium of rights and duties, and allow no privileges to arise on one side and no servitude on the other. "I therefore maintain," he says, "that this is a lamentable contest in which all that we hold dear, speaking of public interests, is at stake, and that the wise policy in regard to it is to minimize to the utmost the relations of the state to industry. As long as there are such relations, every industrial interest is forced more or less to employ plutocratic methods. The corruption is greater, perhaps, on those who exercise them than on the objects of them. *Laissez faire* instead of

[15] "Folkways," pp. 170, 171.

being what it appears to be in most of the current discussions cuts to the very bottom of the morals, the politics, and the political economy of the most important public questions of our time.'' [16]

[16] "Earth Hunger and Other Essays," p. 300.

The amateur social doctors are like the amateur physicians—they always begin with the question of *remedies,* and they go at this without any diagnosis or any knowledge of the anatomy or physiology of society. They never have any doubt of the efficacy of their remedies. They never take account of any ulterior effects which may be apprehended from the remedy itself. It generally troubles them not a whit that their remedy implies a complete reconstruction of society, or even a reconstitution of human nature. Against all such social quackery the obvious injunction to the quacks is, to mind their own business.

What Social Classes Owe to Each Other.

CHAPTER XXII

LAISSEZ FAIRE

The doctrine of *laissez faire* which Sumner advocated was the logical accompaniment of his convictions regarding natural laws, competition, and the state. It is set forth with extraordinary coldness and cruelty in a series of essays originally published by *Harper's Weekly*, in 1883, under the title "What Social Classes Owe to Each Other." These essays created two quite different effects. By a considerable number of people, both in this country and in England and France, who united the scientific point of view with a passion for liberty and justice, they were hailed as one of the strongest statements of the truth with respect to social obligations ever made. To sentimental philanthropists, unscientific reformers, and all who had socialistic leanings they seemed a brutal plea for selfish individualism, disregard of the weak, and free play for the strong. From all such there issued a fierce storm of protest. Even to-day Sumner is frequently painted as heartlessly indifferent to the handicapped and unfortunate, and hostile to all attempts to make this a happier and better world. That indifference to the conditions of his fellow men was something of which Sumner was constitutionally incapable has already been shown. Against the charge that he favored letting things as they are alone, may be put the fact that he spent his life in trying to change them, displaying an unselfishness, devotion, and above all a loyalty to the truth, which few of his critics have ever revealed. While others put forth one project or another for making the world over, Sumner, equally concerned for the good of society, plead for *laissez faire,* because exhaustive investigation and honest reflection persuaded him that this policy alone is conducive to human well-being and in harmony with eternal moral principles.

The degree in which social progress is possible, according to Sumner's view, and what individuals can do to further it, will be outlined in the succeeding chapter. *Laissez faire,* as he used the term, includes avoidance of all anticipatory legislation, of all interference by the state in the industrial organization except such as is necessary to maintain that equilibrium of rights and duties which liberty and justice require, and of all state projects in the interest of "the poor," "the needy," or any class whatsoever.

Anticipatory legislation is both irrational and harmful. History shows that attempts to create future conditions thereby have proved futile. The efforts of those who framed the constitution of the United States to foresee political exigencies and to provide for them were of no avail. The devices against democracy which they set up have all come to naught. "The fathers never intended to have the President elected by a grand democratic *plébiscite,* for they were under impressions which were hostile to democracy, would have held any such project dangerous, if practicable, and would not have judged it likely to produce a good selection. They adopted the device of the electoral college to prevent this. At the fourth election, the first one at which there was a real contest, their plan broke down. It was amended in detail, but in its subsequent working a mass of tradition and unwritten law has grown up upon it which has made it accomplish, only under state limitations, just what they meant to prevent.[1] In regard to patronage, the constitution makers had utopian ideas about the purity and unselfishness in the public service which might be expected in a republic. Dreading executive power, they gave the Senate the right to confirm the appointments of the President. This was a device to prevent patronage. What happened? The arrangement became the means of a shocking abuse of patronage and developed added evils of its own. "On the other hand, many of the provisions which were fought for with the greatest zeal, such as the provision about direct taxes, have proved powerless against advancing opinion. In other respects arrangements which some of the fathers thought essential to the prosperity of the union, such as securing the adherence of the wealthy or attracting the ambitious by titles and orders, have proved of no importance. . . . Thus it has proved, on all sides, that the organic law must move with the life of the nation. Either words change their contents, or interpretations vary, or roundabout methods are invented —in one way or another the nation fits its institutions in spite of all enactments or any pedantic rules of interpretation to its faiths, its tastes, and its needs."[2] In the exploitation of the outlying continents by Europe this truth has been similarly exemplified. The process "has gone on with the majesty and necessity of a process of nature. Nothing in human history can compare with it as an unfolding of the drama of human life on earth under the aspects of growth, reaction, destruction, new development, and high integration. The record shows that the judgments of statesmen and philosophers about this process from its begin-

[1] "The Challenge of Facts and Other Essays," pp. 253, 254.
[2] *Ibid.*, pp. 254, 255.

ning have been a series of errors, and that the policies by which they have sought to control and direct it have only crippled it and interrupted it by war, revolt, and dissension." [2a]

That such should be the result of efforts to fashion future conditions in accordance with theories, or ideals bred in the imagination, is made inevitable by the fact that the organs of the social organization are so interrelated that it is impossible to tell in advance what the effect of any interference will be. Every action is attended by a reaction. This may spread and modify the function of organs seemingly too remote to be influenced. These organs, moreover, are elastic and plastic. "They suffer both temporary and permanent modifications in form and function by their interaction on each other, and by the arbitrary interferences to which they are subjected by legislation or artifice of any kind. It is this elasticity and plasticity of the organs of society which give the social tinker his chance, and make him think that there are no laws of the social order, no science of society, no limits, in fact, to the possibilities of manipulation by 'The State.' He is always operating on the limit of give and take between the organs; he regards all the displacements which he can accomplish as positively new creations; he does not notice at all, and probably is not trained to perceive, the reaction—the other side of the change; he does not understand that he must endure a change on one side for all the change which he effects on the other." [2b]

"Suppose then that we interject into this industrial system some arbitrary interference, in the faith that it will alter the line where opposing interests now touch, and will bring them nearer to what is assumed to be

2a "War and Other Essays," p. 272.
2b "Earth Hunger and Other Essays," p. 285.

justice. Inasmuch as we cannot oversee and compass the industrial system, it is certain that we should work in the dark, and should have no guarantee at all that we had not done the very opposite of what we hoped to do. The instances in history are frequent enough where the masters of society have done this very thing —hurt the very ones they meant to benefit." [3]

If our history had not been written on politics almost exclusively, so that people have not learned to what extent political institutions are determined by economic conditions, it might be more generally appreciated what loss has been sustained by the ignorance, folly, and wickedness of statesmen and social philosophers. "It is manifestly impossible to tell what protection has done for the country unless one is able to form some judgment of what our state would have been to-day if, for the past twenty years, the American people had been allowed, man for man, to earn what they could and keep what they earned. That the accumulation of capital here would have been far greater than it is; that it would have been more equally distributed; that population would have been distributed where it would have been industrially more secure; that laborers would have been more steadily and securely gaining capital, and would have been more contented; that the organization of industry would have been more free and fair; and that the government would have been more sound and pure, are convictions that will be forced upon any candid student of the laws of economic forces and social development." [4] In fact, the greatest reforms which could be accomplished would consist in undoing the work of statesmen in the past, and the greatest difficulty in

[3] "Twentieth Century," April 24, 1890, p. 8.
[4] *North American Review*, September, 1884, Vol. CXXXIX, pp. 294, 295.

the way of reform is to find out how to undo their work
without injury to what is natural and sound. "Human
society tries hard to adapt itself to any conditions in
which it finds itself, and we have been warped and distorted until we have got used to it, as the foot adapts
itself to an ill-fitting boot. Next, we have come to
think that that is the right way for things to be; and it
is true that a change to a sound and normal condition
would for a time hurt us, as a man whose foot has been
distorted would suffer if he tried to wear a well-shaped
boot. Finally, we have produced a lot of economists
and social philosophers who have invented sophisms
for fitting our thinking to the distorted facts."

Whatever hope there may be for eliminating some
of these errors of the past and the establishment of a
healthy social order lies in the acquiring of a science
of society based on observation of phenomena and
study of forces. Any attempt to reconstruct society
on the plan of some enthusiastic social reformer would
simply be repeating the old error and postponing all
chance of real improvement. "Society needs first of
all to be freed from these meddlers—that is, to be let
alone. Here we are, then, once more back at the old
doctrine—*Laissez faire*. Let us translate it into blunt
English, and it will read, Mind your own business." [5]

If attempts of philosophers and statesmen to bring
society into conformity with some preconceived plan
or to make provision for future exigencies are unwise,
interference with the working of natural forces in
trade and industry, according to Sumner, is equally so.
Left alone, these forces will work out the right solution of the problems which arise. State regulation is
bound to be unintelligent and unfair,—unintelligent,
because upon the fundamentals involved there is never

[5] "What Social Classes Owe to Each Other," p. 120.

agreement among those interested. "For instance, when they talk about the labor question they do not agree as to what makes the rate of wages. But how is it possible to advance a step in the discussion of any question about employers and employed without a definite doctrine of what it is that makes the rate of wages? In the discussions about railroads it is constantly assumed that there is some 'cost' which can be taken as a basis for the definition of fair and reasonable rates. On the other hand, it is stoutly asserted that cost in this sense is a myth, and that no cost can be determined which will serve as a basis for any such computation. How can there be any deliberative solution of a practical question as to what railroads and shippers and legislators respectively ought to do, with such discord on the very first notions about the relations of the parties to each other inside the industrial organization? Again, in the discussion about trusts it is asserted that trusts adopt an arbitrary capitalization and then fix the prices of their products at such rates as to pay dividends on the paper capital. On the other hand, it is asserted that there are laws of the market which are imperative in their action and which make it utterly impossible for anybody to do that. In fact, the whole discussion revolves around this issue without ever bringing it out as a definite, independent subject of debate. One or the other view is assumed implicitly, and the discussion moves over secondary and derived applications, while any chance of clearing the matter up is diminished by the odium which is imported into the discussion." [5a]

Furthermore, nature has not given to men individually or as legislative bodies the powers of mind and character which enable them to discern and to do what

[5a] "War and Other Essays," pp. 237, 238.

in justice to all needs to be done. In a democracy the more we try to mold the social organization the greater will be the amount of deliberation and reflection demanded of the masses. It is safe to say that they will not respond. The whole industrial realm, furthermore, is full of conflicts of interest. Parties which have been defeated in the economic struggle, or feel that they have grievances against their rivals, turn to politics for relief. They assail the legislature with complaints and demand that the state shall alter the conditions of industry. The ethical elements in these conflicts of interests are never simple. They generally depend upon the most delicate play of economic forces and individual talent. "When the legislator tries to deal with them so as to do 'justice' he never has the case before him as it is before the mind of a party to the quarrel. In fact it is not possible that he ever could gain such knowledge of it. Some one aspect of the question fills his mind, and it is his prejudices and prepossessions which determine what aspect will win his attention; then he enacts something from the standpoint which he has adopted, and does wrong to all other interests."

But a far more serious objection to interference in industrial matters is the fact that such interference always tends to prevent the state from fulfilling its proper function. Since continual conflict of classes is inevitable, if legislation is employed to regulate according to the wishes of some, then those whose opinions and ambitions are different will, when they get the chance, employ legislation for their own ends. Thus the state will become not the guardian of the interests of all, but the servant of the interests of those best able to control it. "Let the reader note for himself with what *naïveté* the advocate of interference

takes it for granted that he and his associates will have
the administration of the legislative device in their
own hands and will be sure of guiding it for their purposes only. They never appear to remember that the
device, when once set up, will itself become the prize
of a struggle; that it will serve one set of purposes as
well as another, so that after all the only serious question is: Who will get it? Here is another ground for a
general and sweeping policy of non-interference. Although you may be in possession of the power to-day,
and it might suit you very well, either to triumph over
your business rivals and competitors; or to bend to
your will the social organ which stands next to you,
and with which you have the most friction (as, for instance, shippers with transporters); or to see your
pet reform (temperance, for instance) marching on,
you would far better consent to forego your satisfaction, lest presently your rivals, or the railroads, or
the liquor sellers, should beat you in a political
struggle; and then you must suffer wrong and in the
end be forced to give up industrial and persuasive
methods altogether and devote your whole energy to
the political struggle as that on which all the rest
depends." [6]

Indications are abundant that citizens are losing
faith in the state as an instrument for insuring justice
for all. "While it is reaching out on one side to fields
of socialistic enterprise, interfering in the interests
of parties in the industrial organism, assuming
knowledge of economic laws which nobody possesses,
taking ground as to dogmatic notions of justice which
are absurd, and acting because it does not know what
to do, it is losing its power to give peace, order, and
security. The extra-legal power and authority of

[6] "Earth Hunger and Other Essays," p. 287, 288.

leaders over voluntary organizations of men throughout a community who are banded together in order to
press their interests at the expense of other interests,
and who go to the utmost verge of the criminal law,
if they do not claim immunity from it, while obeying
an authority which acts in secret and without responsibility, is a phenomenon which shows the inadequacy
of the existing State to guarantee rights and give security. The boycott and the plan of campaign are certainly not industrial instrumentalities, and it is not
yet quite certain whether they are violent and criminal
instrumentalities by which some men coerce other
men in matters of material interests. If we turn our
minds to the victims of these devices, we see that they
do not find in the modern State that security for their
interests under the competition of life which it is the
first and unquestioned duty of the state to provide.
The boycotted man is deprived of the peaceful enjoyment of rights which the laws and institutions of his
country allow him, and he has no redress. The State
has forbidden all private war on the ground that it
will give a remedy for wrongs, and that private redress
would disturb the peaceful prosecution of their own
interests by other members of the community who are
not parties to the quarrel; but we have seen an industrial war paralyze a whole section for weeks, and it
was treated almost as a right of the parties that they
might find it out, no matter at what cost to by-
standers." [7]

Sumner did not deny, but emphatically asserted, that
it is the duty of individuals to help those less fortunate
than themselves. His private papers show that his
own charities were numerous. Against state aid, however, he rebelled because of its inherent injustice, and

[7] "War and Other Essays," pp. 224, 225.

for the philanthropists and reformers who sought to utilize the machinery of the government to carry out their schemes in behalf of "the poor," "the weak," and "the unfortunate," he had only scorn and rebuke. "The type and formula of most schemes of philanthropy or humanitarianism," he says, "is this: A and B put their heads together to decide what C shall do for D. The radical vice of all these schemes, from a sociological point of view, is that C is not allowed a voice in the matter, and his position, character, and interests, as well as the ultimate effects on society through C's interests, are entirely overlooked. I shall call C the Forgotten Man. For once let us look him up and consider his case, for the characteristic of all social doctors is that they fix their minds on some man or group of men whose case appeals to the sympathies and the imagination, and they plan remedies addressed to the particular trouble; they do not understand that all the parts of society hold together, and that forces which are set in action act and react throughout the whole organism, until an equilibrium is produced by a readjustment of all interests and rights. They therefore ignore entirely the source from which they must draw all the energy which they employ in their remedies, and they ignore all the effects on other members of society than the ones they have in view. They are always under the dominion of the superstition of government, and, forgetting that a government produces nothing at all, they leave out of sight the first fact to be remembered in all social discussion—that the State cannot get a cent for any man without taking it from some other man, and this latter must be a man who has produced and saved it. This latter is the Forgotten Man." [8]

[8] "What Social Classes Owe to Each Other," pp. 123, 124.

"You will find him hard at work because he has a great many to support." He is minding his own business, delving away in patient industry, "paying his taxes, casting his vote, supporting the church and the school, reading his newspaper, and cheering for the politician of his admiration, but he is the only one for whom there is no provision in the great scramble and the big divide." Weighed down with the cost and burden of all the schemes for making everybody happy, with the cost of all public beneficence, with the support of all the loafers, with the loss of all the economic quackery, with the cost of all the jobs, "he is our productive force which we are wasting. Let us take some of the burden off him. Let us turn our pity on him instead of on the good-for-nothing. It will be only justice to him and society will greatly gain by it." [9]

Since *laissez faire* is what the natural order requires if every man is to have all the chance possible to make the most of himself in this world of inequality and the highest civilization is to be achieved and maintained, and since through it alone can practical justice be assured, Sumner was led to make this bold and emphatic statement of conviction:

"I therefore maintain that it is at the present time a matter of patriotism and civic duty to resist the extension of state interference. It is one of the proudest results of political growth that we have reached the point where individualism is possible. Nothing could better show the merit and value of the institutions which we have inherited than the fact that we can afford to play with all these socialistic and semi-socialistic absurdities. They have no great importance until the question arises: Will a generation which can be

[9] See "The Forgotten Man and Other Essays," p. 491 f.

led away into this sort of frivolity be able to transmit
intact institutions which were made only by men of
sterling thought and power, and which can be maintained only by men of the same type? I am familiar
with the irritation and impatience with which remonstrances on this matter are received. Those who know
just how the world ought to be reconstructed are, of
course, angry when they are pushed aside as busy-
bodies. A group of people who assail the legislature
with a plan for regulating their neighbor's mode of
living are enraged at the 'dogma' of non-interference.
The publicist who has been struck by some of the
superficial roughnesses in the collision of interests
which must occur in any time of great industrial
activity, and who has therefore determined to waive
the objections to State interference, if he can see it
brought to bear on his pet reform, will object to absolute principles. For my part, I have never seen that
public or private principles were good for anything
except when there seemed to be a motive for breaking
them. Any one who has studied a question as to which
the solution is yet wanting may despair of the power
of free contract to solve it. I have examined a great
many cases of proposed interference with free contract, and the only alternative to free contract which
I can find is 'heads I win, tails you lose' in favor of
one party or the other. I am familiar with the criticisms which some writers claim to make upon individualism, but the worst individualism I can find in
history is that of the Jacobins, and I believe that it
is logically sound that the anti-social vices should be
most developed whenever the attempt is made to put
socialistic theories in practice. The only question at
this point is: Which may we better trust, the play of
free social forces or legislative and administrative in-

terference? This question is as pertinent for those who expect to win by interference as for others, for whenever we try to get paternalized we only succeed in getting policed." [10]

[10] "War and Other Essays," pp. 225, 226.

If this poor old world is as bad as they say, one more reflection may check the zeal of the headlong reformer. It is at any rate a tough old world. It has taken its trend and curvature and all its twists and tangles from a long course of formation. All its wry and crooked gnarls are therefore stiff and stubborn. If we puny men by our arts can do anything at all to straighten them, it will only be by modifying the tendencies of some of the forces at work, so that, after a sufficient time, their action may be changed a little and slowly the lines of movement may be modified.

The Absurd Effort to Make the World Over.

CHAPTER XXIII

PROGRESS

In a world order such as has been described, what significance has the term "progress"? Obviously Sumner believed that it was within man's power to change things for the better. True, he held up to scorn the great body of reformers and uplifters, but had he not been convinced that gain can be achieved by intelligent, unselfish action, it is inconceivable that he would have endured the toils, run the risks, and made the sacrifices which his career of public service entailed. In what sense, then, is social betterment possible, and in what way can human beings contribute thereto?

It must be recognized, in the first place, that, applied to social customs and institutions, good and bad are relative terms. There is no permanent or universal standard by which right and truth with regard to these matters can be established. They are what they ought to be in proportion as they are adapted to the conditions of the period in which they exist, and since this is a world in which nothing long remains the same, and what the future will bring forth no one can foretell, it is impossible to declare in advance what kind of social arrangement coming days may demand. There is, therefore, no ideal pattern good for all times and places into conformity with which institutions should be shaped. To construct one abstractly, and to put it forward as a "Great Cause," deserving the loyal devotion of all who would have this the best possible world, is both foolish and harmful. We must "abandon all hopes of finding an absolutely 'best' system of government or one which will alter any of the conditions of human life, except by undoing the mischief which mistaken effort may have done. If we study human nature and human history, we find that civil institutions are only 'better' and 'best' relatively to the people for whom they exist, and that they can be so called only as they are more closely adjusted to the circumstances of the nation in question. The *a priori* philosophers have led men astray by their assumptions and speculations, teaching them to look into the clouds for dreams and impossibilities instead of studying the world and life as they are, so as to learn how to make the best of them. We shall discover or invent no system of government which we can carry from nation to nation, counting upon uniform action and results everywhere, as we do, for instance, with a steam engine or a telescope." [1]

All attempt to re-shape society into conformity with ideals evolved out of philosophical speculation or constructed by the imagination, Sumner condemned as destructive to social welfare. It would be unjust, however, to accuse him of throwing contempt upon ideals in general. "What are the proper cases for the use of ideals?" he asks in "Folkways." [2] "Ideals can be useful when they are formed in the imagination of the person who is to realize them by his own exertions, for then the ideal and the program of action are in the same consciousness, and therefore the defects of an ideal are reduced or removed. Ideals are useful (a) in homiletics, which are chiefly occupied with attempts at suggestion. In limited cases a preacher or

---

[1] "The Challenge of Facts and Other Essays," pp. 244, 245.
[2] "Folkways," pp. 201, 202.

teacher can suggest ideals which, if apprehended and adopted, become types toward which young persons may train themselves. Even then these cases merge in the next class. (b) Ideals are useful in self-education. The ideal is then taken up from books or from admired persons by suggestion and imitation, or from auto-suggestion, but generally from a combination of the two. An ideal from auto-suggestion produces enthusiasm. The fantastic character of the ideal, if the person is young, is unimportant. His will is enlisted to work for it. He can constantly compare the ideal with his experience. The ideal is at last shorn down to reality and merges in sober plans of effort. (c) A larger field for ideals is afforded by vanity. As vanity is itself a subjective affection, but one which can awaken only in society, it uses the imagination to suppose cases, plan unlimited schemes, devise types of self-decoration and dreams of superiority, distinction, power, success, and glory. The creations are all phantasms. The ends are all ideals. These ideals may not be extravagant. Vanity generally creates them by raising to a higher pitch some treatment of the body or dress, some admired trait of character, some action which has won glory, or given pleasure and won applause. . . . (d) Ideals also find a great field in marriage. In this case ideals of happiness have powerfully affected the institution at all its stages. Experience of marriage has been partly pleasant and partly the contrary. The experience has stimulated the reflection: How blessed it would be if only this or that unpleasant detail could be corrected! This has led to idealization or the imaginative conception of a modified institution. Our novels now sometimes aid in this idealization. Men loved their daughters with zealous and protective affection long before they loved their wives. The father's love reached out to follow the daughter into matrimony and to secure for her some stipulation which should free wedlock for her from pain or care which other wives had to endure. These stipulations were always guided by idealization. The rich and great were first able to realize the modifications. These then passed into fashion, custom, and the mores, and the institution was perfected and refined by them.''

Ideals which are made the basis of social reconstruction are highly pernicious, however, for they are entirely unscientific. Frequently they are formed in the effort to escape from the hard task of dealing with facts. There is no process by which to reach an ideal and no tests by which to verify it. It is therefore impossible to frame a proposition about it which can be proved or disproved. ''Dogmatic ideals like perfect liberty, justice, or equality, especially if economic and not political liberty, justice and equality are meant, can never furnish rational or scientific motives of action or starting-points for rational effort. They never can enter into scientific thinking since they admit of no analysis and can be tested by no canons of truth. They have no footing in reality. Anybody who says that 'we want to build a republic of educated labor' is not defining a rational program of action. He is only manufacturing turgid phrases. He who says that the state 'ought to balance the motives of interest and benevolence' is not contributing to any sober discussion. He is talking nonsense, since an analysis of 'state,' 'interest,' and 'benevolence' would cause the proposition to fall into contradictions and absurdities. The vice and fallacy of this way of looking at things is that it assumes that men can by thinking things call them into being; or that men can add by thinking to the existing conditions some element which is not in them. All who talk about the 'power of ideas' are more or less under this fallacy. It is a relic of the sympathetic magic of savage men. Serious study of human society shows us that we can never do anything but use and develop the opportunities which are offered to us by the conditions and conjunctures of the moment." [3]

Sumner further states in "The Challenge of Facts" that "the progress which men have made in developing the possibilities of human existence has never been made by jumps and strides. It has never resulted from the schemes of philosophers and reformers. It has never been guided through a set program by the wisdom of any sages, statesmen, or philanthropists. The progress which has been made has been won in minute stages by men who had a definite task before them, and who dealt with it in detail, as it presented itself, without reference to general principles, or attempting to bring it into logical relations to an *a priori* system." [4]

The student of social facts and forces finds it impossible to believe, furthermore, that the world will ever arrive at some happy state where want and hardship are unknown and universal goodness and peace prevail. Such a condition would mean, not quiet and unruffled enjoyment, but stagnation, routine, and decay. It is not in consuming the achievements of the past that either happiness or power is experienced, but in the work of achievement, in the sense of gain and progress. A new measure of energy and strength may be won, but it drives men on to fresh labors and the exhilaration which the struggle they entail imparts. Advantages gained are never permanent. Changes

---

[3] "Earth Hunger and Other Essays," p. 74.
[4] "The Challenge of Facts and Other Essays," pp. 50, 51.

in men and their circumstances are continually taking place, and adjustments must be continually reëstablished. Old evils may be removed, but new ones are forever appearing. How then is it possible to believe that the human race will ever get its work done? Human nature, also, must always be reckoned with, and this in its essentials never alters. Poverty, if conquered and banished, will come again through the vices engendered in a world without poverty, and the conflict will begin once more. "Projects to abolish poverty are worthy of an age which has undertaken to discuss the abolition of disease. Why not abolish death and be as gods once for all? Why not resolve that everybody shall be good and happy? Why not vote that everybody shall have whatever he wants? Why trifle with details? If these agencies can get us anything, they can just as well get us everything. The trouble with creation out of nothing is not to make a universe; it is to make an atom of star-dust." [5]

Nor is there any basis in fact for the modern idea that the world is advancing along some line which is called *progress* toward peace and brotherly love. "We read of fist-law and constant war in the Middle Ages and think that life must have been full of conflicts and bloodshed then: but modern warfare bears down on the whole population with a frightful weight through all the years of peace. Never, from the days of barbarian down to our own time, has every man in a society been a soldier until now: and the armaments of to-day are immensely more costly than ever before. There is only one limit possible to the war preparations of a modern European state; that is, the last man and the last dollar it can control. What will come of the mixture of sentimental social philosophy and warlike

[5] "Earth Hunger and Other Essays," pp. 347, 348.

policy? There is only one thing rationally to be expected, and that is a frightful effusion of blood in revolution and war during the century now opening." [6] That conflict will ever be abolished is unthinkable. "Can peace be universal? There is no reason to believe it. It is a fallacy to suppose that by widening the peace-group more and more it can at last embrace all mankind. What happens is that, as it grows bigger, differences, discords, antagonisms, and war begin inside of it on account of the divergence of interests. Since evil passions are a part of human nature and are in all societies all the time, a part of the energy of the society is constantly spent in repressing them. If all nations should resolve to have no armed ships any more, pirates would reappear upon the ocean; the police of the seas must be maintained. We could not dispense with our militia; we have too frequent need of it now. But police defense is not war in the sense in which I have been discussing it. War, in the future, will be the clash of policies of national vanity and selfishness when they cross each other's path." [7]

When we look back over the stream of history, however, we see a phenomenon to which the term "progress," freed from the popular implications just mentioned, may be applied. It is a progress which is in the nature of things. As human beings from generation to generation have reacted to the facts of existence, increased security and power have resulted, so that there is incalculably more opportunity for self-realization than formerly. The great marvel is that in three or four civilized nations a few million people can so far control the condition of existence that they can live their lives out in comparative peace and

[6] "War and Other Essays," pp. 29, 30.
[7] *Ibid.*, pp. 35, 36.

security. Progress "means winning more social power; it goes along with increase of power and is the proof and the realization of such increase. The arts of life all contribute to the increase. Although it has been said that social power means power of an individual to produce, from the land, a surplus of subsistence beyond his own needs, yet it will not be understood that this power is increased by agricultural improvements only; it is increased by all improvements in any department of industrial effort; it is especially increased by the extension of the cultivated area of the globe, that is, by settling new countries. This last mode of increasing social power is also the easiest." [8]

To this progress can individuals by conscious, intelligent effort contribute? This question must be considered with reference to the mores. Civilization is the product of their evolution. Out of them has come the industrial organization through which capital, the indispensable requisite to all advancement in the arts, has been secured. Not only are capital and the arts affected by the character of the industrial organization itself, but also, as has been shown, by political conditions, by the state, which may interfere detrimentally or may assist by insuring free play to the economic forces, and by prevailing social ideas and customs, all of which are likewise determined by the mores. The evolution of the latter has gone on, for the most part, spontaneously. Human reflection and conscious effort have shaped them only to a comparatively small degree. In what measure is there the possibility of influencing them now in the interests of economic welfare, increased social power, and greater scope for self-realization on the part of the individual?

[8] "The Challenge of Facts and Other Essays," pp. 147, 148.

That the possibility is a limited one, the description of the mores previously given indicates. They are characterized by inertia and rigidity. They coerce each generation. They do not stimulate thought or criticism. They present themselves as final and unchangeable answers to the problems of life. There is in them, however, continual need of change, since the conditions to which they are adaptations are constantly altering. Always is there the danger that they will become stereotyped and lose all relation to expediency. Aberrations occur which demand correction. Along with the need of change in the mores there is also the strain of improvement. If they are imperfectly adapted to satisfying the needs for which they exist, they cause annoyance and pain and tend to change along the lines for which a better adaptation calls.

These characteristics, in Sumner's view, offer some opportunity to influence the character of events and to contribute to the progress of civilization and the advancement of the race. Although man cannot direct the evolution of the mores, by perceiving its trend he can assist it. With the aid of the knowledge which history and science afford, he can make slow and careful corrections and improvements and prevent foolish and harmful interferences with the natural movement of things, so that some confusion and loss will be avoided.

"It is not to be inferred that reform and correction are hopeless. Inasmuch as the mores are a phenomenon of the society and not of the state, and inasmuch as the machinery of administration belongs to the state and not to the society, the administration of the mores presents peculiar difficulties. Strictly speaking, there is no administration of the mores, or it is left to voluntary organs acting by moral suasion. The state administration fails if it tries to deal with the mores, because it goes out of its province. The voluntary organs which try to administer the mores (literature, moral teachers, schools, churches, etc.) have no set method and no persistent effort. They very often make great errors in their methods. In regard to divorce, for instance, it is idle to set up stringent rules in an ecclesiastical body, and to try to establish them by extravagant and false interpretation of the Bible, hoping in that way to lead opinion; but the observation and consideration of cases which occur affect opinion and form convictions. The statesman and social philosopher can act with such influences, sum up the forces which make them, and greatly help the result. The inference is that intelligent art can be introduced here as elsewhere, but that it is necessary to understand the mores and to be able to discern the elements in them, just as it is always necessary for good art to understand the facts of nature with which it will have to deal. It belongs to the work of publicists and statesmen to gauge the forces in the mores and to perceive their tendencies. The great men of a great epoch are those who have understood new currents in the mores. The great reformers of the sixteenth century, the great leaders of modern revolutions, were, as we can easily see, produced out of a protest or revulsion which had long been forming under and within the existing system. The leaders are such because they voice the convictions which have become established and because they propose measures which will realize interests of which the society has become conscious. A hero is not needed. Often a mediocre, commonplace man suffices to give the critical turn to thought or interest. 'A Gian Angelo Medici, agreeable, diplomatic, benevolent, and pleasure-loving, sufficed to initiate a series of events which kept the occidental races in perturbation through two centuries.'[9] Great crises come when great new forces are at work changing fundamental conditions, while powerful institutions and traditions still hold old systems intact. The fifteenth century was such a period. It is in such crises that great men find their opportunity. The man and the age react on each other. The measures of policy which are adopted and upon which energy is expended become components in the evolution. The evolution, although it has the character of a nature process, always must issue by and through men whose passions, follies, and wills are a part of it but are also always dominated by it. The interaction defies our analysis, but it does not discourage our reason and conscience from their play on the situation if we are content to know that their function must be humble. Stoll boldly declares that if one of us had been a judge in the times of the witch trials he would have reasoned as the witch judges did, and would have tortured like them.[10] If that is so, then it behooves us by education and will, with intelligent purpose, to criticize and judge even the most established ways of our time, and to put courage and labor into resistance to the current mores where we judge them wrong. It would be a mighty achievement of the science of society if it could lead up to an art of societal administration which should be intelligent, effective and scientific."[11]

Persons who attempt such assistance of the mores are always handicapped, however, by limitations of mind and knowledge, and especially by the fact that their own ideas and tastes are the products of the

9 Symonds, "Catholic Reaction," Vol. I, p. 144.
10 "Suggestion and Hypnotisms," p. 244.
11 "Folkways," pp. 117, 118.

mores from whose coercion no one can wholly escape. It is only the élite, therefore, who can affect the mores, and they but to a very limited degree. "We are the children of the society in which we are born. It makes us. We are the products of the civilization of our generation. Only a handful of men can react upon the society and the age in which they live so as to modify it at all. They are the very élite of the human race, and after all what they can do is only infinitesimal. Civilization means the art of living on this earth. All men have always been trying to learn it, and all that now is in the order of society is the product of the struggle of ages. It pours along in a mighty flood which bears us all with it; in it are all the efforts, passions, interests, and strifes of men. It is the play of these upon each other which produces the heaving and swaying of the flood and determines its vast modifications of direction. If you come to a faint understanding of this, the man with a scheme in his pocket for the 'reorganization of society' is made to appear very ridiculous." [12]

The more the education given through the home, the school, and the church develops the critical faculty, however, the more will ills be avoided and civilization tend to advance. "Criticism is the examination and test of propositions of any kind which are offered for acceptance, in order to find out whether they correspond to reality or not. The critical faculty is a product of education and training. It is a mental habit and power. It is a prime condition of human welfare that men and women should be trained in it. It is our only guarantee against delusion, deception, superstition, and misapprehension of ourselves and our earthly circumstances. It is a faculty which will

[12] "Earth Hunger and Other Essays," p. 341.

protect us against all harmful suggestions. . . . To act by suggestion or auto-suggestion is to act by impulse. Education teaches us to act by judgment. Our education is good just so far as it produces well-developed critical faculty. The thirteenth century had no critical faculty. It wandered in the dark, multiplying errors, and starting movements which produced loss and misery for centuries, because it dealt with fantasies, and did not know the truth about men or their position in the world. The nineteenth century was characterized by the acquisition and use of the critical faculty. A religious catechism never can train children to criticism. 'Patriotic' history and dithyrambic literature never can do it. A teacher of any subject who insists on accuracy and a rational control of all processes and methods, and who holds everything open to unlimited verification and revision, is cultivating that method as a habit in the pupils. In current language this method is called 'science,' or 'scientific.' The critical habit of thought, if usual in a society, will pervade all its mores because it is a way of taking up the problems of life. Men educated in it cannot be stampeded by stump orators and are never deceived by dithyrambic oratory. They are slow to believe. They can hold things as possible or probable in all degrees, without certainty and without pain. They can wait for evidence and weigh evidence, uninfluenced by the emphasis or confidence with which assertions are made on one side or the other. They can resist appeals to their dearest prejudices and all kinds of cajolery. Education in the critical faculty is the only education of which it can be truly said that it makes good citizens." [13]

The progress of civilization can be assisted also by

[13] "Folkways," pp. 632, 633.

increasing the industrial virtues. Through the development of character capital will be conserved and
increased. Nothing tells on the welfare of man so
much as hard work and self-denial. To cultivate
these is one of the surest ways of overcoming evils
and promoting societal good. "The task of dealing
with social ills is not a new task. People set about
it and discuss it as if the human race had hitherto
neglected it, and as if the solution of the problem was
to be something new in form and substance, different
from the solution of all problems which have hitherto
engaged human effort. In truth, the human race has
never done anything else but struggle with the problem of social welfare. That struggle constitutes history, or the life of the human race on earth. That
struggle embraces all minor problems which occupy
attention here save those of religion, which reaches
beyond this world and finds its objects beyond this
life. Every successful effort to widen the power of
man over nature is a real victory over poverty, vice,
and misery, taking things in general and in the long
run. It would be hard to find a single instance of a
direct assault by positive effort upon poverty, vice,
and misery which has not either failed or, if it has
not failed directly and entirely, has not entailed other
evils greater than the one which it removed. The
only two things which really tell on the welfare of
man on earth are hard work and self-denial (in technical language, labor and capital), and these tell most
when they are brought to bear directly upon the effort
to earn an honest living, to accumulate capital, and
to bring up a family of children to be industrious
and self-denying in their turn.[14] "The sound student
of sociology can hold out to mankind, as individuals

14 "War and Other Essays," pp. 185, 186.

or as a race, only one hope of better and happier living. That hope lies in an enhancement of the industrial virtues and of the moral forces which thence arise. Industry, self-denial, and temperance are the laws of prosperity for men and states; without them advance in the arts and in wealth means only corruption and decay through luxury and vice. With them progress in the arts and increasing wealth are the prime conditions of an advancing civilization which is sound enough to endure.'' [15]

It was in the possibility of furthering human welfare along the lines just indicated that Sumner found the inspiration for his life work. To the development of a science of society he devoted himself with enthusiasm, self-denial, and indefatigable labor, because through it alone can man have the knowledge necessary to escape disastrous errors in relation to societal phenomena and perceive the policies by which human effort should be governed. The arguments of the sentimental school of social philosophers he shattered with hard facts and sound logic, persuaded that their projects were bound to be destructive of the civilization built up by so many centuries of struggle, whose preservation and advancement should be the first concern of all. Against every form of state interference he fought with the same weapons, because such interference is contrary to what a study of the natural order reveals as right, and because it was offensive to his lively sense of justice. For years he taught the youth, endeavoring to make them critical of mind, hostile to all sentimentality, searchers for facts, champions of the truth, conscious of civic responsibility, sturdy of character, because such men have societal value. Thus by nature a preacher, a

[15] "The Challenge of Facts and Other Essays," pp. 51, 52.

reformer, a public servant, he made the intelligent promotion of societal welfare the exclusive aim of his life, sacrificing to it pleasure, recreation, and all else that might interfere with its largest possible realization.

One who aims at glory or fame directly will win only that wretched caricature which we call notoriety. Glory and fame, so far as they are desirable things, are remote results which come of themselves at the end of long and repeated and able exertions.

Discipline.

CHAPTER XXIV

INFLUENCE

The trite statement that influence cannot be measured is particularly true in the case of William Graham Sumner. So many hundreds just starting out on their careers felt the force of his personality, his relations with men and affairs were so numerous and varied, his investigations into the laws and conditions of human life were so thorough and penetrating and his exposition of them so clarifying and convincing, that it is exceptionally difficult to estimate at all adequately how far his life and teachings have determined thought and activities, or to what extent they will mold them in years to come.

In an extraordinary degree his influence sprang from what he himself was. Whether in classroom or faculty meeting or on the platform, he was the rugged personification of truth, of loyalty to the right as it was given him to see the right, of unselfish public spirit; a man of incorruptible integrity whom no flattery or threat or insidious bribe could touch; the relentless foe of all that was mean or false or unjust. Tolerance was not a conspicuous characteristic of Sumner, but except in this respect Huxley's ambition for himself, when he was thirty years old, was realized in his American contemporary: "To smite all humbug, however big; to give a nobler tone to science; to set an example of abstinence from petty personal controversies, and of toleration for everything but lying; to be indifferent as to whether the work is recognized or not, so long as it is done—these are my

497

aims.'' The youth who came into contact with Sumner felt his moral greatness, and it was this that won their unqualified admiration. Unquestionably, large numbers went out from his presence to be bigger and better men and to play a nobler part in public affairs than would have been the case had they never known him. Through his writings, also, the influence of his character worked and still works. They are anything but cold and impersonal. Back of them one always feels the man; they throb with the intensity of his conviction and with moral passion. His essays will live, not only because of the truths they set forth, but because of their scorn, their rebuke, their blows, and their highmindedness.

But it is only when in connection with Sumner's power of character we recall his remarkable skill and force as a teacher that we can begin to appreciate the extent of his influence upon his students. ''It was years,'' says one of them, ''before I could admit that there was any other political economy than that which he taught, which was worthy of the least consideration.'' Those who came under his instruction were grounded in certain principles relating to the state and to citizenship upon which, sometimes consciously and sometimes unconsciously, they acted. Public officials, newspaper editors, lawyers, and business men, although they may have ceased to agree with all of his views, preached and exemplified ''Billy Sumner.''

Scores of letters are in existence, as well as published testimonials, which bear witness to men's keen sense of indebtedness to him. ''It has always seemed to me,'' wrote one lawyer, ''that the test of a great teacher is whether the student who leaves his tutelage goes away a better man than when he came within his

reach. It seems to me to express only the truth when
I say that nearly every man who has come under your
instruction through the years has left you, not only
a better man, but a better man who had learned to
think. This was the concurrence of opinion of three
men—one of the class of '78—one of the class of '95
and one of the class of '05—no later than yesterday.''
From the editor of a well-known daily paper came
this acknowledgment: "I owe to him more than I can
possibly say. What he said, and his way of looking
at things, have stayed with me for thirty years. Time
and again when I have written an editorial I have
wondered what Professor Sumner would think of it.
It is only truth to say that I have tried to be true to
the faith.'' "If you knew how strong an influence
you have on the thinking men who have left Yale in
the last ten years," wrote a former student in 1887,
"you would, I think, sometimes feel repaid for the
apparent waste of energy you so conscientiously put
forth. As for myself, I may say that I owe to you
more intellectual life than to any man living or dead,
except one—John Stuart Mill.'' Another prominent
graduate wrote twenty years later in similar vein:
"I have just finished reading your book 'Folkways.'
It has charmed, delighted, stimulated me. But to say
that, I would not venture to write to you. It may
not, however, be unwelcome to you who have spent
your life in teaching to hear from one who sat under
you half his life ago, one of the long procession who
have passed under your influence, that as I read this
book I realized gratefully how much I owe to the
impetus of your teaching of whatever I have known
of clear thinking and virile views of life.'' A grateful
senior in 1897 thus expressed his appreciation: "I
do not want to leave Yale without thanking you from

the bottom of my heart for the tremendous good I have received from your course this year. Your lectures in societology seem to me the best thing in my whole four years, and I am sure that I shall take from you as a permanent possession, not only a desire to see clearly and to interpret fairly the problems which experience furnishes the intellect, but also the courage to face the greater problems which practical life thrusts upon the will. For it is not simply our minds you have instructed; it is our whole souls you have moved with power in all their relations.''

Although the quality and permanence of Sumner's influence rest primarily upon his character, they do not rest there alone. His moral qualities not only made him a great teacher and inspirer, they also made him an investigator so patient and thorough, so determined not to stop short of fundamental truths, and so desirous of presenting the practical bearing of these clearly and forcefully, that he both contributed to the stock of human knowledge and also furnished effective weapons with which to fight error and dangerous tendencies. More and more is it being recognized that the researches upon which ''Folkways'' is based have brought to light facts concerning society which students, and all interested in the practical work of social betterment as well, cannot afford to disregard. In his essays, and especially in ''What Social Classes Owe to Each Other,'' he presents arguments for individualism and objections to state interference and paternalism which are grounded in the eternal ordering of things and hold good for all places and times. They have never been stated more convincingly and it is impossible to believe that they ever will be. John Graham Brooks says that for many years, publicly and privately, he has ''urged socialists to read—*really* read—Sumner as the most doughty and competent foe with whom they have to reckon.''

The fundamental character of Sumner's work and its permanent and universal value were recognized abroad more quickly, perhaps, than in this country. Many of his writings were at once reprinted in England. ''Protectionism'' was translated into French and Greek; and ''What Social Classes Owe to Each Other,'' into French and German. The two German editions have an introduction by Dr. Theodor Barth, the eminent publicist, prominent among those who consistently opposed Bismarck's protectionist policies. In it he says that while the book naturally reflects American conditions, its author has such a deep comprehension of the subject that ''his reflections are significant for the whole economic culture of our times.'' He also contrasts the natural view of the world which Sumner takes and his candor and straightforward method with the tendencies of German scholarship, declaring that ''the economic intelligence in Germany has succeeded in unraveling the phenomena of economic life to such an extent that, to use a Macaulayan phrase, it has become the dupe of its own ingenuity.'' He points out also that every one who goes to the bottom of things, as Sumner does, has to choose between socialism and individualism. There is no middle course.

In England many of Sumner's writings were widely read and appreciated. A Yale graduate relates that he happened to be taken by a London friend into the Savile Club for dinner, a club whose membership is made up principally of men devoted to arts and letters. At table he sat between his host and an Oxford professor, Edgeworth by name. The latter had re-

cently been in America and had been entertained at
the homes of various well-known professors of Yale
and Harvard. The American referred to several of
these and Professor Edgeworth spoke of them pleas-
antly, but when the name of Professor William G.
Sumner was mentioned his comment was different.
"There," said Professor Edgeworth, "is a man, a
great man, one of the men who knows his subject, one
of the men whose conclusions command respect at
every university in Europe. He is the greatest man
there is at Yale and one of the greatest of Americans,
at least among university men."

The noted economist, Alfred Marshall, wrote Sumner from Oxford: "I have to thank you for your
excellent little book of suggestive questions on economics. I have been using and getting a good many
of my pupils to get your 'Social Classes.' I found
it a most fascinating book, though I am not quite so
thorough an advocate of *laissez faire* as you are."
Upon reading "Bimetallism," James E. Thorold
Rogers, another eminent English scholar, at once
wrote to the *Princeton Review:* "You will perhaps
allow me to congratulate you and the readers of the
Review on the admirable article contributed to it in
your November number by Professor Sumner of Yale
College. I have rarely read anything so sound, so
logical, and so complete, or, I may add, anything
more opportune than the examination which he has
given of a modern heresy in economics. Dealing as
I do with the historical theory of political economy,
I am the more pleased with an essay which, starting
as it does with a few incontestable principles, demonstrates as exactly as would be proved from a history of the currency, the mischievous character of a
proposal which would, were it accepted, be a constant

worry to the most important interests of society. Mr. Sumner has done this service at a time when it was singularly opportune. . . . I hope you will do me the favor of communicating to Professor Sumner my great admiration of his article and my sincere appreciation of its value.''

The following letter from Sir George J. Goschen, holder of many high offices under the English government, indicates that statesmen were as favorably impressed by Sumner's writings as were students.

Seacox Heath,
Hawkshurst,
22 July, '86.

SIR:

I have just read your little book, 'What Social Classes Owe to Each Other,' with very great interest and pleasure. Mr. Albert Grey, M.P., who has just returned from the United States, brought me a copy of it.

I was somewhat surprised to see that the cry for State aid seems to be as pronounced in the United States as with us.

I lately delivered an address on *laissez faire* at Edinburgh and venture to send you a copy, as I gather that you are generally interested in the discussion of these problems.

Yours very faithfully,
GEORGE J. GOSCHEN.

From Herbert Spencer came the two following letters:

38 Queen's Garden,
Bayswater, London,
October 4/83.

DEAR MR. SUMNER:

On my arrival home the other day after a fortnight's absence I found lying for me, among other books, yours

504 WILLIAM GRAHAM SUMNER

on 'What Social Classes Owe to Each Other.' A letter from Youmans had already drawn my attention to it, and I am glad to have a copy. His description leads me to anticipate much pleasure in reading it, and leads me also to rejoice that you are dealing with social questions from so philosophical a point of view.

I fear very much, however, that little can now be done in resisting the communistic tendencies which are daily growing stronger in civilized societies. The wave has become too vast. Every new step makes more difficult any reversal, since the reactive portion of the public becomes weaker and weaker.

However, we can but severally do what in us lies toward checking this disastrous tendency; and it is very satisfactory to me to find that you have issued what I am quite sure will be a telling exposition of rational views.

I hope you are well and prospering in your professorial work. For myself I am sorry to say that ever since my return from America I have been able to do next to nothing; but I am improving a good deal just now and hope shortly to resume work.

Sincerely yours,

HERBERT SPENCER.

A few months later Spencer had read the book as the following letter reveals:

38 Queen's Garden,

Bayswater, London,

Feb'y 28/84.

DEAR PROF. SUMNER:

Thank you for your copy of 'Economic Problems.' When I come to treat of industrial relations and deal with functions as well as structures, I shall doubtless get from it sundry classifications of ideas.

I endeavored to open negotiations between a certain body lately formed here called the Liberty and Property

Defense League, and you, for the purpose of getting a reproduction of your highly useful little book, 'What Social Classes Owe to Each Other.' I have not however succeeded. I wish you could make arrangements for an English edition.

Truly yours,

HERBERT SPENCER.

In France Sumner was held in equally high esteem. The group of individualists and free traders in which the well-known publicist, Yves Guyot, and the economist and translator, Arthur Raffalowich, and his brilliant sister, Sophie, were prominent, looked up to him as an authoritative teacher and inspirer. With the latter Sumner corresponded for a number of years, and the following extracts from her charmingly written letters reveal the regard in which he was held on the Continent, and give some side lights on the man himself.

19 Avenue Hache,

25th February, 1884   Paris.

. . . I am quite ashamed not to have acknowledged yet the attractive, tantalizing, suggestive volume of 'Economic Problems.' I am busy now studying the books and papers you were so kind as to send me, with much pleasure and not without profit I hope, as you will see in the *Journal des Economistes* of April or May.

I heard that M. Courcelle Seneuil—a French economist whose name you know doubtless, on reading the *compte rendu* in which I attempted to give an idea of that charming volume, 'What Social Classes,' asked for the book. After having read it, he was so delighted that he wishes to have it translated into French. If he finds a translator you will hear more of this wish. Words of wisdom would not come amiss just now to Frenchmen and Parisians most of all.

19 Avenue Hache,

June 25th, 1884   Paris.

. . . You may not be aware of it, but among the faithful contributors of the *Journal des Economistes* you have a small body of fanatics, of whom M. Courelle Seneuil is the head, who borrow successively from Mlle. Guillanmin the copy of 'What Social Classes,' and who look forward to what will come next from the same pen. When I hear people say, as they often do, that political economy is dead, that no one really believes in it, I like to think that their prophecies are false, and that a most *eclatant dementi* will come from Yale College.

As you are kind enough to be curious about that anomaly, a woman who takes interest in political economy, I will answer your question to the best of my ability. I was educated in France, but rather as a French boy, than as a French girl, without any accomplishment, learning what is required of lycéens, not from an abstract love of learning, I'm afraid, but for the more practical reason that I wanted to help my brother when he came home tired, and that I forgot everything when it was no more useful to him.

What had a real hold on me was learning English, and I can remember what a deep impression it made on us children, as if we had found what satisfied some mental craving, and made our lives fuller. English literature was like a new and beautiful country, and we plunged into it with the utmost delight. Political economy gave me the same delicious experience of finding what I wanted. It answered so many doubts and puzzles that even the most dry parts were a source of joy which I could not half express. . . .

I am afraid I have lost any good opinion you may have of me by this proof of the feminine perversity that will mix sentiment where it has nothing to do, and is capable of evolving a religious enthusiasm from the dismal science, and I hope you will excuse this egotistical nonsense, and look on it merely as a proof of how I was touched by your too flattering appreciation.

19 Avenue Hache,
Paris.

November 11th, 1885

DEAR SIR:

Have you already given the permission to translate into French your last book on 'Protectionism'? If not, would you give that permission to a French economist, M. Chailley, who is very eager to do that pleasant work? He is a collaborator of the *Journal des Economistes*, the author of a book on the 'Income Tax.' . . .

It would be a happy day for France if your vigorous attack on the common enemy could meet with the reception it deserves—not among the economists—they will recognize with joy its merits—but among the crowd, the victims of a system which they accept blindly. M. Chailley intends, if he has your permission, to publish the translation in very cheap form. That's the only way of hoping for a practical result.

Hotel de la Grande Bretagne,
Nice,
Dec. 25, 1885.

. . . Let me congratulate you on your great knowledge of French economists. I believe you know better what is going on here than very many of us. The book of M. Donnat, which you mentioned in one of your letters, was quite unknown at the librairie Guillaumin, the headquarters of French economists. It was a long time before we could find the book, which is really very interesting.

19 Avenue Hache,
Paris.

January 18, 1887

DEAR SIR:

I heard just now of a funny scene at the Conseil Municipal, which it would be a pity if you did not know, as you were the hero—or the victim of the occasion.

M. Donnat had been quoting your authority—William Graham Sumner, professeur Science Sociale a Yale College, etc. When he had finished Jaffrin jumped up in great triumph: 'You see the Americans are ahead of us. They have professor of social science, and we are only following their example when we say that socialism is scientific and should be taught as such. The time will come when scientific socialism will be taught in our schools, as it is in the United States, by professors of Social Science.' And as he paid no attention to the explanation which was at once given, you may become one of these days the representative of scientific socialism, as Jaffrin has few ideas and keeps close to the few he has.

M. Donnat says he has often spoken of the 'Forgotten Man' to his electors, or in any public meeting, and that it produces a great deal of impression on the crowd. It is a very useful argument and it will become as classical in France as what Bastial used to say: 'Ce qu' on voit et ce qu' on ne voit pas.'

The following appreciation of Sumner from a Frenchman's point of view was written in 1923 by M. Yves Guyot, editor of the *Journal des Economistes* and president of the Société d'Economie Politique de Paris. "My intellectual relations with William Graham Sumner date from more than forty years back. Joseph Chailley's French translation of 'Protectionism' was published in 1886. It was probably about this time that I entered into personal relations with Professor Sumner, by correspondence, but I must have handed over his letters concerning free trade to the Association Libre-Echangiste which then existed. Professor Sumner came to Paris in 1892. I had the pleasure of receiving him at the Ministry

of Public Works. He had just published his great
work, 'The Financier and Finances of the American
Revolution.' His activities entitled him to be elected
a corresponding member of the Académie des Sciences
Morales et Politique. This body is composed of forty-
seven members divided into several sections. That of
Political Economy only comprises eight members and
it cannot itself insure the election of new members
which might be its own candidates. I was unable to
be of any useful assistance to Professor Sumner,
having always acted and written without any regard
for the opinions of the Academy. I mention these
particulars to explain the reason of his non-success.
Had he made an application for one of the vacancies
which occurred later, he would have no doubt been
successful. He did not, however, condescend to any
further steps in the matter.

"I remember the deep impression on me made by
the first lines by Professor Sumner which I read. His
picture of the Forgotten Man was a revelation to
me. Indeed, the part played by this forgotten man
has never been so well characterized and brought out
as by Professor Sumner. How this forgotten man
immediately became my friend! Since Professor
Sumner made me acquainted with him I have never
ceased recommending him to the kind-heartedness and
friendship of all, and I have never stopped trying to
protect him against the enterprises of which he is a
constant victim."

That Sumner's influence has in it the element of
permanence is indicated by the increasing number of
references to his writings which one sees in newspapers, magazines, and books. The "Forgotten Man"
has indeed become a classic, and more and more is it
being appreciated that in his analyses, his conclusions,

and his prophecies, Sumner was right. The *New York World* of September 3, 1922, heads its editorials with one on "The Forgotten Man" and says:

> Nearly forty years ago Prof. William G. Sumner of Yale prepared a lecture entitled 'The Forgotten Man.' That lecture has since taken its place among the classic American contributions to political economy.
>
> 'The Forgotten Man' was never more timely than it is now, and it would be worth hundreds of millions of dollars to the American people if President Harding and Congress could be persuaded to study it until Sumner's thought had become part of their own mental processes.

There follows a quotation from the essay and an exposition of the conditions then existing in the light of it.

In 1917 Mr. Gerhard M. Dahl, then Vice-President of the Chase National Bank, New York, employed this same title, "The Forgotten Man," for an address which was afterwards printed in the *United States Investor*. The address begins with these words:

> MR. PRESIDENT, LADIES AND GENTLEMEN:
> The subject which I have selected to talk to you about for a few moments I have named 'The Forgotten Man.' I have taken this title from a book written by Professor Sumner of Yale University, thirty-five years ago, which is called 'What Social Classes Owe to Each Other.' It is amazing how apt his description of conditions nearly thirty-five years ago is with reference to present-day conditions.

Speaking before the Academy of Political Science in the City of New York, May 23, 1921, Hon. R. C. Leffingwell, at one time Assistant Secretary of the

Treasury, quoted at length from Sumner's essay on "War," and called attention to the fact that these "prophetic words" were written ten years before the outbreak of the great war.

"Folkways" cannot properly be called a popular book, but the increasing number of allusions to it upon which one happens is evidence that its content is finding its way into general use. Even in so unlikely a place as the humorous page of one of the most widely circulated American magazines reference to it was recently made, and also in an editorial in a Toronto paper on "Decency in Dress."

If we turn from clothing to legislation, here, too, we find "Folkways" quoted as an authority. In criticizing the report of a Commission which would have "Congress create by law instanter a new code of living for the sole benefit of labor," the *Wall Street Journal* refers to Sumner's exposition of the "mores," and throws scorn on all attempts to reform existing conditions by arbitrary enactments made in ignorance of fundamental social laws and forces.

Such references as these could be multiplied. They indicate that Sumner has added permanently to the working capital of those who are interested in intelligent social and political activity. The rank which will finally be accorded to him as a sociologist it is too early to assert. Not all the results of his extensive investigations have as yet been made public. It seems altogether probable, however, that Professor Giddings' belief that Sumner will come to be recognized as one of the greatest of sociologists will be justified.

The development of character is the last and highest thing for which we men have to live on earth, and the success with which we develop it depends upon the correctness with which we know the laws of life and morals, and obey them.

The True Aim of Life.

CHAPTER XXV

THE MAN

WILLIAM GRAHAM SUMNER is one of that notable group of men who, favored by the opportunities America offers, have risen in the face of adverse circumstances to a position of prominence and far-reaching influence through sheer ability and force of character. He justified conspicuously, as others of this group have done, the sacrifices and hopes of those who uprooted themselves from Old World surroundings and undertook the laborious and painful task of establishing themselves amid those of the New that their children and their children's children might have a better chance in life.

He was fortunate in his ancestral background. Industry, thrift, persistence, hardiness, and the domestic virtues were ingrained in the stock from which he sprang. Good counsel prevailed and sound principles were inculcated in the home in which he was reared. The educational advantages which this country offers to all, the demand for ability of every kind which its rapid growth has created, and the democratic conditions which distinguish it, made possible the development and expression of his powers. Except for the help of these he was self-dependent and self-made. Opportunities came to him in a remarkable degree, it is true; friends seemed always to appear when he most needed them; but they came because previously he had demonstrated his worth. If we look for the secret of his greatness, we shall find it in his natural endowment, self-discipline maintained by extraordinary power of will, hard work, and high moral purposes.

Nature favored him with physical characteristics which are always an asset to a teacher or public speaker. He was six feet tall with big frame and broad shoulders, but with no suggestion of surplus flesh. He had a large head, strikingly bald, with close-clipped fringe of hair, a conspicuous nose, and piercing eyes. His voice was of iron, and his enunciation deep almost to harshness. In his younger days he walked with great strides and the air of self-confidence and power. Later, after he had been somewhat weakened by illness, he bent forward slightly and was unsteady in the knees, but his appearance and bearing never ceased to command attention and respect. He had a long, nervous hand which was always limp when any one grasped it. Personal contact and familiarity he detested. A colleague once slapped him on the back at parting and said, "Well, Yale has one great professor anyway." Sumner flinched a bit, glanced back at the colleague and remarked disgustedly: "He's a gusher."

With respect to dress he was very particular and during his earlier years followed the styles closely. In the seventies when velveteen jackets were quite the latest thing in gentlemen's attire, he wore one regularly to class, causing comment among the students, who were not accustomed to seeing their professors so modishly dressed. Ordinarily his collar was of the type which has turned down corners and his tie was often passed through an old-fashioned gold ring. He wore eye glasses in class, for which his large nose was well adapted, and would take them off with characteristic gesture when he digressed from the subject he was discussing or became especially interested in some bit of exposition.

Until he broke down in health when he was about fifty years old Sumner paid little attention to his body. He had the Englishman's taste for tea, and often drank five or six strong cups at a meal. During the first years of his professorship he was a heavy smoker and would appear in class with a line of cigars in both upper vest pockets. On September 8, 1879, a date which he never forgot, he gave up tobacco forever. At that time he was consuming about twenty fifteen-cent cigars a day. Looking over the family accounts, he discovered that he was spending annually for these a good portion of what was required to keep the whole household in food. "This is swinish," he exclaimed, and never smoked again. Asked if it was not hard to break off the habit, he replied: "Yes, until I got round the corner." In order to succeed he found it necessary for a period to keep away from clubs and social gatherings.

It was his custom to walk to class, but otherwise he took no exercise for years except during his vacations, and showed little interest in recreation and sports. He played billiards occasionally and now and then indulged in a game of whist. At his doctor's insistence he finally took up bicycle riding, and he rode his wheel as doggedly as he worked, frequently accomplishing trips of fifteen or twenty miles. Clad in an old golf suit, his cap pulled down over his eyes exposing a large area of sun-burned baldness behind, he presented anything but his usual dignified appearance. If a friend accompanied him, he would always keep just a little ahead of his companion, occasionally throwing back some remark difficult to hear or answer, and the latter would generally return home feeling that the outing had been a rather strenuous one. Sometimes Sumner would accompany members of his family to an athletic contest, but apparently he never got over his boyhood conviction that adults ought to be in better business. One day he was standing at the entrance of the Country Club with a friend on crutches who had recently injured a ligament in his leg playing tennis. "I don't see what fun any one can find knocking a small ball through the grass," this person remarked. Sumner said nothing, but looked at him with a quizzical expression on his face. "And I suppose," continued the friend, "that you are thinking how strange it is that any one can get pleasure from knocking a small ball back and forth over a net." "That was just what I was thinking," replied Sumner, and added, "We must be patient with each other."

The small amount of interest he took in college athletics is revealed by a statement which he made in a faculty meeting about the year 1905. Some matter connected with football was being discussed and an appeal was made to Sumner. "What do I know about football?" he growled. "The last game I attended was on Thanksgiving Day, 1876." His ignorance of what was going on in the world of college sports was almost complete. One especially notable Yale athlete, Tom Shevlin, whose face and achievements the newspapers were making widely known was an excellent scholar and in one of Sumner's classes. At the close of a lecture the young man came up to the desk and asked for his mark. Sumner looked down at him and then, much to the amusement of several waiting students, inquired, "Name?" Later he asked another member of the faculty, "Who is this man *Sheldon* anyway?"

Unremitting toil and little attention to physical

needs more than once brought Sumner near the breaking point. When a student abroad and subsequently, when preaching, tutoring, and editing *The Living Church,* his friends had to warn him emphatically that he was undermining his health. In the early nineties he had a serious illness, after which he never commanded his former vigor. Previous to this illness he had suffered from severe attacks of renal colic, and following it there was a hardening of the arteries and a serious heart lesion. He never worried about himself, however, but went on his accustomed way with stoical unconcern. Several trips to Europe and long tramps in Wales, a country of which he was especially fond, gave him some rest and relaxation, but to the end he did little to conserve his strength, pouring all the energy he could summon into the tasks which he had set himself.

On the intellectual side Sumner was vividly alive and insatiably curious. His mind reached out far and in every direction, and with rugged grasp it mastered and exploited whatever it found. In boyhood he turned as naturally and with as eager step to the library as others of his age turned to the fields and the woods. At college he did not confine himself to the studies which the curriculum prescribed, but spent almost all his spare time in reading and independent research. "I mean to learn all I can about everything I can," he wrote to his father while the tedious days of the long trip across the ocean in 1863 wore slowly away, and acting upon this determination he questioned his fellow passengers, listened attentively to the talk of the captain, and acquired practical knowledge in navigation. "When I gave him medicine," said his physician, "he invariably asked what it was, what it was for, and how it was supposed to act. Informed on these matters, he took it faithfully as prescribed."

His curiosity sometimes carried him into surroundings where he seemed oddly out of place. Bob Fitzsimmons once visited New Haven when he was heavyweight champion of America and gave an exhibition in a local theater. One of Sumner's younger colleagues went to see it and the next day rather apologetically told Sumner about it. "I was there," Sumner said. "I have always wanted to see a prize fight, and I thought that probably that was about as near to one as I'd ever get." During a visit to London, his sons relate, he happened upon an open-air meeting conducted by the Salvation Army, and at the invitation of the leader, followed the procession to a hall where workers went about among those present and labored with them personally. A "lassie" talked to Sumner, who sat saying little and with a slight smile on his face, apparently much interested in her methods. Finally, feeling that she was not making much progress, she inquired: "Are you a believer?" Sumner's smile broadened a little and he answered: "Yes, I believe." His inquisitiveness never grew dull and down to old age his mind could not rest from travel. Made weak by time and fate, with heroic heart he still sought to discover and explore.

As a consequence his knowledge from his youth onward was exceptionally broad and diverse. Few men at thirty-two have been recognized as authorities in Hebrew and Greek, and at the same time been considered competent to establish a department of political and social science in a leading university of America. At this period, moreover, he was perhaps equally versed in Biblical history and criticism, for when the first edition of Johnston's Encyclopædia, which appeared in 1876, was being prepared, he was called upon to furnish the articles on "The Bible." At that time had he so desired, he could probably have occupied acceptably a chair of philosophy or theology. In later years he was accustomed to jot down in a book subjects which he hoped to investigate. A few of these will show the range of his inquiries in his special field and incidentally his skill in phrasing: "The Prerogative of Failure," "Envy as a Social Motive," "Happiness Hunting," "The Victories of Rhetoric," "Don Quixote's Political Philosophy," "Can any explanation of the spread of Christianity be found in the mores of the masses in the Hellenic world in the first three centuries of the Christian era?" "Relation of Western Europe and Eastern Asia in the 13th Century," "The Stoic Philosophy and Civil Liberty," "Effect on Industry of Ecclesiasticism," "The Templars as Bankers," "Sanitary Customs and Institutions of the Uncivilized," "Diseases of Poverty, especially of the children of the poor," "The effect of the doctrine that this life is only an introduction to immortality on social rights and duties," "Mica in America."

Although Sumner's mind traveled so broad and varied a territory, he was thorough and honest in the extreme. There were few faults that he hated or condemned more severely than superficiality of thought or slipshod investigation. His most cutting sarcasm was directed toward those who assumed to speak with authority upon matters of which they had but a surface knowledge. He himself compassed sea and land for facts and was unsatisfied so long as there were more to find. He sent to the far corners of the earth for books and information. He acquired one language after another in order to secure first hand acquaintance with customs and thought in all parts of the world. He spared no time or labor to equip himself with whatever he felt might be of assistance to him in his work. "He frequently invited me to see him," wrote Professor Andrew W. Phillips, soon after Sumner's death, "and the burden of the interview so far as catechising me was, 'How would you represent this, that, or the other law of economics by mathematical curves or models, or state the same in mathematical language?' He brought all the German methods to my attention, and we read them together. Along in the early eighties he proposed that we take 118 North College for our *day* study and we kept together there for some years. He went through with Graphic Algebra and Analytical Geometry in a most thorough way, and then took up Calculus and worked at that under my direction for about a year and a half as I recollect it. He had never studied Calculus before. He was very fond of it and expressed himself to the effect that it was the greatest product of the human mind. He studied Williamson's Calculus with me, a hard book, and he spent hours and days and weeks in mastering the problems and ideas."

Sumner's carefulness and patience were extraordinary. A young reporter is said to have asked him why he did not publish more on sociology. "Because," was the gruff rejoinder, "I would rather correct my own mistakes than have other people do it for me." The row after row of classified notes on history, economics, anthropology, and the science of society, which he left at his death, gathered mainly between 1894 and 1907, fill one with amazement. If it were not for the fact that the evidence is there before one, it would be unbelievable that a human being with the varied duties which Sumner assumed, could have been equal to the task of collecting and arranging them. His appreciation of the value of patience and persistence, as well as his capacity for them, is illustrated in a story told by a friend. On Sunday afternoons, when his boys were small, Sumner would take them out for a walk. Frequently they would go down to the railroad where Sumner would explain the working of the switches and other mechanical devices employed in the operation of the trains. An acquaintance once asked him if he thought such young children could understand what he was talking about. "Not the first time," Sumner replied, "nor the second, nor the twentieth perhaps, but in a hundred times, yes." Such infinite patience Sumner brought to every task. He was never dismayed by its size or discouraged by the difficulties and complexities it presented, but with painstaking endurance gave heed to its minutest detail and met its every requirement.

How penetrative, vigorous, and logical his mind was has been pointed out in preceding chapters. He always went directly to the heart of a matter, and kept his eye on the main issue. Irrelevancies he swept ruthlessly aside, and sophistries he exposed with heartless delight. His ability to lay hold of essential facts and point out their necessary bearing once won an intercollegiate debate. "Resolved, that a permament court of arbitration should be established by the United States and Great Britain," was the question to be argued, and in order to assist the team which was to represent Yale a few of the faculty met in Osborn Hall for a discussion of the question. To every one's surprise, Sumner, whose appearance at evening gatherings had been rare on account of ill health, stalked into the room and sat down on the side and in the rear. The first speaker was Professor

Simeon E. Baldwin. At the conclusion of his speech Professor Hadley, who was coaching the team, called upon Professor Sumner. Sumner got up and remarking that if this was a debate he felt he ought to take the position of a debater, went up on the platform and planting himself squarely on his two feet began by saying, "My friend, Mr. Baldwin, has made the following statements," and proceeded to summarize them. "All he has done," Sumner continued, "is to express a pious hope." He then laid down and amplified the two following propositions: first, If people are mad enough they will fight; and second, If they are not mad enough to fight, the ordinary means of diplomacy will suffice. The Yale debaters took their cue from him and won.

In Sumner's mental composition there was nothing of the dreamy or abstractly speculative. On the contrary, the practical predominated. He had the Lancashire intolerance of anything not utilitarian, the Lancashire frugalness and terseness of expression. He was an advocate of simplified spelling and a member of the Orthographic Union formed at Columbia College in 1895. "He used to say that there were three questions to be asked about any production: What is it? How do you know it? *What of it?* Upon the last inquiry he laid particular emphasis. . . . He used to prune the theses written under him of verbiage and slash out inexact expressions, usually making careful emendations, until the pages were scarcely recognizable. For himself, he abjured latinity and chose the tersest and most rugged of Anglo-Saxon terms, using, for an extreme example, a word like leechcraft in place of a more indirect and ponderous term. He hated long and involved sentences, and urged all to be sure to translate German passages that looked as if they were significant, to see if they really were; for, as he said, 'The German language and style lend themselves easily to bathos!' " [1] It was his passion for the clear, definite, and practical, in part at least, which made his attitude toward the metaphysical and intuitional so hostile. He had studied philosophy much as a young man, but as he once expressed it, he "had been engaged in heaving the whole cargo overboard ever since." Down on Fisher's Island one summer a friend who was with him called attention to the holes, swallows' nests, in the side of a cliff near where they were stopping. "Yes," said Sumner, "they remind me of a definition of metaphysics which I once heard. Two men were on a Mississippi steamer passing some clay cliffs full of sparrow-holes when one asked the other what the term 'metaphysics' meant. 'See that cliff,' said the latter. 'See those holes. Well, take away the cliffs and leave the holes, and you have metaphysics.' "

It was characteristic of Sumner, also, always to see the relation of an object or condition to the practical interests of the individual, however remote and forgotten, and generally to the pocketbook of the individual. From Fisher's Island he and a companion once caught sight of the United States warship *Olympia* steaming out of New London Harbor. With her white sides gleaming in the sun she presented a beautiful spectacle, and Sumner's friend commented upon the fact. "Well, take a good look at her," said Sumner, "there's some of your money in her." One of his boys amused him greatly on the occasion of a visit to the circus by displaying the same tendency of mind. He had used some of the money given him to buy a balloon. Suddenly it burst. "There goes your

[1] "War and Other Essays," Introduction, p. xxi.

balloon!'' exclaimed Sumner. ''Yes,'' said the boy, ''and there goes my ten cents.'' As has been pointed out repeatedly in preceding pages, all Sumner's research, writing, and teaching had a practical end in view. He was forever trying to discover that which would contribute to more successful living here upon the earth; laboring to get men to adopt right principles of action; endeavoring to train up youth to go out and be good citizens. His was preëminently a life of service in the interest of a better world.

The assurance which Sumner always displayed, his positiveness of statement, his unconcealed contempt for opinions and theories which he considered superficial, and his matter-of-fact assumption of superior knowledge in his own particular field, led some to charge him with intellectual pride and arrogance. While perhaps he cannot be freed altogether from this indictment, it must also be admitted that he displayed a very fine type of humility. He was always conscious of the limitations of his own knowledge and of the vastness of the unexplored country which stretches out on every side of the thinker and teacher. It was impossible for him not to take a positive position upon any matter which presented itself to him for judgment or action; but he was quick to change in the light of more facts or more mature deliberation. This characteristic was especially evident in faculty deliberations. One day he came into a meeting of the faculty, a little late, and soon made several emphatic statements. For some time he sat in characteristic attitude, coat collar turned up, leaning forward upon his cane, and then made further remarks quite contrary to those he had uttered earlier. ''I don't see how Mr. Sumner reconciles those statements with his former ones,'' commented a professor. ''I don't rec-

oncile them," growled Sumner, "I withdraw the
former." He was always willing to be taught by
those he deemed competent to teach. Furthermore,
he recognized his own tendency to be dogmatic and
the dangers which always threaten men who daily
instruct those who are not in a position to contradict
what is said to them. Dr. Hadley relates an interesting story illustrating this fact and making clear how
Sumner welcomed opposition for his own good. "I
was Labor Commissioner at the time," Dr. Hadley
says, "and had just published my annual report. I
met Sumner one day and he said: 'Hadley, I don't like
your report.' He then went on in his brusque manner
to make the objections which I expected him to make,
and I accepted them without any particular protest.
Not long after I met him again and he said, 'Hadley,
why did you let me talk to you the way I did the other
day?' 'Professor Sumner,' I replied, 'you are fifteen
years older than I am, and about all I know of economics I got from you; why shouldn't you talk as you
did?' 'But look at it from my point of view,' said
he, 'it wasn't good for me. I'm dealing with boys all
the time. I try to get up arguments in class, but
they're one-sided affairs. I know all about the matter
and the boys don't. It isn't good for me to be allowed
to talk that way. Now the next time I do it you say:
'See here, such statements don't go. I'm just as good
a man as you are. Nothing but facts and arguments,
if you please.'"

A delightful picture of Sumner in his study, suggestive of some of the intellectual traits and personal
habits already mentioned, is given by one who was for
some time his secretary, Miss Alice M. Merriman. "I
began work for Professor Sumner," she writes, "in
April, 1895, when he was starting his volume on the

'History of Banking in the United States.' His
method of work, then as always, was to read every
volume he could find which had any bearing on the
subject in hand, making notes from it of any points
which he might wish for either present or future use.
Of course he had employed the same method for years,
and had already collected quantities of notes; but he
went on reading unremittingly and his supply of books
read, and ready for note-making, seemed never to
diminish. From the early part of June he was vir-
tually free from college duties, and from that time
on through the summer, he took an almost savage delight in working as many hours as he could make a
day lengthen into. He was very conscientious, however, about his late afternoon exercise. We were
supposed to make five hours of writing the daily
maximum, but it often ran into six. However, I think
he always went out at 5 o'clock, making that hour the
beginning of his recreation for the day. I imagine it
always closed with dinner at 6:30 or 7, and how late
into the night he read, I can only guess; for the pile
of books was very apt to be restored to its normal
height at my arrival the next morning.

"He was an indefatigable worker—patient, painstaking, and constant, although never giving the appearance of hurry, or of trying to hurry others. I
recall that we had an unusually rainy summer in
1895; perhaps my attention was called to it on account
of our rather frequent stops for thunder showers.
His study was at the top of the house—a large room
with a smaller one adjoining. Here dormer windows
gave light enough for ordinary occasions, but during
a hard shower it was too dark to read or write. I
remember one extremely dark afternoon when he was
particularly anxious to finish something. As the

clouds gathered and darkened everywhere, and the rain poured down, he closed his book with a sigh, and glancing out of the window, said in his dry way: 'I don't believe we needed this.'

"His study was a curious place, reminding one, in mild fashion, of that which Hawthorne describes in one of his books—perhaps 'Septimius Felton'—in that there was always plenty of dust present, though I never came across the spiders! Germ theories were certainly disproved in that study. It was his one room to do as he pleased in; and though members of his family often made strenuous efforts to clear it up for him, they were not encouraged. He had all a man's horror of a broom and dust-cloth, and Thursday mornings I used often to hear him say in a helpless tone: 'Those beastly girls get in here on Wednesdays, and then I never can find anything.' His unfailing thoughtfulness for others was shown many a time by his stopping in the midst of some cherished bit of work to make a fire for me. I hated to have him, and never asked it, for I knew that he hated to stop his work for the purpose; but it was often necessary, and he never flinched, though he frequently went about it with a grim, martyr-like expression on his face.

"His dry sense of humor showed itself frequently and often unexpectedly. One day he was reading a book—doubtless a very learned one, but ambiguously expressed. He pondered awhile over some particularly abstruse sentences, and then laid it aside, saying wearily: 'It seems to me if I knew a thing, I could say it better than that.'

"His combination of real tender-heartedness and almost brusqueness reminded one of the east-wind man in 'Bleak House,' who was always doing some kindness for somebody, but never could stand being thanked for it. He was uniformly kind and thoughtful and courteous in his treatment of me, but I had hard work trying to thank him, and I never could be quite sure whether he heard me or not when I did so. I remember one spring he was apparently very much amused that I thought my presence was rather necessary to see to a little house-cleaning at home. This was a task that his own soul abhorred, and one which he doubtless considered wholly superfluous. However, he made not the slightest objection, and though he may have felt inwardly annoyed at the interruption to his note-making, he let me off with perfect good nature. When I appeared again to take up his work, he seemed quite interested to know if my house-cleaning was done. Another incident rather pleased me, showing at the same time his generosity and his idea of standing out for a principle. Sometimes he let me do my writing at home, as he saw that it was a convenience; but at other times it was necessary that I go to his house. I saw that my car-fares were counting up pretty well, and one day I asked him if he were willing to have me add them to my bill, as I was doing in other cases. 'No,' he said abruptly, 'I am perfectly willing to pay you more, but I don't care where you live—whether across the street or down in West Haven.' I reminded him that a good many days I did his work at home, and hence if he allowed the extra daily, it would come to more in the end. 'I don't care anything about that,' he said gruffly. 'I would just as soon pay more, but I won't pay carfare.' He was always appreciative when any one made the effort to do something for him, whether it turned out very well or not. A case in point was my effort to copy out Russian for his notes. I doubt

if he or any one could read the words, but he took a
grim satisfaction in the attempt.

"His thoroughness was appalling. In connection
with the Boocock Library, he ordered a series of
pamphlets from Germany. I do not remember how
many numbers there were, but it seems to me it was
something like 150, or perhaps more. In stamping
them, I happened to discover that several pages were
omitted from one of the numbers. I called his attention to it, whereat he gave a little growl of disgust
and said: 'Humph! That's just like those Germans.
They go to the ends of the earth to collect information,
and then make a blunder putting their books together.
I want you to go through every one of the numbers
and verify all the pages. Then I will write to the
dealer and make my complaint.' It took a good many
hours to carry out his instructions, and I found nothing amiss with the others, but he was not satisfied
that they were right until a complete inspection had
been made."

The gentler side of Sumner's nature to which this
description alludes was unknown to those whose acquaintance with him was superficial. The impression
prevailed that he was an exceedingly hard man, and
it was not altogether unwarrantable. All his life he
was hard upon himself. With relentless will he held
to the path which duty indicated. As he gave up
smoking, so he gave up everything which seemed at
all inconsistent with reasonableness or right. No consideration of personal comfort, popularity, security,
or material gain did he ever permit to silence him
when he felt he ought to speak, or halt him when he
was convinced he ought to act. For the most part, he
kept his feelings well hidden. Gush and sentimentality he abhorred, and conventions which were hollow

and false he despised. His very devotion to the truth sometimes made him seem heartless, for he would never conceal, or color, or soften facts in order to spare anybody's feelings. He was independent in the extreme, asking no favors and refusing to accept them. He stood upon his own feet and expected others to do likewise. One morning during the last year of his teaching when he was having much difficulty in getting about, he boarded a street car on his way to the college and found every seat taken. One of his graduate students who happened to be in the rear of the car at once got up and offered him a seat, but although it was painful for him to stand and hold on to a strap, no amount of urging could induce Sumner to avail himself of an advantage which had fallen to another. Those were the days when it used to take him five minutes to climb the stairs to his classroom in Osborn Hall. It was pathetic to see him laboriously pulling himself up them, stopping now and then to catch his breath, but it would have been a person who did not know him well who would have had the temerity to offer him assistance. Because he believed that one ought not to lessen another's chance of the largest possible achievement by seeking his aid, and recognized that both justice to all and self-development demand that an individual be thrown upon his own resources, he often seemed unsympathetic and severe to those working under his supervision. Among his graduate students, at a certain period, was a man who wanted to choose for his thesis subject "The Relation of God to the Universe." Sumner offered no objection to the subject, but the student soon got into difficulties and bothered him with frequent visits and inquiries. Finally Sumner got out of patience and said to him: "Don't keep asking me these questions.

Go off and study. Read your books. Then either
you will find the answers for yourself or you will see
how foolish your questions are.'' The student followed this advice and eventually changed his subject
for a very practical one connected with the industrial
organization.

Sumner was also everywhere known as a hard and
relentless fighter. He asked no quarter and he gave
none, frequently saying that any one who begins to
whine when the blows commence to fall ought not to
enter a controversy. It is a question if he was not
prone to apply too harsh terms to those whose views
or policies were repugnant to him. If there was any
respect in which his consciousness of law failed, it
was in his seeming obliviousness to the fact that the
intellectual background, the training, and the general
circumstances of others often made their opinions and
acts as inevitable for them as his own differing ones
were for him.

Toward all guilty of moral laxity and all workers
of iniquity, Sumner was hard as stone. The unscrupulous, the dishonest, the disloyal, the exploiter
of the weak and defenseless, never found leniency in
him. From the conviction, very forcefully expressed
in one of his sermons, that such persons should be
socially ostracized, he did not waver. That he was
not always courteous and that his words and attitude
were sometimes brutal cannot be denied. During the
period that he was a vestryman of Trinity Church a
bitter controversy arose, and at a heated meeting of
the vestry one night a fellow member behaved himself
in a way which disgusted and angered Sumner. On
the following morning that person met him and tried
to begin an explanation of his action of the previous
evening, but Sumner waved him aside with the excla-

mation: "I don't want ever to see you or speak to you again."

A more amusing example of Sumner's roughness is given by Professor Clarence W. Mendell. A meeting of the Yale Chapter of Phi Beta Kappa was soon to be held, and although it was known that Sumner was not in good health and was going out but little, the committee was anxious to have him present and make at least a brief address. Professor Mendell, then a senior, was delegated to interview him on the matter. "I went up to his desk after a recitation," he says, "and in a rather clumsy and verbose manner told him what was wanted, while he sat and glared at me. Receiving no response when I paused, and thinking I might not have made myself clear, I repeated what I had said and enlarged upon it. The brevity of his answer was in striking contrast to my loquaciousness. Leaning towards me when he saw that at length I was entirely through, he roared out just one word, 'NO!' The walk from his desk to the door seemed a mile long."

Outside the college, Sumner's reputation for hardness was due principally to his doctrine of individualism so ruthlessly set forth in his writings and particularly in "What Social Classes Owe to Each Other." Probably there was never a more emotionless statement of the logic of the social situation than this book presents. Such a passage as the following called forth a storm of protest from preachers, social workers, and sentimentalists generally. "Almost all legislative effort to prevent vice is really protective of vice, because all such legislation saves the vicious man from the penalty of his vice. Nature's remedies against vice are terrible. She removes the victim without pity. A drunkard in the gutter is just where

he ought to be, according to the fitness and tendency
of things."[2]

Taken by itself, this statement gives a false idea of
the real Sumner. Hard in theory he unquestionably
was; nevertheless, he often showed a softer, more
sympathetic side. As a matter of fact none would
have been quicker than he to pull a fellow being out
of misery. Many who quote from "What Social
Classes Owe to Each Other," seem never to have
read its final chapter, "Wherefore We Should Love
One Another." In it Sumner states that "a man
who had no sympathies and no sentiments would be
a very poor creature," that men "owe to men in the
perils of this life aid and sympathy," and that "the
law of sympathy by which we share each other's burdens is to do as we would be done by." All charitable
work, however, is to be relegated "to the domain of
private relations, where personal acquaintance and
personal estimates may furnish the proper limitations
and guarantees." Sumner's own private charities
were extensive, but he never let his left hand know
what his right hand was doing. A constant stream
of letters from former students came to him, asking
for information, advice, or assistance in getting positions, and though the answering of these must have
encroached greatly upon the time he wanted to give
to other things, he always replied fully and kindly.
He had great sympathy for young men who really
wanted an education, but were crippled by lack of
funds, and when such cases came to his attention he
did everything in his power to raise the money required or to find means whereby the men could work
their way through college.

Love for children was one of his most conspicuous

[2] "What Social Classes Owe to Each Other," Chapter IX, p. 131.

traits and in their presence he became positively benign. There is little that he would not have tried to do for a child. He hunted the stores through for toys which he thought would please the children of his friends and carefully preserved the little letters of acknowledgment which they sent him. Nothing gave him keener happiness than to join in their play. If he met a nurse maid pushing a baby carriage in his neighborhood, he would stop her, peer smilingly into the carriage, find out to whom the baby belonged, and having fixed its identity in his mind, he never failed to remember it upon subsequent meetings. He was in the waiting-room of his physician one day when the latter's little boy, an extraordinarily beautiful child, broke into the room. When his father appeared from his private office Sumner said to him, "I want you to promise me two things: first, that you will give me a picture of that boy, and second, that you will let him come to see me whenever I send for him." Sumner received the picture and carried it for a long while in his pocketbook, taking it out and gazing at it from time to time with evident delight. When his own grandchildren came his love and solicitude for them were unbounded.

It was in his home life that Sumner's finer qualities revealed themselves most conspicuously. People who saw him in its intimacies were often compelled to revise former opinions of him. This fact is amusingly illustrated by a comment once made by a student who with several others had been invited to the Sumner home for dinner. Bursting into his room upon his return, he exclaimed to a group gathered there: "Say, fellows, do you know Sumner's human; he's kind to his family." No one could be a more devoted husband and father than was he. Womanhood he reverenced and toward it showed something of the chivalry whose spirit is depicted in the legends of King Arthur's court. All the admiration and wor- shipfulness of his nature found expression in his regard for the woman he had chosen as his wife. To the end of his days he never ceased to be a lover. Writing to her after many years of married life from the home of his classmate Dimock, in Coventry, he says: "I have the same room we had before. It is full of you. It makes me feel that I would rather be anywhere with you than anywhere without you." Mrs. Sumner was long a semi-invalid, and her condi- tion was always reflected in Sumner's spirits. If she was better, he was bright and hopeful, and if she was not so well, he was troubled and depressed. Never was he so absorbed in study as to be unmindful of her comfort, nor was any desire of hers too trivial to take him on an errand that might give her satisfac- tion.

His heart was equally bound up in the welfare of his boys, and he always had time to join in their play and assist in their education. "He used to put us on his knees," one of them relates, "and draw amusing pictures for us: he plotted out the heavens and gave us our first lessons in astronomy; and he was our pitcher in games of one-o-cat, always refusing to take his turn at the bat. Later he helped us with our studies, and all the details of Greek and Latin gram- mar and the demonstrations of geometry seemed to be as fresh in his mind as they had ever been." "The famous blizzard of 1888," says Mr. George L. Fox, then rector of the Hopkins Grammar School, "will always be associated in my thought with Professor Sumner. His boys were then in the lower classes of the school. The storm had begun Sunday night and continued with increasing force through Monday. Monday morning his sons with other boys from the outskirts of the city had come bravely to school, plowing with the zest of boyhood through the drifts which had already gathered. About eleven o'clock in the morning I became so alarmed by the increasing size of the drifts and the rising violence of the wind that I assembled the smaller boys, who lived more than half a mile from the school, and dismissed them for the day, urging them to go home as fast as possible and to keep together. Shortly before one o'clock, the regular time for closing, I heard a loud stamping in the front hall, and looking from my room I saw a snow-covered figure, with high top boots and heavy overcoat, neck and face swathed in scarfs. Soon the outer coverings were unrolled and I discovered the familiar face of Professor Sumner, reddened by the wintry blast. When he had gained his breath he quietly remarked, 'I got a little alarmed about the boys, Mr. Fox, so I thought I would come over from the college and see them safely home.' I told him that I was sorry I could not have saved him the trouble, and that I hoped that by this time they were already there. 'All right,' he said, and wrapping himself up again started out in the violent storm. Until I forget that episode I shall always feel like smiling at any reference to the stern, unfeeling severity of 'Billy Sumner.'" It was a not infrequent saying of Sumner's that one of the greatest services a man could render society was to rear up children and send them out into the world well disciplined and capable. It was his happiness to see his own children well established and rendering important service in their several fields. "I have given the

world two good men," he said in his last days, "I am
satisfied."

Although the intellectual and the practical dominated all else in Sumner, he was strongly susceptible
to beauty and grandeur. With the passing of the
years and the continual exercise of the critical faculty he did not suffer that atrophy of the esthetic
sense to which Darwin, whom in many respects
Sumner resembled, perhaps too humbly and with injustice to himself confesses. Like the former, he
found great pleasure and relaxation in novels, which
he read by the score and in many languages, including Russian and Polish; but unlike Darwin, he was
able to read poetry with enjoyment, not only in
his youth, but later. Sophie Rafflavowich, whose
brother, Andre, achieved some eminence as a poet,
used to send specimens of the latter's work to Sumner, who would write her keen and appreciative criticisms. In one of his letters to her he remarks that
the need of the age is for great poets. He was sensitive to grace and beauty in form and movement, and
liked to tell of the appearance made by troops in
training when he was a student in Germany. Their
officers would make them charge over ditches and
fences, and Sumner would describe with grim humor
the ludicrous spectacle they presented, clumsily falling, or hanging like worms on the tops of the obstruc-
tions, and then the harmony of movement and the
surprising gracefulness with which after much practice they would go through the same maneuvers. The
massive and sublime in nature appealed to him
strongly. He liked to lie and look out upon the sea,
and among the mountains of Switzerland, to which
when abroad he was always drawn, he found great

delight and inspiration. He visited the cathedrals and galleries of Europe, but the historical significance of the former was what most appealed to him, and he was more interested in pictures and sculpture as human achievements than as works of art. He enjoyed music. From the opera he got especial pleasure, hearing it in New York frequently, and when abroad, as often as possible. German opera appealed to him most, and Wagner's works he liked best of all, their massiveness and sublimity as well as their legendary setting being suited to his temperament and tastes. He used to go over the libretto very carefully before a performance, his sons recall, making notes on the margin that they might have as little difficulty as possible in following it. He liked to go to the theater, also; and was not above taking part himself in amateur theatricals. One such occasion was on March 4, 1882, when he essayed the rôle of Paul De Verneuil in a French play entitled, "The Grasshopper and the Ants." The other persons in the cast, according to the play bill, were Mr. DuBois, Mrs. Chapman, and Miss Bristol. Those who remember the performance say that Sumner acted with great ease and showed no little histrionic ability.

With all his seriousness, Sumner had a keen sense of humor. He read French plays, classical and modern, with much appreciation of what was amusing in them, and often turned with huge relish to the humorous passages in Shakespeare's writings.

Whatever social proclivities he possessed were not given much play. He went out comparatively little, owing in part, no doubt, to Mrs. Sumner's ill health. When he entertained, as he sometimes did, he was a most agreeable host, and on occasions he would talk with great charm. On the whole, however, the traits

which as a youth held him aloof from others and kept
others at a distance from him, prevailed in his later
years. Several of his classmates were his close, life-
long friends, but he had few intimates. His independence, gruffness, and outspokenness repelled and
intimidated. Judge L. A. Emery once came to New
Haven to visit his son, Professor Henry C. Emery,
who had just joined the Yale faculty. Upon discovering that the latter had been some weeks in the city
without calling upon Sumner, whom the father greatly
admired, he upbraided him roundly and told him that
he wanted him to take him out to see the professor.
The son demurred a little, saying that Sumner was a
very busy man and a bit of a grouch, but as his father
insisted he telephoned Sumner one Wednesday morning stating the situation. "When do you want to
come?" was his gruff question. "Will this afternoon
be convenient?" Professor Emery inquired. "Busy
this afternoon," Sumner answered. "How about to-
morrow afternoon?" "Busy to-morrow afternoon,"
was the reply. "Well, perhaps Friday afternoon,"
suggested Professor Emery. For a moment there
was silence. "Come this afternoon," Sumner growled,
and hung up the receiver. "He saw," said Emery,
"that he couldn't get out of it." When father and
son called, Sumner himself came to the door. Without waiting for an introduction, Judge Emery stepped
forward and said, "Professor Sumner, you don't know
me, but I know you; I'm your forgotten man." The
two quickly got to talking and, says the son, "they
paid no attention at all to me, but spent the entire
afternoon knocking everything that had happened
since the Civil War."

Sumner never severed his connection with the
Christian church. Although he objected strenuously

to being regarded as a minister, feeling that certain characteristics popularly attributed to the clergy as a class would be imputed to him, he remained a priest until his death, carefully sending in his report each year, which was always to the effect that he was occupied with his duties in Yale University. Whatever he may have considered the failings and limitations of the church, he did not cease to regard it as an important agency in developing character and the industrial virtues which he deemed the basis of all social well-being. Perhaps he never forgot that it was the church and a minister that at a critical period in his own youth gave him needed encouragement and set his feet in the path of opportunity and future greatness. Until about 1900 he was a regular attendant at Trinity Church, where his old friend, Dr. Harwood, was so long the rector, and took a rather active part in shaping its policies. "Professor Sumner was a member of the vestry when I came to be an assistant to Dr. Harwood in 1883," writes Dr. Harry P. Nichols, of Holy Trinity Church, New York, "and his voice carried influence. I was called largely to do work among the Yale students, and at the first meeting I had with the vestry he insisted that the salary should be an ample one, that of an associate given a specific work. In all my ministrations, Professor Sumner was my cordial backer. I was often at his house and he gave me the benefit of appreciation and counsel in all my plans. I recall that when I was arranging for an effective organization among the men of the parish, Professor Sumner was quite willing that his name should head the list of officers, although his duties prevented his taking responsible activity in the conduct of the office. The endorsement of any cause by Professor Sumner, particularly a

religious one, counted for much.'' After leaving
Trinity, Sumner's attendance at church was only
occasional, but in the closing years of his life he baptized a little grandson, and not long before his death,
at St. John's Church, he took the Communion.

The religious positiveness which was his when he
came to Yale gradually melted away. As his studies
in the history of man and the origin of human institutions went deeper and deeper it was inevitable that
it should. He faced facts uncompromisingly, anything
vague or intuitional was repugnant to him, and he
was not one to express or hold views for which there
was not concrete proof. ''I never consciously gave
up a religious belief,'' he once said. ''It was as if I
had put my beliefs into a drawer, and when I opened
it there was nothing there at all.'' He never attacked
religion, however, or assumed a controversial attitude
toward it. The fact that he christened his grandchild
and took Communion suggests that deep down in his
nature a modicum of religious faith remained.

Throughout his life, furthermore, he displayed the
spirit of true religion much more conspicuously than
do many theologians and ecclesiastics. He served in
the temple of truth; he practiced self-sacrifice, and
self-denial, and magnanimity; he held the truth to be
all and himself nothing; he was not content simply
to learn, but learned that he might teach mankind.
In his fearless devotion to duty, moreover, and above
all in his often single-handed fight against social and
political sins, he showed all the self-abnegation and
religious passion of a Crusader.

Indeed, it was to his character and high moral
purposes in a considerable degree that Sumner's
greatness was due. He had a mind of exceptional
purity, in which there dwelt no tainted or unseemly

thoughts. He refused to give his approval to a certain textbook when he learned that its author had been guilty of flagrant immorality. In his general austerity and point of view there was much of the Puritan. From boyhood, life was a serious matter to him. There is not much time to live and one must make the most of it. Sloth, frivolity, luxurious self-indulgence, are among the worst of sins. It is the duty of every man to hold himself relentlessly in hand, make the most of his opportunities, and do well the work which is given him to do. He will meet with many temptations and obstacles, but he must fight a good fight, undismayed by indifference and criticism, undiscouraged by disappointment, asking no favors, seeking no praise. Such was the philosophy which Sumner's life embodied. The statement in one of his sermons regarding the extent to which any man can go, if he has a will sufficiently strong, was proved in his own career. He set before himself a great object and made its attainment his exclusive aim, persevering in his devotion to it against all other allurements. He set himself to be one thing and that he was with all his might.

Commendation and praise Sumner never accepted graciously. While probably he was not unappreciative of gratitude and admiration, they seemed always to embarrass and paralyze him. At the close of their course under him, members of the class of 1904 presented him with a loving cup. They had not distinguished themselves as students nor always behaved as they should, and Sumner had frequently shown impatience with them; therefore, as an act of pacification perhaps, and also because they had really liked the course and admired the man, they gave him this evidence of their feeling. The captain of the baseball team was delegated to make the presentation. Accordingly, just before the written test always held at the beginning of the hour, he stepped up to the desk and made his speech, while Sumner sat there with an expression on his face which, as the young man expressed it, "made me feel as if I would like to poke it over to him with a stick." Sumner, evidently disconcerted, took the cup awkwardly, and realizing that some response was necessary, remarked: "I don't often make valedictories, but one seems called for this time." Then a pause. "I've been counting the hours till I got rid of you," he continued. "You seem to want to do the right thing. All I can say is that I will try to think as kindly of you as I can the rest of my life."

At the close of their popular courses it was customary for the students to remain in their seats for a moment or two and cheer the professors. The cheers given by Sumner's two hundred or more students were always loud and prolonged. On such occasions he would never fail to have an exceptionally large amount of writing on the blackboard to erase, and would stand with his back to the class, his head getting redder and redder as the boys continued their cheering; nor did he ever succeed in cleaning the board until they had dispersed.

Sumner never sought honors for himself, or the approval of men. All his thoughts and desires were for the establishment of the principles for which he battled and for the carrying on of the work to which he had given himself heart and soul. A Yale alumnus, happening upon the simple stone which marks Sumner's grave in the country graveyard at Guilford, once expressed the feeling that an imposing monument of some kind ought to be erected in recognition

of his character and worth. For such a memorial
Sumner would have had no wish or liking. He gave
his best to the hundreds of young men who came to
Yale for training, and established a department of
political and social science that they might go forth
with sound economic and social views. His heart was
in that. A memorial which would enlarge and carry
out the work he began would alone be appropriate to
his character and desires.

The display of affection and love which moved
Sumner more probably than any other came at the
close of his career. It was in 1909, his work at Yale
was done, and he was about to be retired. In 1884 the
University of East Tennessee had conferred upon him
the degree of Doctor of Laws. With this exception,
he had received no academic honors. Yale was now
about to confer upon him this same degree. The hall
was filled with two generations of men whom he had
taught and inspired. One after another the candidates were called up and each was greeted with scattering applause. Sumner was last on the list, and
when his name was announced there was a terrific
outburst. Fathers and sons stood up together, clap-
ping their hands, shouting at the top of their voices,
and even waving their hats. Sumner arose and,
somewhat confused and unsteady on his feet, moved
to the center of the stage where he stood bowed over
a little, while the hurricane of cheers continued. It
was evident that he was embarrassed and did not
know what to do; his face grew red, and he pulled
nervously at his mortarboard; but still the racket
kept up. Suddenly the hall was as still as a church,
and Professor William Lyon Phelps, who was intro-
ducing the candidates, began to speak: ''The history
of Professor Sumner's life,'' he said, ''during the last

thirty-seven years is in large measure the history of
Yale. Always a radical"—at the word "radical,"
Sumner straightened his shoulders like a shot, just as
a war horse throws up his head at the sound of a
distant bugle. The audience roared again, the movement was so characteristic of the man, and it was
several minutes before Professor Phelps could go on.
"Always a radical in educational policies," he finally
continued, "head of the liberal element in the faculty,
he has seen Yale change from a conservative to a
progressive institution. If victory is sweet to those
who fight, his heart must be warm." At this statement, Sumner pulled his nose with a nervous jerk, and
for a third time the audience shouted, appreciating
with keen relish that Sumner there on the stage, sniff-
ing at eulogies, was the same man he had always been,
the very embodiment of primeval truthfulness and
ruggedness. "Professor Sumner has combined to an
extraordinary degree the patience of the scholarly
investigator with the fiery zeal of those who love
truth. Like all great teachers and real leaders of
men, he is intensely dogmatic; but his dogmas are not
the result of narrowness or prejudice; they come
from prolonged study and profound thought. His
intellect has broadened, his heart has mellowed, as he
has descended into the vale of years. He has set all
of us a great example—in having a hospitable mind;
a mind not afraid of intellectual consequences, open
to every new idea, and ready to give it glad welcome.
Professor Sumner's books in Political Science and
Societology have made his name known and honored
wherever these studies are followed; but no Yale man,
on hearing Professor Sumner's name, thinks primarily of his books. Men are more important than
books, and it is the virility of this great teacher that

has impressed so many generations of Yale students. He possesses the love, respect and veneration of his former pupils; we do not know 'what social classes owe to each other,' but we do know that many classes at Yale owe Professor Sumner more than can be compassed within the limits of language.'' President Hadley then conferred the degree, and there followed another ovation which lasted for several minutes. When Sumner sat down his eyes were filled with tears.

Letters of congratulation poured in from all over the country. They came from noted educators, statesmen, men prominent in the business world, and from very humble individuals. These touched Sumner deeply and led him to remark to a friend, ''The world's using me pretty well.'' On the evening previous to Commencement he had been the guest of honor at the 1492 dinner, where he had made a delightfully witty speech, saying among other things that although he was to walk the plank the next day, he expected to enter the Carnegie kindergarten and intended to live as long as he could.

The end was now fast approaching, however. Some years before Sumner had gone to his physician and said: ''I want you to listen to my heart.'' ''I examined him,'' says the latter, ''and found that he had a valvular heart lesion and hardening of the arteries. When I had finished he said: 'Well, how long have I got to live?' I told him his condition frankly, but added that with proper care on his part there was no reason why he should not live a good while. 'I don't want any of that stuff,' he growled; 'I want to know how long I've got to live. I'm not afraid to die, in fact I have always had a certain curiosity about death.' 'But I should think you would want to live as long as you can,' I answered. 'Oh, I'm in no hurry to get through,' he replied, 'but if I'm going to die soon, I want to know it. I have my wife to think about and I want to put my house in order; but personally death is no more to me than going upstairs to bed.'" In 1907 he had an attack of temporary paralysis in one leg. On December 31, 1908, he suffered a similar paralysis of the right arm. To Professor Keller he said: "I'm on the home stretch, but don't tell Mrs. Sumner; she has a horror of paralysis and I don't want her worried; she thinks there's some little trouble with an artery in my arm." He kept on with his work as before, however, reading and taking notes by the hour, forcing himself to write out the latter with his left hand until he was able again, though never without difficulty, to use his right. It took him hours to accomplish what formerly had required minutes, but with the unfailing patience and persistence which he had always shown, and with no complaint, he held himself to his tasks.

Faithful to duty to the last, unmindful of himself, and deaf to all remonstrances, he started for New York, ill and weak, in the snowstorm of Monday, December 26, 1909, to deliver the presidential address before the American Sociological Society on "Religion and the Mores." Here at the Murray Hill Hotel, where he always stopped, the final stroke came. For weeks he lay in the Englewood Hospital, his left side paralyzed, tenderly watched over by the members of his family. During all that time, says one of his nurses, he was the "sweetest" patient. "He would try to do anything and take anything that we asked him, but I think the thing that impressed me most was the absolute confidence he had in what we told him." One day toward the end he said to his daughter-in-law, "I'm going down to the Dark River." "Yes,"

she replied, "but love reaches over to the other side."
"We think so," he answered, and after a long pause,
"We hope so."

On April 12, 1910, he died, and three days later,
after a simple service in Battell Chapel such as he
would have wished, his body was borne to the Elliott
family lot in the Guilford cemetery and laid to rest.
He had fought a good fight; he had finished his
course; he had kept the faith.

BIBLIOGRAPHICAL NOTE

An excellent bibliography of Sumner's writings, prepared by Dr. Maurice R. Davie, may be found in "The Forgotten Man and Other Essays." Since it was published a number of other articles have come to light. For the most part they are book reviews and contributions to newspapers and magazines. They add practically nothing to our knowledge of their author.

At the time of his death Sumner was at work upon a Science of Society. He left about fifty drawers containing approximately three thousand notes each, ranging in length from a few lines to two thousand words or more. At least half of these are material which he collected for the book which was to present the ripe fruit of his years of study. The prodigious task of going over these notes and completing the work which Sumner began has been undertaken by Professor Keller, and in the not distant future there will appear a Science of Society in which the results of Sumner's investigations with the deductions to be drawn therefrom will be set forth.

INDEX

THE END